Brookings Papers
ON ECONOMIC ACTIVITY

FALL 2010

DAVID H. ROMER
JUSTIN WOLFERS

Editors

BROOKINGS INSTITUTION PRESS
Washington, D.C.

Copyright © 2011 by
THE BROOKINGS INSTITUTION
1775 Massachusetts Avenue, N.W., Washington, D.C. 20036

ISSN 0007-2303
ISBN-13: 978-0-8157-2157-4

Authorization to photocopy items for internal or personal use or the internal or personal use of specific clients is granted by the Brookings Institution for libraries and other users registered with the Copyright Clearance Center Transactional Reporting Service, provided that the basic fee is paid to the Copyright Clearance Center, 222 Rosewood Drive, Danvers, MA 01923. For more information, please contact CCC at (508) 750-8400. This authorization does not extend to other kinds of copying, such as copying for general distribution, for creating new collective works, or for sale. Specific written permission for such copying must be obtained from the Permissions Department, Brookings Institution Press, 1775 Massachusetts Avenue, N.W., Washington, DC 20036; FAX (202) 536-3623; E-mail permissions@brookings.edu.

Brookings Papers
ON ECONOMIC ACTIVITY

FALL 2010

Editors' Summary — vii

JONATHAN A. PARKER and ANNETTE VISSING-JORGENSEN
The Increase in Income Cyclicality of High-Income Households and Its Relation to the Rise in Top Income Shares — 1
Comments by Rebecca M. Blank and Erik Hurst 56
General Discussion 67

MARIANNE P. BITLER and HILARY W. HOYNES
The State of the Social Safety Net in the Post–Welfare Reform Era — 71
Comments by Christopher Jencks and Bruce D. Meyer 128
General Discussion 142

THOMAS S. DEE and BRIAN A. JACOB
The Impact of No Child Left Behind on Students, Teachers, and Schools — 149
Comments by Caroline M. Hoxby and Helen F. Ladd 195
General Discussion 205

ROCHELLE M. EDGE and REFET S. GÜRKAYNAK
How Useful Are Estimated DSGE Model Forecasts for Central Bankers? — 209
Comments by Ricardo Reis and Christopher A. Sims 245
General Discussion 257

GARY GORTON and ANDREW METRICK
Regulating the Shadow Banking System — 261
Comments by Andrei Shleifer and Daniel K. Tarullo 298
General Discussion 311

JAMES R. HINES JR.
State Fiscal Policies and Transitory Income Fluctuations — 313
Comments by William G. Gale and Brian Knight 338
General Discussion 347

PURPOSE The *Brookings Papers on Economic Activity* publishes research in macroeconomics, broadly defined, with an emphasis on analysis that is empirical, focuses on real-world events and institutions, and is relevant to economic policy. Papers are presented and discussed at conferences twice each year, and the papers and discussant remarks are published in the journal several months later. The intended audience includes analysts from universities, research institutions, governments, and business. The subject matter encompasses all fields of economic inquiry relevant to macroeconomics, including business cycles; development and long-term growth; the distribution of income, wealth, and opportunities; financial markets; international capital and foreign exchange markets; fiscal and monetary policy; international trade; labor markets; the public sector and the welfare state; energy; the environment; political economy; regulation and industrial organization; education; health; and demography.

The conference and the journal are based upon the work partially supported by the National Science Foundation under Grant No. 0752779 and the Alfred P. Sloan Foundation. The papers and discussant remarks reflect the views of the authors and not necessarily the views of the funding organizations or the staff members, officers, or trustees of the Brookings Institution.

CALL FOR PAPERS Although most papers that appear in the *Brookings Papers* are solicited by the editors, the editors welcome submitted proposals. Editorial decisions are generally made about nine months in advance of each conference. Therefore, proposals should be received by December 1 for the following fall conference and by June 1 for the following spring conference. Proposals should be no more than five double-spaced pages and should be sent to brookingspapers@brookings.edu.

ACCESSING THE JOURNAL The full texts of the papers in this issue and all previous issues of the *Brookings Papers on Economic Activity* are now available online at the *Brookings Papers* website, www.brookings.edu/economics/bpea, under "Past Editions." Also visit the *Brookings Papers* website for information about participants in this conference and agendas for upcoming conferences. To purchase print subscriptions or single copies, visit www.brookings.edu/press, or contact the Brookings Institution Press at 866-698-0010 or P.O. Box 465, Hanover, PA 17331-0465. All Brookings periodicals are available online through both the Online Computer Library Center (contact the OCLC subscription department at 800-848-5878) and Project Muse (http://muse.jhu.edu). Archived issues of Brookings journals are also available through JSTOR (www.jstor.org).

EDITORS, PANEL ADVISERS, AND STAFF FOR THE NINETIETH CONFERENCE

Marianne P. Bitler *University of California, Irvine*
Steven J. Davis *University of Chicago*
Thomas S. Dee *University of Virginia*
Rochelle M. Edge *Board of Governors of the Federal Reserve System*
Gary Gorton *Yale University*
Refet S. Gürkaynak *Bilkent University*
Robert E. Hall *Stanford University*
James R. Hines Jr. *University of Michigan*
Hilary W. Hoynes *University of California, Davis*
Erik Hurst *University of Chicago*
Brian A. Jacob *University of Michigan*
Andrew Metrick *Yale University*
Jonathan A. Parker *Northwestern University*
Ricardo Reis *Columbia University*
David H. Romer *University of California, Berkeley*
Annette Vissing-Jorgensen *Northwestern University*
Justin Wolfers *University of Pennsylvania*

Jean-Marie Callan *Brookings Institution*
Michael Treadway *Brookings Institution*
Lindsey B. Wilson *Brookings Institution*

GUESTS WHOSE WRITINGS OR COMMENTS APPEAR IN THIS ISSUE

Henry J. Aaron *Brookings Institution*
Alan J. Auerbach *University of California, Berkeley*
Laurence M. Ball *Johns Hopkins University*
Rebecca M. Blank *U.S. Department of Commerce*
Gary Burtless *Brookings Institution*
Karen Dynan *Brookings Institution*
Kristin J. Forbes *Massachusetts Institute of Technology*
Benjamin A. Friedman *Harvard University*
William G. Gale *Brookings Institution*
Robert J. Gordon *Northwestern University*
Christopher L. House *University of Michigan*
Caroline M. Hoxby *Stanford University*
Christopher Jencks *Harvard University*
Melissa S. Kearney *University of Maryland*
Brian Knight *Brown University*
Donald L. Kohn *Brookings Institution*
Helen F. Ladd *Duke University*
Bruce D. Meyer *University of Chicago*
Adele C. Morris *Brookings Institution*
William D. Nordhaus *Yale University*
Andrei Shleifer *Harvard University*
Christopher A. Sims *Princeton University*
Phillip L. Swagel *University of Maryland*
Daniel K. Tarullo *Board of Governors of the Federal Reserve System*

Editors' Summary

THE BROOKINGS PANEL ON ECONOMIC ACTIVITY held its ninetieth conference in Washington, D.C., on September 16 and 17, 2010, just as the economy was struggling to recover from the Great Recession. The *Brookings Papers* has always strived to provide timely policy analysis, and five of the papers in this volume study aspects of the causes and consequences of this slump. These papers examine the effects of the business cycle on the incomes of the very richest Americans; welfare, welfare reform, and poverty during recessions; the failure of modern macroeconomic models to adequately forecast economic conditions; the role of shadow banking in the financial crisis and the appropriate regulatory response; and expenditures by state and local governments over the business cycle. The remaining paper studies the impact of the No Child Left Behind Act, a far-reaching education reform that will shape the skills of the labor force for years to come.

IN THE FIRST PAPER, Jonathan A. Parker and Annette Vissing-Jorgensen study the cyclicality of income at the very top of the income distribution. The conventional wisdom has been that the brunt of recessions falls on less educated, lower-income workers. Parker and Vissing-Jorgensen show, however, that households in the top 1 percent of the income distribution see their income rise steeply in booms and fall sharply in busts, much more so than the average household. This pattern is robust: it appears regardless of the occupation of the high-earning households and is not driven by the timing of exercising stock options. It is not even confined to the United States: the authors present evidence of similar patterns in Canada. Importantly, they find that consumption as well as income moves with the business cycle among those at the top.

These results do not mean that the conventional wisdom was entirely wrong, however. It remains true that less educated households also suffer disproportionately during recessions, largely because of increased unemployment. The impact of recessions on income is therefore U-shaped across the income distribution: many low-income households are adversely affected, the middle of the distribution is less affected, and the very top of the distribution is hit hard.

Parker and Vissing-Jorgensen's new results are driven in part by their examination of post-1982 data. In earlier years, when top incomes were not so extraordinarily high, they were also less cyclical. Thus, an increase in the cyclicality of high earners corresponded with an increase in their relative incomes. Parker and Vissing-Jorgensen show that this pattern holds across different income groups, across decades, and even across countries: the more unequal the income distribution, the more cyclical is the income of the rich. The authors conclude by developing a theoretical model linking income cyclicality with income inequality. The model suggests that one source of their findings may be progress in information and communications technology, which has enabled very high ability entrepreneurs to leverage their talents, earning them more in good times but exposing them to plummeting demand in bad times.

IN THE SECOND PAPER, Marianne P. Bitler and Hilary W. Hoynes take the opposite perspective from Parker and Vissing-Jorgensen, exploring the cyclicality of well-being among the poorest. The United States has historically protected its poorest citizens from economic fluctuations through a patchwork system of welfare and social insurance programs: Aid to Families with Dependent Children provided cash assistance to poor families with children, while the food stamp program and Medicaid, among others, provided in-kind benefits. Welfare reform in the 1990s overhauled the cash assistance system (now called Temporary Assistance for Needy Families), and researchers have found that participation in this and some other welfare programs has declined since the reform. An unexplored—but currently pressing—question is whether welfare reform has weakened the social safety net, so that it no longer insures poor Americans against large income swings.

Bitler and Hoynes marshal an impressive array of evidence to attack this question, analyzing decades of data and studying numerous indicators of adult and child well-being. They find some evidence that welfare reform has weakened the safety net: poverty (using the official measure, which excludes noncash transfers) has risen more sharply with the unemployment rate in the years after reform than it did in the years before. On the other hand, the authors also find that welfare reform has had no impact on the cyclicality of food consumption, food insecurity, health insurance coverage, household crowding, or health. Reconciling these results, Bitler and Hoynes report that participation in noncash safety net programs generally, and especially the food stamp program, has become much more responsive to economic conditions in the years since welfare reform. On the other hand, participation in cash assistance programs has, if anything, become less responsive to the business cycle. Overall, therefore, Bitler and Hoynes find that cash welfare reform weakened the safety net, but that the food stamp program picked up much of the slack.

IN THE THIRD PAPER, Thomas S. Dee and Brian A. Jacob evaluate the signature education legislation of the last several decades, the No Child Left Behind Act of 2001. This policy brought dramatic changes to the education landscape by instituting regular, high-stakes assessments of students in public schools. Proponents of No Child Left Behind hoped that these high-stakes tests would motivate school districts to improve educational outcomes, thereby aligning the interests of schools and teachers with those of voters and parents. Critics, however, worried that high-stakes testing would distort teacher incentives even further, encouraging them to teach to the test, ignore nontested subject matter, inappropriately place low-achieving students in special needs classrooms, and neglect high-achieving students.

In their thorough evaluation, Dee and Jacob find support for both the proponents and the critics. The authors focus on tests that are not part of the high-stakes tests under No Child Left Behind, and thus are unlikely to be substantially distorted by teaching to the test. They find that No Child Left Behind appears to have had a positive impact on math learning, especially at lower grades and for students from traditionally disadvantaged populations. They find no evidence of an adverse impact on math achievement at either the top or the bottom of the ability distribution; indeed, the evidence suggests that No Child Left Behind had a roughly constant impact across the ability distribution. On the other hand, the policy appears not to have improved reading performance.

Several mechanisms contributed to the improvement in math learning. No Child Left Behind induced schools to spend about $600 more per student per year, Dee and Jacob estimate, with much of the extra money coming from state and local rather than federal sources. This money supported additional instruction as well as education support services. The legislation also led to an increase in the share of teachers with master's degrees.

But some of the critics' fears were justified: schools reduced instruction in social studies and science—nontested subjects—and increased instruction in tested subjects, especially reading.

IN THE FOURTH PAPER, Rochelle M. Edge and Refet S. Gürkaynak study the forecasting performance of the dynamic stochastic general equilibrium (DSGE) models currently fashionable among macroeconomists. DSGE models' emphasis on deep structural parameters, such as individuals' preferences, the available technology, and resource constraints, means that—if the models' underlying assumptions about economic behavior are correct— they are immune to the Lucas critique (that is, the possibility that forward-looking behavior can cause previous patterns to break down in response to policy changes or other developments). Yet their success in predicting macroeconomic movements remains largely unexplored.

The authors focus on the forecasts of the most prominent of these DSGE models for the United States over the period 1992–2006. Consistent with previous evaluations, they find that DSGE models yield forecasts that tend to be less biased and more accurate than the professional forecasts, the Federal Reserve's "Greenbook" forecasts, or purely statistical forecasts. But this is a limited success, as Edge and Gürkaynak find that the DSGE forecasts do *relatively* well only because the performance of all of these forecasts is quite poor. Indeed, the absolute performance of even the DSGE forecasts suggests that, for example, the 95 percent confidence interval around that model's forecasts of annual inflation is 4 percentage points wide, and that most of the time its forecast of annual GDP growth cannot rule out anything from a near-recession to a boom. The slight edge that DSGE forecasts have over other forecasts is therefore not particularly noteworthy, since it involves comparing one weak forecast with others.

The authors argue that the poor performance of all forecasting techniques reflects the time period they study. Because they focus on the Great Moderation period, there is little variation in inflation or GDP growth, and therefore little to forecast. A final thought experiment drives this point home. They ask whether a policymaker considering the 1992–2006 period would have done better adopting any of the forecasts they consider, or, assuming that the policymaker knew the actual mean for that period, using that mean as the forecast. It turns out that the simple average predicts better than any of the forecasts, confirming that none of the forecasts is providing much information.

A more telling evaluation of DSGE models' usefulness must therefore await assessments of their performance in less stable environments. As a step in this direction, Edge and Gürkaynak take a preliminary look at the Great Recession. They present suggestive evidence that the DSGE forecasts were remarkably slow to provide any information concerning the fall in output as the recession unfolded, and that they were outperformed by the other available forecasts in this episode.

IN THE FIFTH PAPER, Gary Gorton and Andrew Metrick examine the "shadow" banking system and consider how it should be regulated. The shadow banking system refers to arrangements or institutions that are economically similar to traditional banking but that operate outside traditional banking arrangements—and, crucially, outside traditional regulation.

Gorton and Metrick begin by documenting the magnitude and sources of the rise in shadow banking and its role in the financial crisis. They describe how a combination of regulatory restrictions on traditional banks, implicit government subsidies of shadow banking (notably through free implicit insurance of money market mutual funds), and financial innovation led to an explosion of shadow banking over the past three decades. They emphasize that one key force behind the growth of shadow banking is special bankruptcy provisions for repurchase agreements ("repos"), which give financial institutions access to a highly liquid source of short-term funding. They also describe how the conjunction of short-term liquid liabilities and long-term illiquid assets left shadow banking vulnerable to panics similar to traditional bank runs, and how such panics were critical in the financial crisis that erupted in the fall of 2008.

The authors then offer both some general principles for regulating shadow banking and a specific proposal to implement those principles. They point out that the critical role of the special bankruptcy provisions for repos gives regulators a powerful lever: by restricting the circumstances under which the bankruptcy safe harbor applies, regulators can shape the system. They argue that much of shadow banking involves sensible arrangements for handling large financial transactions, and thus that regulators should not try to use their powers to force a return to the traditional system. Instead, drawing on lessons from history, they argue that regulation should involve explicit insurance of money market mutual funds that guarantee stable asset values, and stronger collateral requirements for repos and securitization. The specific set of proposals they put forth involve creating new classes of narrow financial institutions for money market mutual funds and for the holding of securitized assets.

IN THE FINAL PAPER, James R. Hines, Jr. studies expenditure by state and local government over the business cycle. As Hines observes, more than 40 percent of total government expenditure comes from state and local rather than federal government. Since fiscal policy is a key tool for managing aggregate demand, how states and local governments respond to recessions is a key component of the fiscal policy response to the business cycle.

Whereas federal expenditure is clearly countercyclical, rising during recessions and falling (relative to GDP) during booms, Hines shows that aggregate state and local government expenditure hardly responds when GDP falls below its potential. Unlike the federal government, most states have balanced budget requirements that limit their ability to borrow during recessions. Countercyclical state fiscal policy therefore requires strong discipline; states need to save during the good times so they can spend in the bad.

Hines suggests, however, that poor governance in some states contributes to making their expenditure actually procyclical. States that rank higher in corruption, a proxy for more general incompetence, tend to have especially procyclical expenditure. Corroborating this story, Hines finds further evidence that states in general lack strong discipline in the fact that they have a high propensity (perhaps 80 percent) to spend out of federal grants. Whereas a rational state government would save the federal money, states apparently cannot help but spend the cash they have on hand. But this policy vice suggests a policy remedy: federal grants to state governments may be an effective way to stimulate aggregate demand during recessions.

JONATHAN A. PARKER
Northwestern University

ANNETTE VISSING-JORGENSEN
Northwestern University

The Increase in Income Cyclicality of High-Income Households and Its Relation to the Rise in Top Income Shares

ABSTRACT We document a large increase in the cyclicality of the incomes of high-income households, coinciding with the rise in their share of aggregate income. In the United States, since top income shares began to rise rapidly in the early 1980s, incomes of those in the top 1 percent of the income distribution have averaged 14 times average income and been 2.4 times more cyclical. Before the early 1980s, incomes of the top 1 percent were slightly less cyclical than average. The increase in cyclicality at the top is to a large extent due to increases in the share and the cyclicality of their earned income. The high cyclicality among top incomes is found for households without stock options; following the same households over time; for post-tax, post-transfer income; and for consumption. We study cyclicality throughout the income distribution and reconcile our findings with earlier work. Furthermore, greater top income share is associated with greater top income cyclicality across recent decades, across subgroups of top income households, and, in changes, across countries. This suggests a common cause. We show theoretically that increases in the production scale of the most talented can raise both top incomes and their cyclicality.

Since the early 1970s, economic inequality in the United States—as measured by the distribution of wages and salaries, or of income more broadly, or of consumption expenditure—has been steadily increasing.[1] The consensus explanation for the general increase in inequality is that skill-

---

1. For wages and salaries this change was first documented by Bound and Johnson (1992) and Katz and Murphy (1992). The increase that began in the 1970s and 1980s continued

biased technological change has raised the earnings of individuals with more skills, as measured, for example, by education. However, accompanying this steady rise in inequality has been a much larger and more rapid increase in the income share of those at the very top of the income distribution. The share of (non-capital gains) income accruing to those in the top 1 percent of the income distribution increased from 8 percent in the early 1980s to 18 percent in 2008; the income share for those in the top 0.01 percent increased from around 0.7 percent to 3.3 percent over the same period (Piketty and Saez 2003, Saez 2010). Both the suddenness and the magnitude of these increases have shifted perceptions about the importance of technological change as the cause of increased income inequality generally and raised the possibility of an important role for other factors, such as "changes in labor market institutions, fiscal policy, or more generally social norms regarding pay inequality" (Piketty and Saez 2003, p. 3).

In this paper we bring together evidence from a variety of datasets to show that, as first argued in Parker and Vissing-Jorgensen (2009), another fundamental shift has occurred across the U.S. income distribution. During the past quarter century the incomes of high-income households have become much more sensitive to aggregate income fluctuations than previously. Before the early 1980s, the incomes of high-income households were more often than not less cyclical than the income of the average household. But since around 1982 the incomes of the top 1 percent have become more than twice as sensitive to aggregate income fluctuations as the income of the average household.

The fact that this increase in the cyclicality of income of the top 1 percent coincides with the increase in their income share suggests that a common cause underlies both phenomena. We provide further evidence for a link between increased income inequality and increased income cyclicality at the top by documenting, first, that across *income groups* within the top 1 percent, higher average income is associated with higher income cyclicality in the 1982–2008 period; second, that across *decades* since the 1970s, cyclicality of the top 1 percent increases decade by decade as that group's income share increases; and third, across *countries,* increases in income

---

through the 1990s and into the 2000s in the top half of the wage distribution (Autor, Katz, and Kearney 2008). On increasing inequality in consumption, see Cutler and Katz (1991), Attanasio and Davis (1996), and Heathcote, Perri, and Violante (2010). Although the survey information on households suggests that the increase in the overall distribution of inequality in expenditure has been significantly less than that observed for income, this may partially be an issue of measurement of expenditure (see, for example, Aguiar and Bils 2010).

cyclicality of the top 1 percent are highly correlated with increases in their income share.

We argue that these facts are not inconsistent with the hypothesis that the increase in top income shares was caused by rapid technological progress in information and communications technologies (ICT) since the early 1980s. If improvements in ICT have increased the ability of the most talented workers to handle more work or to scale their ideas by working with more production inputs, then the ICT revolution could have caused the incomes of the highest paid both to rise and to become more sensitive to economic fluctuations. The intuition is that individuals who have less decreasing returns to scale will operate at a greater scale (that is, with more production inputs) and have lower ratios of gross revenue to production costs, and therefore have greater sensitivity of earnings to business cycles.

Expanding on these contributions, we begin in section I by focusing on the details of the change in income cyclicality of top income groups in the United States. We use the Statistics of Income (SOI) data of Thomas Piketty and Emmanuel Saez (Piketty and Saez 2003, Saez 2010), which are based on tax records, to show that the average income (before taxes and transfers and excluding capital gains) accruing to those in the very top of the income distribu-tion has moved substantially more (in percentage terms) than the overall average in each boom and each recession since 1982, on average rising 5.0 percentage points more per year in each boom and falling 3.7 percentage points more per year in each recession. Before 1982, however, this was not the case.

This high cyclicality is not simply due to capital or entrepreneurial income. High-income tax units (one or more individuals filing a single return) tend to have a significant share of income from wages and salaries (including bonuses), and this type of income has roughly the same exposure to fluctuations as their nonwage income. Wage and salary income is also a major source of the change in cyclicality of top incomes. Before 1982 the wage and salary income of high-income tax units was roughly acyclical, but since 1982 it has been highly cyclical. Also, we show that the top 1 percent of earners come from a broad range of industries and occupations, and we argue that no one industry's or occupation's pay structure is driving our finding.

Further, we provide three pieces of evidence that although high-income households are more likely to have stock options, our main finding is not driven by the potentially endogenous timing of the exercise of stock options. First, in the period since 1997 for which we have data, only about 22 percent of households in the top 1 percent have stock options (that is, were given stock options during the preceding year or owned stock options when surveyed), and income cyclicality of households in the top 1 percent is roughly similar if one leaves out households with stock options. Second, for a sample of top corporate executives for whom we have information about the value of options granted, we find that income calculated by including options only when granted, rather than when exercised, is highly cyclical. To be clear, this evidence in no way rules out a causal explanation that involves a general rise in pay for performance—indeed, options income is highly cyclical for those who have options, and bonus income may serve a similar purpose for those in the top 1 percent without options income. Our point is simply that the high cyclicality of the wage and salary (and overall) income of the top 1 percent is not spuriously generated by a correlation between the timing of options exercise and aggregate fluctuations. Third, as a further piece of evidence that the high cyclicality is neither due to endogenous timing of income without economic significance nor due to other measurement problems in income data, we show that the cyclicality of the *consumption* of households in the top of the consumption expenditure distribution—specifically, the top 5 percent by initial consumption—is also more than twice that of the average household.

Additional evidence confirming the high cyclicality of top incomes comes from verifying the out-of-sample forecasts made in Parker and Vissing-Jorgensen (2009) based on cyclicality estimates that excluded the recent recession. Income data for 2008 and consumption expenditure data through February 2009 show sharp declines for the top 1 percent during the recent recession, consistent with these predictions.

How does this new fact relate to the prior literature that concludes that low-income households bear the brunt of recessions and benefit the most from expansions? In section II, using data from the Current Population Survey (CPS), we show that the incomes of low-education households are more cyclical than those of high-education households and that the greater cyclicality of the top 1 percent does not appear in the CPS before 1982. Further, looking at the whole distribution using a dataset from the Congressional Budget Office that merges the CPS with the SOI tax data on high incomes, we find that the sensitivity of the wage and salary income of households in the bottom two quintiles to fluctuations in aggregate income is slightly higher than that of households in the third and fourth quintiles and than that of households from the 80th to the 99th percentiles.

However, in the public CPS data for the period since 1982, when one ranks by percentile in the income distribution, the top 1 percent have a higher cyclicality than even the lowest education group (those with less than a high school diploma). The cyclicality of the top 1 percent is even higher when measured using the CPS top 1 percent income series constructed by Richard Burkhauser and coauthors (2008, 2009) from underlying CPS data not subject to the top coding applied to the public files. Thus, top incomes are highly cyclical, but it is harder to observe this high cyclicality in the publicly available CPS data alone because of top coding, and because cyclicality is high only for very high income households. We conclude that across the distribution of incomes, cyclicality is asymmetrically U-shaped: it is higher for the bottom quintiles than for the middle and the upper-middle class, but much higher for the top 1 percent, and especially for the very highest incomes.

Different cyclicalities of taxes and transfers at different points in the income distribution can lead to differences in cyclicality between pre-tax, pre-transfer cash income and disposable (post-tax, post-transfer) income. We show that taxes and especially transfers significantly reduce the cyclicality at the bottom of the income distribution while making less difference to the cyclicality of the very top. Thus, the cyclicality of top 1 percent incomes relative to the rest of the population is even greater for disposable income than it is for pre-tax, pre-transfer income.

Having established and explored our main finding for the United States, in section III we present evidence from Canada, which has a different tax system, slightly different culture, and better available information on top incomes from tax records. In the Canadian tax data, top income cyclicality is quite similar to that in the United States during the past quarter century. Further, in the Canadian data we are able to follow families across years (that is, we use panel data). Families in the top 1 percent of the income distribution in one year have income changes to the next year that are almost twice as cyclical as for the average. This higher cyclicality for the top 1 percent is similar in repeated cross-sectional data and in panel data, suggesting that the availability of only repeated cross-sectional data in the U.S. tax data is unlikely to substantially affect the estimated U.S. cyclicalities.

Section IV presents evidence of a strong link between increased income inequality and increased income cyclicality at the top by exploiting variation across groups, decades, and countries. We split the top 1 percent into three groups (percentiles 99–99.9, 99.9–99.99, and 99.99–100) and document for the period since 1982 that across these groups, the higher the average income, the higher the income cyclicality. Furthermore, calculating cyclicalities by decade since 1970, we show that for a given top group, as its income share increases, the cyclicality of its income increases. Finally, comparing the period 1970–82 with the period 1982–2007 using data for 10 countries, we find that those with larger increases in the income share of the top 1 percent also have larger increases in the income cyclicality of the top 1 percent.

The link between increased inequality and increased cyclicality suggests a common cause of the two phenomena. In section V we argue that the increase in cyclicality is not inconsistent with an explanation of the increase in top income shares based on market-driven changes in incomes rather than, for example, changes in social norms. Specifically, we outline an explanation for both phenomena based on the rapid improvements in ICT in recent decades. Skill-biased technological progress that takes the form of lowering the degree of decreasing returns to scale for the highest-skill individuals naturally leads to increases in both the incomes and the income cyclicality of these individuals.

We emphasize that our results do not imply that the utility or happiness of high-income households is more cyclical that that of the average household. In fact, if risk aversion is lower at high expenditure levels, the utility of high-income households may be less cyclical than that of lower-income households, even with higher income cyclicality. Instead, our main finding establishes a new fact that is informative about changes in incomes and the labor market for high earners and of particular relevance for theories of the recent rise in income shares of high-income households.

I. The Changing Cyclicality of High Incomes

In this section we document the changing cyclicality of the income that accrues to top percentile groups in the income distribution, using the Statistics of Income data compiled by Piketty and Saez (2003) and extended by Saez (2010). In doing so, we study the timing of the change in cyclicality documented by Parker and Vissing-Jorgensen (2009). We show that the dramatic increase in the cyclicality of high incomes started in the early 1980s, and that this increase is significantly due to earned income and not just due to the (potentially endogenous) timing of executive stock option compensation.

I.A. The Main Facts

The main advantage of the Piketty-Saez data is that since they are based on administrative data from the Internal Revenue Service (IRS) on individual income tax returns, they provide extensive and accurate measurement of the very top of the income distribution. However, since some low-income households do not file tax returns (and even fewer did in the earlier years covered by the data), there is little detail on the low end of the income distribution. Piketty and Saez use aggregate personal income data from the national accounts to calculate aggregate taxable income up to 1944; after 1944 they use the available tax return data plus an assumption about the incomes of nonfilers. Using these data, Piketty and Saez track the trend in the income share of the top 1 percent, 0.1 percent, and 0.01 percent of the income distribution, information simply not available in survey-based datasets on wages and incomes. The detail available on tax returns allows the measurement of pre-tax, pre-transfer cash income excluding realized capital gains. We exclude capital gains because our focus is on the timing of income, and the data contain only measures of realized capital gains, not capital gains as they accrue.

The data have some shortcomings, however. First, income excludes income paid as benefits (such as employer-paid health benefits and contributions to pensions) and excludes the employer share of payroll taxes (Social Security, Medicare, and unemployment taxes). Second, the unit of observation in these data is a tax unit, not an individual or a household. There has been a steady downward trend in the number of individuals per tax unit over time. This is a concern for measurement of trends if this ratio changes unevenly across income groups, but it poses less of a concern for our measurement of business cycle exposure. Third, the data are repeated cross sections and contain little information on demographics or other information that could allow one to track income changes for a constant population of households. Thus, the changes in income we report are based on income and income rank for groups of households that overlap but are not completely identical across years.[2]

Finally, incomes as reported to the IRS may be affected by tax reforms and by a variety of tax avoidance and tax evasion activities such as non-reporting of income, sheltering of income in 401(k)s, and changes in the reporting of income between closely held business profits and personal income. Tax reforms pose a particular concern since they cause changes in total reported taxable income that are potentially different across different filers. To the extent that such changes disproportionately affect high-income filers, this creates an artificially high correlation between changes in aggregate reported taxable income and changes in the reported taxable income of top income filers. To avoid this problem, we do not measure cyclicality from correlations with tax return–based aggregates, but instead use

---

2. We address each of these issues in our analysis of the Canadian data below and argue that focusing on a constant set of households does not lead to materially different results for the income cyclicality of the top 1 percent.

aggregates from the national income and product accounts (NIPA; see the online data appendix for details).[3] Given this solution, tax reforms as well as the other data issues likely pose larger problems for measuring long-term trends than for measuring cyclicalities (see Reynolds 2007 and Piketty and Saez 2007).

We begin our analysis of these data by reporting the percent growth in income across each boom and recession since 1917, where "boom" and "recession" are defined, respectively, as periods during which NIPA real income per tax unit, before taxes and transfers and excluding capital gains, was increasing, and periods during which it was decreasing. Generally, these periods line up with recessions and expansions as identified by the Business Cycle Dating Committee of the National Bureau of Economic Research.

The dramatic increase in the exposure of high-income tax units to economic fluctuations began in the early 1980s. Table 1 shows the annualized percent change in average income per tax unit for all tax units, for the top 1 percent of the distribution, and for fractional percentiles within the top 1 percent. The final column reports the difference (in percentage points) between this annualized change for the top 1 percent and that for all tax units. Since 1982 the incomes of high-income households have risen more in booms and fallen less in recessions than the average income. According to the final column, since the end of the 1981–82 recession, the average income accruing to the top 1 percent of the income distribution has moved substantially more (in percentage terms) than the overall average in every boom and every recession, on average rising 5.0 percentage points more per year in each boom and falling 3.7 percentage points more per year in each recession.

Further, although one might think it natural for high incomes to be more cyclical, this was not so in the past. In the postwar period before 1982, the incomes of high-income households more often than not moved less (again

---

3. In our analysis this seems to be an important issue only for the 1986 tax reform (top group cyclicalities are higher in the 1980s if a tax-based measure of aggregate income is used). For the 1993 tax reform, Goolsbee (2000) provides evidence that executives timed the exercise of their options to take advantage of lower tax rates in 1992, thus seemingly raising aggregate income in 1992 at the expense of income in 1993. In the NIPA data, aggregate income growth was marginally negative from 1992 to 1993. To avoid artificially overstating our claim about extreme growth rates for top groups, we include 1993 as a boom year in table 1. Note, however, that Hall and Liebman (2000) argue that the high incomes in 1992 may not have been tax motivated, and they show that income shifting is not evident in response to two tax reforms of the 1980s.

Table 1. Changes in Real Income per Tax Unit by Income Group in Expansions and Recessions, 1917–2008
Percent per year except where stated otherwise[a]

Period	All tax units	Top 1 percent	99.0th–99.9th percentile	99.9th–99.99th percentile	Top 0.01 percent	Change for top 1 percent minus change for all tax units (percentage points)
\multicolumn{7}{c}{Expansions (periods with increasing aggregate personal income per tax unit)}
2003–07	1.8	7.8	5.6	8.7	13.9	6.0
1991–2000	2.6	5.8	4.4	7.5	9.0	3.2
1982–89	2.2	7.9	6.0	10.7	14.3	5.7
1980–81	0.8	−2.7	−3.3	−1.3	−0.7	−3.5
1975–79	1.6	1.4	0.9	2.4	3.7	−0.2
1958–73	2.6	1.9	2.0	1.6	1.0	−0.8
1954–57	3.7	2.6	3.1	1.0	2.0	−1.1
1949–53	5.0	−0.1	0.9	−2.0	−4.1	−5.1
1947–48	1.4	4.7	3.3	8.4	7.5	3.3
1938–44	11.0	3.6	4.5	3.0	−0.7	−7.4
1933–37	8.3	9.3	9.7	9.1	7.8	1.0
1924–29	1.8	4.3	3.0	4.1	10.4	2.5
1921–23	12.1	10.3	9.9	9.7	14.1	−1.8
\multicolumn{7}{c}{Recessions (periods with decreasing aggregate personal income per tax unit)}
2007–08	−2.6	−8.4	−6.7	−8.9	−12.7	−5.8
2000–03	−2.3	−5.8	−4.3	−7.7	−8.3	−3.5
1989–91	−1.7	−3.5	−2.2	−6.0	−5.6	−1.8
1981–82	−1.4	2.4	0.3	4.6	15.7	3.9
1979–80	−2.7	−0.9	−1.5	−0.5	3.6	1.8
1973–75	−4.5	−2.5	−3.2	−1.2	1.9	2.0
1957–58	−1.9	−4.7	−4.3	−5.7	−6.1	−2.8
1953–54	−1.1	2.2	2.5	0.2	3.7	3.2
1948–49	−2.3	−4.1	−4.1	−5.3	−1.2	−1.8
1944–47	−5.5	−0.4	0.6	−2.6	−2.4	5.1
1937–38	−8.0	−17.7	−14.4	−22.6	−24.0	−9.7
1929–33	−9.5	−12.8	−11.8	−12.5	−17.7	−3.4
1923–24	−1.2	7.5	6.0	8.8	13.3	8.7
1917–21	−7.6	−10.5	−6.1	−13.2	−22.0	−2.9

Sources: National Income and Product Accounts data, Piketty and Saez (2003), and Saez (2010). See the online appendix (www.brookings.edu/economics/bpea, under "Conferences and Papers") for details.

a. Geometric annual averages calculated over the indicated period. Income is real pre-tax, pre-transfer income excluding capital gains and per tax unit; the same measure is used to define income groups.

in percentage terms) than the income of the average household. In the postwar period (1947 on) up to 1982, the incomes accruing to the top 1 percent co-moved less with the business cycle than did the income of the average household in 9 of the 12 booms and recessions. Relative to total income per tax unit, income accruing to the top 1 percent of tax units on average rose by 1.2 percentage points per year *less* in each boom and fell by 1.1 percentage points per year *less* in each recession. The difference between this period and the post-1982 period is economically large. Finally, in the pre-1947 period, for which the data are of poorer quality and, after 1941, influenced by wartime policies, the income accruing to the top 1 percent does not appear systematically more or less cyclical than that of the average household.

A striking feature of this change, to which we later return, is that it coincides almost exactly with the acceleration in the share of income accruing to the highest earners documented by Piketty and Saez (2003). In their data the income share of the top 1 percent reached its minimum at 7.7 percent in 1973, grew slightly to equal 8.0 in 1981, and then started rising rapidly to reach 17.7 percent in 2008. The coincident timing of the increase in top income shares and the increase in top income exposure to fluctuations suggests a common cause, as we discuss in sections IV and V.[4]

Notice from table 1 that, consistent with an out-of-sample forecast in Parker and Vissing-Jorgensen (2009), incomes of the top 1 percent fell substantially more than the average income in the recent recession—at least based on 2007–08 growth rates—with an 8.4 percent fall (again in real per-tax-unit terms) for the top 1 percent compared with a 2.6 percent fall for the average tax unit. The fall for the top 0.01 percent is even larger, at 12.7 percent. We emphasize that these numbers exclude capital gains and thus to a large extent are driven by wage and salary income, which fell by 3.3 percent from 2007 to 2008 for the average tax unit, by 6.0 percent for the top 1 percent, and by 17.5 percent for the top 0.01 percent. (We elaborate on the role of earned income for the top income groups below.)

Hereafter we will characterize the cyclical exposure of any income group i by a measure of its income cyclicality we call beta, which is the coefficient

---

4. Top income shares were also large in the prewar period, a period in which we do not find evidence for higher cyclicality of the incomes of the top 1 percent. Piketty and Saez (2003) argue that different factors drove the income shares of the top 1 percent during the period of declining inequality and during the period of increasing inequality; see our discussion in section IV. See also Kuznets (1953).

on the logarithmic change in income per member in the total population (Y) in a regression where the dependent variable is the log change in income per member of income group i (Y_i):

(1) $$\Delta \ln Y_{i,t+1} = \alpha_i + \beta_i \Delta \ln Y_{t+1} + \varepsilon_{i,t+1}.$$

Beta is thus the elasticity of the income per member of group i with respect to average income, so that if average income growth is 1 percent, we expect the income of group i to grow by β_i percent.

The top panel of table 2 presents our main findings on the change in cyclicality in terms of beta for the top 1 percent of the distribution and within subgroups of the top 1 percent across periods. The betas of the top 1 percent and the top 0.01 percent of tax units are 2.39 and 3.96, respectively, for the post-1982 period.[5] These levels of cyclicality represent very large increases relative to prior periods: in the periods before 1982, the betas of all top income groups are less than 1, except for the top 0.01 percent for the period 1917–47.

The second panel of table 2 shows how much more income those in the top 1 percent and its subgroups received relative to the average household. These ratios are calculated from the group income shares (group income share/group size). Income per tax unit in the top groups was relatively high in 1917–47 (income per tax unit for the top 0.01 percent was 194 times the average income), was relatively lower in 1948–82 (65 times the average for the top 0.01 percent), and has been relatively high again since 1982 (207 times the average for the top 0.01 percent). In 2008 the top 1 percent included all tax units with incomes above $342,000; the threshold for the top 0.01 percent was $6.4 million. Average income for these two groups was $906,000 and $17.1 million, respectively, in that year.

The different betas and the larger share of income earned by top groups together translate into a disproportionate fraction of aggregate income changes falling on high-income households. To estimate the average fraction of aggregate income changes borne by a group, we regress (dollar change in real group income per tax unit) × (group share of population)/(lagged aggregate real income per tax unit) on the growth rate of aggregate income per tax unit. Across all groups, the numerators sum to the total real dollar

---

5. It is worth clarifying that there is no mechanical tendency for a group to become more exposed to the cycle as its income share increases, but in fact the opposite. In the limit, as a group's income becomes a larger and larger share of all income, its exposure to the aggregate tends toward 1.

Table 2. Cyclicality of Real Income per Tax Unit, by Income Group, 1917–2008[a]

Period	All tax units	Top 1 percent	99.0th–99.9th percentile	99.9th–99.99th percentile	Top 0.01 percent
		Income cyclicality (beta)[b]			
1982–2008	1.00	2.39	1.75	3.08	3.96
		(0.57)	(0.38)	(0.80)	(1.11)
1947–82	1.00	0.72	0.81	0.63	0.02
		(0.20)	(0.16)	(0.36)	(0.36)
1917–47	1.00	0.90	0.82	0.94	1.12
		(0.17)	(0.14)	(0.20)	(0.31)
		Ratio of group average income to average for all tax units			
1982–2008	1.0	13.6	9.2	36.2	206.6
1947–82	1.0	8.7	7.1	18.7	64.6
1917–47	1.0	15.4	10.7	42.6	194.4
		Fraction of aggregate income change borne by group[c]			
1982–2008	1.00	0.266	0.117	0.082	0.067
		(0.059)	(0.024)	(0.019)	(0.018)
1947–82	1.00	0.056	0.046	0.010	–0.000
		(0.016)	(0.010)	(0.007)	(0.002)
		Alternative measures of beta[b]			
Regressing group income growth on median income growth					
1982–2008	0.98	2.27	1.78	2.73	3.43
	(0.14)	(0.77)	(0.51)	(1.10)	(1.49)
1967–82	0.93	0.52	0.64	0.32	–0.19
	(0.13)	(0.25)	(0.19)	(0.44)	(0.58)
Regressing group income growth on unemployment rate					
1982–2008	–0.023	–0.058	–0.043	–0.076	–0.091
	(0.004)	(0.018)	(0.012)	(0.025)	(0.035)
1948–82	–0.021	–0.015	–0.017	–0.013	–0.006
	(0.002)	(0.005)	(0.004)	(0.009)	(0.009)

Sources: Authors' regressions using data in table 1, with additional data for median income growth and the unemployment rate. See the online appendix for details.

a. Standard errors are in parentheses.

b. Coefficient on the log growth rate of average income per tax unit for all tax units (top panel) or on the log growth rate in median household income or on the change in the unemployment rate (bottom panels), in a regression where the dependent variable is the log growth rate of average income per tax unit in the indicated group.

c. Coefficient on the growth rate of average aggregate income per tax unit in a regression where the dependent variable is (change in group average income per tax unit) × (group share of population)/(lagged aggregate average income per tax unit).

change in income per tax unit, so the regression coefficients across a complete set of nonintersecting groups would sum to 1. Since 1982 the fractions of income changes borne by the top 1 percent and the top 0.01 percent are 26.6 percent and 6.7 percent—27 times and 670 times their shares in the population—respectively (third panel of table 2).

We emphasize that the increase in top income cyclicality is robust to using other measures of aggregate fluctuations. The fourth panel of table 2 measures cyclicality by beta with respect to changes in median household income (as calculated by the Census Bureau using the CPS) and with respect to changes in the aggregate unemployment rate. In both cases, measured cyclicality of the top 1 percent is lower than that for all tax units in the early period; from there it more than triples, reaching more than double that of the average tax unit in the recent period.

Furthermore, these changes in cyclical exposure represent actual increases in the cyclical volatility of high incomes. That is, the rise in the cyclical exposure of the top 1 percent is much greater than the decline in total income volatility that occurred in the Great Moderation. In the Piketty-Saez data, the standard deviation of the log change in the average income of the top 1 percent rose significantly, from 0.039 during 1947–82 to 0.085 during 1982–2008; the corresponding numbers for the top 0.01 percent are 0.059 and 0.155, respectively. In terms of cyclicality, the standard deviation of the cyclical component $\beta_i \Delta \ln Y_{t+1}$, rose also for all top income groups, as the standard deviation of $\Delta \ln Y_{t+1}$ fell only from 0.029 to 0.023, a much smaller (percentage) fall than the rise in the β_is in table 2. Thus, for the top 1 percent, the standard deviation of the cyclical component $\beta_i \Delta \ln Y_{t+1}$ rose from 0.021 during 1947–82 to 0.055 during 1982–2008.

I.B. Wages and Salaries

To reiterate, in all of these results, the incomes of high-income groups are measured as cash income before government transfers and taxes, and the income changes are not contaminated by any endogenous timing of realizations of income reported as capital gains. That said, our results so far include income from all other taxable sources: wage and salary income (including bonuses and most stock options), entrepreneurial income, dividends, interest, and rental incomes. We now show that our main findings are driven to a large extent by the changing cyclicality of wage and salary income. We also document that they are not driven by potentially endogenous timing of stock options (more exercising of stock options in booms) or solely due to people with stock options.

Table 3 shows, for the postwar period up to 1982 and the period since, the average share of each group's income that is from each source as defined by the IRS (top panel) and the cyclicality of each type of income (bottom panel). This table documents three main points. First, in the period since 1982, wage and salary income accounts for only a slightly lower share of total income (60 percent) for the top 1 percent than for the average

Table 3. Composition of Income and Cyclicality of Income Growth, by Top Income Group and Income Source, 1947–82 and 1982–2008[a]

	1947–82					1982–2008				
Income source	All tax units	Top 1 percent	99.0th–99.9th percentile	99.9th–99.99th percentile	Top 0.01 percent	All tax units	Top 1 percent	99.0th–99.9th percentile	99.9th–99.99th percentile	Top 0.01 percent
	Average share of income from indicated source									
Wages and salaries	71.9	45.2	49.4	38.8	20.3	67.3	60.3	67.4	53.5	40.0
Entrepreneurial	13.1	28.3	31.2	23.7	11.1	10.2	22.8	19.5	25.8	32.0
Dividends	3.5	17.5	11.1	27.1	56.2	5.0	6.8	5.1	8.4	12.3
Interest	8.2	5.3	5.0	5.8	6.9	15.3	7.7	6.2	8.9	12.2
Rent	3.4	3.8	3.4	4.6	5.4	2.1	2.4	1.9	3.5	3.5
	Beta of group's income from indicated source									
Total income	1.00	0.72	0.81	0.63	0.02	1.00	2.39	1.75	3.08	3.96
		(0.20)	(0.16)	(0.36)	(0.36)		(0.57)	(0.38)	(0.80)	(1.11)
Wages and salaries	1.12	0.36	0.44	0.20	−0.54	0.87	2.38	1.32	3.61	6.20
	(0.05)	(0.14)	(0.13)	(0.27)	(0.85)	(0.06)	(0.58)	(0.31)	(1.08)	(1.93)
Entrepreneurial	1.39	1.87	2.08	1.82	−1.54	1.33	2.07	2.29	0.76	1.53
	(0.25)	(0.68)	(0.59)	(0.99)	(2.52)	(0.33)	(1.31)	(1.13)	(2.91)	(1.78)
Dividends	1.16	0.85	0.96	0.83	0.62	1.24	2.65	3.37	2.33	1.64
	(0.29)	(0.38)	(0.39)	(0.68)	(0.34)	(0.57)	(1.26)	(0.97)	(1.62)	(1.93)
Interest	0.00	−0.10	−0.14	−0.04	0.06	1.54	4.52	4.41	5.24	3.84
	(0.19)	(0.48)	(0.44)	(0.66)	(0.80)	(0.39)	(1.28)	(1.18)	(1.22)	(1.71)
Rent	0.62	−0.44	−0.17	−0.73	−1.14	−1.36	−0.26	−0.49	−0.37	−0.54
	(0.41)	(0.87)	(0.98)	(0.93)	(1.53)	(1.29)	(1.61)	(3.61)	(2.07)	(1.54)

Sources: See table 1. See the online appendix for details.

a. Income is total pre-tax, pre-transfer income excluding capital gains. Standard errors are in parentheses.

household (two-thirds). Wages and salaries are a smaller but still significant share of income for the top 0.01 percent (40 percent).

Second, and more important, since 1982 the wage and salary income of high-income groups is much more cyclical than that for all tax units. To maintain comparability across types of income and in the definition of an economic fluctuation, for all types we define cyclicality with respect to fluctuations in NIPA aggregate pre-tax, pre-transfer income excluding capital gains per tax unit. Since 1982 the wage and salary income of the top 1 percent has a cyclicality of 2.4, and that of the top 0.01 percent a cyclicality of 6.2, compared with a cyclicality of less than 1 for all tax units. The cyclicality of wage and salary income of the top 1 percent is about the same as that of their overall income (and thus as the average cyclicality of their other types of income), whereas the cyclicality of wage and salary income of the top 0.01 percent exceeds that of all their other types of income.

Third, the change in cyclicality of the top 1 percent since 1982 is to a large extent driven by the rise in the share of wages and salaries in their total income and the change in its cyclicality, with a smaller role for increased cyclicality of dividend and interest income. The top panel of table 3 shows that the share of wage and salary income in the incomes of the top 1 percent rose by 15 percentage points across periods. The bottom panel shows a dramatic increase in the cyclicality of the wages and salaries of the top 1 percent, from 0.4 in the 1947–82 period to 2.4 in the 1982–2008 period. Across periods there is also a substantial increase in the cyclicality of dividend and interest income for the top 1 percent, but these two sources are smaller shares of income. The cyclicality of entrepreneurial income for the top 1 percent is relatively stable, at around 2 for both 1947–82 and 1982–2008. For the top 0.01 percent, the change in cyclicality is more widespread across categories, but again the largest role is played by wage and salary income.

We next investigate the role of stock options in our findings. The rise of stock options coincides with the rise of income inequality, and the vast majority of stock options are nonqualified options, which are treated for tax purposes as wage and salary income when exercised.[6] Because our

---

6. Qualified stock options are taxed as capital gains when exercised and the stocks received are sold, provided that they are held for a year and that the stocks purchased with them are held for another year. The gain resulting from the difference between the strike price and the market price, however, can count toward income for purposes of the alternative minimum tax. We do not deal here with the accounting treatment of stock options for financial reporting, which differs from the tax treatment for the individual; for example, it allows corporations to deduct more on their tax returns than they expense on their financial statements.

analysis so far is based on tax return data, it includes income from non-qualified options in wage and salary income. We are concerned that either endogenous timing of the exercise of stock options (if more are exercised in booms) or a correlation between stock market performance and aggregate income might make our measure of realized top incomes excessively procyclical even if actual economic earnings were not. Thus, we address two questions concerning options. First, is income from options sufficiently prevalent in the top 1 percent to be the main driver of high wage and salary cyclicality? Second, do we still find high cyclicality of top incomes if we include options in income when granted (at values determined by the Black-Scholes model) instead of when exercised (as in the tax data)?

To address the first question, we use the Survey of Consumer Finances (SCF) for 1998, 2001, 2004, and 2007, which contains information on wealth and income (for the preceding calendar year) for a stratified random sample of households that oversamples rich households. These years of the SCF also include the responses to two survey questions about stock options. The first asks whether the household received stock options during the past year, and the second asks whether the household has a valuable asset not otherwise recorded in the interview and then asks the household to state what it is, with stock options being one possible response. SCF data are not top coded, with the exception that a household is dropped if it has a net worth greater than the least wealthy person in the Forbes list of the wealthiest 400 people in the United States.[7] On average across the four survey years, only 22 percent of households in the top 1 percent of the income distribution had stock options. Furthermore, the cyclicality of income growth (of non-capital gains income, based on aggregate income calculated from SCF data and using 3-year real log growth rates) is around 1.8 both for all households in the top 1 percent and for households in the top 1 percent without stock options. This indicates that income from stock options is not driving our main findings.

To answer the second question, we use data on executive compensation from ExecuComp, which are available for 1992 to 2009. Our sample definition is described in the online data appendix (at www.brookings.edu/economics/bpea, under "Conferences and Papers"). The average number of executives covered in our sample is 6,216 per year. The top panel of table 4 shows that in these data the average total executive compensation (in real 2008 dollars) was $1.6 million in 1992 based on the value

---

7. This should not affect our results substantially, since the top 400 families correspond to only a small fraction of even the top 0.01 percent.

Table 4. Cyclicality of Income of Corporate Executives, 1992–2009

	1992	2009
	Millions of 2008 dollars	
Average real total compensation		
Based on value of options granted[a]	1.45	2.43
Based on value of options exercised[b]	1.63	2.39
	Percent	
Average share of total compensation by component, based on value of options granted[c]		
Salary	32.6	20.2
Bonus	18.6	5.6
Stock grants	7.0	29.3
Option grants	29.6	19.4
Other[d]	12.2	25.6
	Beta	Standard error
Cyclicality of component income growth[e]		
Based on value of options granted		
Total compensation	2.89	0.86
Salary	−0.12	0.13
Bonus	1.01	0.93
Stock grants	2.82	1.02
Option grants	5.36	1.70
Other[d]	0.97	1.57
Based on value of options exercised		
Total compensation	4.39	1.15
Option grants	10.86	2.24
Excluding options		
Total compensation	1.01	0.62
	2007–08	2008–09
	Percent	
Growth rate of total real compensation		
Based on value of options granted	−8.3	−5.3
Based on value of options exercised	−20.1	−18.2

Sources: Authors' calculations using ExecuComp data. See the online data appendix for details.

a. ExecuComp series tdc1.

b. ExecuComp series tdc2.

c. Average compensation from the indicated component divided by average total compensation. Numbers may not sum to 100 because of rounding.

d. For example, nonequity incentive plan compensation.

e. Estimation based on log growth and excluding the 2005–06 growth rate, which may be affected by changes in reporting requirements in 2006.

of options exercised. Using the group income cutoffs in the Piketty-Saez data, on average across 1992–2009, 81 percent of the ExecuComp executives were in the top 1 percent, and 7 percent were in the top 0.01 percent.[8] The second panel of the table shows that the executives received a substantial fraction of their income in the form of options. The table also reports betas for each income component (calculated from annual averages of each type of income across executives). The beta of overall compensation is 2.9 based on the value of options granted, and 4.4 based on the value of options exercised. Given that only a small fraction of those in the top 1 percent have stock options income (according to the SCF data) and that the beta of executive compensation based on the value of options granted is about two-thirds that based on the value of options exercised (as calculated from the ExecuComp data), we conclude that endogenous timing of options is not likely to have substantially affected our beta estimates for wages and salaries using the Piketty-Saez data.

Interestingly, these findings do not imply that options are not critical for the income cyclicality of top earners who do receive stock options. For executives in the ExecuComp data, options income does drive the high cyclicality of their wage and salary income: their beta of compensation excluding options is around 1. That is, the cyclical component of their income is (granted) options. For these results to be consistent with our results from the SCF, however, it must therefore be that nonoptions wage and salary income is highly cyclical for top earners without options. Bonuses or other incentive pay may play a central role for these households, but our data sources (aside from ExecuComp) do not separately break out bonuses.

A final observation can be made from the ExecuComp data. Table 4 also shows the growth rates of real compensation for executives in this sample for 2007–08 and 2008–09. The negative growth rates for 2007–08 of −8.3 percent and −20.1 percent (depending on which options data are used) confirm the finding based on the data for all top 1 percent tax units in table 1 that top income groups were hit harder by the recent recession than the average household. For 2008–09 the executives in the ExecuComp data did much worse than the average tax unit (for which we estimate, using NIPA data, that wage and salary income fell by 5.3 percent

---

8. With an average of 137 million tax units across 1992–2009, the top 1 percent consists of, on average, 1,370,000 households, and the top 0.01 percent of, on average, 13,700 households. Households headed by executives represented in ExecuComp thus make up a tiny fraction of both the top 1 percent and the top 0.01 percent.

in real per-tax-unit terms) when we measure income including the value of options exercised, but similar to the average tax unit when we use the value of options granted.[9]

I.C. Who Is in the Top 1 Percent?

To further understand what drives the higher cyclicality of income of the top 1 percent, it is useful to document the characteristics of families in that group and how these have changed across periods. Since this is not feasible in the Piketty-Saez data, we use the March CPS public use microdata files. We study the characteristics of families and their heads for the entire population and for the top 1 percent using pre-tax, post-transfer family income excluding capital gains.[10] Table 5 reports statistics averaged across the 5 years ending in 1982 and across the 5 years ending in 2008.

Heads of families in the top 1 percent tend to be slightly older than the average, are more likely to be married, and are less likely to be retired. They are more likely to be white, self-employed, and more educated. Perhaps surprisingly, the top 1 percent are widely dispersed across industries and occupations. This makes it less likely that a particular industry or occupation is driving most of the high cyclicality of incomes among this group. For example, it is unlikely that the increased cyclicality of the top 1 percent is due only to more of them being employed in finance today than earlier, or to incomes in financial occupations having become more cyclical (although finance may be more important for the top 0.01 percent), for two reasons. First, the share of the top 1 percent in finance (and related industries) is only 16 percent even at the end of our sample period, up by about 4.4 percentage points from the early 1980s. Therefore, whether one assumes that the beta of incomes in the finance industry is constant but that more of the top 1 percent are now employed in finance, or one allows the beta of finance to increase, the beta for finance in the post-1982 period would have to be at least 11 in order for finance to explain

---

9. The more meaningful comparison here is probably the one based on value of options exercised, since NIPA wages and salaries are based on that concept (see Moylan 2008). The treatment of options in the NIPA is unlikely to materially affect our results, since options income is only a tiny fraction of overall NIPA income. Furthermore, as shown in the bottom panel of table 2, our main results are very similar when we use unemployment or median income to measure aggregate fluctuations.

10. We use this definition of income to match with previous work using the CPS, since comparability is important for our analysis in section II.A.

Table 5. Demographic, Educational, and Occupational Characteristics of Heads of Families in the Top 1 Percent of the Income Distribution, 1978–82 and 2004–08[a]

Characteristic	Top 1 percent[b]		All families	
	1978–82	2004–08	1978–82	2004–08
	Units as indicated			
Demographics				
Average age	50.7	47.8	45.1	46.9
Percent with children under 18	37.9	50.6	51.5	46.4
Average no. of children under 18	0.7	1.0	1.0	0.9
Percent married	97.8	97.0	87.3	84.6
Percent retired	7.0	12.3	14.8	29.6
Percent white	95.9	88.3	87.6	81.7
Percent self-employed	39.4	27.8	11.6	9.1
	Percent of all family heads			
Education				
Less than high school	5.3	1.3	30.2	12.1
High school diploma	15.6	9.8	33.2	31.3
Some college	13.7	13.0	18.0	27.5
College degree	31.6	33.1	12.3	18.6
Post-college education	33.7	42.8	6.3	10.5
Industry				
Manufacturing and construction	22.0	11.8	28.3	14.9
Finance, insurance, and real estate	11.6	16.0	3.9	5.2
Professional services	24.7	41.8	11.4	23.0
Wholesale and retail trade	13.3	9.2	12.8	9.7
Other	28.4	21.3	43.5	47.1
	1982–85	*1998–2001*	*1982–85*	*1998–2001*
Occupation[c]				
Executive, administrative, or managerial	34.7	35.5	10.8	12.3
Professional specialty	29.6	32.1	9.4	11.6
Sales	16.0	13.1	8.3	8.4
Other	19.7	19.3	71.6	67.7

Sources: Authors' calculations using Census public use data from the March CPS files from 1979 to 2009, referring to the previous year's income and labor force characteristics. See the online data appendix for details.

a. "Families" excludes people not living with someone related to them by blood or marriage. This definition includes about 90 percent of households in the top 1 percent of the income distribution and 76 percent of households in the general population (as determined from the 1995 Survey of Consumer Finances). Reported percentages and averages are averaged across years in the indicated period.

b. As defined by CPS family income (pre-tax, post-transfer income excluding capital gains).

c. We use a common occupation coding for income years 1982–2001.

the increase in beta of the entire top 1 percent from 0.7 to 2.4 (top panel of table 2).[11]

Second, to the extent we can estimate betas of the top 1 percent at the industry or occupation level, we find no evidence that the beta for those in finance is dramatically larger than the betas of other top 1 percent households.[12] Jon Bakija, Adam Cole, and Bradley Heim (2010) provide data for the top 1 percent and the top 0.1 percent that are comparable to the data from Piketty and Saez but contain information about occupations (coded from taxpayer responses to the occupation question on Form 1040). We use their data for 1993, 1997, 1999, and 2001–05 to calculate log growth rates (annualized in the case of 4- or 2-year periods) and regress these on aggregate log growth rates (using the same aggregate variable we used earlier). Four occupations account for more than 5 percent of tax units in the top 1 percent and the top 0.1 percent. These are "executives, managers, and supervisors (non-finance)," "financial professions, including management," "lawyers," and "medical." Using these data, we estimate a beta of 1.99 for the full top 1 percent, and betas for the four subgroups listed of 1.96, 2.34, 1.67, and 0.71. For the top 0.1 percent we estimate a beta of 2.82 for the full group and betas of 2.27, 3.08, 3.60, and 2.34 for the four main subgroups (all estimates listed have associated t statistics of 2 or more). With the exception of medical occupations within the top 1 percent, this suggests that betas are high across all the largest subgroups of the top 1 percent and the top 0.1 percent.

I.D. Consumption

We next turn to the question of whether the high cyclicality of income for high-income households leads to a high cyclicality of consumption

---

11. We calculate this as follows. Let a' and a denote the share of the top 1 percent employed in finance during 1982–2008 and 1947–82, respectively, and let β' and β denote the income cyclicality of the top 1 percent in these two periods. If the beta of those in the top 1 percent not employed in finance was constant at 1, then $a'\beta' + (1 - a') = 2.4$ and $a\beta + (1 - a) = 0.7$, and thus $a'\beta' - a\beta - (a' - a) = 1.7$. Suppose (based on table 5) that $a' = 0.16$, and assume (to give finance its best chance at being the explanation) that $a = 0.06$ (lower than the pre-1982 value from table 5). Then $0.16 \times \beta' - 0.06\beta = 1.8$. Consider two possible cases: If $\beta = \beta'$, then $\beta' = 18$. Alternatively, if $\beta = 1$, then $\beta' = 11.6$.

12. The CPS data (described in more detail in section II) are problematic for this purpose because values assigned to top-coded observations are not industry specific, implying that betas for top 1 percent households across industries could spuriously look similar. With that important reservation, we find that within each of the four industries listed in table 5, betas for families in the top 1 percent are much larger than for the average family, and the top 1 percent finance industry beta is roughly similar to that for the nonfinance industries taken as a group.

spending. Evidence on this question constitutes a further test of our main finding, as well as of the extent to which consumption is smoothed across these income changes, as would be the case for insurable changes in income or endogenous timing of income. Unfortunately, high-income groups are generally thought to be underrepresented in the Consumer Expenditure Survey (CE), and some CE consumption categories are top coded.[13] Furthermore, in order to have a sufficient number of households, our analysis here focuses on the top 5 percent of CE households rather than the top 1 percent. Nonetheless, our analysis shows higher cyclicality for high-consumption households.

We use the CE data to construct measures of household-level spending from January 1982 to February 2009 for different groups ranked by their expenditure level in the quarter before the interview. Our consumption measure is nondurables plus some services; the main categories of excluded services are health care, education, and housing (except for the nondurable and service components of household operations). We deflate the reported consumption values using the Bureau of Labor Statistics (BLS) price index for nondurables. For each household we calculate log-consumption growth rates from one quarter to the next and average these across households in a given group (using survey weights). We then calculate annual log growth rates by summing four quarterly log growth rates. For each group we run a time-series regression of the four-quarter log growth rates in consumption per household on the log growth rate of one of four different series (in separate regressions): NIPA pre-tax, pre-transfer income; NIPA disposable (that is, post-tax, post-transfer) income; NIPA personal consumption expenditures (PCE) on nondurables and services; and CE average consumption for all households (using our consumption definition). For comparability across regressions in table 6 and for comparability with the earlier tables, the first three regressions all use the same price deflator, the CPI series from Piketty and Saez, whereas the regression with CE average consumption as the explanatory variable uses the BLS deflator (since both the left- and the right-hand-side variable are based on the same consumption measure).

Table 6 shows that the sensitivity of the consumption of households in the top 5 percent of the distribution (ranked by initial consumption) to

---

13. Because of the way the CE is structured, the respondent's burden rises with expenditure: more time is required to report more expenditure. Further, there is evidence that underreporting rises with expenditure. See, for example, Aguiar and Bils (2010).

Table 6. Cyclicality of Real Consumption among All Households and the Top 5 Percent, January 1982–February 2009[a]

Measure	All households	Top 5 percent
Ratio of group average consumption to average consumption of all households	1.00	2.52
Beta from regression of consumption on:[b]		
NIPA pre-tax, pre-transfer personal income	0.58	1.94
	(0.14)	(0.50)
NIPA post-tax, post-transfer personal income	0.61	2.60
	(0.23)	(0.61)
NIPA nondurables and services consumption	1.17	4.80
	(0.27)	(0.97)
CE consumption for all households	1.00	2.38
		(0.30)
Fraction of total CE consumption fluctuations borne by group[c]	1.00	0.32
		(0.04)

Sources: Authors' calculations and regressions using data from the Consumer Expenditure Survey (CE).

a. Consumption includes expenditure on nondurable goods and some services. Groups are defined based on their consumption in the previous survey interview. Changes for all variables in all regressions are measured as 4-quarter log growth rates. Standard errors are in parentheses.

b. Each beta is the coefficient on the log change in the indicated aggregate in a regression where the dependent variable is the log change in consumption per household in the indicated group.

c. Coefficient on the growth rate of aggregate CE consumption per household in a regression where the dependent variable is (change in group average consumption per household) × (group share of population)/ (lagged aggregate average consumption per household).

aggregate income fluctuations is between 1.9 and 2.6, depending on the income measure used, whereas the sensitivity to aggregate consumption fluctuations is almost 5.[14] This compares with a sensitivity of the consumption of the full set of CE households that is substantially less than 1 with respect to NIPA incomes.

The implications of this higher cyclicality are borne out in the expenditure response of high-consumption households to the recent deep recession. Figure 1 shows that CE consumption in the recent recession fell substantially more for high-expenditure households—more than 10 percent from 2007 to 2008—than the average for all households. This finding is

---

14. The sensitivities of top household consumption to NIPA consumption are a bit lower than similar statistics for a shorter sample reported in Parker and Vissing-Jorgensen (2009). The difference is due not to differences in the samples, but rather to the price index used: Parker and Vissing-Jorgensen (2009) used a PCE deflator to deflate NIPA consumption, whereas the results reported here use the CPI series from Piketty and Saez.

Figure 1. Cumulative Change in Log Real Expenditure per Household, 2005–09ᵃ

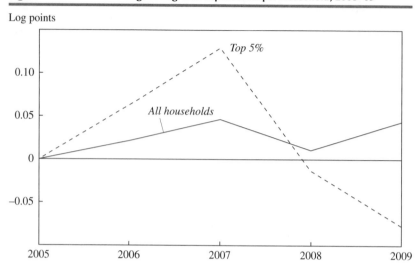

Source: Authors' calculations using Consumer Expenditure Survey data for 2005 to February 2009.
a. Annual values are within-year averages (using survey weights) of quarterly consumption (multiplied by 4). The consumption measure is nondurables and some services. Households are sorted on the basis of current consumption.

consistent with the out-of-sample forecast in Parker and Vissing-Jorgensen (2009).[15]

These results provide additional evidence that the high cyclicality of top incomes is not due to the endogenous timing of compensation but instead affects the standard of living for top income households. We emphasize, however, that a given percent decline in expenditure presumably has greater welfare implications for a low-expenditure household than for a high-expenditure household. This point, along with the lack of foundation for interpersonal welfare comparisons, suggests that one should not conclude that high-income households suffer more from recessions than do low-income households.

---

15. For better readability, the figure focuses on annual data, calculated as within-year averages (using survey weights) of quarterly consumption values across households in a given group (multiplied by 4). Furthermore, because we are interested in showing levels of growth rates, not only their betas with respect to aggregates, we sort households according to current consumption rather than consumption in the previous quarter. The latter method is theoretically more meaningful but, with measurement error in consumption, leads to a mechanical negative bias in growth rates for top groups. As discussed in Parker and Vissing-Jorgensen (2009), this does not affect the estimation of betas when log growth rates are used, but it would bias this figure.

To conclude, we find a dramatic increase in the cyclicality of top incomes. This increase occurs for total (non-capital gains) income as well as for wage and salary income alone, and top groups' expenditures are also highly cyclical during the post-1982 period. Furthermore, the top 1 percent are active in a wide range of industries and occupations, making it less likely that a particular industry or occupation is driving most of the high cyclicality of top groups' incomes.

II. Cyclicalities across the Full Income Distribution and the Impact of Transfers, Taxes, and Capital Gains

In this section we use data on the entire distribution of incomes across households to reconcile our findings with the conventional wisdom that low-income households are the most affected by booms and recessions and that this greater sensitivity is due to higher cyclicality of hours worked among this group. Further, in studying the entire distribution, we also characterize how the tax-and-transfer system changes the cyclicality of take-home income. Finally, we track individual families rather than the income distribution across years as an alternative to using repeated cross-sectional data.

II.A. Relating Our Findings to the Conventional Wisdom

Previous studies have shown that the incomes of low-income households are more cyclical because unemployment falls primarily on low-wage workers (Clark and Summers 1981, Kydland 1984), whereas the wages of low-wage households have approximately the same exposure to the business cycle as those of high-wage households (Solon, Barsky, and Parker 1994). The flip side is that economic booms raise the standard of living of low-income households by more than they do high-income households (Card and Blank 1993, Hines, Hoynes, and Krueger 2001). Rebecca Blank (1989, p. 142), for example, concludes that "the income distribution narrows in times of economic expansion." There are three reasons why the conventional wisdom might not have detected the high cyclicality of top incomes: first, the time period, since high-income cyclicality began to rise only in the 1980s; second, the focus on broad groups, since cyclicality is high only for the very top of the distribution; and third, the top coding of incomes in conventional survey datasets, since this masks changes in income at the top end of the income distribution.

To begin, we track income groups using the March CPS public use microdata files for 1968–2008. The definition of income is the standard Census definition, namely, pre-tax, post-transfer income excluding capital gains, and the unit of observation is a Census-defined family.[16] We drop changes across years with major top code changes, and we note that after 1996 the data report the mean income for families above the top-coded amount, whereas before they simply report the income top code amount in place of actual income when top coded.

Following some of the earlier literature, the top panel of table 7 shows the cyclicality of incomes of low-education families (which are typically also lower-income families) and high-education families (typically higher-income families). Families are categorized according to the characteristics of the head, and we examine cyclicality with respect to average CPS income and the NIPA pre-tax, pre-transfer income (excluding capital gains) measure used in the earlier tables. Even during the period from 1982 on, there is some evidence that the conventional facts about cyclicality hold in that low-education households are more exposed to economic fluctuations than high-education households.

Turning to the top 1 percent, we show in the sixth column of table 7 that from 1968 to 1982, incomes in the top 1 percent of the distribution in the CPS were less cyclical than the average, with a beta of roughly 0.6. Thus, the previous literature is entirely correct about the early part of the period it studies. But when one focuses on the top 1 percent in the period since 1982 (next column), the cyclicality of that group's income is estimated to be 1.97 or 1.00, depending on the measure of income used—estimates as large as those for families with less than a high school education. The higher top 1 percent cyclicality after 1982 is presumably due to the later period, to increases in the top code level at several points over the years, and, after 1996, to the increased variability in amounts reported for top-coded observations.

Finally, we use a measure of the top 1 percent income share in the CPS constructed by Burkhauser and others (2008, 2009) using internal Census Bureau data for the CPS. These data measure top 1 percent income shares more accurately than is possible with the top-coded, publicly released microdata because the internal data are subject only to high-end censoring due to the number of digits allocated to the internally recorded income variable. That said, there are a number of additional issues with the accuracy of internal CPS top income data, and the series of Burkhauser and coauthors does

---

16. This definition has the benefit of dropping households consisting of unrelated individuals, but the disadvantage of dropping single individuals without children. The latter account for only about 10 percent of households in the top 1 percent, but 24 percent of the general population, according to the 1995 SCF.

Table 7. Cyclicality of Income by Education and of Top 1 Percent, Using CPS Data[a]

	Cyclicality by level of education, using public use data on families, 1982–2008					Cyclicality of top 1 percent			
						Using public use data on families		Using public use and internal data[b]	
Beta	Less than high school	Some high school	Some college	College graduate	More than college	1968–82	1982–2008	1982–2006, series 1	1982–2006, series 2
With respect to CPS income	1.52	0.94	0.91	1.08	0.73	0.55	1.97	2.57	2.44
	(0.19)	(0.13)	(0.14)	(0.14)	(0.21)	(0.30)	(0.75)	(0.58)	(0.35)
With respect to NIPA income	0.85	0.67	0.67	0.78	0.63	0.64	1.00	1.81	2.18
	(0.34)	(0.19)	(0.20)	(0.22)	(0.23)	(0.46)	(0.83)	(0.84)	(0.62)

Source: Authors' regressions using Census CPS data and data from Burkhauser and others (2010).

a. Public use data are March CPS public use data files from 1968 to 2009; see the online data appendix for further details. When using these data, we drop changes across the following years with major top code changes: 1980–81, 1983–84, 1994–95, and 2001–02. In addition, when using internal CPS data for households (series 1) we drop changes for 1992–93, when the Census allocated more digits to the internal record that stores the income series; series 2, covering tax units, is adjusted for this jump. We do not use income data for 1973–75 because the 1975 data are missing weights, and the 1973 and 1974 data have more than 1 percent of income data top coded. Income for defining the top 1 percent and in the regressions is CPS family income, which is pre-tax, post-transfer income excluding capital gains. Standard errors are in parentheses.

b. Data are based on internal CPS files and are from Burkhauser and others (2010), provided (in updated version) by the authors. Series 1 from Burkhauser and others (2010) measures the top 1 percent income share in the distribution of households, and series 2 measures top 1 percent income share in the distribution of tax units.

not show as significant an increase in top income shares as the tax data (see Burkhauser and others 2008, 2009, and Atkinson and others 2010). Despite these caveats, as displayed in the last two columns of table 7, these internal CPS survey data show an even higher cyclicality of the top 1 percent than the public data, and one that is very similar to that of the Piketty-Saez data from table 3.[17]

The previous literature, furthermore, shows that the cyclicality of the incomes of low-income families is largely due to the cyclicality of their hours worked. We now show that hours cyclicality plays only a minor role for the cyclicality of the top 1 percent. First, using all families in the CPS, we calculate average usual hours worked per week in each year for different income groups. For each group we regress the change in log average hours on the change in log real NIPA income (pre-tax, pre-transfer income, excluding capital gains), using data for 1982–2008. The cyclicality of hours for the top 1 percent is 0.26 (but with a standard error of 0.30), which is similar to the cyclicality of hours for all families, which we estimate to be 0.22 (with a standard error of 0.06). Thus, although the results are weak statistically, there is no evidence of a different cyclicality in hours for the top 1 percent. Second, we use the CPS hours data to adjust our measure of the wage and salary income of the top 1 percent from the Piketty-Saez data. We regress log growth in wages and salaries on log growth in hours and use the residual in place of the original wage and salaries series in our analysis of cyclicality. The cyclicality of "hours-adjusted" wages and salaries is estimated to be 2.2 for the top 1 percent, only slightly lower than the cyclicality of the unadjusted series, which is 2.4 (table 3). A similar exercise for the bottom quintile (using merged SOI-CPS data on the bottom quintile's income, as described in the next subsection) finds that most of the cyclicality for that group is in fact due to the cyclicality of hours worked, consistent with the previous literature.[18] Our analysis implies that, in contrast with the bottom end of the distribution, most of the cyclicality of the

---

17. To use these data, which report "true" (internal CPS) income shares, we infer the missing amount of income of the top 1 percent (denoted x) and thus also the missing amount from total income in the public CPS (denoted Y) from the relationship $(Y + x) \times$ (internal CPS income share) $= (Y^{1\%} + x)$, where $Y^{1\%}$ is the total income of the top 1 percent of families in the public data. Burkhauser and others (2010) provide two series for the internal CPS top 1 percent income share, one based on households and one based on tax units. Since neither matches our choice of CPS unit of analysis perfectly, we show results based on both.

18. Castro and Coen-Pirani (2008) provide further analysis of the cyclicality of hours, focusing on a comparison of college-educated with non-college-educated individuals.

top 1 percent is due to fluctuating payments for work rather than fluctuating hours worked.

We conclude that our results on income cyclicality both by education group in the CPS and for the top 1 percent before 1982 support the conventional view that low incomes are more cyclical. However, after 1982, even in this conventional survey dataset which has top-coded incomes, high income cyclicality is observable for the top 1 percent, and even higher cyclicality can be measured from versions of the data not subject to the top coding imposed on the public release files. Furthermore, this high cyclicality does not appear to be driven by cyclicality in hours worked, as it is for the bottom income groups. We now turn to a dataset from the Congressional Budget Office (CBO) that combines information from the CPS and the SOI data and allows us to study the entire distribution of income without the confounding issues of top coding.

II.B. Cyclicalities across the Full Income Distribution

To study the complete income distribution, this subsection employs a dataset from the Congressional Budget Office (2008) that merges data from the IRS SOI and data from the CPS to estimate average household income for different groups of households in different years. The two most important differences between the SOI-CPS data from the Congressional Budget Office and the SOI data used in tables 1, 2, and 3 are the unit of analysis and the definition of income used to sort households. The unit of analysis is the household in the SOI-CPS data and a tax unit in the SOI data. In terms of income, in the SOI-CPS data, households are sorted on pre-tax income per effective householder *including* transfers and capital gains, whereas in the Piketty-Saez SOI data, tax units are sorted on pre-tax income *excluding* transfers and capital gains. Our online data appendix provides further details.

The SOI-CPS data confirm our earlier findings for top income groups for this different set of choices about income measurement and unit of analysis. Table 8 shows statistics on the income distribution and cyclicality across the first four quintiles, in detail for the top quintile, and then in further detail for the top 1 percent. Focusing first on wages and salaries and on pre-tax, pre-transfer income excluding capital gains, as in all our analysis up to this point, we find (top panel) that the top 1 percent in the SOI-CPS data earn about 11 times, and the top 0.01 percent about 150 times, the average income; both these results are fairly similar to those reported in the second panel of table 2. The second panel of table 8 shows that all household groupings except the top 1 percent get 60 to 70 percent of their

Table 8. Cyclicality of Income by Measure of Income and Income Group, Merged IRS SOI and CPS Data, 1982–2005[a]

Measure or source of income	All households	Lowest quintile	Second quintile	Middle quintile	Fourth quintile	80th–90th percentile	90th–95th percentile	95th–99.0th percentile	Top 1 percent	99.0th–99.9th percentile	99.9th–99.99th percentile	Top 0.01 percent
					Ratio of average income in group to average for all households							
Pre-tax, pre-transfer excluding capital gains	1.00	0.17	0.47	0.76	1.14	1.58	2.04	3.05	10.96	5.77	29.42	150.59
Pre-tax, post-transfer excluding capital gains	1.00	0.23	0.51	0.79	1.12	1.52	1.96	2.91	10.31	5.47	27.55	140.68
Pre-tax, post-transfer including capital gains	1.00	0.22	0.49	0.75	1.08	1.47	1.92	2.94	12.80	6.37	36.42	242.46
Post-tax, post-transfer including capital gains	1.00	0.26	0.54	0.80	1.10	1.46	1.86	2.78	11.17	7.14	31.14	206.14
					Average share of indicated source in pre-tax, pre-transfer income excluding capital gains (percent)							
Wages and salaries	67.20	61.89	67.55	69.45	72.14	72.85	70.30	62.44	44.20	65.83	38.18	26.54
Pensions	5.02	3.09	4.44	6.25	5.84	5.53	5.45	4.71	1.85	3.22	1.16	0.39
Proprietors' and other business income	6.54	5.27	4.07	3.22	3.09	3.80	5.56	11.44	21.33	26.57	23.66	24.14
Interest and dividends	6.92	3.02	3.08	4.15	4.47	4.88	6.49	10.05	18.72	21.52	21.75	25.31
In-kind income	6.67	20.94	13.30	9.28	6.79	5.25	4.38	3.21	1.03	1.93	0.42	0.06
Imputed taxes	6.95	5.61	5.90	6.16	6.34	6.37	6.46	6.65	11.01	11.08	12.69	21.65
Other	0.69	0.16	1.65	1.50	1.32	1.27	1.33	1.50	1.87	2.28	2.17	1.88
Pre-tax, pre-transfer income excluding capital gains	100.00	100.00	100.00	100.00	100.00	100.00	100.00	100.00	100.00	100.00	100.00	100.00

	C1	C2	C3	C4	C5	C6	C7	C8	C9	C10	C11	C12
Cash transfers	7.27	40.43	18.23	10.35	5.87	3.72	3.02	2.38	0.87	1.59	0.37	0.11
Capital gains	5.13	0.36	0.37	0.49	0.77	1.32	2.35	5.90	31.39	23.34	41.52	92.48
Taxes	24.22	10.16	15.55	18.71	21.21	23.51	25.25	28.08	41.22	43.37	45.90	62.78
Post-tax, post-transfer income including capital gains	88.19	130.63	103.04	92.14	85.43	81.53	80.12	80.19	91.05	109.97	95.99	129.81
Beta of indicated income source or measure with respect to aggregate (NIPA) pre-tax, pre-transfer income excluding capital gains												
Wages and salaries	0.83	0.79	1.00	0.63	0.78	0.70	0.44	0.67	2.40	1.40	4.15	5.88
	(0.08)	(0.38)	(0.34)	(0.18)	(0.11)	(0.16)	(0.14)	(0.15)	(0.84)	(0.59)	(1.27)	(2.34)
Pre-tax, pre-transfer income excluding capital gains	0.90	0.76	0.90	0.66	0.69	0.67	0.67	1.01	2.16	0.77	3.07	3.33
	(0.12)	(0.32)	(0.27)	(0.13)	(0.08)	(0.12)	(0.10)	(0.16)	(0.73)	(0.77)	(1.00)	(1.71)
Pre-tax, post-transfer income excluding capital gains	0.78	0.41	0.61	0.48	0.59	0.61	0.66	1.01	2.16	0.78	3.06	3.34
	(0.11)	(0.24)	(0.20)	(0.11)	(0.08)	(0.10)	(0.09)	(0.16)	(0.72)	(0.74)	(0.99)	(1.70)
Pre-tax, post-transfer income including capital gains	1.07	0.45	0.64	0.51	0.63	0.68	0.79	1.24	3.28	1.82	4.16	5.47
	(0.22)	(0.24)	(0.20)	(0.11)	(0.08)	(0.12)	(0.12)	(0.26)	(1.03)	(0.48)	(1.62)	(2.09)
Post-tax, post-transfer income including capital gains	0.91	0.38	0.50	0.40	0.49	0.51	0.65	1.11	3.48	2.35	4.56	6.09
	(0.21)	(0.24)	(0.19)	(0.12)	(0.10)	(0.12)	(0.14)	(0.29)	(1.16)	(0.77)	(1.81)	(2.30)
Fraction of aggregate (merged IRS SOI and CPS) income change borne by indicated group												
Pre-tax, pre-transfer income excluding capital gains	1.00	0.034	0.097	0.115	0.158	0.107	0.064	0.132	0.288	0.048	0.098	0.065
		(0.011)	(0.022)	(0.018)	(0.016)	(0.013)	(0.011)	(0.014)	(0.049)	(0.016)	(0.016)	(0.017)
Post-tax, post-transfer income including capital gains	1.00	0.016	0.041	0.056	0.100	0.075	0.063	0.140	0.482	0.185	0.159	0.161
		(0.013)	(0.020)	(0.018)	(0.018)	(0.011)	(0.009)	(0.012)	(0.052)	(0.020)	(0.018)	(0.022)

Sources: Authors' calculations and regressions using IRS SOI and CPS data merged by the Congressional Budget Office. See the online data appendix for details.

a. Income measures are average income per household. The distribution of income is measured across individuals and is based on household pre-tax, post-transfer income including capital gains, with income adjusted for household size by dividing by the square root of the number of people in the household. Standard errors are in parentheses.

income from wages and salaries. This number drops to 44 percent for the top 1 percent, and 27 percent for the top 0.01 percent.[19] The first two rows of the third panel confirm our main findings on the post-1982 cyclicality of top income groups (compare this panel with the second panel of table 3). For the top 1 percent, both wages and salaries and overall pre-tax, pre-transfer income (excluding capital gains) per householder are more than twice as cyclical as the average income of all households, and for households in the top 0.01 percent, both wages and salaries and overall income are more than three times as cyclical as the average.[20]

Second, the first two rows of the third panel of table 8 show that the incomes of households in the bottom two quintiles are a bit more cyclical than those of households from the middle quintile up to the 90th to 95th percentile. Thus, even in this period of high exposure of very high income groups, households in the lowest income quintile still have a slightly higher cyclicality of income than households in the middle and upper-middle parts of the distribution, but a much lower cyclicality than those at the top end.[21]

In sum, the recent cyclicality of wages and salaries and pre-tax, pre-transfer income is asymmetrically U-shaped, higher for the bottom two quintiles than for the middle and upper-middle part of the income distribution, and dramatically higher for the top 1 percent and the top 0.01 percent.

II.C. Cyclicality and Transfers, Taxes, and Capital Gains

The different levels and cyclicalities of the incomes of different groups in the income distribution lead to different levels and cyclicalities of taxes and transfers, and therefore different cyclicalities of disposable income and ultimately of consumption. In this section we document that taxes and transfers reduce the cyclicality of income except at the very top. We also investigate the role of capital gains.

---

19. The somewhat smaller role of wages for the top groups than in the top panel of table 3 is probably due to the fact that households in the SOI-CPS data are sorted by an income measure that includes capital gains.

20. For comparability with earlier tables, the right-hand-side variable in this panel is (as in tables 1, 2, and 3) the log growth rate in real NIPA pre-tax, pre-transfer income per tax unit, excluding capital gains. The alternative would be to use the aggregate income from the SOI-CPS data. This leads to similar results.

21. The cyclicality of the bottom quintile in the SOI-CPS data is not as high as one might have expected from the cyclicality of low-education households in the CPS. When using CPS data with families sorted on income rather than education, we find a cyclicality for the bottom quintile in the CPS that is similar to that found for the bottom quintile in the SOI-CPS data.

First, the top two panels of table 8 show that adding transfers to our definition of income raises the incomes of the lowest quintile substantially but makes only a small difference to the incomes further up the distribution; the ratio of top income to average income falls slightly, since aggregate income is higher when transfers are included. Next, adding capital gains to income works the same way at the other end of the distribution, increasing the incomes of the top groups and so raising their relative incomes, while lowering the relative incomes of the bottom groups. Finally, subtracting taxes lowers the incomes of the top groups the most and so raises the relative incomes of the bottom quintiles.

Second, the third panel of table 8 shows that the income cyclicalities of the bottom income groups are significantly reduced by transfers, which are large for the bottom quintile (about 40 percent of pre-tax, pre-transfer, pre-capital gains income) and countercyclical. The cyclicality of income for the bottom quintile falls from 0.76 to 0.41 as a result of transfer income alone, and that of the second quintile falls from 0.90 to 0.61. Third, capital gains increase cyclicality for all groups, and the importance of capital gains rises steadily with income, corresponding to the larger fraction of income coming from capital gains for higher-income groups. Including capital gains raises the income cyclicality of the top 1 percent from 2.2 to 3.3.[22] Finally, taxes modestly lower the cyclicality of income for groups below the 99th percentile, while increasing cyclicality for the top 1 percent.

The fourth panel of table 8 summarizes the impact of different income levels and cyclicalities by calculating the fraction of aggregate income changes borne by each group. On average, the top 1 percent bears 29 percent of changes in aggregate pre-tax, pre-transfer income excluding capital gains, and as much as 48 percent of changes in aggregate post-tax, post-transfer income including capital gains.[23]

Overall, the cyclicality of the middle income groups is more stable across different income measures than that of the top and bottom of the income distribution. The cyclicality of the lowest income groups is significantly reduced by transfers, and that of the top income groups is significantly raised by including realized capital gains.

---

22. Notice that the betas reported in the third panel of table 8 are all with respect to aggregate pre-tax, pre-transfer income excluding capital gains.

23. In order for these fractions to sum to 1 across groups, we base aggregate income changes on aggregates from the SOI-CPS data themselves. To avoid potential biases in our estimates of betas from having SOI-based data on both the left- and the right-hand side of the regression, we omit the growth rates for the years around the 1986 tax reform (1985–86, 1986–87, and 1987–88).

II.D. The Cyclicality of Same-Family Income

So far, because we use datasets that have good coverage of the top end of the income distribution, our analysis measures the cyclicality of the average income of the top 1 percent of the income distribution rather than the cyclicality of a given set of tax units or households. The top 1 percent of the distribution contains somewhat different people from year to year. Could the cyclicality of the change in incomes of the group of people that start in the top 1 percent be different from the cyclicality of the distribution that we have estimated so far? Such a difference could arise, for example, from a correlation between individual income risks and aggregate fluctuations. We have already provided, in our consumption analysis in section I.D, some evidence of high cyclicality in data covering a constant set of households from one period to the next. Here we further investigate the cyclicality of same-family income in two ways.

First, we link families across our March CPS extracts (which we also used in section II.A) for 1982–2009. In each year we categorize families into percentiles based on the entire distribution of families, and then we take the subsample of those that can be tracked to the following survey year and calculate the change in average income for each income group from this set of families. Thus, we calculate the annual log change in average income for groups of families that, in the first year of the change, are all within a certain part of the income distribution. Because of the small number of families in the top 1 percent that can be linked across years, the standard errors of the cyclicalities estimated for the top 1 percent in regressions parallel to those in table 7 are very large, around 1.6. For the top 5 percent, the sample is larger and the standard errors are somewhat smaller. The cyclicalities of same-family incomes for the top 5 percent are estimated to be 1.46, with a standard error of 0.80, with respect to average CPS income and 0.80, with a standard error of 0.86, with respect to NIPA income.

Second, in the next section we turn to tax data in which we can track the same families over time. Doing so requires using tax data from another country, but one that has also had an increase in top income inequality.

We can summarize the main results of sections II.A through II.D as follows: First, it is harder to observe high income cyclicality in the top 1 percent in the public use CPS data, because of top coding and the fact that cyclicality is high only for very high income families. Second, in looking at the entire distribution of incomes, the cyclicality of pre-tax, pre-transfer incomes excluding capital gains is asymmetrically U-shaped: it is slightly higher for the bottom two quintiles of the income distribution than for the next groups up to around the 95th percentile (and even up to the 99th percentile when focusing on wages and salaries), and very high for the top 1 percent and especially the top 0.1 and 0.01 percent. Third, transfers significantly reduce cyclicality at the bottom of the income distribution, essentially equating cyclicality across the distribution except for the top. The realization of capital gains raises the cyclicality of incomes at the very top even higher; taxes generate a small additional increase in cyclicality at the top.

III. Canada

Saez and Michael Veall (2007) show that Canada has also had a large increase in income inequality at the high end of the income distribution that roughly coincides temporally with the U.S. increase but is slightly less extreme. Canada has a slightly different tax system and culture but presumably is affected by the same changes in economic factors, such as technology and trade, as the United States. Thus, to provide another observation on the cyclicality of top incomes and to provide information about possible causes, we analyze the cyclicality of Canadian top incomes. There are also a number of ways in which the Canadian data are better than the U.S. data, most notably in that we can track the same families across years.

Our data come from the Longitudinal Administrative Databank, which contains records for 20 percent of all tax returns filed in Canada from 1982 to 2007. Working with Statistics Canada, we extracted information on the average incomes of families in different groups in the income distribution, both as repeated cross sections and tracking the families in different groups in the income distribution in a given year into the following year, as we were able to do with a subset of the CPS.[24] Further, we obtained data on income by source, as in the SOI data from Piketty and Saez, and on taxes and transfers, as in the SOI-CPS data from the CBO. We asked Statistics Canada to rank households and construct groups based on income calculated from pre-tax, pre-transfer income excluding capital gains.

Table 9 summarizes our results on the cyclicality of pre-tax, pre-transfer income excluding capital gains for different income groups in Canada with respect to aggregate Canadian income fluctuations for both sampling

---

24. The Canadian tax system is based on the individual, so tracking families involves summing income across family members (legal and common law spouses and children) if more than one live at the same address.

Table 9. Cyclicality of Income by Measure of Income and Income Group in Canada, 1982–2007[a]

Measure or source of income	All families	Lowest quintile	Second quintile	Middle quintile	Fourth quintile	80th–90th percentile	90th–95th percentile	95th–99.0th percentile	Top 1 percent	99.0th–99.9th percentile	99.9th–99.99th percentile	Top 0.01 percent
	\multicolumn{12}{c}{Ratio of average income in group to average for all families}											
Pre-tax, pre-transfer excluding capital gains	1.00	0.04	0.32	0.73	1.26	1.85	2.43	3.41	8.81	6.99	20.12	70.59
Pre-tax, post-transfer excluding capital gains	1.00	0.21	0.43	0.76	1.19	1.70	2.20	3.07	7.86	6.25	17.90	62.66
Pre-tax, post-transfer including capital gains	1.00	0.22	0.43	0.75	1.18	1.68	2.19	3.10	8.34	6.59	19.38	65.82
Post-tax, post-transfer including capital gains	1.00	0.26	0.49	0.80	1.19	1.65	2.09	2.87	6.89	5.57	15.27	50.77
	\multicolumn{12}{c}{Average share of indicated source in pre-tax, pre-transfer income excluding capital gains (percent)}											
Wages and salaries	78.4	65.7	59.5	74.2	83.2	86.2	85.5	77.9	60.5	58.1	65.0	70.0
Pensions	5.5	18.0	14.5	9.8	5.5	3.5	2.9	2.9	2.2	2.5	1.7	0.7
Business and professional income	5.6	−20.1	6.2	4.7	3.6	3.4	4.0	8.2	17.4	21.0	10.6	3.0
Interest and dividends	6.6	27.9	11.6	6.6	4.5	4.1	4.6	7.0	14.6	13.1	17.4	21.2
Other investment income	3.9	8.5	8.2	4.7	3.2	2.8	2.9	4.0	5.3	5.2	5.4	5.1
Pre-tax, pre-transfer income excluding capital gains	100.0	100.0	100.0	100.0	100.0	100.0	100.0	100.0	100.0	100.0	100.0	100.0
Cash transfers	12.8	571.3	51.3	16.8	7.0	3.5	2.2	1.5	0.7	0.8	0.4	0.1
Capital gains	3.5	27.1	4.0	2.6	2.1	2.1	2.5	4.2	9.4	8.8	11.6	8.3
Taxes	21.5	9.0	10.7	16.1	19.6	21.5	23.0	26.0	35.9	34.2	40.1	40.3
Post-tax, post-transfer income including capital gains	137.8	707.3	166.0	135.5	128.7	127.2	127.7	131.6	145.9	143.9	152.1	148.6

Beta with respect to average pre-tax, pre-transfer income excluding capital gains for all families												
Pre-tax, pre-transfer income excluding capital gains	0.94 (0.13)	6.21 (1.27)	1.86 (0.31)	1.06 (0.16)	0.73 (0.10)	0.64 (0.09)	0.64 (0.09)	0.75 (0.11)	1.58 (0.29)	1.26 (0.21)	2.17 (0.45)	2.98 (0.85)
Pre-tax, post-transfer income excluding capital gains	0.71 (0.11)	0.36 (0.33)	0.80 (0.21)	0.67 (0.15)	0.59 (0.10)	0.59 (0.09)	0.62 (0.10)	0.74 (0.11)	1.57 (0.29)	1.25 (0.21)	2.16 (0.45)	2.97 (0.85)
Pre-tax, post-transfer income including capital gains	0.79 (0.11)	0.43 (0.31)	0.85 (0.19)	0.71 (0.13)	0.64 (0.09)	0.64 (0.09)	0.67 (0.10)	0.84 (0.11)	1.84 (0.39)	1.50 (0.29)	2.63 (0.62)	3.02 (0.91)
Post-tax, post-transfer income including capital gains	0.71 (0.12)	0.37 (0.32)	0.72 (0.20)	0.63 (0.15)	0.61 (0.12)	0.61 (0.10)	0.63 (0.10)	0.77 (0.13)	1.64 (0.48)	1.33 (0.40)	2.51 (0.77)	2.24 (0.95)
Same-household beta with respect to average pre-tax, pre-transfer income excluding capital gains												
Pre-tax, pre-transfer income excluding capital gains	0.90 (0.13)	7.40 (3.29)	1.73 (0.36)	1.01 (0.15)	0.77 (0.11)	0.70 (0.12)	0.72 (0.16)	0.93 (0.23)	1.58 (0.35)	1.48 (0.35)	2.20 (0.46)	1.60 (0.93)
Pre-tax, post-transfer income excluding capital gains	0.68 (0.12)	0.51 (0.71)	0.86 (0.26)	0.65 (0.15)	0.60 (0.11)	0.60 (0.12)	0.64 (0.15)	0.87 (0.23)	1.56 (0.34)	1.45 (0.34)	2.18 (0.46)	1.59 (0.93)
Pre-tax, post-transfer income including capital gains	0.76 (0.12)	0.57 (0.72)	0.90 (0.26)	0.71 (0.15)	0.65 (0.10)	0.66 (0.12)	0.70 (0.15)	1.00 (0.23)	1.82 (0.41)	1.68 (0.38)	2.54 (0.54)	1.85 (1.07)
Post-tax, post-transfer income including capital gains	0.69 (0.12)	0.50 (2.53)	0.83 (0.94)	0.68 (0.44)	0.61 (0.64)	0.62 (0.25)	0.64 (0.15)	0.88 (0.12)	1.58 (0.13)	1.48 (0.17)	2.38 (0.25)	1.02 (0.49)

Source: Authors' calculations and regressions using data extracts from the Longitudinal Administrative Databank at Statistics Canada.
a. Individuals are summed within families, and families are ranked by pre-tax, pre-transfer income excluding capital gains in each year. Aggregate income is market income (personal income less transfers) per family. All betas for income measures that include capital gains exclude changes to and from 1994, because that year is an outlier due to a change in tax law (see Saez and Veall 2007). Standard errors are in parentheses.

procedures (same households from year to year, and not). First, focusing on wages and salaries and pre-tax, pre-transfer income excluding capital gains, the top panel of table 9 shows (comparing with table 2) that the ratio of income of the top 1 percent to average income is somewhat lower in Canada than in the United States, although this point should be qualified by possible differences in tax laws and tax avoidance by high-income households between the two countries.[25]

Second, comparison of the second panel of table 9 with table 3 shows that the top 1 percent in Canada and in the United States get similar shares (about 60 percent) of their income from wages and salaries. However, in Canada the top 0.01 percent get about 70 percent of their income from wages and salaries, compared with only 40 percent in the United States (from table 3).

Third, turning to our main point of interest, the third panel of table 9 shows that top incomes in Canada, as in the United States, are highly cyclical in the period since 1982. In Canada the top 1 percent and the top 0.01 percent have cyclicalities of 1.6 and 3.0 in the recent period, slightly lower than the corresponding cyclicalities in the United States (top panel of table 2), which are 2.4 and 4.0, respectively. The next two sections argue that this pattern across the two counties—higher cyclicality for those at the top of the income distribution—is representative of a close relationship and potentially a common cause of both high income shares and high cyclicality at the top in the period since the early 1980s.

Fourth, table 9 also shows the effect of capital gains, taxes, and transfers in Canada. Looking across rows in the third panel reveals that in Canada the government has little effect on the cyclicality of incomes at the top of the distribution. At the bottom, however, the effect of transfers is far larger in Canada than in the United States (table 8). The beta for the lowest income quintile before taxes and transfers is over 6, compared with 0.76 for the United States, whereas that after transfers is 0.36, quite similar to the 0.41 in the U.S. data. Although one might be tempted to credit the Canadian welfare state, it seems unlikely that the United States and Canada are truly so different in the exposure of pre- versus post-transfer incomes. Instead, the large impact of transfers on the cyclicality of the bottom group in Canada is likely due to very low average pre-tax, pre-transfer

25. We compare the Canadian data with our results in tables 2 and 3 rather than table 8 because tables 2 and 3 (like the Canadian data) are based on sorting households using pre-tax, pre-transfer income excluding capital gains, whereas the data underlying table 8 are available only sorting households using pre-tax, post-transfer incomes including capital gains.

incomes for this group (with very low average incomes, even moderate transfers can change the cyclicality substantially). Lower pre-tax, pre-transfer incomes for the bottom group in Canada are due in large measure to the Canadian groups being defined in terms of an income measure that excludes transfers, and to the SOI-CPS data in table 8 excluding households with negative income from the bottom income category.

Finally, the bottom panel of table 9 shows that in Canada the income changes from one year to the next that occur for those households who are in the top 1 percent in the first year also have a high cyclicality with respect to changes in aggregate Canadian income, roughly similar to that found in the third panel using repeated cross-sectional data. This is something we could not observe in the U.S. tax data. Thus, the cyclical exposure from one year to the next for families that start in the top 1 percent of the income distribution (but who may fall elsewhere in the distribution in subsequent years) is similar to the cyclical exposure of the annually reported top 1 percent of the income distribution (a group that contains somewhat different families from year to year). This is less so, however, for the top 0.01 percent. The three groups of families that start in the various income groups within the top 1 percent (bottom panel) have similar cyclicalities, whereas for the same three groups in the annually reported top 1 percent of the distribution (third panel), the top 0.01 percent have (economically) significantly higher cyclicality than the other two groups. Nonetheless, the fact that we estimate high cyclicalities for the top 1 percent in both cross-sectional data and panel data is evidence against the hypothesis that the cyclicality of top incomes in panel data in the United States would be quite different from what we have estimated from repeated cross-sectional data. To conclude our discussion of the bottom panel of table 9, we note that the roles of taxes, transfers, and capital gains are broadly similar to those in the third panel.

IV. The Empirical Link between Income Cyclicality and Income Shares at the Top

Having explored in detail the rise in the cyclicality of high incomes in the last three decades, we now show that this increase is closely related to the rise in the share of income accruing to the top of the income distribution. Specifically, we present three pieces of evidence that *the higher the level of income inequality, the higher the income cyclicality of the rich.* We exploit variation across groups, time, and countries. First, in the post-1982 period, the higher a group is in the income distribution (within the top 1 percent),

Figure 2. Income Share of the Top 1 Percent, 1917–2008

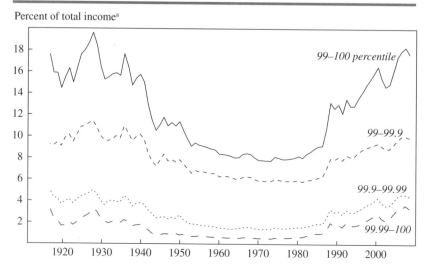

Source: Piketty and Saez (2003), updated by Saez (2010).
a. Income is defined as pre-tax, pre-transfer income excluding capital gains.

the higher is that group's income cyclicality. Second, across decades, as the income share of a given top group increases, the cyclicality of its income increases, consistent with the fact that the increase in the income share of the top 1 percent starts at almost exactly the same time as the increase in the income cyclicality of that group. Third, across countries, those with larger increases in the income share of the top 1 percent have experienced larger increases in the income cyclicality of the top 1 percent. This tight empirical link between inequality and cyclicality at the top end of the income distribution in the past quarter century strongly suggests that these two phenomena share a common cause.

Before we turn to this evidence, figure 2 complements the basic facts displayed in tables 1 and 2 by plotting the income shares from the Piketty-Saez data.[26] These data show both that the dramatic rise in top income shares started in the early 1980s, when cyclicality also increased, and that cyclicality and the income share of the top income groups are not linked in the first half of the 20th century. Top income shares were large in the prewar period, a period in which we do not find evidence of higher cyclicality of the incomes of the top 1 percent. Piketty and Saez (2003) argue that

---

26. As in tables 1, 2, and 3, these shares are for income excluding capital gains, and the data come from Piketty and Saez (2003) as updated in Saez (2010).

different factors drove the income shares of the top 1 percent during the period of declining inequality than during the later period of increasing inequality. They argue that the decline in the income share of the top 1 percent, and of the highest-income groups within the top 1 percent, from around 1928 to around 1970 was driven in large part by declines in capital income (income from dividends and interest), which were in turn due to a combination of the Great Depression and the large tax increases enacted to finance the war; these included large increases in corporate income taxes that almost mechanically reduced distributions to stockholders. In contrast, an increase in wage and salary income is the key driver of the more recent increase in the income share of the top 1 percent. The lack of correspondence between top 1 percent income share and income cyclicality together with the different income composition in the earlier period suggests that the decline in top income shares from 1928 to 1970 was not driven by the same factors as the more recent increases. This is consistent with our explanation for the recent changes: the ICT revolution did not happen in reverse in the early to middle part of the 20th century.

Our first piece of additional evidence of a link between the cyclicality and the income shares of the top 1 percent is that, for groups further up the income distribution within the top 1 percent, there is both a larger income share (relative to the size of the group) and a larger income cyclicality during the period since 1982. Figure 3 graphs the cyclicality of income over the period 1982–2008 for each income group (using data from tables 2 and 3 and the same calculations for other income groups) against the time-series average of the log ratio of that group's average income to the average income of all tax units.[27] The first panel of figure 3 focuses on pre-tax, pre-transfer income excluding capital gains, and since we argue that the high cyclicality of wage and salary income is a key driver of the high overall cyclicality of the incomes of the top 1 percent, the second panel focuses on wage and salary income alone. It is apparent from both graphs that groups higher up in the income distribution within the top 1 percent have both higher ratios of income to average income and higher income cyclicality. Inequality at the top is extreme: the incomes of the top 0.01 percent are on average 212 times the average income (see the second panel of table 2). Similarly, cyclicality at the top is extreme: that of the top 0.01 percent is about four times that of the average (six times when one focuses on

---

27. The betas depicted are from table 3 and are based on growth rates for 1983–2008. The average log income ratios are calculated as the time-series average of the log income ratio (average group income for the year to average income for all tax units for that year), using income ratios for the initial year of each growth rate used (1982–2007).

Figure 3. Betas and Log Ratios of Group Income to Average Income, by Income Group, 1982–2008[a]

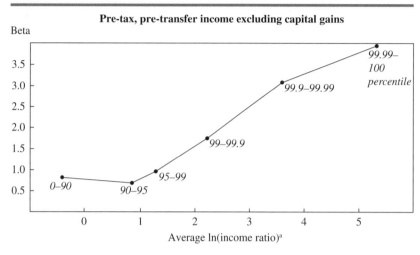

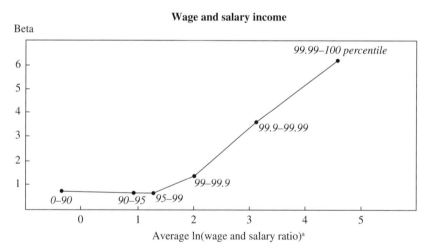

Source: Authors' calculations based on data from Piketty and Saez (2003), extended by Saez (2010).
a. Average across years of the log of the group's average income divided by aggregate average income.

wages and salaries only). This again suggests a link between the level of income inequality and income cyclicality.

A simple statistical description of the relationship is that β in equation 1 is a function of the average log income ratio: $\beta_i = \lambda_0 + \lambda_1 (1/T) \Sigma \ln(Y_{i,t}/Y_t)$, where the summation is across the T years for each income group i, so that equation 1 becomes

(2) $$\Delta \ln Y_{i,t+1} = \alpha_i + \beta_i \Delta \ln Y_{t+1} + \varepsilon_{i,t+1} =$$
$$\alpha_i + \lambda_0 \Delta \ln Y_{t+1} + \lambda_1 \left[\Delta \ln Y_{t+1} (1/T) \Sigma \ln\left(Y_{i,t}/Y_t\right)\right] + \varepsilon_{i,t+1}.$$

We estimate this relationship by stacking data for percentiles 0–90, 90–95, 95–99, 99–99.9, 99.9–99.99, and 99.99–100 using the growth rates for 1983–2008, for a total of 156 observations. Using pre-tax, pre-transfer income excluding capital gains results in an estimate of λ_1 of 0.65. Using wage and salary data results in an estimate of λ_1 of 1.61. Both estimates are significant at the 1 percent level, showing that cyclicality increases with income share across groups.

Second, over time since top income shares first began to rise, as a group's income share has increased, so has its cyclicality. To show this, we estimate betas for each high-income group and decade since the 1970s, and the time-series average of the log ratio of that group's average income to the average income of all tax units for each group and decade. Figure 4 plots decadal betas against decadal average log income ratios. Again the top panel focuses on pre-tax, pre-transfer income excluding capital gains, and the second panel on wage and salary income. For each group, both cyclicalities and average log income ratios increase over time, leading to a positive association between a group's cyclicality and its average income ratio. This pattern is present both in overall income and in wage and salary income. Notice that when one connects the points by decade, as is done in figure 4, rather than by group, it becomes clear that the relationship between average log incomes and cyclicalities is strengthening over time: no relationship was apparent in the 1970s, whereas a strong relationship is observed in the 2000s.

A statistical description of the relationship underlying figure 4 is that β in equation 1 is a function of the log income ratio, now allowing for time-series variation in the ratio, so $\beta_i = \lambda_0 + \lambda_1 \ln(Y_{i,t}/Y_t)$. Equation 1 then becomes

(3) $$\Delta \ln Y_{i,t+1} = \alpha_i + \beta_i \Delta \ln Y_{t+1} + \varepsilon_{i,t+1} =$$
$$\alpha_i + \lambda_0 \Delta \ln Y_{t+1} + \lambda_1 \left[\Delta \ln Y_{t+1} \ln\left(Y_{i,t}/Y_t\right)\right] + \varepsilon_{i,t+1}.$$

We estimate this relationship separately for each of the three subgroups of the top 1 percent—percentiles 99–99.9, 99.9–99.99, and 99.99–100—using the growth rates for 1970–2008. We include $\ln(Y_{i,t}/Y_t)$ itself as an additional regressor to avoid potentially spurious significance of the variable of interest, $\Delta \ln Y_{t+1} \ln(Y_{i,t}/Y_t)$. Using pre-tax, pre-transfer income excluding

Figure 4. Betas and Log Ratios of Group Income to Average Income across Decades[a]

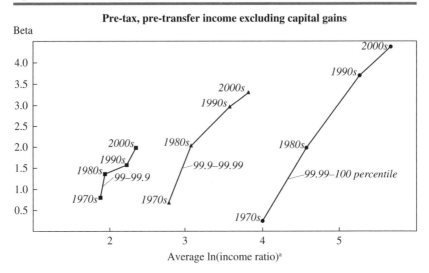

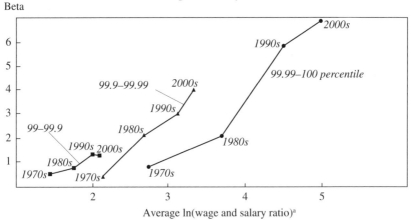

Source: Authors' calculations based on data from Piketty and Saez (2003), extended by Saez (2010).
a. Average across years of the group's average income divided by aggregate average income.

capital gains results in estimates of λ_1 of 2.09 ($t = 1.75$) for percentiles 99–99.9, 2.37 ($t = 2.01$) for percentiles 99.9–99.99, and 2.48 ($t = 2.35$) for percentiles 99.99–100. Using wage and salary data results in estimates of λ_1 of 1.46 ($t = 2.25$), 2.86 ($t = 2.31$), and 3.03 ($t = 2.60$) for the three groups, respectively. This confirms, using time-series variation in income shares (log income ratios) within groups, that higher income shares are associated with higher cyclicality.

Third, we show that the countries with the largest increases in the income shares of the top 1 percent also have experienced the largest increases in the cyclicality of incomes of that group. We use the dataset constructed from tax records from Atkinson, Piketty, and Saez (2010), which contains annual time-series data for the incomes of the top 1 percent for 22 countries. We focus on relating changes in top income shares to changes in top income cyclicality rather than on post-1982 levels of each variable, because of the differences in tax systems across countries and the consequent differences in measurement of top income shares, as well as the host of other differences that exist across countries.[28] We estimate income cyclicality for the top 1 percent in the period from 1982 onward (the period for which we found higher top 1 percent income cyclicality for the United States) and for the period 1970–82 (as a benchmark period). Of the 22 countries, we exclude 6 (Australia, Finland, Germany, New Zealand, Norway, and the United Kingdom) for which income measures include capital gains and 1 (Switzerland) for which incomes are not available at an annual frequency.[29] Furthermore, we require countries to have at least five observations of growth rates in the 1970–82 period and five in the 1982–2007 period, leading us to drop another 5 countries (Argentina, China, Indonesia, Netherlands, and Spain). This leaves 10 countries (Canada, France, India, Ireland, Italy, Japan, Portugal, Singapore, Sweden, and the United States). The original data for Canada extend only to 2000, but we obtained data up to 2007 from Michael Veall.[30] As shown in figure 5, there is a positive relationship between the increase in top 1 percent beta and the increase in top 1 percent income shares. The fitted value is from an ordinary least

---

28. An example is whether the unit of analysis is the family or the individual. See Atkinson, Piketty, and Saez (forthcoming), table 3 and related text.

29. We include Finland in the set for which incomes include capital gains. Although it is possible to calculate top 1 percent income shares from the original article (Jantti and others 2010), it appears infeasible to calculate aggregate totals that fully exclude capital gains.

30. The updated data from Veall start in 1982. We use the original data for earlier years and the updated data from 1982 on, with growth rates always calculated using income data from the same dataset. In the dataset from Atkinson, Piketty, and Saez (2010), U.S. aggregate income is based on tax records. This may bias upward the beta of the top 1 percent in the period that includes the 1986 tax reform (if incomes are distorted by tax reform effects more for the top 1 percent than for other groups). We therefore drop the growth rates for 1987 and 1988 for the United States but could alternatively use NIPA aggregate income as in our earlier analysis (the 1986 growth rate is not an outlier in this dataset).

Figure 5. Changes in Betas and Changes in Income Shares of the Top 1 Percent in 10 Countries, 1970–2007[a]

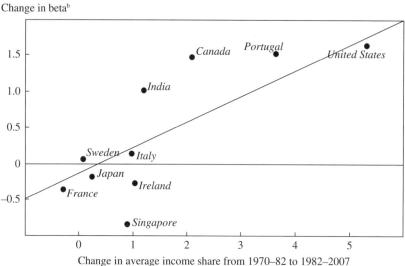

Source: Authors' calculations based on data from Atkinson, Piketty, and Saez (2010).
a. Line represents fitted value.
b. Beta for the top 1 percent for 1982-2007 minus beta for the top 1 percent for 1970–82.

squares regression relating the change in top 1 percent beta to the change in average top 1 percent income shares. The slope coefficient in this regression is 0.42 (the heteroscedasticity-robust standard error is 0.07) and the R^2 is 0.64.

Overall, these three different approaches all suggest that in recent decades, the greater is the top 1 percent income share, the higher is income cyclicality for those in the top 1 percent.

V. Technological Change and Changes in High-Income Shares and Cyclicality

This section argues using a simple example that increases in the scale at which top earners operate naturally lead to increases in both income and income cyclicality at the top of the distribution. We do not provide additional tests to support this interpretation of the facts. Instead we intend in this section to put forward an additional theory, to be considered in future work, about the underlying economic drivers behind these two phenomena.

V.A. Existing Theories for Increasing Top Income Shares

The leading explanation for the broad increase in wage and income inequality that started in the 1970s is that technological change over this period has complemented the skills of highly skilled workers (see, for example, Autor, Katz, and Kearney 2008, Acemoglu and Autor 2010). There is also evidence that changes in economic institutions or regulation (such as minimum wages and unionization) have increased income inequality at the lower end of the distribution. At the very top of the distribution, Piketty and Saez (2003) argue that the speed and size of the increases in relative earnings are inconsistent with the main existing theories based on skill-biased technological change, and that the evidence from top income shares may instead suggest an important role for changing social norms with respect to high earnings. Finally, there is a well-developed literature on the rise in relative compensation for a subset of top earners, namely, corporate chief executive officers (CEOs). Several explanations have been proposed for the rise in relative CEO pay, including a shift in social norms regarding compensation, an increase in managerial power (rent extraction, captured boards), a shift in demand from specific to general skills, an increase in the size of firms, and skill-biased technological change (Kaplan and Rauh 2010, Bertrand 2009).

Top executives are, however, a minority of highly compensated individuals. Steven Kaplan and Joshua Rauh (2010) document that only about 5 percent of earners in the top 0.01 percent are executives of nonfinancial firms. They also show that investment bankers, other financial asset managers (at hedge, venture capital, private equity, and mutual funds), lawyers, and to a smaller extent athletes and celebrities all make up significant fractions of the top income groups.[31] Kaplan and Rauh argue that the fact that pay has increased dramatically at the top in each of these sectors is evidence against the first three explanations above. Neither social norms nor increased managerial power seems relevant for the pay of many occupations among top earners, such as hedge fund managers, and specific rather than general skills seem more important for lawyers, hedge fund managers, investment bankers, and professional athletes. Expanding on the argument of Xavier Gabaix and Augustin Landier (2008) that increased CEO pay can be explained by increased firm size, Kaplan and Rauh further show

---

31. Bakija and others (2010) provide much more detailed occupational information, indicating that another large subgroup within the highest income groups is people in medical occupations.

that the leading financial services firms, law firms, and hedge, venture capital, and private equity funds have grown larger over time (measured by inputs or output). This does not fully explain the increase in CEO pay (and the top 1 percent income share), however, since average firm size was increasing before 1980, too. What is needed to explain these facts is that the impact of firm size on top 1 percent pay is higher than it was before, as might arise from skill-biased technological change favoring those at the top. This would amount to a mix of the last two theories listed above.

Of these existing theories, which also predict an increase in the income cyclicality of top earners? The canonical theories of skill-biased technological change require a separate assumption that the technology that complements skill has a very cyclical impact on those at the top of the income distribution.[32] Other theories of rising pay at the top similarly require additional assumptions—that the ability of CEOs to "steal" is cyclical or that norms about pay are highly cyclical (for example, because high pay or conspicuous consumption is more stigmatized during recessions).

Although changing institutions and regulations, power structures, or norms may have a role in the changes we have observed, we argue that these changes are not inconsistent with a theory of skill-biased technological change—specifically, changes in ICT—in which these changes have increased the scale at which the top earners operate. We show theoretically that if advances in ICT have increased the ability to scale the application of high skills, this naturally implies both that top incomes will rise and that fluctuations in demand over the business cycle will affect the incomes of the highest-skill individuals disproportionately. The next subsection describes this mechanism, leaving empirical tests or calibrations for future work.

V.B. A Theory of Why Very High Income Individuals Have Higher and More Cyclical Incomes than in the Past

The rise of ICT has allowed the most skilled in any given occupation to apply their talents more broadly, for example, to manage more workers and capital, to entertain more people, or to write more papers. Thus, ICT has lowered the extent to which quality declines when more output is produced; in other words, it has made marginal revenue curves decline more

---

32. One approach would be to assume that the latest technologies that complement the skills of the most highly paid are tied to new investment (in physical capital of higher quality, in equipment and software, or in organizational capital). Then, since investment is highly procyclical, skill-biased technological change could lead to both higher incomes and higher cyclicality of incomes for those with the highest skills.

slowly with output. This change has raised the operational scale and the earnings of the most skilled. The highest earners tend to have larger fluctuations in their earnings than the rest of the population because those who operate at a large scale naturally have lower profit margins and so are more exposed to cyclical fluctuations.

The following simple model formalizes this argument and illustrates how those with higher incomes tend also to have more cyclical incomes.[33] Let each worker produce earnings according to

(4) $$py - ci = Ai^{\alpha} - ci,$$

where $0 < \alpha < 1$ and $\alpha A > c$. Further assume that workers earn the full net revenue they contribute to the firm, so that earnings are $\pi = Ai^{\alpha} - ci$. Very highly skilled workers have higher α than they had in the past, whereas changes in α for lower-skilled workers are zero or comparatively small. A higher α means that a worker's marginal product diminishes less rapidly as the input i increases. The assumption $\alpha A > c$ ensures that high-α workers earn more than low-α workers. The key change in our earnings function that generates both increased cyclicality and increased earnings shares for highly skilled workers is our conjecture that growth in ICT has increased α for very highly skilled workers during the period since 1982.

Three different interpretations of our revenue or earnings function are useful. First, the most obvious interpretation is that all workers produce output of identical quality, but the best produce more for given inputs and have less diminishing returns to scale. In our equations this corresponds to i being inputs, $y = i^{\alpha}$, $p = A$, and c being the price of the inputs. In this interpretation the ICT revolution increases the returns to scale (that is, reduces the degree of decreasing returns to scale) of the best workers and allows them to work with more inputs; for example, a CEO can manage a larger company.

A second interpretation of equation 4 is that ICT has changed markets so that highly skilled workers are more like superstars in the sense of Sherwin Rosen (1981). That is, highly skilled workers produce the same number of units of output for given inputs as other workers, but as they produce more output, the quality of that output declines more slowly than that of other workers does. As in Rosen (1981, p. 849), "superior talent stands out and does not deteriorate so rapidly with market size as inferior talent does." In this interpretation the ICT revolution has lowered how quickly

---

33. Our earnings function is in the spirit of the equilibrium model of Lucas (1978).

quality declines with output for the best workers. In our equations this corresponds to i being both input and output ($y = i$), the price p being a function of quality that decreases with output as $p(y) = Ay^{\alpha-1}$ (so $py = Ai^\alpha$), and c being the marginal cost of producing another unit of output. For example, the top lawyers (in the post-1982 world) may be able to write more briefs without the quality of their legal advice suffering as much as would be the case for less skilled lawyers (for example, because of the impact of ICT on the ease with which case histories can be researched).

A final and closely related interpretation is that of an asset manager paid based on performance. In this interpretation let i be assets under management, c the expected return investors can earn elsewhere, and Ai^α the (risk-adjusted) trading profits of the fund.[34] The earnings equation then captures the idea that the best fund managers are increasingly able to invest more money without the returns on their investments deteriorating as much as for other fund managers.

Given our assumptions, the optimal level of i is

(5)
$$i^* = (A\alpha/c)^{1/(1-\alpha)},$$

with associated earnings for the worker of

(6)
$$\pi = (A\alpha/c)^{1/(1-\alpha)} c(1-\alpha)/\alpha.$$

Equation 6 delivers our two main results.

First, because workers with higher α earn higher incomes (by assumption), income inequality and top income shares increase when the α of top earners increases. In equation 6, $d\pi/d\alpha > 0$. This occurs because highly skilled workers generate more revenue for given inputs, and they are optimally matched with more inputs because they have less decreasing returns to scale.

Second, an increase in the α of high-α workers increases the cyclicality of their earnings. Assume that business cycle fluctuations are driven by fluctuation in A, representing either market demand shocks or technology shocks. The percentage change in profits depends on α as

(7)
$$d\ln \pi/d\ln A = 1/(1-\alpha),$$

---

34. This structure corresponds to a setting with no management fees and a 100 percent carry, but the results should generalize to a more standard contract with a 2 percent fee and 20 percent carry.

which is positive and increasing in α. Thus, the cyclicality of the earnings of a worker increases if the worker's α rises. Note that d lnπ/d lnA does not depend on whether i is adjusted optimally in response to the change in A, since by the envelope theorem, dπ/di = 0 at the initial value of A. Thus, the high cyclicality of earnings is driven not by a higher cyclicality of inputs, but by the increased sensitivity of earnings to demand that comes from working with a higher level of inputs. That said, the input scale of more highly skilled workers is more cyclical in this model; it is just not the cause of greater income cyclicality.

The intuition for the different cyclicalities is that more highly skilled workers optimally are working with more inputs (interpretation 1) or producing more output (interpretations 2 and 3). Their revenue is similarly sensitive to fluctuations as those of lower-skill individuals, since fluctuations in A affect the revenue of each worker proportionately. However, for highly skilled workers, costs are higher relative to revenue, so ci is more substantial relative to Ai^{α} for these workers. This makes their earnings, $\pi = Ai^{\alpha} - ci$, more cyclical. For low-skilled workers, inputs are small relative to revenue, so fluctuations in earnings are in percentage terms more similar to fluctuations in revenue.

VI. Conclusion

Coinciding with the increase in the income share of top earners since the early 1980s has been an increase in the cyclicality of the incomes of top earners. The high cyclicality that we document for top incomes, including wages and salaries, appears to be linked empirically to increases in the income shares of top earners, based on variation over time, across groups of top earners, and across countries. This increased cyclicality and its link to increased income shares should contribute to a better understanding of the reasons behind the increase in top income shares.

We propose that the information and communications revolution provides a natural way to think about how technological change may have raised both top income shares and top income cyclicality. The change in technology that we suggest—increased scale or increased "superstar"-type production by top earners—generates a simple connection between income shares and cyclicality, in that the earnings of those operating on a larger scale naturally become more sensitive to the business cycle. Our brief analysis of our posited mechanism leaves open the question of how well it can quantitatively match the documented changes in cyclicality over time and across countries.

ACKNOWLEDGMENTS For helpful comments we thank the editors, our discussants Rebecca Blank and Erik Hurst, as well as Jeff Campbell, Xavier Gabaix, Takashi Yamashita, participants at the Brookings Panel conference, and seminar participants at Kellogg School of Management and the Federal Reserve Banks of Cleveland and Chicago. We thank David Autor and Melanie Wasserman for help with the CPS files. We thank Brian Murphy and Habib Saani of Statistics Canada for help with the Longitudinal Administrative Databank. We thank Jeff Larrimore for providing the data from Burkhauser and others (2008, 2009) and Michael Veall for providing data from Saez and Veall (2007) updated to 2007. We thank the Zell Center and Kellogg School of Management for funding. Nicolas Ziebarth provided excellent research assistance.

The authors report no relevant potential conflicts of interest.

References

Acemoglu, Daron, and David Autor. 2010. "Skills, Tasks and Technologies: Implications for Employment and Earnings." Working Paper no. 16082. Cambridge, Mass.: National Bureau of Economic Research.

Aguiar, Mark, and Mark Bils. 2010. "Has Consumption Inequality Mirrored Income Inequality?" Working paper. University of Rochester.

Atkinson, Anthony B., Thomas Piketty, and Emmanuel Saez. Forthcoming. "Top Incomes over a Century or More." *Journal of Economic Literature.*

Attanasio, Orazio, and Steven J. Davis. 1996. "Relative Wage Movements and the Distribution of Consumption." *Journal of Political Economy* 104, no. 6: 1227–62.

Autor, David H., Lawrence F. Katz, and Melissa S. Kearney. 2008. "Trends in U.S. Wage Inequality: Revising the Revisionists." 2008. *Review of Economics and Statistics* 90, no. 2: 300–23.

Bakija, Jon, Adam Cole, and Bradley T. Heim. 2010. "Jobs and Income Growth of Top Earners and the Causes of Changing Income Inequality: Evidence from U.S. Tax Return Data." Working paper. Williams College (November).

Bertrand, Marianne, 2009. "CEOs." *Annual Review of Economics* 1: 1.1–1.29.

Blank, Rebecca M. 1989. "Disaggregating the Effect of the Business Cycle on the Distribution of Income." *Economica* 56, no. 222 (May): 141–63.

Bound, John, and George Johnson. 1992. "Changes in the Structure of Wages in the 1980's: An Evaluation of Alternative Explanations." *American Economic Review* 82, no. 3: 371–92.

Burkhauser, Richard V., Shuaizhang Feng, Stephen P. Jenkins, and Jeff Larrimore. 2008. "Estimating Trends in US Income Inequality Using the Current Population Survey: The Importance of Controlling for Censoring." Working Paper no. 14247. Cambridge, Mass.: National Bureau of Economic Research (August).

———. 2009. "Recent Trends in Top Income Shares in the USA: Reconciling Estimates from March CPS and IRS Tax Return Data." Working Paper no. 15320. Cambridge, Mass.: National Bureau of Economic Research (September).

Card, David, and Rebecca M. Blank. 1993. "Poverty, Income, Distribution, and Growth: Are They Still Connected?" *BPEA*, no. 2: 285–339.

Castro, Rui, and Daniele Coen-Pirani. 2008. "Why Have Aggregate Skilled Hours Become So Cyclical since the Mid-1980s?" *International Economic Review* 49, no. 1: 135–84.

Clark, Kim B., and Lawrence H. Summers. 1981. "Demographic Differences in Cyclical Employment Variation." *Journal of Human Resources* 16, no. 1: 61–79.

Congressional Budget Office. 2008. *Historical Effective Tax Rates, 1979 to 2005: Supplement with Additional Data on Sources of Income and High-Income Households,* and *Methodology.* Washington (December). www.cbo.gov/publications/collections/tax/2009.cfm.

Cutler, David M., and Lawrence F. Katz. 1991. "Macroeconomic Performance and the Disadvantaged." *BPEA,* no. 2: 1–74.

Gabaix, Xavier, and Augustin Landier. 2008. "Why Has CEO Pay Increased So Much?" *Quarterly Journal of Economics* 123, no. 1: 49–100.

Goolsbee, Austan. 2000. "What Happens When You Tax the Rich? Evidence from Executive Compensation." *Journal of Political Economy* 108, no. 2 (April): 352–78.

Hall, Brian J., and Jeffrey B. Liebman. 2000. *The Taxation of Executive Compensation*. Tax Policy and the Economy series, vol. 14. Cambridge, Mass.: National Bureau of Economic Research.

Heathcote, Jonathan, Fabrizio Perri, and Giovanni L. Violante. 2010. "Unequal We Stand: An Empirical Analysis of Economic Inequality in the United States, 1967–2006." *Review of Economic Dynamics* 13, no. 1 (January): 15–51.

Hines, James R., Hilary Hoynes, and Alan B. Krueger. 2001. "Another Look at Whether a Rising Tide Lifts All Boats." In *The Roaring Nineties: Can Full Employment Be Sustained?* edited by Alan B. Krueger and Robert Solow. New York: Russell Sage Foundation.

Jäntti, M., M. Riihelä, R. Sullström, and M. Tuomala. 2010. "Trends in Top Income Shares in Finland." In *Top Incomes: A Global Perspective*, edited by A. B. Atkinson and T. Piketty. Oxford University Press.

Kaplan, Steven N., and Joshua Rauh. 2010. "Wall Street and Main Street: What Contributes to the Rise in the Highest Incomes?" *Review of Financial Studies* 23, no. 3: 1004–50.

Katz, Lawrence F., and Kevin M. Murphy. 1992. "Changes in Relative Wages, 1963–87: Supply and Demand Factors." *Quarterly Journal of Economics* 107, no. 1: 35–78.

Kuznets, Simon. 1953. *Shares of Upper Income Groups in Income and Savings*. New York: National Bureau of Economic Research.

Kydland, Finn E. 1984. "Labor-Force Heterogeneity and the Business Cycle." *Carnegie Rochester Conference Series on Public Policy* 32: 173–208.

Lucas, Robert E., Jr. 1978. "On the Size Distribution of Business Firms." *Bell Journal of Economics* 9, no. 2 (Autumn): 508–23.

Moylan, Carol E. 2008. "Employee Stock Options and the National Economic Accounts." *Survey of Current Business* 88, no. 2 (February): 7–13.

Parker, Jonathan A., and Annette Vissing-Jørgensen. 2009. "Who Bears Aggregate Fluctuations and How?" *American Economic Review* 99, no. 2 (May): 399–405.

Piketty, Thomas, and Emmanuel Saez. 2003. "Income Inequality in the United States, 1913–1998." *Quarterly Journal of Economics* 118, no. 1: 1–39.

———. 2007. "Response by Thomas Piketty and Emmanuel Saez to: The Top 1% . . . of What? By Alan Reynolds." University of California, Berkeley.

Reynolds, Alan. 2007. "Has U.S. Income Inequality Really Increased?" *Policy Analysis* 586 (January 8): 1–24.

Rosen, Sherwin. 1981. "The Economics of Superstars." *American Economic Review* 71, no. 5 (December): 845–58.

Saez, Emmanuel. 2010. "Tables and Figures Updated to 2008." University of California, Berkeley (July). elsa.berkeley.edu/~saez/TabFig2008.xls.

Saez, E., and M. R. Veall. 2007. "The Evolution of High Incomes in Canada, 1920–2000." In *Top Incomes over the 20th Century: A Contrast between Continental European and English-Speaking Countries,* edited by A. B. Atkinson and T. Piketty. Oxford University Press.

Solon, Gary, Robert Barsky, and Jonathan A. Parker. 1994. "Measuring the Cyclicality of Real Wages: How Important Is Composition Bias?" *Quarterly Journal of Economics* 109, no. 1 (February): 1–25.

Comments and Discussion

COMMENT BY
REBECCA M. BLANK[1]   This paper by Jonathan Parker and Annette Vissing-Jorgensen is highly interesting. Its primary conclusion, that incomes have become markedly more cyclical at the very top of the income distribution in the past 25 years, is surprising and intriguing. The paper presents a new fact about the world that was not previously known, and this makes it likely that the paper will stimulate further research and debate.

For an empirical economist, there is much to like in this paper. The authors do an extremely thorough job of data analysis. They use multiple datasets to confirm and test their results, with substantial attention to proving the robustness of what they find. Any careful reader will come away impressed by the serious data work in the paper and persuaded that the cyclicality of incomes among the top 1 percent of U.S. households has indeed increased. That said, as with most papers that uncover new facts, there is more work to be done to understand and interpret this result, so that it informs the theoretical framework that economists use when thinking about income generation, inequality, and macroeconomic change.

It is important to be clear about what the results in this paper do *not* show. The greater cyclicality that the authors discuss appears to be focused at the very top of the income distribution, particularly among the top 1 percent of households. Hence, this result does not overturn the frequently noted result that incomes are more cyclical among lower-income families than among higher-income families. On average, income in the bottom quintiles is more cyclical than in the middle quintile, as the authors' table 8 demonstrates. Furthermore, the authors reiterate the fact that the cyclical

---

1. These comments reflect the personal opinion of the author and do not necessarily represent the views of the Department of Commerce or the U.S. Government.

nature of unemployment, in particular, seems to lead to income cyclicality among lower-income families.

On the question of who is most hurt by cyclical downturns, nothing in this paper refutes the widely held belief, buttressed by substantial evidence, that lower-income families (particularly those headed by someone with less education, working in a lower-wage job) experience greater economic deprivation in a recession than do other families. These families experience a disproportionate share of unemployment and are more likely than other families to need government assistance to survive economically during bad economic times. The fact that income and consumption patterns (as the authors show) are also highly cyclical at the very top of the income distribution is less likely to signal deprivation, although it may well create real stress within these families. Households in the top 1 percent of the income distribution have substantial savings and assets and can smooth their consumption if they wish. This means that the consumption cyclicality that they experience (matching their income cyclicality) is best viewed as an economic choice on their part. In contrast, consumption cyclicality among very poor families who have no savings is much more likely to be an involuntary and unavoidable response to changes in earnings and income.

It would therefore be inaccurate to interpret the results in this paper as saying something about well-being. Parker and Vissing-Jorgensen are clear on this point, but it is worth stressing nonetheless. The results in this paper do, however, inevitably raise the question of why this cyclicality has increased among households at the very top of the income distribution, particularly given the close relationship between rising cyclicality and increases in absolute levels of inequality, which the authors document. At the end of the paper, Parker and Vissing-Jorgensen present a theory that focuses on changes in information and communications technologies (ICT) that have increased the ability of highly skilled persons to leverage their skills and expand their income, leading to rising inequality. The authors' model suggests that this exposes them to greater cyclical fluctuations.

I find this model a plausible story, although it is just that at the moment—a possible story, without supporting evidence. To investigate whether the data support this theory, one would want to look at changes in earnings levels and cyclicality among high-earning workers who might have greater "leverage" due to the ICT revolution, and among those who might be less affected by this phenomenon. Unfortunately, when one is exploring a phenomenon that is primarily visible in only the top 1 percent of the population, such investigations are hard to pursue.

What is happening in ICT may be only part of the change in the economic environment facing top-earning workers. The expanded global markets in which more and more companies are operating also provide scope to utilize the gains from ICT that did not exist before. It might have been useful for the authors to say more about globalization and how it relates to their theory.

My biggest hesitation about the causal hypothesis that Parker and Vissing-Jorgensen present is that it is unclear to me why it would be limited to workers at the extreme top of the income distribution. Both the greater global marketplaces and the expanded possibilities created by new ICT should have benefited many higher-skilled workers. The authors' results suggest that the increased income cyclicality they observe is closely related to cyclicality in wages and salaries among the topmost earners and does not reflect rising cyclicality in hours of work or in other forms of income. At a minimum, this suggests that compensation among the very top earners is more tied to overall economic performance than it is among workers even slightly lower in the earnings distribution. Perhaps additional theoretical structure is needed to explain why compensation practices at the very top differ from those even a little lower on the wage spectrum.

For instance, one question I would be very interested in knowing more about is how compensation packages for top earners differ across industries and occupations. Although Parker and Vissing-Jorgensen indicate that the top 1 percent of earners are spread across industries (table 5 in their paper), my guess is that there may be different compensation practices for (say) those who manage money for large manufacturing firms than for those who manage the firm's operations. And the ability of new ICT to enlarge the possible value generated by these different top managers might also vary. It may take a series of more micro-focused case studies, looking at very highly paid senior people in a selected group of industries and occupations, to better understand and investigate both the authors' theory and their empirical results.

Let me close with a comment about the data. As the authors note, it is extremely difficult to study the phenomenon of income cyclicality at the top because very few of the available datasets are large enough to produce a reasonable-sized sample among the top 1 percent of earners. And very few available datasets are accurate enough to produce informative data about that group, even if their samples were larger. Among survey statisticians there is widespread concern about lower survey response rates among the extremely wealthy. (Of course, sample weighting techniques can adjust for this, but a small number of observations with larger weights will lead to less accuracy.)

In addition, noisy data can lead to a top 1 percent sample that includes households whose actual income would not place them in this category. For all of these reasons, annual cross-sectional datasets based on relatively small samples of the population (such as the Current Population Survey or the Consumer Expenditure Survey) are probably of limited value in addressing the questions raised by this paper. For this reason, I would place less reliance on tables 5 and 6, which use those data, than on other results in the paper. Even if one combines a number of years' data together to produce a larger sample, data reliability questions may still pose problems for the researcher.

This means that there are probably two datasets best suited to look at this small sliver of the population: the Statistics of Income data, which the authors use intensively, and the American Community Survey (ACS). The ACS, which the authors do not use, replaced the old "long form" of the decennial census after the 2000 census. It collects information monthly on a wide variety of indicators (including income, earnings, and family composition) from a random sample of families. In any one year, the ACS samples a little over 1.9 million households. Although the ACS lacks data from before the 2000s, and so cannot be used to investigate long-term trends in cyclicality, it can be used to look in much greater depth at who the families and individuals are at the very top of the income distribution in recent years, and at how different types of households and families responded to the Great Recession. Those who want to explore these issues further should think about the possibilities provided by the ACS for this research question.

Overall, this is a fine paper. In some ways it merely adds to the puzzle of why and how inequality and earnings among very top earners have changed over the past 25 years. But by adding a new fact about income cyclicality, and closely linking that fact with rising incomes among these earners, the paper provides information that will help economists winnow out the various theories that have been proposed to explain widening inequality. The most believable explanations will be those that explain both the rising levels of income and the rising income cyclicality in this group.

COMMENT BY
ERIK HURST This paper by Jonathan Parker and Annette Vissing-Jorgensen documents an interesting, important, and novel set of facts pertaining to the cyclicality of income for very high income individuals. The paper shows that in recent years, households in the top 1 percent of the income distribution have much more cyclical incomes than most other households. Additionally, the paper shows that this high relative cyclicality

is a relatively recent phenomenon, that it moves in lockstep (decade by decade) with the well-documented increase in income inequality driven by the increasing income share for these households, and that it is robust to controlling for stock options, household fixed effects, and taxes and transfers. The facts are very carefully documented, and I have no comments whatsoever on the existing empirical work in the paper.

The second part of the paper lays out a simple theory to explain these facts. In particular, it asks what factors could possibly result both in an increasing share of income earned by very high income individuals and in an increasing cyclicality of income for those individuals. The authors propose a model where information and communications technologies have increased the optimal production scale for the most talented individuals. Nothing in the paper convincingly supports or convincingly refutes this theory. Rather, as the authors note, it is simply one theory that could simultaneously generate increasing income inequality and increasing cyclicality among those with very high incomes.

My comments are structured in two parts. First, I want to emphasize that the authors make no claims about the welfare costs of recessions. They are very clear about this. However, it is a point worth reemphasizing so that the paper's implications are not misconstrued. Second, I will offer some new facts related to the changing nature of compensation that took place for higher-income households during this period. In particular, bonus income increased in importance for high-income households during the 1990s and early 2000s. As I show below, bonus income is much more cyclical than other types of income and is more closely associated with the finance industry than with other industries.

WHAT THIS PAPER IS NOT ABOUT. Upon reading this paper, one is tempted to use the facts that it documents to make statements pertaining to the distributional costs of business cycle fluctuations. The authors caution readers against making such types of calculations. I want to underscore this point.

The authors show (convincingly) that the cyclicality of income is much higher for those with very high incomes than for other income groups and that this cyclicality has been increasing over time. Do these results imply that the cost of business cycles, in terms of standard utility-based measures of welfare, is higher for those with very high incomes than for those at other points of the income distribution? Do the results imply that over the last two and a half decades, those with very high incomes are bearing an increasing brunt of business cycle variation in terms of changes in welfare? The answer to both of these questions is a resounding no. Variations in income (and, to a lesser extent, in consumption) do not map directly onto variations in standard, utility-based measures of welfare. Households with sufficient wealth can self-insure against income fluctuations by accumulating and then drawing down assets. Households can maintain consumption flows despite variation in consumption outlays by delaying the replacement of durables, and even some goods traditionally defined as nondurable, such as clothing or vacation spending, have aspects of durability. Finally, given standard assumptions about household preferences, concave utility functions imply that a given change in expenditure will have a much smaller effect on utility for individuals with very high expenditure than for individuals with lower expenditure.

Two other facts need to be emphasized. First, households with very high incomes may have anticipated the increase in risk to their incomes that the authors document, and if so, one would expect them to have demanded compensation for bearing that risk. This could explain the fact that those with very high incomes are earning higher returns on their labor and simultaneously facing more variable labor income streams. The story is analogous to the difference between investing in stocks and investing in bonds. If the earnings of those with very high incomes have become more stock-like (taking more of an equity stake in their employing firm through their labor investments), it is not surprising to see them bearing more risk and receiving higher returns. Second, and a related point, the variation in income for these households could be either transitory or permanent. In order to compute standard welfare calculations using income and expenditure data (even if one could measure the service flow of expenditure correctly), one needs to know whether the observed variation in income was perceived as a transitory shock or as a permanent shock. To the extent that business cycle variation implies differences in expectations about the evolution of the permanent component of income for individuals at different points of the income distribution, welfare calculations again become complicated.

Collectively, the results in this paper do not suggest that the brunt of business cycles in terms of changing well-being is being disproportionately borne by those with very high incomes in recent periods. What the paper does show is that the income of those at the top of the income distribution has become more cyclical. I view these results as potentially informative about the changing nature of compensation in the economy over the last few decades, not as an input into how we think about the distributional costs of cyclical variation. Like the authors, I would caution readers against using the paper's results to draw conclusions about how cyclical variations affect well-being for individuals at different points of the income distribution.

THE INCREASING IMPORTANCE OF BONUS INCOME AT THE TOP. The paper left me with a few lingering questions about which components of earnings are driving the results. First, how important are bonuses for individuals at the top of the income distribution? Second, are bonuses more important for individuals in some professions than in others? Third, has the composition of bonus-receiving professions been changing over time? Fourth, is bonus income more cyclical than other types of income? Finally, can bonuses help explain the correlation between the increased share of income and the increased cyclicality of income for very high income households?

Some of these questions are hard to answer with existing datasets. I will try to provide some information on some of these questions using data from the Panel Study of Income Dynamics (PSID), and will then discuss further why bonus income could help explain the facts documented in the paper. I wish to emphasize that these PSID results are meant to be only suggestive. The PSID is not an ideal dataset for analyzing the earnings behavior of very high income households, because of its limited sample size.

The PSID disaggregates labor earnings into the following categories: regular wage and salary income, bonus income, income from commissions, tips, overtime compensation, and business income. For my analysis I use data from the 1995, 1997, 1999, 2001, 2003, 2005, and 2007 waves of the PSID, and I pool bonus and commission income together, because commissions, like bonuses, could be related to work effort and could vary with the state of the aggregate economy. I restrict the sample to male heads of households between the ages of 16 and 70 who were currently employed and had positive earnings during the preceding year. The earnings reports I use are total earnings (from all sources) within a particular category from the preceding year. For example, bonus earnings reported in the 1995 wave of the PSID refer to all bonuses earned during calendar 1994. All earnings data are converted into 2000 dollars, when applicable.

To compute earnings percentiles, I rank all earnings for individuals within the sample separately for each year. Given the sample sizes, I classify households into the top 2.5 percentiles (the richest households), percentiles 2.5–5.0, percentiles 5.0–10.0, and the bottom 90 percentiles. I look at three measures: the share of households receiving either bonus or commission earnings, the share of total earnings that come from either bonus or commission earnings, and the fraction of household heads who work in the finance industry. As it turns out, the inclusion of commissions adds lit-

Table 1. Importance of Bonus Income across the Income Distribution, Pooled Years[a]
Percent

Indicator	Labor earnings percentiles			
	Bottom 90	5–10	2.5–5	Top 2.5
Fraction receiving bonus income, all heads of household	9	19	22	29
Share of bonus income in total income, all heads of household	1	3	4	8
Share of bonus income in total income, bonus recipients only	11	17	20	28
Sample size	25,028	1,117	542	533

Source: Author's calculations using data from the 1995, 1997, 1999, 2001, 2003, 2005, and 2007 waves of the Panel Study of Income Dynamics.

a. Sample includes all currently employed male heads of household between ages 16 and 70 who had positive income in the preceding year. Percentiles are defined within each year separately. All differences are statistically significant from each other except for the 5–10 percentile and 2.5–5 percentile comparisons.

tle to the analysis; essentially all the results are driven by bonuses rather than commissions, and therefore in what follows I refer to the sum of bonus and commission income simply as bonus income.

My table 1 shows, first, the fraction of household heads in each of the above percentile ranges who received bonus income. These results pool the data across all years. Only 9 percent of household heads in the bottom 90 percentiles of the income distribution received bonus income. For the other income groups, the fraction receiving bonus income rises with income, reaching 29 percent in the highest income group. The table also shows the average fraction of income that comes from bonuses across all households within the different percentile ranges. This is calculated as the simple average of the bonus share across all individuals within each range. This share likewise increases as one moves up the earnings ladder. For example, the average individual in the top 2.5 percentiles gets about 8 percent of earnings from bonuses, compared with 1 percent for the average individual in the bottom 90 percentiles. Finally, the third line of table 1 shows the average bonus share for those households who reported positive bonus income. The conclusion from table 1 is that bonus income is more important for higher-earning than for lower-earning households.

Figure 1 shows the time-series patterns in the bonus share of earnings for household heads in the bottom 90 percentiles and for those in the top 2.5 percentiles. The figure shows a dramatic increase in the share of income earned from bonuses between 1994 (from the 1995 survey) and

Figure 1. Share of Income from Bonuses, 1995–2007

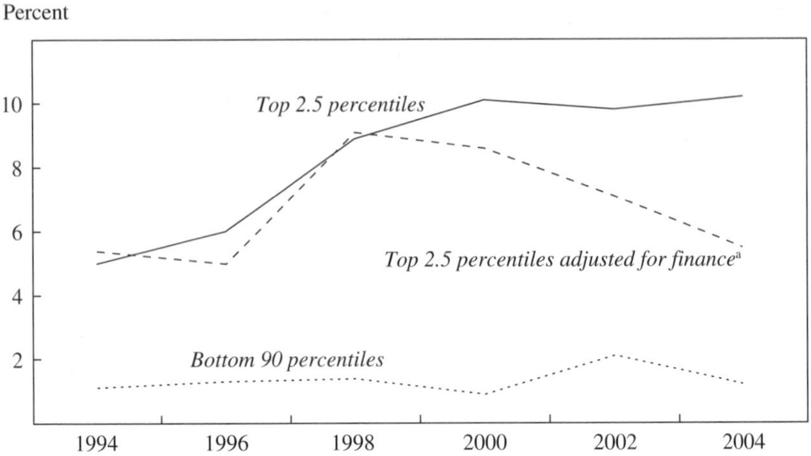

Percent

[Chart showing three lines from 1994 to 2004:
- Top 2.5 percentiles: rises from about 5 in 1994 to about 10 by 1998, stays near 10 through 2004
- Top 2.5 percentiles adjusted for finance[a]: rises from about 5 to about 9 by 1998, then declines to about 6 by 2004
- Bottom 90 percentiles: flat around 2 throughout]

Source: Author's calculations using data from the 1995, 1997, 1999, 2001, 2003, 2005, and 2007 waves of the Panel Study of Income Dynamics.

a. Plot of the coefficients on the year dummies in the regression reported in the second results column in table 2. Sample includes all currently employed male heads of household between ages 16 and 70 who had positive income in the preceding year.

2004 (from the 2005 survey) for the latter group. For example, whereas in 1994 roughly 5 percent of this group's earnings came from bonuses, in 2004 that figure was roughly 10 percent. In contrast, those in the bottom 90 percentiles show no discernable trend in the share of income earned from bonuses.

To summarize, the PSID results show that the share of income from bonuses among households at the top of the income distribution was increasing at the same time that these households, according to the data that the paper uses, were seeing both an increased share of total income and an increased cyclicality of income. This suggests that the rise in bonus income among these households may relate to the patterns documented by Parker and Vissing-Jorgensen.

Is there a statistical relationship between the receipt of bonus income and working in the finance sector? Steven Kaplan and Joshua Rauh (2010) show that individuals in the finance sector increased their share in the very top of the income distribution during the 1990s and the early 2000s. The same patterns hold in the PSID data. In 1994, 12 percent of individuals in the top 2.5 percent of the income distribution were in the finance industry; by 2004 this figure had risen to nearly 18.5 percent.

Table 2. Regressions Explaining Bonus Income with Finance Industry Employment and Income, Pooled Years[a]

	Dependent variable		
		Bonus share of total income	
Independent variable	Dummy for positive bonus	All heads of households	Bonus recipients only
Dummy for employment in finance industry	0.075 (0.026)	0.041 (0.012)	0.159 (0.052)
Dummy for income in top 10 percentiles	0.103 (0.021)	0.024 (0.007)	0.057 (0.030)
Dummy for income in top 2.5 percentiles	0.087 (0.026)	0.043 (0.017)	0.084 (0.047)
Constant	0.091 (0.004)	0.009 (0.001)	0.104 (0.009)
Sample size	27,220	27,220	2,902

Source: Authors' regressions using data from the 1995, 1997, 1999, 2001, 2003, 2005, and 2007 waves of the PSID.

a. Sample includes all currently employed male heads of household between ages 16 and 70 who had positive income in the preceding year. Percentiles are defined within each year separately. Robust standard errors are in parentheses.

Table 2 shows the results of three regressions. Each regresses some measure of the importance of bonus income on a dummy variable indicating whether the individual is in the finance industry, a dummy for whether the individual is in the top 10 percent of the income distribution, and a dummy for whether the individual is in the top 2.5 percent of the income distribution. (If the individual is in the top 2.5 percent, both the top 10 percent dummy and the top 2.5 percent dummy have a value of 1.) I run these regressions on the entire pooled sample. As the table shows, being in the finance industry increases the likelihood of receiving a bonus, the share of income that comes from bonuses, and the share of income coming from bonuses conditional on receiving a bonus.

Given that the finance industry has been increasing in importance over time, a natural question is how much of the increasing share of bonus income for those individuals with very high income during the 1990s and early 2000s (documented above) was simply due to the increasing prominence of individuals in the finance industry in that group. To address this, I run two regressions on a sample that includes only those individuals in the top 2.5 percentiles of the income distribution. The first simply regresses the share of income from bonuses on year dummies. The second regresses the same dependent variable on year dummies, a dummy for whether the individual was in the finance industry, and an interaction of the finance dummy with the year dummies. Figure 1 also plots the coefficients on the year dummies from these regressions and shows that a substantial part of the increase in the bonus share of earnings for this group, particularly after 1998, was due to the increasing importance of the finance industry.

The PSID data do not go back far enough in time to allow a full analysis of the cyclicality of bonus income. However, it is not a leap to think that bonus income is more cyclical than other types of income, given that it is usually linked to firm performance or profits. If that is the case, then as bonus income has been a more important component of income for those with very high incomes, this could be a cause of the increased cyclicality of income for these individuals.

What can the increasing importance of bonus income reveal about the relationship between the rising share of total income accruing to very high income individuals and the increased cyclicality of income for these individuals? One possibility is that the facts documented in the paper are simply driven by the increasing share of very high income individuals working in the finance industry. On average, individuals employed in finance receive a larger share of their income as bonuses, and they are more likely to be represented among the very rich. Although this is likely to be some of the story, it is not the entire story. As shown in the paper, some evidence suggests that it is unlikely that the compositional switch within the group of very high income individuals toward finance solely explains their results.

The rise in importance of bonus income does reveal that the nature of compensation has been changing. Ex ante, higher-income individuals are relying more on bonus income as a form of compensation. Bonus income is more risky than some other forms of compensation in that it is directly tied to firm profits. To be willing to bear this risk, these high-income individuals need to be compensated for it. As a result, the shift toward bonus income can be consistent with the rising share of income for these households as well as with the increased cyclicality. But why has the compensation structure changed such that those who had very high incomes to begin with are willing to bear this additional income risk? Are such risk-sharing agreements efficient, in that they better align incentives between the high-income workers and the firm? Are the high-income workers becoming synonymous with the firm itself? If these workers are now willing to take on more risk of the firm's profitability, does that imply that the other workers are now facing less risk? Does it imply that other *investors* in the firm are facing less risk? The facts in this paper should be leading economists to ask a whole new series of questions about the allocation of risk within the economy.

SUMMARY. Overall, this is a very nice paper. The methodology is well executed, and the results are well documented. The question remaining is what is driving those results. The paper proposes one story. But there is nothing in the paper that confirms (or contradicts) this story. It appears that the changing nature of compensation of very high income individuals in the form of the rising importance of bonus income is potentially part of the story. The facts documented in the paper, collectively, should point researchers toward addressing a whole series of interesting questions.

REFERENCE FOR THE HURST COMMENT

Kaplan, Steve, and Joshua Rauh. 2010. "Wall Street and Main Street: What Contributes to the Rise in the Highest Income?" *Review of Financial Studies* 23, no. 3: 1004–50.

GENERAL DISCUSSION George Perry observed that developments in the financial sector can largely explain the sharp rise in economy-wide inequality between 1982 and 2008 that the authors analyze. In the authors' data, wages and salaries of the top 0.1 percent of the income distribution were $183 billion higher in 2008 than if they had just kept up with the average rise since 1982. Wages and salaries per worker in finance rose nearly twice as much as the economy-wide average over this period, and total wages and salaries in finance in 2008 were $154 billion higher than if the per worker average had simply kept up with the rest of the economy. Hedge funds, which were in their infancy at the start of the 1980s, managed an estimated $2.5 trillion in 2008, which would account for roughly $100 billion of financial wages and salaries that year. Hedge funds are also characterized by high earnings volatility, as are other leveraged financial activities that generate very high incomes and greatly expanded over this period. All this suggests that finance is not just part of the income distribution story but the dominant part. Economies of scale have always existed in finance. What has changed in the financial sector is the increasing application of leverage and risk.

Refet Gürkaynak found one of the most fascinating findings in this paper to be that not just income, but also consumption, has become more volatile at the top of the income distribution. That finding is surprising, because one would think that individuals at the very top also have sufficient wealth to smooth their consumption. He further suggested that the paper's findings might be explained in terms of the standard risk-return relationship in finance. If a greater proportion of an individual's compensation is in the form of bonuses, which are more volatile than wages and salary, that individual would have to be compensated more on average to be willing to accept that risk.

Benjamin Friedman was likewise fascinated by the finding of higher consumption volatility at the high end. He proposed three potential explanations. First, available statistics other than those from tax records (which do not report consumption directly) are unreliable at the extremes, and so the finding might simply be spurious. Second, even though people at the top of the income distribution also have higher wealth-to-income ratios, much of that wealth is in illiquid form and so might not be available to smooth consumption. Third, consumption by people at the very top may be lumpier. Whatever the explanation, it was a puzzling finding that seemed to go against accepted knowledge. Erik Hurst added that even if consumption is volatile for the really wealthy, their utility is probably not much affected. Happiness data show that happiness is not more volatile for the very rich than for other households.

William Nordhaus thought that what might be going on at the very top end is that some people are able to impose a "tax" on the profits of companies that they control, in the form of bonuses, stock options, or perks. Because profits are cyclical, this income will also be cyclical. To the extent that compensation structures are becoming more incentive-based, moving away from a fixed base pay, this should contribute to making top incomes more cyclical. Nordhaus was also concerned that capital gains are a very large omitted part of income. To the extent that some cyclicality of the capital gains component is not getting measured, that would be another explanation for the paper's finding.

James Hines noted that the Tax Reform Act of 1986 changed not only tax rates but also the definition of taxable income. Some of the difference in the proportion of income going to the very top depends on this definitional change. Also, because tax rates on the very rich are much lower today than in earlier decades, the rich have less incentive to avoid classifying some income as taxable income. The estate tax, which has seen an extreme reduction recently, also bears on the decisionmaking of top income groups. Assets can now be given to a trust in the name of a child and will not show up as income.

Gary Burtless argued that another important change was in the incentive to hold income within corporations as opposed to organizing the firm so that the income is immediately treated as though distributed to all of the owners. Before the Tax Reform Act of 1986, there was a strong incentive for corporate income to be held within companies rather than distributed to rich shareholders; after the reform, this incentive changed. Many companies were reorganized so that company income was taxed only once, as personal income to shareholders. Income at the top might be more cyclical today in part because some income was formerly sheltered within the corporation. Under current law, all the cyclicality in that corporate income will be reflected directly in the owner's personal income tax.

Robert Gordon noted that the share of total executive income taking the form of stock options rose dramatically during the 1990s. Also, the two big recent episodes of stock market volatility were synchronous with the business cycle, making it difficult to distinguish between its role and that of the stock market cycle. Gordon suggested that quite a bit of the increase in top income cyclicality might be due to the increased dependence of very top income earners on stock options. He proposed as a possible explanation a general increase in the market power of managers, which could help to explain both the increase in inequality and the increased downward responsiveness of labor hours to the decline in output, as has occurred in the last two recessions. The question was how much of this shift in market power is due to growing strength at the top versus growing weakness at the bottom. It could be that the eroding market power of workers at the bottom created a vacuum, and the top moved in.

Karen Dynan was interested in how the authors' findings related to the so-called Great Moderation. If top income groups accounted for a greater share of total income in this period, and at the same time were experiencing greater income volatility, how does that square with the stylized fact of greater moderation in the macroeconomy, and how might that inform the understanding of that period?

Justin Wolfers found the paper's analysis to be extremely thorough across datasets, and the results as reliable as they could be given certain weaknesses in the data. He also noted that the main finding is not only well supported, but surprising. Two years ago, if someone had surveyed 100 labor economists and asked them whether rich people were more likely than others to get hurt by recessions, the majority, he believed, would have said no. Wolfers also suggested further testing the theory using data from the so-called Great Compression of the 1920s through the 1950s—a period that also saw a large shift in income inequality but in the opposite direction.

Robert Hall observed that the rational thing to do when one's lifetime resources change immediately and dramatically is to change one's consumption immediately and dramatically. There is no reason to think that high-income households would act any differently in such circumstances. Following up on Gürkaynak's point about the risk-return relationship, Hall noted that there is also a lot of evidence that ordinary wages contain an insurance element, especially among longer-term workers, who are typically insulated from layoffs. Somebody has to stand on the other side of this insurance deal. To the extent that that somebody is the high-income shareholders of the same firms, this could explain the observed volatility of their incomes.

Bruce Meyer reported that a student of Anthony Atkinson had found that high-income shares of total income rise dramatically after financial crises. This result comes from 50 years of data from many countries. He wondered how much of what the paper found to be going on is about the timing of income changes in response to financial shocks.

Laurence Ball thought the facts reported in the paper were basically right, and he agreed with Perry that hedge funds must be a big part of the story. But he also wondered how precisely hedge funds might be driving the observed change in cyclicality. Possible explanations included regulatory changes, changes in social norms, changes in tax rates, or some combination of those elements.

MARIANNE P. BITLER
Federal Reserve Bank of San Francisco

HILARY W. HOYNES
University of California, Davis

The State of the Social Safety Net in the Post–Welfare Reform Era

ABSTRACT The 1996 welfare reform led to sweeping changes to the central cash safety net program for families with children. Along with other changes, the reform imposed lifetime time limits for receipt of cash welfare, effectively ending its entitlement nature for these families. Despite dire predictions, previous research has shown that program caseloads declined and employment increased, with no detectible increase in poverty or worsening of child well-being. We reevaluate these results in light of the severe 2007–09 recession. In particular, we examine how welfare reform has altered the cyclicality of the response of caseloads and family well-being. We find that use of food stamps and noncash safety net program participation have become significantly more responsive to the economic cycle after welfare reform, rising more when unemployment increases. By contrast, we find no evidence that cash welfare for families with children is more responsive, and some evidence that it might be less so. We find some evidence that poverty increases more with increases in the unemployment rate after reform, and none that it increases less. We find no significant effects of reform on the cyclical responsiveness of food consumption, food insecurity, health insurance, household crowding, or health.

The Personal Responsibility and Work Opportunity Reconciliation Act of 1996 made sweeping changes to the central cash safety net program in the United States. The Aid to Families with Dependent Children (AFDC) program had provided cash benefits to low-income, primarily single-parent families with children since 1935 and had come to be almost synonymous with "welfare." After 60 years with minimal changes, President Bill Clinton made good on his pledge to "end welfare as we know it," signing the 1996 legislation and thereby eliminating AFDC and replacing it with Temporary Assistance for Needy Families. TANF, or welfare as we know it now, imposes stringent work requirements, sanctions for noncompliance, and lifetime time limits for receipt of welfare. Importantly, the imposition of time limits effectively ended the entitlement nature of cash welfare for poor families with children.

In the wake of this landmark welfare reform legislation, a widespread concern was that the new policy would lead to increases in poverty and deprivation among disadvantaged families. Literally hundreds of studies evaluated the impacts of welfare reform on family and child well-being. A broad summary of that voluminous literature is that the reform led to a significant reduction in welfare participation and an increase in female employment, with little consistent evidence that it also led to an increase (or a decrease) in poverty or contributed materially to the observed decline in child poverty.[1] However, the literature also shows that the strong labor market of the late 1990s, along with the dramatic expansion of "in work" aid for low-income families with children through the Earned Income Tax Credit (EITC), may have softened the initial impact of welfare reform (Meyer and Rosenbaum 2001, Grogger 2003). Thus, at the end of the great expansion of the 1990s, cash welfare caseloads had fallen by more than 50 percent from their peak in 1994, to levels not seen since 1970. Between 1992 and 2000, the employment rate of single women with children increased by 15.3 percentage points, from 69.4 percent to 84.7 percent, and the child poverty rate declined by 6.1 percentage points, from 22.3 percent to 16.2 percent.

Of course, the expansion of the 1990s eventually ended. The nation entered a short recession in 2001, followed by a relatively weak expansion. Then, in December 2007, what has been called the Great Recession began, which was deeper and longer than any other postwar downturn to date. In this contraction and its aftermath, the national unemployment rate increased by more than 5 percentage points, from 5.0 percent in December 2007 to 10.1 percent in October 2009, exceeding the largest increase previously seen in the postwar era, that during the deep, back-to-back recessions of the early 1980s. Incomes are down, poverty is up, and participation in government assistance to families through use of unemployment benefits and food assistance has risen substantially. By contrast, TANF caseloads have remained relatively flat.

Our paper enters at this point. We seek to evaluate the impact of welfare reform on disadvantaged families in the Great Recession. It is well known

1. Comprehensive reviews can be found in Blank (2002) and Grogger and Karoly (2005). The research summarized there focuses on the effects of reform on program participation, income and earnings, consumption, child outcomes, and a host of other measures.

that economic downturns adversely affect employment, income, and family well-being, and that they have larger negative impacts on those with less education and skill (Hoynes 2000, Hines, Hoynes, and Krueger 2001). Here we ask whether the impact of the economic cycle on disadvantaged families has changed with welfare reform. With welfare today providing less protection than before, are economic shocks causing more-adverse outcomes? We focus on the nonelderly and in particular on families with children. This is a natural choice given that our paper studies the effects of reform of the cash assistance system that is exclusively targeted to families with children.[2] In an effort to broadly capture the possible effects of reform, we look not only at use of cash welfare but also at family well-being measures and other aspects of the safety net. Outcomes we examine include poverty (both official and alternative measures), earnings and income, participation in food stamps, participation in Supplemental Security Income (SSI) and disability income, receipt of child support or alimony income, whether individuals live in public housing or get a rent subsidy, food consumption, food insecurity, health insurance coverage, health status, measures of crowding (such as "doubling up"), and the presence of single female-headed family units. We use both administrative data and household survey data to assemble a comprehensive picture of family well-being in the wake of welfare reform.

We begin in section I with a descriptive and expansive look at expansions and contractions from 1979 to the present. For each contraction or expansion, we report data on *changes* in spending on government assistance programs (cash welfare, unemployment insurance, and food assistance), in spending on the EITC, in family employment and poverty, in measures of housing stress, in health insurance coverage and access, and in family consumption. In so doing, we pay particular attention to how the changes during the recent recession compare with those during the early-1980s recessions. In section II we step back and provide a brief description of welfare and the safety net for low-income families more broadly, with a focus on recent important changes.

The descriptive approach of the paper's first two sections, although informative about the basic facts, does not allow us to identify the role that welfare reform has played in causing the observed changes in outcomes. We turn to this question in section III, where we present our core findings about how welfare reform has affected the relationship between the economic cycle and family well-being among the disadvantaged. To identify the impact of welfare, we take advantage of the rich variation across states

---

2. The effect of the Great Recession on the operation of the safety net for the elderly is also an important topic, but not one within the scope of this paper.

in the timing and severity of economic cycles and welfare reform. Our econometric model is a basic state-year panel where we regress various family outcomes on the unemployment rate, a measure of welfare reform, and the interaction between the two. The estimated coefficient on the interaction term identifies how welfare reform has affected the impact of the cycle on family well-being.

This approach allows us to estimate how an increase in a state's unemployment rate affects outcomes among the disadvantaged, and how those impacts changed with the dramatic reform to welfare. We believe ours to be the first paper to address this issue. We utilize data from many sources in order to provide a comprehensive evaluation. We start with administrative data on participation in AFDC and TANF and on food stamp caseloads, to document the "first stage" of the policies. We then analyze data from 30 years of the March Current Population Survey Supplement (CPS), which allow us to examine impacts on various family and household measures of well-being, including earnings and income, poverty, living arrangements and housing stress, program participation beyond AFDC/TANF and food stamps, health insurance coverage, and health status. Finally, we present results for food consumption, using data from the Panel Study of Income Dynamics, and for food insecurity, using data from the food security supplements to the CPS.

In section IV we reexamine the effects of welfare reform and how welfare participation responds to the business cycle. First, we briefly touch on what is known about the response of public assistance and the safety net to the recession of 2001. Then we revisit the topic of reductions in welfare participation with reform, and in particular whether they have been driven by changes in eligibility (that is, by reduced access) or changes in take-up. We then go on to explore what is known about those single, nonworking women who before reform were at risk of being on welfare but are no longer on welfare (known as "disconnected women" in a growing literature). Section V concludes.

Using both administrative and survey data, we find that both food stamps and a broader measure of safety net participation (one that excludes cash welfare for families with children and Medicaid) have become more responsive to the economic cycle after welfare reform. Although always countercyclical, both of these measures increase more with unemployment after welfare reform. All measures of poverty (official and our own alternative measure) are also countercyclical, and the likelihood of having an income under 150 percent of the official poverty threshold is significantly more countercyclical after reform. By contrast, there is no evidence that cash welfare for families with children is more responsive after reform, and some evidence that it might be less so. We find that reform has had no significant effects on the cyclical responsiveness of food consumption, food insecurity, receipt of child support or alimony, receipt of SSI or disability insurance benefits, health insurance coverage, household crowding, or health.

I. The Business Cycle, the Safety Net, and Family Well-Being

In this section we examine the changes in government assistance and family outcomes that have occurred historically across expansions and contractions in the United States. Figure 1 traces our measure of the economic cycle—the unemployment rate—annually from 1962 to 2009. During the recent recession, which officially began in December 2007, the unemployment rate rose from 5 percent to a peak of 10.1 percent in October 2009. Although the recession officially ended in June 2009, the unemployment rate remains high, at 9.6 percent in September 2010 (seasonally adjusted). In terms of the annual averages shown in figure 1, unemployment in that recession increased from 4.6 percent in 2007 to 9.3 percent in 2009. In our analysis we compare results for the recent recession with those for the early 1980s, when two recessions in quick succession led to an increase in the annual unemployment rate from 5.8 percent in 1979 to 9.7 percent in 1982.

Figure 1 also depicts two measures of the poverty rate (the share of the population living in poverty), also on an annual basis. We view the poverty rate as a central measure of family well-being and thus rely on it heavily in our work. Official poverty status in the United States is determined by comparing total pre-tax family cash income with a poverty threshold, which varies by family size, number of children, and the presence or absence of elderly persons. (Thus, all persons in the same family have the same poverty status.) In 2009 the poverty threshold for a family of four (two adults, two children) was roughly $22,000. This measure of resources has numerous drawbacks. Notably, there is no geographic variation in the threshold, despite wide variation in costs and wages across regions, and the thresholds are based on outdated household budgeting rules of thumb, which fail to adjust for changes in many categories of expenses (such as shelter, clothing, work-related expenses, medical expenses, and utilities) and thus do not currently reflect actual needs. Also, the thresholds are updated annually by the consumer price index for all urban consumers (CPI-U), a measure of inflation that may not well capture changes in prices paid by disadvantaged families caused by changes in the basket of goods they consume. Further, family cash income is not a complete measure of

Figure 1. Unemployment Rate and Overall Poverty Rates, 1962–2009[a]

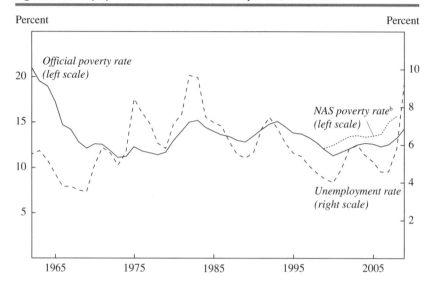

Sources: See the appendix.
a. Rates are annual averages. Poverty rates are calculated as the share of all persons living in families with income below the official or the NAS alternative poverty line.
b. Measure uses the MSI-NGA-CE version of NAS tabulations. See the appendix for details.

family resources. It excludes noncash government transfers (such as food stamps, housing subsidies, and housing vouchers), certain subtractions from income (such as income and payroll taxes), and certain additions to income (such as the EITC) made through the tax system. These limitations in the official poverty definition have been noted by many, and a recent National Academy of Sciences (NAS) panel made recommendations for revisions (Citro and Michael 1995). Throughout the paper we make use, to the fullest extent possible, of an alternative poverty definition using a comprehensive post-tax, post-transfer income concept. Of particular relevance for our work is the measurement of noncash benefits, the EITC, and taxes.[3]

---

3. The official poverty thresholds were developed in 1963 and 1964 and adopted in 1969, and official statistics are available back to 1959. The thresholds have been adjusted each year to reflect changes in the cost of living, using the CPI-U, but otherwise have changed little since their creation. The Census Bureau is developing a supplemental poverty measure to be published in addition to the official measure. The supplemental measure is intended to incorporate many of the suggestions of the NAS report on the poverty measure. The Census Bureau and the Bureau of Labor Statistics have long examined various alternative measures of both income and thresholds and have published various experimental series (for example, Dalaker 2005); they have also explored whether the NAS recommendations could be implemented (for example, Garner and Short 2008).

Figure 1 shows that poverty in the population as a whole declined substantially between the early 1960s and the mid-1970s, with shorter periods of increases and decreases since that time. In the recent recession the official poverty rate increased by 1.8 percentage points, from 12.5 percent in 2007 to 14.3 percent in 2009. The fact that unemployment did not improve in late 2009 and early 2010 suggests that poverty will likely increase further before it declines. The figure also plots, for the years for which data are available (1999–2008), an alternative poverty measure suggested by the NAS, which incorporates noncash transfers, taxes, out-of-pocket medical expenditure, and work-related deductions in income and includes consumption-based measures in the thresholds. Poverty by this measure is higher than by the official measure but follows a very similar trend.[4]

Given our focus on the effects of welfare reform on the nonelderly, we show in figure 2 the official poverty rate for children, as well as that for all nonelderly persons, from 1980 to 2009. In 2009, 15.1 percent of nonelderly persons, and 20.7 percent of children, were poor. The figure also plots the unemployment rate, with shading for years when contractions occurred,[5] and shows that poverty rates are countercyclical, rising in downturns and falling in expansions. These simple time series do not reveal any obvious evidence of a change in the cyclicality of poverty following welfare reform; that is, it does not appear that poverty more closely tracks the unemployment rate after 1996 than before. One can, however, see that the strong expansion of the late 1990s was associated with decreases in both the unemployment rate and poverty.

Table 1 provides more detail on economic circumstances and well-being in contractions and expansions, both before and after welfare reform. The contractions and expansions are the same as those depicted in figure 2. The first column reports changes during 1979–82, a period that includes the two back-to-back recessions. The next four columns report changes for the contractions of 1989–92, 2000–03, and 2007–09; in the last of these, a few measures (EITC spending, NAS alternative poverty,

---

4. In our own empirical analysis of the March CPS data below, we are able to construct a consistent alternative poverty measure for calendar years 1980–86, 1988–90, and 1991–2008. Because of Census data limitations at the time of writing, the Census tabulations for the NAS measure as well as our own tabulations of alternative poverty are not yet available for 2009.

5. The official NBER recession dating is monthly, whereas most of our analyses in the paper rely on annual data. Therefore we constructed an annual series for contractions based on the official monthly dates, augmented by examination of the peaks and troughs in the national unemployment rate. See the appendix for a comparison of NBER monthly recession dating and our annual contraction dating.

Figure 2. Unemployment Rate and Child and Nonelderly Poverty Rates, 1980–2009[a]

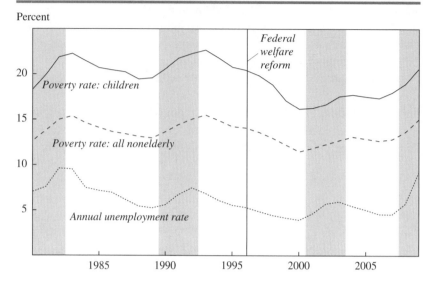

Sources: See the appendix.

a. Rates are annual averages. Poverty rates are calculated as the share of children or of nonelderly persons living in families with income below the official poverty line. Shading indicates years of labor market contraction as defined in the appendix.

and food insecurity) are available only through 2008. The final three columns present changes during the three expansions depicted in figure 2: 1982–89, 1992–2000, and 2003–07. We view these tabulations as interesting and descriptive, but again it is difficult to reach conclusions about how cyclicality has changed because one cannot distinguish the cycle from the aggregate trend.

The first row of table 1 reports the change in the annual unemployment rate in each contraction and expansion. During the 2007–09 recession, the unemployment rate increased by 4.7 percentage points, compared with an increase of 3.9 percentage points between 1979 and 1982 and even smaller increases during the 1989–92 and 2000–03 contractions. The next panel documents how spending on the key cash and near-cash government assistance programs (the latter comprising food stamps, unemployment insurance, and the EITC) changed across cycles. Both food stamps and (especially) unemployment insurance show countercyclical spending. Of particular interest is the 68 percent increase in real food stamp spending per capita between 2007 and 2009. Expenditure for the EITC does not appear to follow a countercyclical pattern, although with major expan-

Table 1. Changes in Unemployment, Safety Net Program Expenditure, and Family Well-Being across Contractions and Expansions[a]

Percentage points except where stated otherwise

	Contractions				Expansions		
Statistic	1979–82	1989–92	2000–03	2007–09[b]	1982–89	1992–2000	2003–07
Change in unemployment rate (annual average)	3.9	2.2	2.0	4.7[b]	−4.4	−3.5	−1.4
Changes in real safety net expenditure per capita (in percent)							
AFDC/TANF assistance payments	−14	10	−17	−2	−2	−63	−24
AFDC/TANF total expenditure	n.a.	n.a.	−3	8	n.a.	−17	−13
Food stamps	11	48	36	68	−10	−48	19
Unemployment insurance, state regular plus extended	n.a.	52	84	150	−56	−41	−33
Unemployment insurance, all	n.a.	132	132	277	n.a.	−61	−47
EITC	−37	68	9	−0.4[c]	171	84	7
Changes in family well-being: employment and poverty							
Official poverty rate, all persons	3.3	2.0	1.2	1.8	−2.2	−3.5	0.0
Official poverty rate, children	5.5	2.7	1.4	2.7	−2.3	−6.1	0.4
Official extreme poverty rate, children	n.a.	2.1	1.2	1.5	−1.7	−3.4	−0.1
NAS alternative poverty rate, all persons	n.a.	n.a.	1.0	0.6[c]	n.a.	n.a.	1.6
Share of single women with children with job last week	−1.9	−1.4	−3.3	−3.9	3.0	14.6	0.5
Share of single women with children out of labor force last week	−0.8	0.7	0.6	0.4	−0.8	−11.9	1.8
Share of children receiving any non-AFDC/TANF, non-Medicaid safety net benefit	n.a.	4.3	1.3	4.5	−2.2	−3.9	−1.1

(continued)

Table 1. Changes in Unemployment, Safety Net Program Expenditure, and Family Well-Being across Contractions and Expansions[a] (*Continued*)

Percentage points except where stated otherwise

Statistic	Contractions				Expansions		
	1979–82	1989–92	2000–03	2007–09	1982–89	1992–2000	2003–07
Changes in family well-being: consumption and food insecurity							
Real consumption by lowest income quintile (percent)							
Total consumption	n.a.	−7.8	−3.5	2.0	n.a.	15.6	−1.8
Food consumption	n.a.	−9.3	11.3	11.5	n.a.	−3.9	−15.3
Share of households experiencing food insecurity	n.a.	n.a.	n.a.	3.2[c]	n.a.	n.a.	0.2
Changes in family well-being: demographic and housing stress							
Share of children living in female-headed family	2.9	1.7	0.4	0.2	1.4	−0.7	0.8
Share of children living in household with more than one family	2.9	1.0	−0.1	0.2	0.3	0.0	1.0
Changes in health insurance and access							
Share of nonelderly persons uninsured	1.9	1.2	−0.3	1.0	1.7	0.0	0.1
Share of persons who delayed care or had no care because of cost	n.a.	n.a.	1.4	3.4	n.a.	n.a.	0.8
Homelessness (change in number of persons)							
Persons on the street at a given point in time	n.a.	n.a.	n.a.	−41,000	n.a.	n.a.	n.a.
Persons ever using shelter or transitional housing over past year	n.a.	n.a.	n.a.	−30,000	n.a.	n.a.	n.a.
Families ever using shelter or transitional housing over past year	n.a.	n.a.	n.a.	62,000	n.a.	n.a.	n.a.

Sources: Various published sources and authors' calculations from March Current Population Survey data. For details on sources and methods, see the appendix.
a. n.a. = not available.
b. Change from 2007 to 2008 is 1.2 percentage points.
c. Change from 2007 to 2008.

sions in the program in 1986, 1990, and 1993, it is hard to distinguish any impact of the cycle (Eissa and Hoynes 2006).

Perhaps surprisingly, the data on cash welfare expenditure (AFDC and TANF) do not show a clear countercyclical pattern. Cash welfare payments per capita increased during the 1989–92 contraction (by 10 percent) but *decreased* during the contractions of 1979–82 (by 14 percent), 2000–03 (17 percent), and 2007–09 (2 percent). However, the more comprehensive TANF total assistance measure, which includes cash and noncash assistance, increased by 8 percent in the 2007–09 recession.[6] Less surprisingly, cash payments decreased during each of the three expansions. Previous research shows that some of the decreases in periods of contraction are the result of structural, policy-driven declines in expenditure (for example, expenditure was lower because of rules cutting eligibility in 1981 and because of welfare reform in the late 1990s) in excess of countercyclical increases in expenditure. This illustrates the limitations of this exercise: simple descriptive comparisons of expenditure across contractions and expansions are not definitive in identifying the effects of welfare reform on the responsiveness of the safety net.

We postpone until the next section a detailed discussion of welfare, other safety net programs, and the recent reforms. However, to provide a context for the material presented in the remaining panels of table 1, here we present a demographic profile of cash welfare recipients. In particular, table 2 reports characteristics of families with any cash welfare income (AFDC or general assistance) in 1995, on the eve of federal welfare reform. For comparison, we also present the same characteristics for all families with children in 1995 and for families receiving cash welfare at the end of the period, in 2009.[7] In 1995 almost 70 percent of heads of

---

6. After welfare reform, states had flexibility to spend federal block grant funding on not only cash assistance, but also other noncash aid such as subsidized child care, transportation, and education and training. The total expenditure series includes spending from all sources. We discuss this further below.

7. These calculations are based on the 1996 and 2010 March CPS, which collects information on current living arrangements and on income, transfers, and health insurance coverage for the preceding calendar year. Like all sample surveys, the CPS relies on self-reports, and as in many such surveys, income is underreported. The degree of underreporting varies both over time and across types of income as well as by recipiency and total dollar amounts. (Weinberg 2004 summarizes some of the issues; see also specific studies such as Meyer, Mok, and Sullivan 2009, Wheaton 2007, and Bitler, Currie, and Scholz 2003.) In part because of this concern about the validity of self-reports of income from public assistance and other programs, we also present results using administrative counts.

Table 2. Characteristics of Families Receiving Public Assistance Income in 1995 and 2009, and of All Families in 1995[a]

Percent except where stated otherwise

Characteristic	Families with children receiving cash welfare, 1995[b]	All families with children, 1995[c]	Families with children receiving cash welfare, 2009[b]
Heads of family			
Percent white, non-Hispanic	39.0	69.7	37.5
Percent black, non-Hispanic	33.9	13.6	34.4
Percent Hispanic	21.5	12.0	23.9
Percent female	78.4	36.7	82.2
Percent with <12 years education	40.5	15.8	33.8
Percent with exactly 12 years education	34.0	31.8	33.4
Percent with >12 years education	25.5	52.4	32.8
Percent never married	37.6	8.8	45.1
Percent divorced, separated, or widowed	34.7	18.4	27.4
Percent married	27.7	72.9	27.6
Average age (years)	33.9	38.2	35.4
Percent insured	96.6	85.6	94.4
Percent working last week	30.6	80.3	34.1
Percent out of the labor force last week	56.0	14.3	49.1
Families			
Percent in household receiving food stamps	86.5	14.4	82.1
Percent in household in public or subsidized housing	32.8	6.0	32.1
Percent in household owning home	16.6	64.3	19.9
Percent with child insured	98.9	87.4	99.1

Sources: Authors' tabulations of 1996 and 2010 March CPS data.

a. Demographics and living arrangements are as of the time of the survey (March 1996 or 2010); income and program receipt refer to calendar year 1995 or 2009.

b. Families with at least one child and receiving public assistance income (AFDC, TANF, or general assistance).

c. All families with at least one child.

families with cash welfare income were unmarried single women, about 40 percent were non-Hispanic whites, 34 percent were non-Hispanic blacks, and 22 percent were Hispanic.[8] These figures changed little between 1995 and 2009. Compared with all families with children, the welfare population is more likely to be black or Hispanic, less educated, unmarried, and female headed, with the head out of the labor force. In addition, table 2 shows that most families receiving cash welfare also participate in other government programs: in 1995, 87 percent of these families received food stamps, and 33 percent lived in government-subsidized housing. (Not shown in the table is that 90 percent of the heads and 97 percent of the children were on Medicaid—or, for the children only, the State Children's Health Insurance Program—13 percent received cash assistance through the SSI program, and 65 percent participated in the free and reduced-price school meals program.)

Historically, families do not mix welfare and work (31 percent of recipients were working at the time of the 1995 survey, and 56 percent were out of the labor force), but the tabulations for 2009 suggest that combining welfare and work has increased somewhat since welfare reform.[9] Those who did work before welfare reform tended to work in poorly paid occupations (Burtless 1997). Also worth noting is that among a given entry cohort into welfare, a large share will be on welfare for a short time, but a large share of the current welfare caseload is made up of long-term recipients, who tend to be even less attached to the labor force than other recipients (see, for example, Bane and Ellwood 1994). Ellwood (1986) reports that 34 percent of first-time AFDC recipients had not worked in the previous 2 years, and 18.4 percent of these new recipients had a disability that limited work.

---

8. It may seem surprising that we find just over a quarter of families receiving welfare to have married heads. However, under AFDC, states could offer benefits to support children in two-parent families where the primary earner was unemployed (in 1995, these families accounted for 7 percent of cases; U.S. House of Representatives 1996), and under TANF, many of the eligibility rules distinguished far less between two- and one-parent families. Further, because family structure is measured as of March whereas income is measured for the preceding calendar year, some share of individuals may have gotten married after having been on cash assistance.

9. In these tabulations, a family is identified as a welfare recipient if it received any public assistance income (AFDC/TANF or other) during the previous calendar year. We measure employment as of the week before the survey. (We can also measure any employment during the last calendar year.) Consequently, because one cannot tell from the CPS whether people had earnings when they were also receiving cash assistance, the CPS does not allow for identification of simultaneous welfare and work status.

With these facts in mind, we return to table 1, which also presents changes across contractions and expansions for a broad array of outcomes relevant for the welfare population. Data on most outcomes are not available for all time periods, and many are available only after welfare reform. All of the poverty measures are strongly countercyclical. For example, the official poverty rate for children increased by 5.5 percentage points in the 1979–82 recession, and by 2.7 percentage points between 2007 and 2009. Poverty declined in two of the three periods of expansion, the exception being the 2003–07 expansion, when child poverty increased by 0.4 percentage point. Extreme child poverty, defined as the share of children in families with income below 50 percent of the official poverty threshold, declined across all expansions. The NAS alternative poverty measure seems to fluctuate less with the cycle. (As noted above, the NAS alternative poverty measure is not yet available for 2009, so the statistic for the recent recession is of limited value.)

Employment of single mothers exhibits a procyclical pattern, declining by 3.9 percentage points in the recent recession, compared with 1.9 percentage points in the 1979–82 contraction. This suggests a greater sensitivity to the cycle after welfare reform, which is consistent with an increase in rates of attachment to the labor market among potential welfare recipients. We also consider a more comprehensive measure of receipt of safety net benefits that includes a broad array of public assistance programs (but excludes AFDC/TANF, general assistance, and Medicaid). This broad safety net participation measure is very strongly countercyclical, increasing by a striking 4.5 percentage points in the recent contraction after declining in the 1992–2000 expansion by a similar amount.[10]

Mindful of the importance of looking at measures that capture well-being rather than resources, in the remainder of the table we present changes in consumption expenditure (in real 2009 dollars per capita from the Consumer Expenditure Survey), in food insecurity, in "doubling up" and homelessness, and in health insurance coverage and access. Our consumption measures are for individuals in the lowest 20 percent of consumer units by pre-tax income, and notably, changes in these measures do not show a consistent pattern across the contractions and expansions. Food insecurity, data for which are available only for the later period, shows an

---

10. This measure takes a value of 1 for any household where a member is reported as participating in food stamps, SSI, public housing or rental subsidies, free or reduced-price school lunches, or energy assistance during the calendar year before the survey.

increase of 3.2 percentage points in the recent contraction; this is particularly striking given that the data are available only through 2008.[11]

The share of children living in a female-headed household and the share "doubling up" (living in households with two or more families, a measure of housing stress) also do not exhibit strong patterns across cycles. Curiously, homelessness, data for which are available only for the most recent period and for a sample of shelters, seems to have declined in the recent recession, although the number of homeless *families* increased. Delay of or failure to get medical care due to cost, a measure of health care access, rises in both contractions for which data are available; health insurance coverage, however, shows no clear cyclical trend.

To illustrate in more detail the degree of protection that cash welfare and food stamps provide in recessions, the top panel of figure 3 shows the total number of unemployed persons, the cash welfare (TANF) caseload, and the food stamp caseload by month from January 2007 to the present. We normalize all series to 1 in December 2007, the official start of the recent recession, and demarcate the official end of the recession in June 2009.[12] The figure shows that food stamp caseloads have expanded significantly with the recession whereas TANF caseloads have changed very little. The middle panel of figure 3 depicts the same three series (substituting AFDC for TANF) for the second of the two early-1980s recessions, which officially began in July 1981, and the bottom panel does the same for the recession that began in July 1990. These graphs suggest that cash welfare caseloads are less responsive to the economic cycle than are food stamp caseloads and that neither program responded much during the 1981–82 recession.

Finally, another way to assess the role of the safety net is to examine the sources of income for the disadvantaged during a contraction. The top panel of figure 4 shows the share of total income (which here includes both cash income and the value of food stamps) by source for all households in poverty in 1982 and 2008; the bottom panel provides the same information for households in extreme poverty (income below 50 percent of the official

---

11. Food security is a measure of households having enough nutritionally adequate and safe foods or having assured ability to acquire acceptable foods in socially acceptable ways (for example, not through emergency food supplies or scavenging). Haider (2006) describes advantages and disadvantages of this measure of well-being, which contains a psychological component.

12. These figures update earlier graphs from a presentation by LaDonna Pavetti, "Responding to Increasing Need: Assessing TANF's Responsiveness during Hard Economic Times," Center for Budget and Policy Priorities, June 3, 2010.

Figure 3. Unemployment, Cash Welfare Caseloads, and Food Stamp Caseloads in Three Recessions[a]

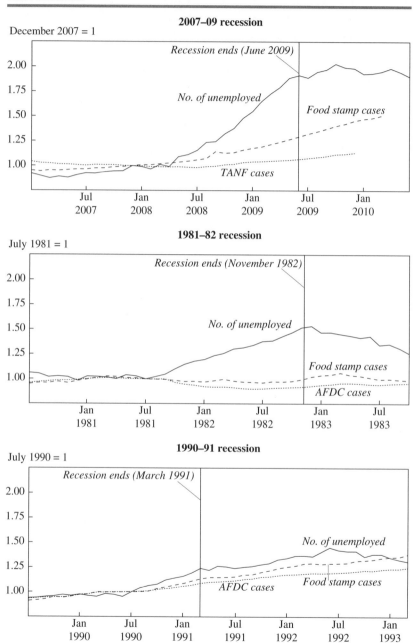

Sources: See the appendix.
a. All series are normalized relative to their level at the beginning of the recession.

Figure 4. Composition of Income by Source for Households below the Official Poverty Line, 1982 and 2008[a]

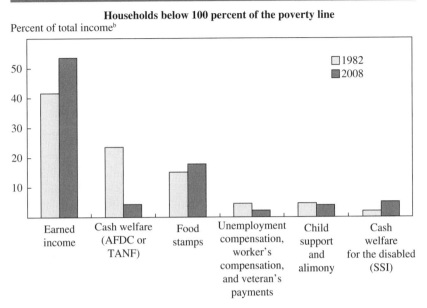

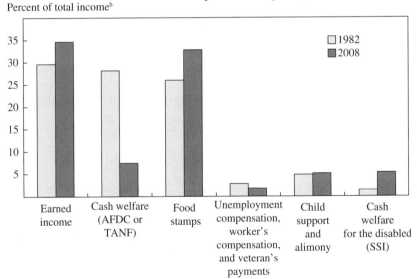

Source: Authors' calculations from 1983 and 2009 March CPS data.
a. Data refer to 1982 and 2008 calendar-year income. Samples include only households with children, and poverty is evaluated at the household level. Percentages do not sum to 100 because some income sources are excluded.
b. Total income includes the value of food stamps received.

poverty threshold).[13] This figure clearly shows the declining role of cash welfare as a countercyclical income source for the poor and the increasing roles played by food stamps, earnings, and SSI.[14]

Several important points emerge from this analysis. Overall, use of a broad measure of the safety net (excluding Medicaid and cash assistance for families with children), poverty, food insecurity, and health care access show strong countercyclical patterns. The nature of changes in demographic stress, homelessness, and consumption across the cycle is less clear. Unfortunately, many of the outcomes of interest exhibit either secular trends (for example, children living with single female family heads, percent uninsured) or policy-driven structural changes (for example, expansions in the EITC, welfare reform–induced reductions in use of cash welfare), or both. These other factors make it difficult to draw conclusions from table 1 (or figure 3) concerning cycles, the disadvantaged, and welfare reform, as it is hard to separate the role of the aggregate cycle from that of other factors affecting the trends in outcomes. To take just one example, it is well understood that, as alluded to above, AFDC caseloads declined in 1981 as a result of changes in the benefit reduction rate that reduced eligibility for many recipients (Moffitt 1992, U.S. General Accounting Office 1985). This obviously complicates the interpretation of figure 3 and table 1. Rebecca Blank expresses our concerns well:

> Note that the back-to-back recessions in the early 1980s caused a mild uptick in caseloads, but this was quickly aborted when legislative changes in Reagan's first term ended AFDC eligibility for about 15 percent of the caseload.... This policy change makes it difficult to do any quick "eyeball" comparisons between the recession effects of the early 1980s and the early 1990s on caseloads. (Blank 2001, p. 87)

In sum, the data in table 1 provide a useful description of changes in well-being in the recent recession. However, to make more definitive conclusions about how the cyclicality of outcomes has changed after welfare reform, we defer to our regression results below, where we are able to separate out secular trends from the cycle.

II. The Elements of the Safety Net before and after Reform

Before discussing our regression results, we step back and provide some more background on welfare and welfare reform. Cash welfare is not the only government assistance program for low-income families with chil-

---

13. We are unable to update this figure to 2009 because the amount of food stamps per household has not yet been released by the Census Bureau as of this writing.

14. The share of income provided by food stamps might increase mechanically if families leave welfare and do not replace all of their welfare income, because the food stamp program reduces benefits by 30 cents for each dollar of other income.

Table 3. Expenditure on and Participation in Cash or Near-Cash Safety Net Programs, 2009, and Children Removed from Poverty, by Program, 2009[a]

Program	Thousands	Total benefit payments (millions of dollars)	Average monthly benefit (dollars)	Estimated no. of children removed from poverty (millions)
Cash welfare (TANF)[b] (cases)	1,796	9,324	397	0.8
Food stamps (cases)	15,232	50,360	276	2.2
EITC[c] (tax filing units)	24,757	50,669	171	2.6
Cash welfare (SSI, nonaged caseload)	6,407	41,023	517	1.0
Unemployment compensation (persons)				
Regular state benefits	n.a.	79,600	1,335	n.a.
Extended benefits	n.a.	7,574	n.a.	n.a.
Emergency benefits	n.a.	44,246	n.a.	n.a.
Total	5,757	131,420	n.a.	n.a.

Sources: For children removed from poverty see Sherman (2009). For all other sources see the appendix.
a. Data refer to calendar 2009 and are in 2009 dollars except where noted otherwise.
b. Data refer to fiscal 2009.
c. Data refer to 2008 and are in 2008 dollars.

dren. In our analysis of the impact of the cycle on disadvantaged families, we seek to understand how both cash welfare and the other elements of the safety net may have affected family well-being. Therefore, here we describe not only cash welfare and welfare reform but also, briefly, the other safety net programs and their recent reforms.

Table 3 presents an overview of participation and spending in the central cash and near-cash safety net programs for low-income families with children. The two primary programs are TANF (the cash welfare program that replaced AFDC as described above) and the food stamp program (now called the Supplemental Nutrition Assistance Program). The food stamp program is by far the larger of the two, especially since welfare reform: in 2009, 15 million families or single individuals received food stamps, at a cost of $50 billion (all dollar figures in this paragraph are in current dollars), compared with fewer than 2 million families receiving cash welfare, at a cost of $9 billion. The EITC provides tax-based aid for low-income working families with children, and in 2008, the most recent year for which data are available, 25 million families received the EITC, at a total tax cost of $51 billion. SSI is another cash welfare program, one that primarily serves poor elderly and disabled adults but is also received by disabled children in some poor families. Finally, unemployment compensation is obviously a critical element of the safety net and is *the* central income replacement program in recessions. This program differs from the others in that it is a social insurance program, with eligibility determined by work history and not conditioned on current income. Unemployment compensation consists of several different programs, including regular state benefits, state extended benefits (which generally kick in when a state's unemployment rate exceeds a preset threshold), and the federally financed emergency benefits program (which is currently in place and extends benefits well beyond the normal maximum period of receipt of 26 weeks). In 2009, on average, about 6 million persons in a given week received some form of unemployment compensation, at a cost of over $131 billion for the year).

Average monthly payments per recipient family in 2009 were $397 for TANF and $276 for food stamps. EITC credits in 2008 averaged $2,046 per year, or $171 per month. By contrast, regular state weekly unemployment compensation payments in the fourth quarter of 2009 averaged $308 per week ($1,335 per month). The final column in table 3 reports results from a recent Center for Budget and Policy Priorities study (Sherman 2009) on the number of children that each of these programs lifted out of poverty in 2005. The EITC leads, having lifted 2.6 million children out of poverty, followed by food stamps at 2.2 million, and then by SSI and TANF, which each removed about 1 million children from poverty.[15]

Our analysis focuses on cash welfare (TANF) and food stamps, but in our analysis of family income and poverty, we indirectly analyze the impacts of all the programs listed in table 3 as well as broader measures of any safety net use that encompass other programs, such as the free and reduced-price school lunch program and public housing and rental vouchers.[16]

---

15. These calculations for poverty alleviation perform the hypothetical exercise of eliminating one program at a time while maintaining all of the others. The exact numbers differ somewhat from study to study; for another set of estimates see Meyer (2010). Of course, EITC eligibility rules mean most EITC benefits are received by individuals near the poverty line, thus making it more likely for the EITC to lift families out of poverty. Other programs such as AFDC/TANF have eligibility thresholds further from the poverty line, making it less likely they will lift families out of poverty.

16. Other cash or near-cash programs of relevance for families with children include public housing and vouchers and rent subsidies, other nutrition programs (the National School Lunch and Breakfast programs, WIC), energy assistance, and state general assistance programs. In addition, Medicaid provides health insurance for poor children and families, and higher-income (but still low-income) children are eligible for SCHIP.

II.A. Eligibility Rules, Benefits, and Recent Reforms for the Key Safety Net Programs

CASH WELFARE. At the national level, cash welfare for low-income families started with the AFDC program, created by the Social Security Act of 1935. The program was jointly funded by the state and federal governments (with a higher federal matching rate for lower-income states). States had authority to set benefit levels, but the federal government dictated most of the remaining eligibility and benefit rules. A family was eligible if it satisfied income and asset tests, and assistance was primarily limited to single women with children.[17] The benefits were structured in a manner typical for income support programs: if a family had no income, it received the maximum benefit or "guarantee." As the family's earnings (or allowable income) increased, the benefit was reduced by the benefit reduction rate or clawback rate, which created an implicit tax rate on earned income. Historically, this rate has varied between 67 and 100 percent, providing a strong disincentive for work (Moffitt 1983). This fact attracted little attention in the program's early decades, when very few mothers participated in the labor market. Over time, however, concerns about the work disincentive (and about the disincentive to form two-parent families) grew, and interest in reforming the program followed.

The modern era of welfare reform began in the early 1990s, when many states were granted waivers to modify their AFDC programs.[18] About half of the states implemented some sort of welfare waiver between 1992 and 1995. On the heels of this state experimentation, the Personal Responsibility and Work Opportunity Reconciliation Act (PRWORA) was enacted in 1996, replacing AFDC with TANF. The key elements of reform in the state waivers and the TANF legislation included work requirements, lifetime time limits on the duration of welfare receipt, financial sanctions for failing to adhere to the work requirements or other rules, and enhanced

---

17. More precisely, a family had to show that the children were deprived of parental support by the absence, incapacitation, or (in some states and some periods) unemployment of one parent. In practice, throughout its history more than 90 percent of the AFDC caseload consisted of single mothers (see U.S. Department of Health and Human Services 2008, appendix A, table TANF-1). Large changes in the mid-1960s expanded the program considerably for unmarried mothers.

18. The 1990s reforms were by no means the first reforms of AFDC. Without a doubt, however, they were the furthest reaching, and today "welfare reform" generally refers to those changes.

earnings disregards.[19] These changes were designed to facilitate the transition from welfare to work and to reduce dependence on cash welfare. The time limits were an important provision in that they eliminated the entitlement nature of the program. States have considerable discretion in setting policies under TANF, but by federal law, programs must include work requirements and lifetime time limits of 5 years or less for the vast majority of recipients.[20] The character of federal funding also changed from an (uncapped) matching formula under AFDC to a (capped) block grant under TANF.

An advantage for identifying the effects of these recent reforms is that both the timing and the type of welfare reform varied considerably across states in the 1990s. Some states reformed their programs through waivers, in advance of the 1996 law. Other states reformed their programs later, when required by PRWORA, with the last state implementing TANF in January 1998. Under PRWORA, states continue to vary in their length of time limits, types of sanctions, and so on. For example, Gilbert Crouse (1999) reports that before PRWORA, 15 states had waivers approved with time limits on receipt, 19 had waivers approved that enhanced their earnings disregards, and 28 had waivers approved that included sanctions for noncompliance. Although PRWORA imposed time limits for federally funded welfare on all states, some states use their own funds to pay benefits beyond the federal time limit. This state variation in the timing and severity of reform has been widely exploited in empirical studies of welfare reform (see reviews in Blank 2002 and Grogger and Karoly 2005), and we will make use of this variation as well.

TANF provides benefits only to families with quite low incomes, and eligibility cutoffs and benefit levels leave recipients substantially below the poverty line. Before welfare reform, under AFDC, the median state provided benefits to families with income up to 70 percent of the poverty guideline, and the median state's benefit level for a family of three was

---

19. Enhanced earnings disregards refer to changes in the benefit formula to reduce the rate at which earnings are "taxed" by the welfare system and thus increase incentives to work. Other changes adopted by some states include expanding eligibility for two-parent families, "family caps" (freezing benefits at the level associated with current family size), and imposing residency and schooling requirements for unmarried teen recipients. For a detailed discussion of the policy changes, see Blank and Haskins (2001) and Grogger and Karoly (2005).

20. The 5-year lifetime limit on receipt of federal TANF assistance applies to adult-headed families, but the law allowed states to exempt from this limit for hardship reasons up to 20 percent of their total caseload.

about 36 percent of the 1996 poverty guideline (U.S. House of Representatives 1996).[21] Benefits varied widely across states; for example, in 1996 maximum benefits for a family of three were $120 per month in Mississippi and $607 per month in California. As part of their welfare reforms, to improve financial incentives to make the transition from welfare to work, many states decreased the implicit tax rate on earned income within the TANF program, allowing individuals to have much higher earnings before losing all their welfare benefits. Despite these expansions in the amount of earned income that families could keep while on welfare, total benefits remain low.

FOOD STAMPS. The Supplemental Nutrition Assistance Program, like TANF, is a means-tested program (eligible families and individuals must satisfy income and asset tests) in which benefits are subject to a ceiling and reduced with earned income. The similarities end there, however. First, the food stamp program is a federal program, with all funding (except for 50 percent of administrative costs) provided by the federal government. Second, unlike virtually all other cash assistance programs, food stamps are not limited to certain targeted groups such as families with children, the elderly, and the disabled. Third, the benefit reduction rate is relatively low (30 cents per dollar earned), and the income eligibility threshold is relatively high (130 percent of the poverty guideline). The lower benefit reduction rate means that the food stamp program serves not only the nonworking poor (those receiving cash welfare) but also the working poor. Recipients are allowed to use their benefits to buy a wide array of food items (although not prepared foods), and studies show that the behavioral response to food stamps is similar to the response to cash (Fraker and others 1992, Hoynes and Schanzenbach 2009, Ohls and others 1992). Food stamp benefits today are disbursed with debit cards rather than paper vouchers as in the past.

Unlike cash welfare, the food stamp program has remained relatively unchanged over time. The income eligibility cutoff and benefits are adjusted for changes in prices each year, and the actual benefit formula (and thus the implicit tax rate) has changed very little over time. However, important limitations to the program were introduced under PRWORA: legal immigrants

---

21. Note that eligibility for many federal safety net programs is based on poverty guidelines, which are simplified versions of the Census poverty thresholds, varying by fewer dimensions and made available earlier in the year. Poverty guidelines vary by number of persons and are different for Alaska and Hawaii than for the rest of the states and the District of Columbia. See aspe.hhs.gov/poverty/figures-fed-reg.shtml.

were deemed ineligible, and most childless, jobless adults between 18 and 50 could receive only 3 months of food stamps in any 3-year period.[22] The 2002 farm bill reinstated benefits for legal immigrants, and the 2009 federal stimulus bill temporarily suspended the 3-month limit for childless, jobless adults. The stimulus bill also provided a temporary increase in maximum benefits of roughly $25 per month, at a cost of $6 billion in 2009 (Pavetti and Rosenbaum 2010).

Since welfare reform (and perhaps even before it), the food stamp program is unambiguously the key safety net program and the only one that is "universal" (that is, based only on economic need) and that has a fully funded entitlement. Caseloads and benefits adjust automatically with demand (increasing in recessions), and costs are uncapped.

UNEMPLOYMENT INSURANCE. As already noted, unemployment insurance is a social insurance program that provides temporary and partial earnings replacement for involuntarily unemployed individuals with a recent employment history. As a social insurance program, unemployment insurance is not means tested, and eligibility is a function of earnings history. States administer their programs and set payroll taxes and benefit levels. Workers' wages are subject to tax while employed, and unemployed workers receive benefits for a fixed duration, with replacement rates (the ratio of benefits to most recent earnings) averaging 47 percent since 1995 (U.S. Department of Labor 2010). The extended benefit program extends receipt of unemployment compensation beyond the 26-week maximum when state unemployment rates or the share of the insured population claiming benefits is high. Funding for the extended program is shared by the states and the federal government. In most major downturns, Congress has enacted emergency extensions to unemployment insurance, such as the current program, which in most states extends benefits up to 99 weeks. Recently, these emergency extensions have been fully federally funded.

Although unemployment compensation plays a central role in recessions, it is often not considered part of the safety net because it primarily provides insurance and is funded through worker contributions. We mention it here for three reasons. First, given the increase in employment

---

22. Technically, the 3-months-in-3-years limitation applied to able-bodied adults aged 18–49 with no dependents who were not working, in a work program, or doing workfare. Individuals are exempt if they are caring for a child, are unable to work, or are pregnant. States can exempt 15 percent of individuals and can get this provision waived if the state unemployment rate is above 10 percent or if the state is eligible for state extended unemployment benefits or there are not enough jobs.

among the potentially welfare-eligible population since TANF's passage (see the discussion of figure 6 below), unemployment compensation may be increasing in importance for low-income families. Second, although the insurance is not means tested, replacement rates fall as earnings rise, providing greater protection for lower-wage workers. Third, the emergency federal benefit extensions tend to be explicitly countercyclical and are passed by Congress in response to bad economic times. Although these emergency programs are typically short lived, when in effect they account for a large share of total spending on unemployment compensation. Table 3 shows that in 2009, emergency benefits were about $44 billion, compared with a combined $87 billion for regular and extended benefits.

THE TRANSITION FROM OUT-OF-WORK TO IN-WORK ASSISTANCE. As discussed above, the EITC is one of the most costly cash or near-cash assistance programs. It functions as an earnings subsidy and as such is extended only to working families. The expansion of the EITC, facilitated through tax acts in 1986, 1990, and 1993, has featured prominently in the movement toward more "in-work" assistance in the safety net. However, the emergence of TANF has also been an important part of this transition. Virtually all TANF policies—the work requirements, the time limits, and the lowering of the benefit reduction rate—are designed to increase work. In addition, under TANF, states have the flexibility to use their federal block grant funding toward assistance other than periodic cash benefits: examples include child care subsidies as well as transportation, training, and diversion payments.[23] To illustrate the importance of these trends, figure 5 shows real spending per capita from 1980 to 2009 for families receiving cash grants through AFDC/TANF as well as total TANF expenditure per capita and total EITC tax cost per capita. (We also show spending on food stamps per capita because this program, too, serves the working poor.) The expansion of the EITC between 1986 and 1998, coupled with the decline in cash welfare expenditure beginning with the waivers of the early 1990s, represents a tremendous change in the incentives faced by low-income families with children. Importantly, the post–welfare reform trend in total TANF expenditure presents a somewhat different picture concerning welfare funding than the trend for cash grants only—in fact, total funding has been more or less constant (in real terms) over the last 10 or more years. Unfortunately, the state reporting requirements for noncash TANF expenditure are minimal,

---

23. Diversion payments are one-time payments made in lieu of monthly benefit payments at the recipient's request.

Figure 5. Real Expenditure per Capita on Cash and Near-Cash Safety Net Programs, 1980–2009[a]

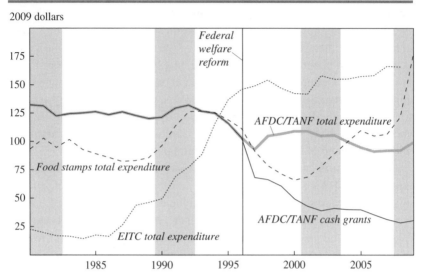

Sources: See the appendix.
a. Shading indicates years of labor market contraction as defined in the appendix.

and thus very little is known about who receives this funding and what it is spent on.[24] Nonetheless, these changes illustrate an important transition from out-of-work aid to in-work aid for low-income families with children.

The result of these policy changes, coupled with the strong labor market of the late 1990s, was a historic increase in employment for single women with children. Figure 6 presents, for 1980–2009, the percentages of three groups of women aged 20–58 with any weeks of work in the last year: sin-

---

24. In the March CPS from 2001 to 2009, individuals were asked whether they had obtained transportation assistance or child care assistance so that they could work or go to school or training; they were also asked whether they had obtained job readiness training or attended a job search class or job club or participated in GED classes or a community service job as a condition of receiving cash assistance. We combined these into two household-level variables. Although these activities need not all be funded by TANF, surely some are. From 2000 to 2008, 2.5 percent of households included someone getting child care assistance or transportation assistance; 3.4 percent of households had someone in job readiness, job search, GED classes, or community service, compared with 3.8 percent of households in which one or more members received public assistance income. Furthermore, most of the households with cash welfare did not get either of the two other supports, and vice versa; among households with a child under 18, only 30 percent of those getting cash welfare had someone getting one of these other noncash benefits, while of those getting the noncash benefits, only 21 percent got public assistance income.

Figure 6. Female Employment Rate by Marital Status and Presence of Children, 1980–2009[a]

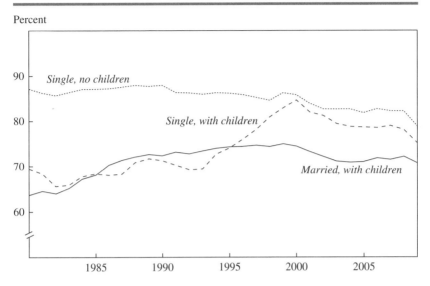

Source: Authors' calculations from 1981–2010 March CPS data.
a. Employment is measured annually and defined as having worked any weeks during the calendar year before the survey year. The sample includes women aged 20–58.

gle women heading families with children, married women with children in the family, and single women without children in the family. Between 1992 and 2000 the employment rate of single women with kids rose by 15 percentage points; the other groups saw minimal changes. This trend suggests that outcomes for these single-woman-headed families will be more procyclical, given their increased connection to the labor market.

II.B. Cycles and Participation in Safety Net Programs

Figure 7 presents cash welfare and food stamp caseloads from 1980 to 2009. These data come from administrative sources rather than self-reports from household surveys (see the data appendix for details). To account for changes in population over this period, we show the ratio of the caseload to the total population.[25] Several observations can be made. First, throughout

---

25. The caseload is essentially a count of families or households, whereas the denominator is a count of persons. Although it might be more intuitive to put the number of recipients in the numerator, the caseload measure is more commonly used to abstract away from changes in the size of families receiving benefits. In practice, trends in the ratio of recipients to population look quite similar to those presented here.

Figure 7. Cash Welfare and Food Stamp Caseloads, Administrative Data, 1980–2009[a]

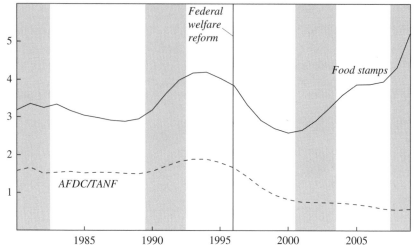

Sources: See the appendix.
a. Shading indicates years of labor market contraction as defined in the appendix.

the pre– and post–welfare reform periods, many more families received food stamps than received cash welfare. Second, cash welfare caseloads dramatically declined in the period around welfare reform and have remained low since. Third, compared with cash welfare, the food stamp caseload shows a stronger countercyclical tendency, at least during the early part of the period.[26] Fourth, since 2000 the trend in the TANF caseload bears little relationship to the national business cycle. Notably, the TANF caseload increased by very little in the recent recession, as figure 3 showed, despite unemployment rates reaching over 10 percent in many states.[27]

---

26. Over the early 2000s, and culminating in provisions included in the 2002 farm bill, the U.S. Department of Agriculture implemented a number of provisions to expand food stamp access by allowing more state policy choices in recertification and reporting and funding some outreach. Klerman and Danielson (2009) look at the effects of these changes and changes in the labor market on food stamp caseloads through 2004.

27. Toward the end of the period depicted in figure 7, in order to remain in compliance with various TANF requirements, many states moved portions of their caseloads off TANF and into new, "solely state-funded" programs. Data collected by LaDonna Pavetti of the Center for Budget and Policy Priorities suggest that these programs are relatively small and show small increases in the recent recession.

Figure 8. Multiple Safety Net Program Participation, 1980–2009[a]

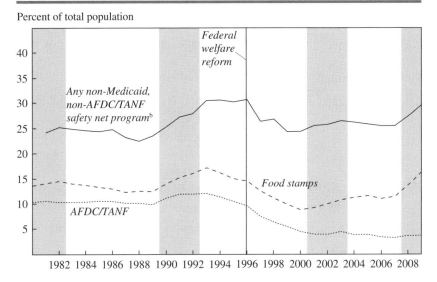

Source: Authors' calculations from 1981–2010 March CPS data.
a. Samples include only households with children, and program participation is evaluated at the household level. Shading indicates years of labor market contraction as defined in the appendix.
b. Households in which someone participated in food stamps, the free or reduced-price school lunch program, or SSI or received public housing or a government rental subsidy or energy assistance.

In figure 8 we return to our broader measure of safety net benefits (excluding Medicaid and cash welfare for families with children; see table 1), which we construct from the 1981–2010 March CPS data. Other than an increase in the early 1990s, followed by a decline, this more comprehensive measure of safety net participation also shows a fair amount of cyclical variation.[28]

Why might it make sense that the food stamp program and our broader measure of the non-AFDC/TANF, non-Medicaid safety net are more countercyclical than cash welfare? As mentioned above, the implicit tax rates in cash welfare are high, much higher than those in the food stamp program. It is much more common for families with food stamps to also have earned income, whereas this is relatively uncommon for cash welfare recipients (see table 2).

28. We also include household participation in cash welfare and food stamps, as measured in the CPS, in figure 8. We find it encouraging that the trends in participation are so similar to those seen in the administrative data.

One should be cautious about drawing conclusions from national trends, however. The problem, as noted in section I, is that it is difficult to distinguish between changes due to labor market fluctuations and changes due to reforms in the programs themselves. For example, the fall in the cash welfare caseload in the late 1990s has been shown to be a function of both the strong economy and welfare reform (for example, see Council of Economic Advisers 1997, Blank 2001, and Ziliak and others 2000). To separate out the impact of welfare reform from labor market fluctuations, our empirical model will use disaggregated data and take advantage of rich variation in cycles and reform across states and time.

III. Welfare Reform and the Impact of the Business Cycle on Family Well-Being

In this section we present our central empirical results on the impact of welfare reform on family well-being over the business cycle. These are new results that build on the models used in two separate literatures: the first examines the impact of the cycle on family economic outcomes and on different demographic groups (for examples, see Hoynes 2000 and Hines, Hoynes, and Krueger 2001), and the second the impacts of welfare reform (see reviews by Blank 2002 and Grogger and Karoly 2005). Clearly, the fact that the safety net provides less than perfect insurance implies that a recession will lead to reductions in family well-being, as measured by increases in poverty, reductions in consumption, increases in doubling up, and so on. What we want to examine is how welfare reform has affected that tendency.

A standard approach in both of these literatures is to use variation across states to distinguish the impact of labor market cycles from that of policy changes. We adopt that approach here as well. In particular, we estimate the following model:

(1) $$y_{st} = \alpha + \phi UR_{st} + \theta REFORM_{st} + \delta UR_{st} \times REFORM_{st} + \gamma_s + \lambda_t + \eta_s t + \varepsilon_{st},$$

where s indexes states, t indexes years, UR is the unemployment rate, and $REFORM$ is a measure of welfare reform.[29] Our equation controls for state

---

29. We have also explored other measures of the cycle, including other labor market measures (employment-to-population ratios or employment growth) and, alternatively, GDP growth, which maps more naturally onto the official recession dating. Although the magnitudes differ, the qualitative conclusions are similar to those reported here.

fixed effects (γ_s), year fixed effects (λ_t), and linear time trends for each state ($\eta_s t$). When we use household survey data, we also control for demographics (X_{ist}, where i indexes households). Standard errors allow for arbitrary correlation within states. The main specifications for administrative caseloads are at the monthly level, and for them t denotes months rather than years.

We begin by analyzing the administrative caseload data on AFDC/TANF and food stamps and then move on to a wide range of family well-being measures based on the March CPS. Using the CPS, we examine impacts on official poverty, our own alternative measure of poverty, program participation (single programs as well as multiple programs), living arrangements (female-headed families), employment among female heads of family units, measures of housing stress (doubling up, households containing subfamilies, and others), health insurance coverage, receipt of child support or alimony, and general health. Finally, we present estimates for food insecurity and, using data from the Panel Study of Income Dynamics, family food consumption. Caseload models are weighted by the total population, and the survey data models are weighted using the survey-provided weights.

The model controls for a main effect for welfare reform and a main effect for labor markets (the unemployment rate). The parameter of interest is δ, the interaction between the reform variable and the unemployment rate, which measures how the impact of the cycle on outcome y changes with welfare reform. With controls for fixed state effects and fixed time (year or month) effects, our estimates are identified off of changes within states over time. This type of model is commonly known as a difference-in-differences model.[30]

This model, by controlling for an unrestricted time trend (λ_t), captures any elements that are common to all states in a given year. A downside of this approach is that the time effects absorb some features of the national cycle. However, the benefit of this approach is that it allows us to identify the impacts of welfare reform separately from labor market fluctuations. To illustrate the variation we are using, figure 9 presents a series of scatterplots of state data in which each state's population is represented by the size of the circle centered on the data point for that state. The horizontal

---

30. Our central parameter, on the interaction between the unemployment rate and welfare reform, would still be identified if reform were captured by a national pre-versus-post-1996 variable (because the unemployment rate still varies by state). However, we use state variation in reform, which we view as a more credible source of identification.

Figure 9. Change in Unemployment Rate, Change in Welfare Caseloads, and Change in Child Poverty during Labor Market Contractions, by State[a]

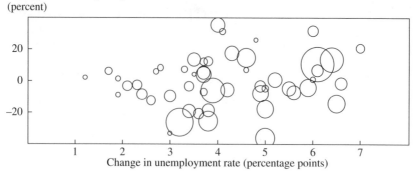

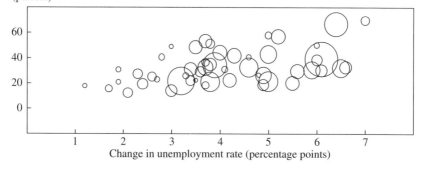

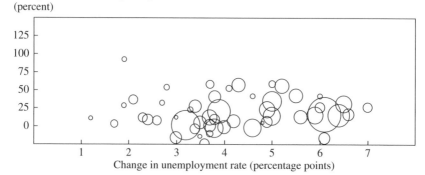

Figure 9. Change in Unemployment Rate, Change in Welfare Caseloads, and Change in Child Poverty during Labor Market Contractions, by State *(Continued)*

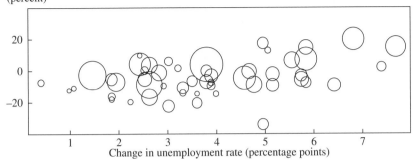

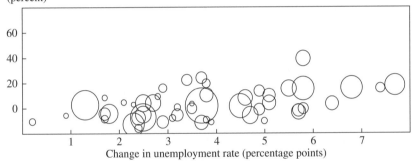

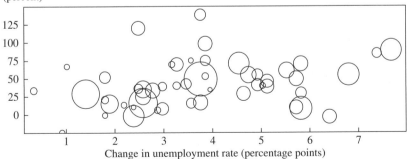

Sources: See the appendix.

a. The center of each circle plots the change in the unemployment rate and the percent change in caseloads or the child poverty rate for one U.S. state between the peak and the trough of the indicated contraction. Circle sizes are proportional to state populations. Official child poverty is calculated by the authors using the 1980, 1983, 2008 and 2010 March CPS and family-level poverty.

b. Food stamp caseloads are not available for 1979, so the percentage change in the caseload between 1980 and 1982 is shown instead.

axis in each panel plots the change in state annual unemployment rates (in percentage points) over a contraction, and the vertical axis a change in a state outcome (in percent) over the same period. The first three panels present data for 2007–09, and the next three panels for 1979–82. For each cycle we show the percent change in cash welfare caseloads per capita (top panels), the percent change in food stamp caseloads per capita (middle panels),[31] and the percent change in official child poverty rates (bottom panels). We have forced the scales to be the same for each of the two contractions for each outcome to provide better comparisons across contractions. The figure reveals considerable variation in the depth of the recessions across states. For example, between 2007 and 2009, state changes in the unemployment rate ranged from about 1 to 7 percentage points, and the change in child poverty varied from a reduction of 25 percent to an increase of nearly 100 percent. Further, the figure shows a positive correlation between the severity of a recession and the increase in official child poverty and program caseloads per capita.

We explore the effects of three measures of welfare reform. First, we use a state pre-versus-post design where *REFORM* equals 1 if the state has implemented a waiver or has implemented TANF, and zero otherwise.[32] Second, we use an explicit categorization of states based on their TANF and waiver policies, focusing on two policy dimensions: the length of time limits and the severity of sanctions. We adopt definitions and data from Caroline Danielson and Jacob Klerman (2004) in constructing these variables.[33] We define time limits as *short* (less than 48 months), *long* (48 months or longer), or *adult* (time limits remove only adults from aid), with the omitted group being state-year cells with no time limits (either pre-PRWORA AFDC rules or no time limit under TANF). We define financial sanctions as *full* (immediate, full family sanction) or *gradual* (gradual, full family sanction), with the omitted group being weak sanctions (either AFDC sanctions or, under TANF, sanctions no more stringent than the AFDC sanctions).

---

31. Because our data on food stamp caseloads begin in 1980, the second middle panel measures the percent change in food stamp caseloads between 1980 and 1982, but the change in unemployment rates from 1979 to 1982.

32. Whereas the timing and the presence of waivers vary considerably across states, TANF implementation varies minimally, as all states implemented TANF in late 1996, 1997, or 1998. See table 1 of Bitler, Gelbach, and Hoynes (2006) for implementation dates and an example of a paper using this identification strategy.

33. We thank Caroline Danielson of the Public Policy Institute of California for generously providing us with their data and coding.

With the administrative monthly caseload data, we use the policies in place that month. For CPS outcomes measured over the last calendar year, such as program participation, income, poverty, and health insurance coverage, the main reform variable is measured as the share of the past calendar year during which reform was in place, and the time limit and sanction policies are coded according to what was in place in December of the preceding year. For the other outcomes measured at the time of the CPS survey (living arrangements, health status), welfare reform is measured by whether the policy was in place as of March of the survey year.

III.A. Safety Net Caseloads

Table 4 presents estimates of the model using administrative data on participation in the cash welfare and food stamp programs. The dependent variable is caseloads per capita at the state-month-year level for 1980 through 2009. State monthly unemployment rates are seasonally adjusted (but the results are very similar if we use non–seasonally adjusted unemployment). We view the results here as a sort of "first stage": they are useful to establish the basic relationship between welfare reform and the cyclicality of safety net programs for low-income families. Additionally, these caseloads are measures from administrative data and do not suffer from underreporting. Thus, they provide us with a valuable benchmark for understanding whether the underreporting documented by Bruce Meyer, Wallace Mok, and James Sullivan (2009) and others has implications for analysis using state-year panels with state and year fixed effects.[34] Finally, considerable attention has been given to the rise in food stamp caseloads in the recent recession,[35] yet no prior research has identified whether welfare reform contributed in any way to that rise.

Table 4 reports the coefficients on the state unemployment rate and the interaction between the unemployment rate and welfare reform. We present three specifications, one for each of the reform variables we discuss above. The dependent variable is the ratio of the caseload to the population (multiplied by 100), and the unemployment rate is measured in percent.

---

34. Weinberg (2004) discusses a host of such studies related to underreporting in the CPS and other Census surveys; Wheaton (2007) documents underreporting of benefit receipt in the CPS.

35. Jason DeParle and Robert Gebeloff, "Food Stamp Use Soars, and Stigma Fades," *The New York Times,* November 29, 2009.

Table 4. Regressions Estimating Impacts of the Business Cycle and Welfare Reform on Cash Welfare and Food Assistance Caseloads[a]

	\multicolumn{6}{c}{Dependent variable}					
	AFDC/TANF caseload-population ratio × 100			Food stamp caseload-population ratio × 100		
Independent variable	4-1	4-2	4-3	4-4	4-5	4-6
State unemployment rate	0.058***	0.066***	0.065***	0.171***	0.187***	0.159***
	(0.010)	(0.011)	(0.013)	(0.027)	(0.024)	(0.020)
Unemployment rate × any reform	0.012			0.050		
	(0.023)			(0.042)		
Unemployment rate × short time limit		−0.026			0.020	
		(0.022)			(0.059)	
Unemployment rate × long time limit		−0.039*			0.000	
		(0.020)			(0.045)	
Unemployment rate × adult time limit		−0.046***			−0.173***	
		(0.015)			(0.036)	
Unemployment rate × full sanction			−0.018			0.138**
			(0.013)			(0.056)
Unemployment rate × gradual sanction			−0.010			0.105
			(0.019)			(0.063)
Mean of dependent variable	1.234	1.234	1.234	3.499	3.499	3.499
No. of observations	18,360	18,360	18,360	18,417	18,417	18,417
Adjusted R^2	0.95	0.95	0.95	0.9	0.91	0.91

Source: Authors' regressions. See the appendix for details on data sources and coding of welfare reforms.

a. Regressions were performed on monthly data on program caseloads per capita by state and year from January 1980 through December 2009 (for AFDC/TANF) and January 1980 through March 2010 (for food stamps). Observations for food stamp cases are missing for Vermont for October 1988 through September 1996. Models also include a full set of time fixed effects, state fixed effects, state-specific linear time trends, and main effects for welfare reform. Welfare reform policies are state policies in place in the month before the caseload month. Asterisks indicate statistical significance at the ***1 percent, **5 percent, and *10 percent level.

For cash welfare caseloads (column 4-1), the coefficient of 0.06 implies that a 1-percentage-point increase in the unemployment rate leads to an increase in the scaled AFDC/TANF caseload-population ratio of 0.06, which, relative to the mean of 1.2, implies an effect size of 4.7 percent. Interestingly, food stamp caseloads (column 4-4) show a similar effect size: the coefficient of 0.17 scaled by the mean of 3.5 implies an effect size of 4.9 percent.

A negative coefficient on the interaction between the unemployment rate and reform implies that welfare reform led to a reduction in the cyclicality of program participation, and a positive coefficient implies an increase (since program participation is expected to be, and is, countercyclical). We expect that the impact of short time limits on cyclicality should exceed (in magnitude) that of long time limits, and both should be larger in magnitude than the effect of the omitted group of no time limits. Adult time limits are generally the least stringent of the three; however, this measure ignores the length of the time limit, which also might be important. We expect the impact of full sanctions on cyclicality to be greater in magnitude than the impact of gradual sanctions, and both should be larger than the effect of the omitted group of no sanctions.

With the exception of the "any reform" specification, the results for AFDC/TANF caseloads (columns 4-1 to 4-3) imply that welfare reform is associated with a *decrease* in the cyclicality of cash welfare. With the exception of the adult time limit, the results for food stamp caseloads (columns 4-4 to 4-6) imply that welfare reform led to an *increase* in the cyclicality of food stamp receipt. However, only 4 of the 12 interaction coefficients reach statistical significance at the 10 percent level or better, and only 3 do so at the 5 percent level or better. Clearly, there is no evidence that welfare reform led to cash assistance caseloads being significantly more cyclically responsive.

Our results are highly robust to several alternative specifications not reported here. We find similar results if we use lagged unemployment rates and if we allow a more flexible state trend (quadratic rather than the linear trends in the main specification). Further, we find no evidence of nonlinear impacts of unemployment rates—we had conjectured that an increase in unemployment from a higher base might lead to larger effects. The results are very similar if we use only data from the 1989-2010 period. Finally, both the food stamps and cash welfare results are robust to adding controls for the state maximum real AFDC/TANF benefits for a family of three. (Benefit levels are an important state cash welfare policy variable that changes throughout the pre– and post–welfare reform period.)[36]

We conclude from these results that the unemployment rate has a positive, significant, and robust effect on cash welfare and food stamp caseloads. Further, welfare reform is generally associated with reductions in the cyclicality of cash welfare participation and increases in the cyclicality of food stamp participation, although not all interactions reach statistical significance.[37]

III.B. Outcomes for Households and for Single Female Family Heads Using the March CPS

We next analyze data from the pooled 1980–2010 March CPS surveys. Our primary focus is on outcomes for single female–headed families with children (table 5) and on households containing at least one child under 18 (tables 6 and 7). We estimate equation 1 and include controls for the race or ethnicity, sex (where appropriate), age, and education of the woman or the household head. We also examine impacts on various subsamples, including single female family heads with 12 or fewer years of education, households whose head has 12 years of education or fewer, and households with at least one family unit with a single female head and a child. These alternative subsamples are intended to select groups that are relatively more disadvantaged and more likely than the general population to have been at risk of participating in the safety net in general, and cash welfare in particular.

We start by examining impacts on earnings, income, and cash welfare income for a sample of single mothers with children. This is a useful starting place because many prior studies have shown that welfare reform has led to increases in employment for this group (see Blank 2002 for a review). These results (reported in table 5) show robust and statistically significant evidence that cash welfare income is countercyclical and that earnings and income are procyclical. A 1-percentage-point increase in the

---

36. We thank Rebecca Blank for suggesting that we control for this variable, especially since our time period 1980–2009 contains a long period before welfare reform. Our results are also unchanged if we incorporate the solely state funded program caseload (data obtained from LaDonna Pavetti and starting in 2006) into our measure of state cash welfare caseloads.

37. We also examined similar models for unemployment compensation and found stronger countercyclical responses than of cash welfare or food stamps to the unemployment rate (not surprisingly) but no evidence that the use of unemployment compensation over the business cycle has been affected by welfare reform.

Table 5. Regressions Estimating Impacts of the Business Cycle and Welfare Reform on Earnings and Income for Single Female Family Heads with Children[a]

	Dependent variable								
	Annual public assistance income			Annual wage and salary income			Total annual family income		
Independent variable	5-1	5-2	5-3	5-4	5-5	5-6	5-7	5-8	5-9
State unemployment rate	78*** (20)	91*** (14)	81*** (16)	−214*** (56)	−277*** (73)	−250*** (70)	−297*** (76)	−390*** (72)	−357 (50)
Unemployment rate × any reform	−4 (28)			−356* (200)			−423* (218)		
Unemployment rate × short time limit		−99*** (24)			−498** (212)			−403 (250)	
Unemployment rate × long time limit		−63** (28)			−245 (255)			−276 (251)	
Unemployment rate × adult time limit		−109*** (25)			142 (296)			47 (303)	
Unemployment rate × full sanction			−23 (27)			−353 (222)			−394** (177)
Unemployment rate × gradual sanction			13 (26)			−493** (191)			−409** (194)
Mean of dependent variable	1,224	1,224	1,224	17,866	17,866	17,866	26,465	26,465	26,465
Adjusted R^2	0.19	0.19	0.19	0.19	0.19	0.19	0.23	0.23	0.23

Source: Authors' regressions.

a. Regressions are performed on data from the 1980–2010 March Current Population Surveys; outcomes refer to the preceding calendar year and thus cover 1980–2009. Observations are by family, and the sample includes single female family heads living with a child. Models also include year fixed effects, state fixed effects, state-specific linear time trends, main effects for welfare reform, and demographic controls for race/ethnicity, age, and education of the woman. The main reform variable is measured as the share of the past calendar year that the reform was in place, and the time limit policies were coded according to what was in place in December. Number of observations is 181,353 in all regressions. Asterisks indicate statistical significance at the ***1 percent, **5 percent, and *10 percent level.

unemployment rate leads to a $78 (in 2009 dollars, or about 6 percent) increase in yearly public assistance income in the any-reform specification. The same increase in unemployment leads to about a 1 percent decline in wage and salary income and a 1 percent decline in total (nuclear) family income in the any-reform specification. Further, the interactions between welfare reform and unemployment are largely negative, 8 of the 12 interactions are statistically significant at the 10 percent level or better, and 7 are significant at the 5 percent level or better. A negative coefficient implies that welfare reform led to a *decrease* in the cyclicality for cash welfare income (since the main effect on unemployment is positive, showing that cash welfare receipt is countercyclical) and an *increase* in the cyclicality for earnings and total income (since the main effect is negative, showing that earnings and total income are procyclical). This is important because if earnings are more procyclical after reform—falling more in the recent recession than they would have before reform—then greater countercyclicality in the safety net is necessary to maintain the same level of well-being. This combination (less insurance through cash welfare and more vulnerability in recessions) suggests a bad combination of effects. To get a sense of the magnitudes of the interaction coefficients for the any-reform specifications, a 1-percentage-point increase in the unemployment rate after reform would lead to an additional decrease in public assistance income of $4, or about 0.3 percent (with a 95 percent confidence interval of −4.9 to 4.3 percent), an additional decrease in wage and salary income of $356, or about 2.0 percent (95 percent confidence interval of −4.2 to 0.3 percent), and a decrease in total family income of $423, or about 1.6 percent (95 percent confidence interval of −3.3 to 0.1 percent). These findings suggest that increases in unemployment such as that during the recent recession could lead to economically meaningful decreases in earnings and income in the wake of reform. In results not shown, coefficients on the unemployment rate and its interaction with reform are larger in magnitude (more negative) for wage and salary income and for total income for the sample of low-education single female family heads.

Table 6 presents results for our central measure of family well-being, the poverty rate, for all households with children. We present results using both the official poverty measure and our alternative measure, and we measure poverty at the household level. We construct our alternative poverty measure using the existing official thresholds and an expanded measure of household income, which adds to money income the cash value of food stamps, school lunches, and housing subsidies and subtracts pay-

Table 6. Regressions Estimating Impacts of the Business Cycle and Welfare Reform on Poverty[a]

	Dependent variable: share of all households with children in indicated group					
	By official poverty measure			By alternative poverty measure		
Independent variable	Below 50% of poverty line	Below 100% of poverty line	Below 150% of poverty line	Below 50% of poverty line	Below 100% of poverty line	Below 150% of poverty line
State unemployment rate	0.0030***	0.0064***	0.0073***	0.0014***	0.0057***	0.0075***
	(0.0005)	(0.0008)	(0.0011)	(0.0004)	(0.0008)	(0.0013)
Unemployment rate × any reform	0.0007	0.0023	0.0036**	0.0007	0.0013	0.0027
	(0.0012)	(0.0016)	(0.0018)	(0.0008)	(0.0022)	(0.0019)
Mean of dependent variable	0.059	0.150	0.249	0.029	0.123	0.263
No. of observations	759,990	759,990	759,990	682,762	682,762	682,762
Adjusted R^2	0.10	0.19	0.23	0.03	0.15	0.22

Source: Authors' regressions.

a. Regressions are performed on data from the 1981–2010 March CPS; outcomes refer to the preceding calendar year and thus cover 1980–2009 (except for alternative poverty, which covers only 1980–86, 1988–89, and 1991–2008). Observations are by household, and the sample includes all households with a child under 18. Models also include year fixed effects, state fixed effects, state-specific linear time trends, main effects for welfare reform, and demographic controls for race/ethnicity, age, sex, and education of the household head. The main reform variable is measured as the share of the past calendar year that the reform was in place, and the time limit policies are coded according to what was in place in December. Asterisks indicate statistical significance at the ***1 percent, **5 percent, and *10 percent level.

roll taxes and net federal and state taxes (including the EITC).[38] To explore outcomes across the distribution, we look at the fractions of households below 50 percent of the poverty threshold (extreme poverty) and below 100 and 150 percent of the poverty threshold, using total household cash income and our alternative measure of resources including some transfers and taxes. Here we present results for our pre-versus-post measure of welfare reform, where reform is defined as any reform. For each specification we report the coefficients on the main effect for the unemployment rate and its interaction with the welfare reform variable.

Table 6 shows that higher unemployment rates lead to statistically significant increases in official and alternative poverty as well as in the fractions of families below 50 percent and 150 percent of the poverty threshold, using either measure. The any-reform results consistently show that the countercyclicality of poverty increased after welfare reform (positive interaction added to the positive main effect). This is true for our preferred, alternative poverty measure, it holds across all levels of poverty, and the effect sizes are fairly similar across the different poverty measures (all between 1 and 2.5 percent of the mean of the dependent variable). Interestingly, the results reach statistical significance only for 150 percent of official poverty. (Results using time limits or sanction severity are less consistent.) For the low-education household head sample, the findings (not shown in the table), are similar, the magnitudes are about the same as a share of the mean, and the positive interaction coefficient is statistically significant at the 5 percent level for 150 percent of official poverty, and at the 10 percent level for 150 percent of alternative poverty.

Table 7 presents our final set of results for CPS outcomes. The top panel shows results for any household participation in AFDC/TANF, food stamps, SSI, and the broader safety net (non-Medicaid, non-AFDC/TANF safety net benefits). The bottom panel shows the household measures for "anyone uninsured last year," for demographic stress (more than one family in the household, at least one of which has a child), for the presence of any female family head in the household, and for the presence of a woman in the household who is "disconnected" by Blank and Brian Kovak's (2008)

---

38. We constructed this alternative measure ourselves, making every effort to maintain consistency over time while including as many components of CPS experimental poverty measures as possible (see, for example, Dalaker 2005). This measure is available only for a subset of survey years: 1980–87, 1989–90, and 1992–2008 (2009 calendar-year data had not been released at the time of this writing).

Table 7. Regressions Estimating Impact of the Business Cycle and Welfare Reform on Safety Net Participation and Household Well-Being[a]

	Dependent variable: probability that household received indicated assistance[b]			
Independent variable	Any public assistance	Any food stamps	Any SSI	Any non-Medicaid, non-AFDC/ TANF safety net benefit
State unemployment rate	0.004*** (0.001)	0.010*** (0.002)	−0.001 (0.0004)	0.008*** (0.002)
Unemployment rate × any reform	0.005 (0.003)	0.008** (0.003)	0.0004 (0.001)	0.008** (0.003)
Mean of dependent variable	0.122	0.199	0.044	0.387
No. of observations	378,067	378,067	378,067	361,340
Adjusted R^2	0.17	0.17	0.04	0.21
	Dependent variable: probability that household had indicated characteristic[b]			
	Anyone lacks health insurance	Household contains >1 family	Any family head is female	Any family head is a disconnected woman[c]
State unemployment rate	0.006** (0.003)	0.002** (0.001)	−0.0004 (0.001)	0.0003 (0.0005)
Unemployment rate × any reform	0.001 (0.003)	0.001 (0.001)	0.004 (0.003)	0.001 (0.001)
Mean of dependent variable	0.357	0.092	0.293	0.041
No. of observations	346,817	381,817	381,817	381,817
Adjusted R^2	0.09	0.13	0.46	0.05

Source: Authors' regressions

a. Regressions are performed on data from the 1980–2010 March CPS. Program participation and lack of insurance refer to the preceding calendar year and thus cover 1980–2009; living arrangements refer to the time of the survey. Observations are by household, and the sample includes all households with a child under 18 headed by someone with a high school education or less. Models also include year fixed effects, state fixed effects, state-specific linear time trends, main effects for welfare reform, and demographic controls for race/ethnicity, age, sex, and education of the household head. For outcomes measured over the last calendar year, the main reform variable is measured as the share of the past calendar year that reform was in place, and the time limit policies are coded according to what was in place in December of that year. For outcomes measured at the time of the survey, welfare reform is measured by whether the policy was in place as of March of the survey year. Asterisks indicate statistical significance at the ***1 percent, **5 percent, and *10 percent level.

b. Sample consists of households with children whose head has less than 12 years of education.

c. Defined similarly to Blank and Kovak (2008) as a single female family head aged 18–58 living with a child, with no income from public assistance or earnings.

definition.[39] To focus on a group with higher likelihood of being affected by welfare, all of the outcomes in this table are estimated on the sample of households with children where the head has 12 years of education or less.

To begin, we use our CPS sample to examine participation in cash welfare and food stamps. We present these results for two reasons. First, given concerns about underreporting in the CPS, it is informative to compare these results with those from the administrative data. If they are similar, it lessens our concern about the importance of underreporting in a pooled cross-sectional analysis with demographic controls and state and year fixed effects.[40] The qualitative conclusions using the CPS sample match those from the administrative results well: cash welfare and food stamps are both countercyclical (with a positive main effect on unemployment), and the magnitudes are in the same ballpark as those for the administrative data. A 1-percentage-point increase in unemployment leads to about a 0.4-percentage-point increase in the probability that someone in the household had cash assistance income last year (this is about a 3.3 percent increase). The same increase in the unemployment rate leads to a 1.0-percentage-point increase in the probability that someone in the household got food stamps last year (about a 5 percent increase). The coefficients on the interaction of reform and the unemployment rate are also positive in both regressions, and the pattern of significance is similar to that in the administrative data (the p-value for the interaction for welfare is 0.105, and that for food stamps is 0.023).[41] The effect of a 1-percentage-point increase in the unemployment rate on food stamp receipt is about a

---

39. More precisely, our definition approximates Blank and Kovak's definition 1, in which a disconnected woman is a single female family head aged 18–58 living with a child, with no income from public assistance or earnings. We also explored two other definitions. The first defines a disconnected woman as a single female family head aged 18–58 living with a child and earning less than $2,000 a month while receiving income from public assistance of less than $1,000 a month (both figures in 2009 dollars); the second adds the restriction that real monthly income from SSI is less than $1,000. Results were similar across measures.

40. For another approach to dealing with underreporting in a recent analysis of trends in poverty, see Scholz, Moffitt, and Cowan (2009).

41. They should not be identical for the following reasons. First, the administrative data are monthly and define the main reform variable as a dummy for implementation by a particular month, whereas the CPS data are annual and the reform variable is the share of the calendar year that reform was in place. Second, the sample in the administrative regressions is everyone (with the dependent variable having the total caseload in the numerator and total population in the denominator), whereas the CPS sample is households with children and a low-educated head (with the dependent variable being the presence or absence of someone in the household receiving the benefit). Third, the CPS welfare variable includes other forms of public assistance such as general assistance.

4 percent increase after reform. Our conclusion from these specifications is unchanged from that from the administrative caseloads: both programs are cyclically responsive, but only the food stamp program has become significantly more so after reform.

In separate analyses we find that SSI bears little relationship to the business cycle and that this does not change with welfare reform. The final column in the top panel of table 7 reports results for our comprehensive measure of safety net benefits that includes many public assistance programs (but excludes AFDC/TANF, general assistance, and Medicaid). The results here are very clear: overall safety net participation is strongly countercyclical (the main effect is positive and significant, and a 1-percentage-point increase in unemployment leads to about a 2.1 percent increase in receipt), and the cyclicality significantly increases after welfare reform (the interaction is positive and significant, and again a 1-percentage-point increase in unemployment after reform leads to an additional 2.1 percent increase in receipt). The picture that emerges is that although the effect of cash welfare protection (follow-ing increases in unemployment) has fallen or stayed the same after reform, protection through other safety net programs is increasing.

The bottom panel of table 7 presents other household outcomes. The propensity to be uninsured and the rate of doubling up increase with unemployment, yet the propensity for the household to contain a female head or a disconnected woman does not vary significantly over the cycle. Interestingly, all of the interactions are positive, implying that welfare reform is associated with an increase in the cyclicality of these adverse outcomes. However, these results are only suggestive, as none reaches statistical significance. We also considered a host of other outcomes, none of which showed significant changes in their cyclicality after reform, including the presence of disability income in the household, the presence of any related subfamily with a child, the presence of more than one family with a child, health, and the other measures of disconnected women (results available from the authors on request).

III.C. Other Outcomes

The CPS income and poverty measures that we described above are important for capturing the economic well-being of families affected by welfare reform, whereas some of the other outcomes matter for capturing other dimensions such as health insurance coverage or doubling up. A limitation of the income and poverty results is that it is well known that welfare and other government transfers are underreported in the CPS and other household surveys (Meyer, Mok, and Sullivan 2009). This is what motivated our use of both administrative data and an alternative measure of poverty in the micro data. Furthermore, households may save or borrow and may receive private transfers that are not well measured in household survey data.

One common alternative measure of well-being considered in the development literature is consumption, which may be easier to measure than income and poverty in some contexts. Meyer and Sullivan (2008) have used expenditure and time use as alternative measures of well-being and have shown that among single woman-headed families, those low in the income distribution and low in the expenditure distribution experienced different changes from the 1990s to the 2000s. The public use version of the Consumer Expenditure Survey does not contain state identifiers and is available only through the first quarter of 2009, and so we leave these data to be analyzed in future work.

We estimated models for food expenditure using data from the Panel Study of Income Dynamics (available only through 2005). We estimated equation 1 on a sample of female heads of household aged 25–61 living with children, for the period 1980–2005. These results, not shown here, show that increases in the unemployment rate lead to reductions in food consumption, with no evidence that the cyclicality changed with reform (although these estimates had large standard errors relative to the estimated coefficients). We also estimated models for food insecurity, data for which come from the December CPS supplements.[42] The drawback of the food insecurity measures is that because they are consistently available only from 2001 on (our sample goes through 2008), nearly all the variation with which reform's effects on cyclicality are identified is cross-sectional, and thus we do not focus on them.

IV. Discussion

Prior work indicates that participation in cash welfare has decreased with the transition from AFDC to TANF (Council of Economic Advisers 1997, Ziliak and others 2000, and more recently Danielson and Klerman 2008). Why this is so is not fully understood, but possibilities include an interest in "banking" benefits for the future (see, for example, Grogger and Michalopoulos 2003), the burden of complying with work requirements, individuals being removed from the rolls because they reached the time limits, changes in what the state spends TANF money on, and so on. This

---

42. Craig Gundersen and Feeding America generously provided us with tabulations on state-year rates of food insecurity.

might lead one to anticipate that the cyclical response of cash welfare would be less strong after welfare reform.

Our view of the results is that cash welfare has indeed become less cyclical after reform, or at least has not become more cyclical, although we caution that our estimated coefficients do not uniformly support this view and that few reach statistical significance. By contrast, our findings for food stamps and a broader measure of "any safety net participation except for AFDC/TANF and Medicaid" suggest an increased sensitivity to the business cycle after reform; for both of these, participation is countercyclical (rising when unemployment rates rise) and becomes more so after reform.

The descriptive evidence about the role that eligibility and take-up play in informing these findings is informative. Our own descriptive work and that of others (for example, Zedlewski 2008) suggest that use of cash assistance did not increase in either the mild recession of 2001 or the most recent recession (with the caveat that unemployment may not have peaked yet). The available evidence suggests that the decline in caseloads after welfare reform (and the lack of increase in the post–welfare reform recessions) is explained almost completely by declines in take-up rather than declines in eligibility (for example, because recipients reached their time limits). The U.S. Department of Health and Human Services (2008) estimates that eligibility for cash welfare has fluctuated within a relatively narrow range, from 5.7 million families in 1995 to 5.1 million in 1999, 4.6 million in 2001, 4.8 million in 2003, and 5.3 million in 2005 (the most recent year available; all years in this paragraph are fiscal years).[43] By contrast, take-up rates have fallen steeply, from 84 percent in 1995 to 48 percent in 2001, 46 percent in 2003, and 40 percent in 2005. At the same time, the number of households eligible for food stamps went up from 15 million in 1995 to 15.2 million in 2001, 17.9 million in 2003, and 18.1 million in 2005, while take-up declined from 69 percent in 1995 to a low of 48 percent in 2001 before rising to 59 percent in 2005. This suggests that the cyclical response in caseloads after welfare reform is driven primarily by changes in take-up.

It would be of interest to know about the effects of the Great Recession on the outcomes of groups who are no longer participating in welfare as well as those that are. Unfortunately, not only is it hard to statistically

---

43. These estimates are based on the Urban Institute's TRIM3 microsimulation model, which uses March CPS data (adjusted for nonresponse) and simulates eligibility for AFDC/TANF. The report also presents results from a Mathematica microsimulation model of food stamp eligibility (Cunnyngham, Castner, and Schirm 2010).

identify groups who would have been at high risk of participating but are no longer doing so, but many of the outcomes of interest are not well measured or are measured only in small samples. Thus, we again turn to descriptive evidence.

To the extent that women were able to leave welfare through employment, have they been able to stay employed through recessions? Robert Lerman (2005) finds that single mothers lost some ground during the 2001 recession but still were more likely to be employed or in the labor force than before welfare reform. Are workers who might end up unemployed able to access other parts of the safety net such as unemployment compensation? Christopher O'Leary (2010) presents findings from administrative data about experiences of welfare recipients from four states who left welfare for work: 79 percent experienced a new spell of unemployment within 3 years, yet only 24 percent of these applied for unemployment insurance (far below application rates in the general population), and only 50 percent of the applicants eventually received unemployment insurance benefits (also low relative to the general population). In our pooled March CPS data, about 11 percent of households with children who had some public assistance income from 1979 to 2009 also had income from workers' compensation, unemployment compensation, or veterans' payments. This fraction ranged from 7.3 percent of households in 2007 to 16 percent in 2009.

What about the most disadvantaged? Concern has been growing about the part of the pre-reform welfare caseload that was least ready to work. Several recent studies have addressed the experience of so-called disconnected women, single female heads of families with children who neither are participating in cash welfare (TANF and sometimes SSI as well) nor have substantial earnings. Some share of this group is undoubtedly made up of welfare leavers, and some of the leaver studies can inform us about this group. Blank and Kovak (2008) find that among single female-headed families with children with incomes under 200 percent of the poverty line, 20 percent are disconnected. How these families are surviving is a puzzle. More data and research are needed in order to know how to address this issue.

V. Conclusion

The passage of the 1996 welfare reform act led to sweeping changes to the central cash safety net program for families with children, replacing the AFDC program with TANF. The key provisions of that law included work requirements, financial sanctions for noncompliance, and a lifetime time limit for receipt of cash welfare. The imposition of lifetime time limits is particularly noteworthy because it overturned more than 60 years of entitlement to cash welfare for low-income families with children. Despite dire predictions of rising poverty and deprivation, previous research has shown that with reform, caseloads declined and employment increased, with no detectible increase in poverty or reduction in child well-being.

Several important factors likely contribute to explaining "why the experts were wrong." It turns out that as welfare reform hit, earnings subsidies for low-income families with children were rising through expansions in the EITC. Further, the labor market of the first 5 years after welfare reform offered the most favorable conditions for low-skilled workers in many decades. Finally, it seems that the new and stringently applied pro-work policies led to larger behavioral responses than had been expected based on models of the pre–welfare reform period.

This paper has reevaluated welfare reform in light of the severe recession that began in December 2007. In particular, we have examined how reform has altered the cyclicality of the response of program caseloads and family well-being. We find that TANF provides less protection, or at least no more protection, in an economic downturn than the AFDC program that preceded it, but that the noncash welfare safety net (and especially food stamps) is providing significantly more protection. In our analyses using both the official measure and our own alternative measure of poverty, the point estimates imply that the increase in poverty in an economic downturn is greater after welfare reform than it would have been before reform. These results are only suggestive, given that few are statistically significant, but the findings are statistically significant and robust for the propensity to live in a household with income under 150 percent of the official poverty line. We find no significant effect of reform on the cyclical responsiveness of food consumption, food insecurity, or health, or on a number of other measures including doubling up, lack of health insurance, and presence of a single female family head.

Overall, we find no evidence that the prevalence of negative family or household well-being in an economic downturn has improved after welfare reform, and some weak evidence that it has worsened. Further, it appears that food stamp benefits are playing an important role in mitigating adverse impacts on income in post–welfare reform recessions. This suggests a policy recommendation for continued current funding of the food stamp program, should these results hold up with more data and for a broader range of outcomes.

A limitation to our work derives from the fact that we (and others) find a portion of children to be living in families that are "disconnected," with limited income and limited use of public support. Ideally, we would zero in on this particularly fragile group. However, doing this would require better data on family consumption, child and family well-being, and other child outcomes as well as on family histories of welfare and other public assistance and employment and income for large samples of families with children by state and year, and these data are not available.

APPENDIX
Data and Sources

Contractions and Expansions: For table 1 we identified changes over contractions as the range of years from an unemployment low (in terms of the annual unemployment rate) to an unemployment high, and expansions as the range from an unemployment high to an unemployment low. Necessarily, then, the periods of expansion and contraction overlap by one year. Each contraction corresponds to a recession (in one case to two recessions) as identified by the Business Cycle Dating Committee of the National Bureau of Economic Research. We pooled the two early-1980s recessions, and the data end in 2009. The contraction periods are 1979–82 (corresponding to the NBER recessions of January to July 1980 and July 1981 to November 1982), 1989–92 (NBER recession of July 1990 to March 1991), 2000–03 (NBER recession of March to November 2001), and 2007–09 (NBER recession of December 2007 to June 2009). The expansion periods are thus 1982–89, 1992–2000, and 2003–07. The end date of 2009 for the most recent contraction may end up not being the peak annual unemployment period, but 2009 is the last year for which the bulk of our data are available. In figures 2, 5, 7, and 8 we have shaded periods of contraction; for these we drop the first one-year period (the unemployment rate low) and thus those periods are 1980–82, 1990–92, 2001–03, and 2008–09.

AFDC/TANF Administrative Data on Caseloads and Expenditure: AFDC caseloads were downloaded from the web site of the Office of Family Assistance, U.S. Department of Health and Human Services (DHHS) at www.acf.hhs.gov/programs/ofa/data-reports/caseload/caseload_archive. html, and TANF caseloads (which, beginning in 2000, include Separate State Program/Maintenance of Effort cases) from www.acf.hhs.gov/programs/ofa/data-reports/index.htm. Both measure average monthly caseloads during the year. Unpublished data on AFDC cash expenditure (and combined AFDC/TANF expenditure) for 1980–2000 were provided by Don Oellerich in the Office of the Assistant Secretary for Planning Evaluation at DHHS. TANF expenditure data are from the DHHS website at www.acf.hhs.gov/programs/ofs/data/index.html. TANF cash expenditure is defined as the figure in the second data column (line 5a, "Basic Assistance") of table F-3, "Combined Spending of Federal and States Funds with ARRA Funds Expended . . . in FY 2009." TANF total expenditure includes all expenditure (maintenance of effort from the state and federal sources, including separate state programs, combined federal and state expenditures on assistance, nonassistance, and both together, as reported in table F, "Combined Spending of Federal and State Funds Expended in FY [year]." Federal stimulus expenditure under the American Recovery and Reinvestment Act of 2009 (ARRA) is included in the 2009 data. AFDC cash assistance numbers for 1979 came from the Green Book of the U.S. House Committee on Ways and Means (waysandmeans.house.gov/singlepages.aspx?NewsID=10490). The average monthly TANF benefit (used in table 3) is the average family benefit for 2006, expressed in 2009 dollars, from DHHS (2008), appendix A, table TANF-6. All AFDC and TANF data are for the month or the fiscal year (which ends on September 30).

Food Stamp Administrative Data on Caseloads and Expenditure: Caseloads and expenditure by month for calendar years 1980–2009 and for January through March 2010 come from unpublished U.S. Department of Agriculture (USDA) data generously provided by Katie Fitzpatrick and John Kirlin of the Economic Research Service, USDA. Table 1 presents average monthly caseload and total annual payments.

Unemployment Insurance Administrative Data on Caseloads and Expenditure: Data for calendar years 1980 (or in some cases a later starting date) through 2009 are unpublished data provided by the Office of the Chief Economist at the U.S. Department of Labor. The average benefit is the weekly average benefit amount for 2009Q4 from the website of the Employment and Training Administration at the U.S. Department of Labor, at workforcesecurity.doleta.gov/unemploy/content/data_stats/datasum09/DataSum_2009_4.pdf.

Unemployment for the United States and by State: The number of unemployed and the unemployment rate for the nation as a whole and for each state, annually and by month, come from the Bureau of Labor Statistics' Current Population Survey, accessed at www.bls.gov/cps/ and www.bls.gov/lau/. The monthly numbers are seasonally adjusted.

Population for the United States and by State: U.S. population data are from the annual *Economic Report of the President,* accessed at www.gpoaccess.gov/eop/2010/B34.xls. State population data are from the National Cancer Institute's SEER (Surveillance Epidemiology and End Results, at seer.cancer.gov/popdata/download.html) for 1980–2007, and from the U.S. Census Bureau for 2008 on.

Deflator: The CPI-U is from the *Economic Report of the President,* accessed at www.gpoaccess.gov/eop/tables10.html.

Census Poverty Rates: Official poverty, all persons, and official poverty, children, come from the U.S. Census Bureau, "Income, Poverty, and Health Insurance Coverage in the United States: 2009," report P60-238, tables B-1 and B-2. NAS alternative poverty numbers come from the U.S. Census Bureau web site, at www.census.gov/hhes/www/povmeas/web_tab4_nas_measures_historical.xls, "Official and National Academy of Sciences (NAS) Based Poverty Rates: 1999 to 2008." We report the series MSI-NGA-CE, in which imputed out-of-pocket medical expenses are subtracted from income (MSI), no geographic adjustments are made (NGA), and the thresholds are based on consumption data from the Consumer Expenditure Survey (CE).

EITC: Data on the annual number of recipients and the total tax cost (including refundable and nonrefundable portions) of the EITC for 1980–2008 are from the Tax Policy Center's "Tax Facts: Historical EITC Recipients" for fiscal 1976–2010, downloaded from www.taxpolicycenter.org/taxfacts/displayafact.cfm?Docid=37.

SSI: Data on number of recipients (those who received any payment during the year), total benefit payments, and average monthly benefit are from Social Security Administration (2010) and refer to federal plus state supplementation program.

Other sources for tables 1 and 3 include the following:

—*Consumption:* statistics for expenditure by "Quintiles of income before taxes," published by the Bureau of Labor Statistics and available at www.bls.gov/cex/csxstnd.htm.

—*Food insecurity:* based on Food Security Supplements to the December Current Population Survey for 2001–2008, compiled by Craig Gundersen and Feeding America and graciously shared with us by Gundersen.

—*Health insurance and delayed/didn't get care because of cost:* data published by the Centers for Disease Control in "Health Insurance Coverage Trends, 1959–2007" (www.cdc.gov/nchs/data/nhsr/nhsr017.pdf) as well as annual reports based on the National Health Interview Survey

("Summary Health Statistics for the U.S. Population: National Health Interview Survey," various years).

—*Homeless:* from the Office of Community Planning and Development, U.S. Department of Housing and Urban Development, "Annual Homeless Assessment Report to Congress," for 2007 and 2009.

ACKNOWLEDGMENTS We thank the editors, Sandy Jencks, Bruce Meyer, Rebecca Blank, Karl Scholz, Dan Wilson, Bart Hobijn, Mary Daly, Rob Valletta, and Caroline Danielson; seminar participants at the Federal Reserve Bank of San Francisco; and Brookings Panel conference participants for helpful suggestions. We thank Jessamyn Schaller, Danielle Sandler, Ankur Patel, Ted Wiles, and Joyce Kwok for excellent research assistance. We also thank Robert Moffitt, Jim Ziliak, Donna Pavetti, Patty Anderson, Rob Valletta, Don Oellerich, John Kirlin, Caroline Danielson, Paige Shevlin, David Langon, and Katie Fitzpatrick, who generously shared data and expertise on administrative and labor market data. The views in this paper are solely the responsibility of the authors and should not be interpreted as reflecting the views of the Federal Reserve Bank of San Francisco or the Board of Governors of the Federal Reserve System.

The authors report no relevant potential conflicts of interest.

References

Bane, Mary Jo, and David T. Ellwood. 1994. *Welfare Realities: From Rhetoric to Reform.* Harvard University Press.

Bitler, Marianne P., Janet Currie, and John Karl Scholz. 2003. "WIC Eligibility and Participation." *Journal of Human Resources* 38: 1139–79.

Bitler, Marianne P., Jonah B. Gelbach, and Hilary W. Hoynes. 2006. "Welfare Reform and Children's Living Arrangements." *Journal of Human Resources* 41, no. 1: 1–27.

Blank, Rebecca M. 2001. "What Causes Public Assistance Caseloads to Grow?" *Journal of Human Resources* 36, no. 1 (Winter): 85–118.

———. 2002. "Evaluating Welfare Reform in the United States." *Journal of Economic Literature* 40, no. 4 (December): 1105–66.

Blank, Rebecca M., and Ron Haskins, eds. 2001. *The New World of Welfare.* Brookings.

Blank, Rebecca M., and Brian K. Kovak. 2008. "Helping Disconnected Single Mothers." Policy Brief no. 10. National Poverty Center, University of Michigan.

Burtless, Gary T. 1997. "Welfare Recipients' Job Skills and Employment Prospects." *The Future of Children* 7, no. 1 (Spring): 39–51.

Citro, Constance F., and Robert T. Michael, eds. 1995. *Measuring Poverty: A New Approach.* Washington: National Academy Press.

Council of Economic Advisers. 1997. "Technical Report: Explaining the Decline in Welfare Receipt, 1993–1996." Washington (May 9).

Crouse, Gil. 1999. "State Implementation of Major Changes to Welfare Policies, 1992–1998." Washington: U.S. Department of Health and Human Services. aspe.hhs.gov/hsp/Waiver-Policies99/policy_CEA.htm.

Cunnyngham, Karen E., Laura A. Castner, and Allen L. Shirm. 2010. "Empirical Bayes Shrinkage Estimates of State Supplemental Nutrition Assistance Program Participation Rates in 2005–2007 for All Eligible People and the Working Poor." Princeton, N.J.: Mathematica Policy Research.

Dalaker, Joe. 2005. "Alternative Poverty Estimates in the United States: 2003." Current Population Report P60-227. Washington: U.S. Bureau of the Census.

Danielson, Caroline, and Jacob Alex Klerman. 2004. "Did Welfare Reform Cause the Caseload Decline?" Working Paper WR-167. Santa Monica, Calif.: RAND Corporation.

———. 2008. "Did Welfare Reform Cause the Caseload Decline?" *Social Service Review* 82, no. 4: 703–30.

Eissa, Nada, and Hilary W. Hoynes. 2006. "Behavioral Responses to Taxes: Lessons from the EITC and Labor Supply." *Tax Policy and the Economy* 20: 73–110.

Ellwood, David T. 1986. "Targeting 'Would-Be' Long-Term Recipients of AFDC." Princeton, N.J.: Mathematica Policy Research (January).

Fraker, Thomas M., Alberto P. Martini, James C. Ohls, Michael Ponza, and Elizabeth A. Quinn. 1992. *The Evaluation of the Alabama Food Stamp Cash-*

Out Demonstration, Vol. 1: *Recipient Impacts.* Princeton, N.J.: Mathematica Policy Research.

Garner, Thesia I., and Kathleen S. Short. 2008. "Creating a Consistent Poverty Measure over Time Using NAS Procedures: 1996–2005." Working Paper no. 417. Washington: U.S. Bureau of Labor Statistics and U.S. Census Bureau.

Grogger, Jeffrey. 2003. "The Effects of Time Limits, the EITC, and Other Policy Changes on Welfare Use, Work, and Income among Female-Headed Families." *Review of Economic and Statistics* 85, no. 2: 394–408.

Grogger, Jeffrey, and Lynn A. Karoly. 2005. *Welfare Reform: Effects of a Decade of Change.* Harvard University Press.

Grogger, Jeffrey, and Charles Michalopoulos. 2003. "Welfare Dynamics under Time Limits." *Journal of Political Economy* 111, no. 3: 530–554.

Haider, Steven J. 2006. "A Comparison of Surveys for Food Insecurity and Hunger Measurement." Discussion paper prepared for the National Academy of Sciences Panel on Food Insecurity and Hunger Measurement. Michigan State University.

Hines, James R. Jr., Hilary Hoynes, and Alan B. Krueger. 2001. "Another Look at Whether a Rising Tide Lifts All Boats." In *The Roaring Nineties: Can Full Employment Be Sustained?* edited by Alan Krueger and Robert Solow. New York: Russell Sage Foundation.

Hoynes, Hilary W. 2000. "The Employment, Earnings, and Income of Less Skilled Workers over the Business Cycle." In *Finding Jobs: Work and Welfare Reform,* edited by Rebecca M. Blank and David Card. New York: Russell Sage Foundation.

Hoynes, Hilary W., and Diane Whitmore Schanzenbach. 2009. "Consumption Responses to In-Kind Transfers: Evidence from the Introduction of the Food Stamp Program." *American Economic Journal: Applied Economics* 1, no. 4 (October): 109–39.

Klerman, Jacob Alex, and Caroline Danielson. 2009. "Determinants of the Food Stamp Program Caseload." Contractor and Cooperator Report no. 50. Washington: Economic Research Service, U.S. Department of Agriculture.

Lerman, Robert. 2005. "How Did the 2001 Recession Affect Single Mothers?" Single Parents' Earnings Monitor no. 3. Washington: Urban Institute.

Meyer, Bruce D. 2010. "The Effects of the Earned Income Tax Credit and Recent Reforms." *Tax Policy and the Economy* 24: 153–80.

Meyer, Bruce D., and Dan T. Rosenbaum. 2001. "Welfare, the Earned Income Tax Credit, and the Labor Supply of Single Mothers." *Quarterly Journal of Economics* 116, no. 3 (August): 1063–1114.

Meyer, Bruce D., and James X. Sullivan. 2008. "Changes in the Consumption, Income, and Well-Being of Single Mother Headed Families." *American Economic Review* 98, no. 5 (December): 2221–41.

Meyer, Bruce D., Wallace K. C. Mok, and James X. Sullivan. 2009. "The Under-Reporting of Transfers in Household Surveys: Its Nature and Consequences." Working Paper no. 15181. Cambridge, Mass.: National Bureau of Economic Research.

Moffitt, Robert. 1983. "An Economic Model of Welfare Stigma." *American Economic Review* 73, no. 5 (December): 1023–25.

———. 1992. "Incentive Effects of the U.S. Welfare System: A Review." *Journal of Economic Literature* 30, no. 1 (March): 1–61.

Ohls, Jim C., Thomas M. Fraker, Alberto P. Martini, and Michael Ponza. 1992. "The Effects of Cash-Out on Food Use by Food Stamp Program Participants in San Diego." Washington: Office of Analysis and Evaluation, Food and Nutrition Service, U.S. Department of Agriculture.

O'Leary, Christopher J. 2010. "Unemployment after Welfare Reform." *Employment Research Newsletter* 17, no. 2. Kalamazoo, Mich.: W.E. Upjohn Institute for Employment Research.

Pavetti, LaDonna, and Dorothy Rosenbaum. 2010. "Creating a Safety Net That Works When the Economy Doesn't: The Role of the Food Stamp and TANF Programs." Washington: Center on Budget and Policy Priorities.

Scholz, John Karl, Robert Moffitt, and Benjamin Cowan. 2009. "Trends in Income Support." In *Changing Poverty, Changing Policies*, edited by Maria Cancian and Sheldon Danziger. New York: Russell Sage Foundation.

Sherman, Arloc. 2009. "Safety Net Effective at Fighting Poverty but Has Weakened for the Very Poorest." Washington: Center for Budget and Policy Priorities (July 6).

Social Security Administration. 2010. *SSI Annual Statistical Report, 2009*. Washington (September).

U.S. Department of Agriculture. 2010. *Food Security in the United States: Measuring Household Food Security*. Washington: Economic Research Service, U.S. Department of Agriculture. www.ers.usda.gov/Briefing/FoodSecurity/measurement.htm, accessed August 14, 2010.

U.S. Department of Health and Human Services. 2008a. *Temporary Assistance for Needy Families Program (TANF): Eighth Annual Report to Congress*. Washington: Administration for Children and Families, Office of Family Assistance, U.S. Department of Health and Human Services. www.acf.hhs.gov/programs/ofa/data-reports/annualreport8/TANF_8th_Report_111908.pdf.

———. 2008b. *Indicators of Welfare Dependence: Annual Report to Congress 2008*. Washington.

U.S. Department of Labor. 2010. *Unemployment Insurance Chartbook*, Section A-16. www.doleta.gov/unemploy/chartbook.cfm, accessed September 7, 2010.

U.S. General Accounting Office. 1985. "An Evaluation of the 1981 AFDC Changes: A Final Report." GAO/PEMD-85-4. Washington (July 2).

U.S. House of Representatives. 1996. *Background Material and Data on Programs within the Jurisdiction of the House Committee on Ways and Means*. Washington: Committee on Ways and Means, U.S. House of Representatives.

Weinberg, Daniel H. 2004. "Income Data Quality Issues in the Annual Social and Economic Supplement to the Current Population Survey." Washington: U.S. Census Bureau.

Wheaton, Laura. 2007. "Underreporting of Means-Tested Transfer Programs in the CPS and SIPP." *Proceedings of the American Statistical Association,* Social Statistics Section, pp. 3622–29.

Zedlewski, Sheila. 2008. "The Role of Welfare During a Recession." Urban Institute Recession and Recovery Report no. 3. Washington: Urban Institute.

Ziliak, James P., David N. Figlio, Elizabeth E. Davis, and Laura S. Connolly. 2000. "Accounting for the Decline in AFDC Caseloads: Welfare Reform or the Economy?" *Journal of Human Resources* 35, no. 3: 570–86.

Comments and Discussion

COMMENT BY
CHRISTOPHER JENCKS   Marianne Bitler and Hilary Hoynes have provided the most comprehensive treatment to date of how low-income families with children fared during the first 3 years since the recent recession began. Their primary goal, however, is not to chronicle what happened to these families but to investigate whether they would have fared better if the pre-1996 welfare system had still been in place. Simply tracking what has happened to these families since 2007 is a challenging task, partly because there are dozens of potentially relevant indicators and no agreement about their relative importance, and partly because the U.S. statistical system takes so long to produce many of these indicators. Figuring out what would have happened in the absence of welfare reform is even more challenging, because the details of this counterfactual are so uncertain. I take up these two issues in turn.

WHAT HAPPENED BETWEEN 2007 AND 2010? According to the National Bureau of Economic Research, the economy began to contract in December 2007 and began to grow again in July 2009. But for families that derive most of their income from the labor market, what matters is not whether the economy is contracting or expanding, but whether demand for workers is growing fast enough to provide jobs for a growing population of adults who want work. Bitler and Hoynes therefore use the unemployment rate to estimate the impact of the business cycle on family income and other measures of well-being.

If we judge by official statistics on employment and population growth, the number of would-be workers has grown faster than the number of jobs since the summer of 2007, and the gap continued to widen even after the official unemployment rate peaked in October 2009. The official unemployment rate began to decline in the fall of 2009 because more unemployed workers stopped searching for jobs and were therefore dropped from the official unemployment count. If the job market tightens, most of these "discouraged" workers will start looking again. That means they must be taken into account both when we assess how many families have been affected by the downturn and when we estimate how many additional jobs would be needed to get the unemployment rate down to the level that prevailed in the middle of 2007.

One imperfect way to address this problem is to assume that the overall fraction of adults who want a job is likely to be about the same when unemployment returns to its prerecession level as it was before the recession began. If that is the case, the size of the labor force as a share of the adult population should yield a better picture of how far the nation is from full employment at any given point in a downturn than the official unemployment rate does. In 2007 civilian employment averaged 146.0 million and unemployment averaged 7.1 million, so the total civilian labor force averaged 153.1 million people, or 66.0 percent of all U.S. residents over the age of 16. In November 2010, just before this comment was written, seasonally adjusted employment was 138.9 million, unemployment was 15.1 million, and the civilian labor force was 64.5 percent of the population over 16. If 66.0 percent of those over the age of 16 still wanted jobs of the kind that were available in 2007, and only 138.9 million people had jobs, roughly 18.7 million people who would have taken a job in 2007 were unemployed in November 2010. If we define the "unemployed" in this way, the "true" unemployment rate in November 2010 was 11.8 percent. Making the same calculation for October 2009, when the official unemployment rate peaked, the "true" unemployment rate was then 11.5 percent. At some point job growth will presumably begin to exceed growth in the number of would-be workers, but no one knows when that will be.

Bitler and Hoynes focus primarily on how rising unemployment affected low-income families with children. The official child poverty rate rose 2.7 percentage points between 2007 and 2009 (see their table 1 and U.S. Bureau of the Census 2010, table B-2). However, the official poverty rate suffers from several problems that make it an unreliable guide to trends in material hardship (Jencks, Mayer, and Swingle 2004). One well-known problem is that poverty rates are calculated using family rather than household income, and the Census Bureau defines a family as including only household members related by blood, marriage, or adoption. Thus, if an unmarried mother has a live-in boyfriend, the Census Bureau does not count his income when it determines whether the mother and her children are poor. This rule makes mothers cohabiting with working boyfriends look poorer than they are. In bad times, however, this rule hides the increase in child poverty that occurs when live-in boyfriends lose their jobs.

Another well-known problem is that the official poverty rate ignores both taxes (notably the earned income tax credit, or EITC) and noncash government benefits such as Medicaid, food stamps, and housing subsidies, all of which play a critical role in the well-being of low-income families. This approach to measuring income inflates the child poverty rate even more than ignoring live-in boyfriends, but it biases the estimated impact of unemployment on poverty only when taxes or noncash benefits change at the same time as unemployment. Bitler and Hoynes show that spending on per capita on Temporary Assistance for Needy Families (TANF) did not substantially increase between 2007 and 2009 but that spending per capita on food stamps rose by two-thirds (see their table 1). Ignoring this increase presumably tends to offset the bias created by ignoring any decline in income from live-in boyfriends who become unemployed. Because of these and other problems, Bitler and Hoynes calculate an adjusted poverty rate, but it is available only through 2008. They also try to check their conclusions against more direct measures of material hardship. I focus here on hardship in three domains: food, housing, and health care.

FOOD. Every December the Census Bureau's Current Population Survey includes a "food security" supplement designed by the U.S. Department of Agriculture. This supplement asks families about their food expenditure, their use of food pantries, and their ability to buy as much food as they think they need. The median family with children reported weekly spending per person of $33 in both 2007 and 2009 (Nord, Andrews, and Carlson 2008, p. 24; Nord and others 2010, p. 25).[1] Since food prices rose about 3 percent over those 2 years, $33 bought about 3 percent less (or at least less desirable) food in 2009 than in 2007. Median expenditure per person was only about $2 per week lower among families headed by a single mother and only $1 per week lower among families with incomes below the poverty line, presumably because the reported median is quite close to an eligible family's food stamp budget.

---

1. This finding should be treated cautiously. Measured in current dollars, the median for all families with children was $33.33 per person in both years. This presumably reflects the fact that the median family had three members and reported spending $100 a week in both years. But because many families round their estimates of grocery spending to easily remembered numbers, far more families report spending $100 a week than, say, $97 or $103. As a result, the median may remain the same for a long time even if the full distribution is shifting to the left or right.

Median spending does not tell us how many families with children had trouble getting enough to eat. In rich countries like the United States, few families experience protracted periods of hunger or malnutrition, but many families experience occasional crises when they cannot afford to buy enough food, and some experience such crises fairly often. According to the food security survey, 7.8 percent of children lived in families that reported having turned to food pantries for help at some point during 2009, compared with only 5.3 percent during 2007. The fraction of all families reporting that there had been times when the food they bought "didn't last" and they "didn't have money to get more" rose from 12 percent to 16 percent between 2007 and 2009. Over the same period, the fraction of families reporting that an adult in the family was hungry and "didn't eat because there wasn't enough money for food" rose from 3.3 percent to 4.6 percent, and the fraction reporting that they had not eaten for a whole day rose from 1.3 percent to 1.7 percent (Nord and others 2010, p. 45).

HEALTH. People's health can suffer for many reasons during an economic downturn. In the United States many people lose their health insurance soon after they lose their job. Some even lose their health insurance without losing their job, because their employer stops offering coverage. The fraction of Americans with employment-based insurance fell from 59.3 percent in 2007 to 55.8 percent in 2009 (U.S. Census Bureau 2010, table C-3). Public programs picked up some of those who lost their private coverage, but the fraction without any heath insurance rose from 15.3 percent to 16.7 percent. Among children, however, Medicaid expansion cut the proportion who were uninsured from 11.0 percent in 2007 to 10.0 percent in 2009.

A large body of research has shown that even in countries with universal health insurance, workers' health tends to deteriorate if they lose their job. This is also true in the United States. However, Christopher Ruhm (2003) has shown that when one looks at the entire population rather than just the unemployed, mortality rates actually fall faster when the economy is contracting than when it is growing. This is true not only in the United States but in other high-income countries as well (Gerdtham and Ruhm 2005). At least in the United States, the pattern seems to be linked to the fact that heavy drinking, smoking, auto accidents, air pollution, and overtime work also decline during downturns (Ruhm 2005).

It is too soon to be sure whether this benign effect of economic austerity recurred between 2007 and 2009. Thus far the evidence is mixed. On the one hand, provisional data from the National Center for Health Statistics (NCHS, various years) indicate that infant mortality declined only modestly, from 6.7 to 6.6 deaths per 1,000 live births, between 2003 and 2007, a time when unemployment was falling, but that it declined three times as fast, from 6.6 to 6.3 per 1,000, between 2007 and 2009. That is consistent with Ruhm's earlier findings. Age-adjusted estimates for the rest of the population are not yet available.[2]

HOUSING. When unemployment rises, some families cannot pay their mortgage or their rent and instead double up with relatives or friends. One would expect doubling up to have been especially common in 2007–09, since the collapse of the housing bubble led to more foreclosures and evictions during these years than at any time since the 1930s. The U.S. Census Bureau (2010) reported an 11.6-percentage-point rise between March 2008 and March 2010 in the number of households that included more than one family. Apparently, however, very few of these families included children, since Bitler and Hoynes report in their table 1 that the fraction of children living in a household that included more than one family rose only 0.2 percentage points. It is hard to know what this measure means, since they report a smaller annual increase between 2007 and 2009 than between 2003 and 2007, when unemployment was falling. Average household size, which rose 1.1 percent between March 2007 and March 2010 (from 2.558 persons to 2.585 persons) may be a better measure of doubling up.[3] Indeed, the increase in household size may underestimate the amount of doubling up, because the number of births was 4.1 percent lower in 2009 than in 2007. In due course, moreover, many families tire of sharing their home with another family, especially if it includes children. Not surprisingly, the U.S. Department of Housing and Urban Development (2010) estimates that the number of families with children in shelters for the homeless also rose, from 131,000 in January 2007 to 170,000 in 2009.

Taking all this evidence together, it seems clear that both the fraction of families that sometimes had trouble getting enough to eat and the fraction with serious housing problems rose between 2007 and 2009, which is consistent with what one would expect based on both the rise in unemployment and the rise in the official poverty rate. Mortality rates appear to have fallen appreciably for infants, but there is no reliable evidence yet for adults.

---

2. Provisional data on mortality from all causes that are not adjusted for the aging of the population indicate that the mortality rate fell more slowly between 2007 and 2009 than between 2003 and 2007. However, age-adjusted mortality is falling faster than unadjusted mortality, so conclusions based on the provisional data are very risky.

3. Household size is estimated using the ratio of persons to households in U.S. Census Bureau (2010), tables B-1 and A-1. The estimates shown there are for March 2009, when the survey was conducted.

COMMENTS and DISCUSSION 133

WOULD THINGS HAVE BEEN BETTER UNDER THE OLD WELFARE SYSTEM? Bitler and Hoynes's main goal is to figure out whether families with children would have fared better during the current downturn if the pre-1996 welfare system had still been in place. They use standard econometric methods to address this question, comparing trends within states before and after each state implemented welfare reform. Their results suggest that the effect of unemployment on child poverty was somewhat greater after welfare reform, but their estimates have large standard errors, and in five out of six cases the confidence interval includes zero (see their table 6). Nonetheless, since the primary goal of welfare reform was to make single mothers more dependent on earnings and less dependent on "handouts," and since the clearest consequence of the new law was to reduce the number of families getting a monthly welfare check, from 4.5 million in fiscal 1996 to 2.1 million in fiscal 2002, Bitler and Hoynes's expectation that child poverty should have become more sensitive to labor market conditions seems plausible, and nothing in their findings suggests that it is wrong. That said, three comments are in order.

First, from a policy perspective it is not clear why we should even be investigating the impact of welfare reform. Even if Bitler and Hoynes and other researchers were finding that welfare reform had terrible consequences for millions of children, the chances that legislators would respond by bringing back anything like the old AFDC (Aid to Families with Dependent Children) regime are close to zero. Legislators might try to help single mothers in other ways, such as by providing jobs and child care for all single mothers or guaranteeing all low-income single mothers a housing subsidy, but bringing back AFDC would be a nonstarter.

Second, it is not clear what "welfare reform" really includes in Bitler and Hoynes's analysis. They treat the states that introduced more stringent requirements than those traditionally allowed by AFDC as having begun welfare reform when their federal waiver was approved. However, the new federal rules established in 1996 under the Personal Responsibility and Work Opportunity Reconciliation Act (PRWORA), which replaced AFDC with TANF, were far more stringent than the rules introduced by states under pre-1996 waivers. Welfare waivers were also contemporaneous with increases in the EITC between 1993 and 1996 that made work a more attractive alternative to welfare.

Furthermore, states did not implement the new TANF rules immediately. States made it progressively harder for new applicants to get on the rolls, and they enforced their time limits more assiduously over time. These efforts to keep cutting the rolls year after year were motivated partly by state leg-

Table 1. Changes in Unemployment and in Child Poverty during Upturns and Downturns, 1996–2009

	1996	2000	2003	2007	2009
Unemployment (percent)	5.4	4.0	6.0	4.6	9.3
Child poverty (percent)	20.5	16.2	17.6	18.0	20.7
	1996–2000	2000–03	2003–07	2007–09	
Change in unemployment	−1.4	+2.0	−1.4	+4.7	
Change in child poverty	−4.3	+1.4	+0.4	+2.7	
As ratio to change in unemployment	3.07	0.70	−0.29	0.57	

Sources: *Economic Report of the President 2010*, table B-35; U.S. Bureau of the Census (2010), p. 56.

islators' desire to show their commitment to "work, not welfare," and partly by the threat of federal sanctions if states did not reduce the rolls more every year. As a result, the number of families getting TANF benefits fell by about half a million a year between fiscal 1996 and fiscal 2000 (from 4.5 million to 2.3 million). Some of this steady decline was surely due to the tightening labor market, but unemployment fell only from 5.4 percent to 4.0 percent between 1996 and 2000, and the labor force participation rate rose only from 66.8 percent to 67.1 percent. The welfare rolls fell by another 200,000 between 2000 and 2002, even though unemployment was higher in 2002 than it had been in 1996 (5.8 percent versus 5.4 percent).

This history suggests that the effects of the EITC and PRWORA unfolded gradually rather than instantaneously. When welfare reform is gradual and the lags are uncertain, disentangling the effects of reform from the effects of the EITC and unemployment is extremely difficult, and it is no surprise that most of Bitler and Hoynes's coefficients have large standard errors. My table 1 provides a simple illustration of the underlying problem by showing how child poverty changed between 1996 and 2009 as the unemployment rate rose and fell. To minimize the problem of lags, I focus on peak-to-trough and trough-to-peak changes in unemployment.

From 1996 to 2000 unemployment fell only 1.4 percentage points while child poverty fell 4.3 percentage points, suggesting a very strong postreform effect of full employment on child poverty. But after 2000 the relationship between unemployment and child poverty weakened. Unemployment rose 2.0 percentage points between 2000 and 2003, but child poverty only rose 1.4 percentage points. Between 2003 and 2007 unemployment fell as much as it had between 1996 and 2000 (1.4 percentage points), but child poverty rose from 17.6 percent to 18.0 percent. By 2007, therefore, the link between child poverty and the labor market was looking quite tenuous. However, the recent recession has provided a fourth test of the link, and it points to a more cautious conclusion. The official unemployment rate rose from 4.6 percent in 2007 to 9.3 percent in 2009, and each 1-percentage-point rise in unemployment was associated with an increase in child poverty of 0.57 percentage point, which is fairly similar to the association during the rise in unemployment between 2000 and 2003.

The fact that the relationship between unemployment and child poverty varies so much could have numerous causes. First, the big drop in child poverty between 1996 and 2000 reflected the fact that PRWORA and the EITC induced more single mothers to look for work, and tight labor markets helped them find it. Second, wages near the bottom of the distribution rose. At the 20th percentile of the combined distribution for men and women, for example, real wages rose 11 percent between 1996 and 2000, which was the only period of sustained increase between 1973 and 2007 (Economic Policy Institute 2009, table 3.5). These factors could also explain why child poverty was lower during 2001–03, a period of relatively high unemployment, than it had been in the early 1990s. The fact that child poverty hardly dropped at all after 2003, when unemployment began to fall, is harder to explain.

Bitler and Hoynes try to deal with these problems by looking at trends across the 50 states rather than within the United States as a whole. Their estimates therefore rely on the average relationship between trends in unemployment and child poverty within states. Nonetheless, their estimates have large standard errors and are seldom statistically significant. My tentative conclusion is thus that we are still some distance from identifying all the factors that affect either official child poverty rates or the authors' adjusted rates. The same conclusion probably holds for the direct measures of children's well-being that both they and I discuss.

REFERENCES FOR THE JENCKS COMMENT

Economic Policy Institute. 2009. *The State of Working America 2008/2009*. Washington. Data available at www.epi.org/resources/datazone_dznational/.

Gerdtham, Ulf-G., and Christopher J. Ruhm. 2006. "Deaths Rise in Good Economic Times: Evidence from the OECD." *Economics and Human Biology* 4, no. 3: 298–316.

Jencks, Christopher, Susan E. Mayer, and Joseph Swingle. 2004. "Can We Fix the Federal Poverty Measure so It Provides Reliable Information about Changes in Children's Living Conditions?" Harvard University, University of Chicago, and Wellesley College.

National Center for Heath Statistics. Various years. "Births, Marriages, Divorces, and Deaths: Provisional Data." National Vital Statistics Reports. Washington.

Nord, Mark, Margaret Andrews, and Steven Carlson. 2008. "Household Food Security in the United States, 2007." Report no. 65. U.S. Department of Agriculture, Economic Research Service.

Nord, Mark, Alisha Coleman-Jensen, Margaret Andrews, and Steven Carlson. 2010. "Household Food Security in the United States, 2009." Report no. 108. U.S. Department of Agriculture, Economic Research Service.

Ruhm, Christopher J. 2003. "Good Times Make You Sick." *Journal of Health Economics* 22, no. 4: 637–58.

———. 2005. "Healthy Living in Hard Times." *Journal of Health Economics* 24, no. 2: 341–63.

U.S. Census Bureau. 2010. "Income, Poverty, and Health Insurance Coverage in the United States: 2009." *Current Population Reports,* series P60-238. Washington.

———. 2010. "Webinar on 2009 Income, Poverty and Health Insurance Estimates from The Current Population Survey." (Washington, D.C. September 16).

U.S. Department of Housing and Urban Development. 2010. "The 2009 Annual Homeless Assessment Report to Congress." Office of Community Planning and Development. Washington.

COMMENT BY

BRUCE D. MEYER   This paper by Marianne Bitler and Hilary Hoynes examines the important question of how the social safety net has changed over time and how these changes have affected the well-being of families. Many indicators suggest that the safety net has changed substantially. Whether in terms of program caseloads or in terms of expenditure, over the past 15 years or so, Aid to Families with Dependent Children (AFDC) and its successor Temporary Assistance for Needy Families (TANF) have become much less important, while the earned income tax credit (EITC) and the food stamp program (today known as the Supplemental Nutrition Assistance Program, or SNAP) have steadily expanded. More recently, enrollment in and spending on unemployment insurance (UI) skyrocketed in the Great Recession.

The paper begins with nice descriptions of the main programs that provide for the disadvantaged, focusing on AFDC/TANF, food stamps, and UI. The program rules are carefully summarized, and recent changes to these rules are described in detail. The focus on these programs partly flows from the authors' decision to examine the nonelderly exclusively. The study also focuses on nonmedical assistance. If one is concerned about where the current safety net might be failing to serve the disadvantaged, cash or near-cash assistance to the nonelderly is likely to be the right place to look. Robert Moffitt and John Karl Scholz (2010) have noted that recent increases in income support have been focused on very poor elderly, disabled, and childless families through the Social Security (both its old-age and its disability components), Supplemental Security Income (SSI), and health programs. In contrast, very poor families with children have seen a decline in expenditure due to lower receipt rates of AFDC/TANF and food stamps, although recently SNAP caseloads have risen considerably.

The paper also focuses on how the safety net for the nonelderly has responded to the recession, rather than on how those disadvantaged by persistently poor skills, disability, or old age have fared in recent years. The paper's analysis thus concentrates on those likely to be hurt given the differing trends in government spending by demographic group, and given that the economy is in the midst of its most severe downturn since the Great Depression. The authors' conclusions about the functioning of the safety net will not be applicable to the elderly or to those among the nonelderly who are suffering more long-term disadvantage.

It is also worth stepping back and thinking about the ways a recession can hurt the disadvantaged. The most obvious way is through the loss of employment and a decline in earnings among the employed. Thus, the recession is likely to have its largest effects on those who depend on employment, namely, the able-bodied nonelderly. Another way to characterize the trends in income support in recent years is as a shift in support from the nonworking poor to the working poor (Moffitt 2003, 2007). Given this shift, one might be especially worried if the recession leads to a loss of benefits for the working poor, such as from the EITC, as employment falls. Other effects of the recession on the disadvantaged might include a reduced likelihood of marriage and higher rates of marital dissolution (although Hellerstein and Morrill 2010 provide evidence that divorce is procyclical), both of which might impoverish single adults and their families. Finally, one might see a decline in private transfers and other support for the poor.

A basic question that the paper could address more directly is how one should go about assessing the state of the safety net. Presumably, economists and policymakers would like to know how the safety net cushions any income shocks and prevents them from leading to a fall in family well-being. To examine this question, we first need to assess the extent of the shocks to income. We also need to decide how to measure family well-being. We could measure well-being using income, which has a long tradition. But income often only translates roughly into well-being, because families save and borrow. Furthermore, most families, even most poor families, have substantial nonfinancial assets: homes, cars, and other durables. Depending on their stock of these assets, a change in income will have different effects on their well-being. Finally, income is often misreported in household surveys, especially among the most disadvantaged households. Only half of food stamp and welfare dollars are reported in the main survey used by the authors, the Current Population Survey (Meyer, Mok, and Sullivan 2009, Meyer and Goerge 2010). The reporting of private transfers is likely worse. Consumption data are a good alternative to income data, given that recent research shows that consumption is better measured than income at the bottom and that low consumption is more closely associated with deprivation than is low income (Meyer and Sullivan 2003, forthcoming-b). Other dimensions to well-being might also be of concern. If families have less nonmarket time (including leisure), or if access to medical care has changed, for example, then well-being is affected.

Factors other than the safety net might also have changed in the Great Recession in ways that affect family well-being. The years leading up to the recession as well as the recession years themselves were a period of atypically slow employment growth. In addition, tighter credit and the sharp decline in housing prices imply that many households can no longer borrow or access housing equity in bad times, which suggests that the recession may have done more damage than its depth alone would indicate. Thus, it seems likely that the effect of changes in the safety net may be difficult to separate from that of other changes in economic conditions.

The paper reports three main sets of empirical results. The first summarizes aggregate changes in a number of measures of economic conditions, benefit receipt, and well-being both in the recent recession and in earlier contractions and expansions. Among the most important findings from this analysis are that even though unemployment rose more in the recent recession than in the 1979–82 recession, official poverty rose less, and total consumption and food consumption in the bottom income quintile actually went up. Also, food stamp receipt rose much more in this recession than in past ones. These initial results do not indicate a newly permeable safety net.

The second set of results describes the responsiveness of state program caseloads and individual reported receipt of benefits to state unemployment rates. The paper argues that food stamp caseloads and receipt have become more sensitive to unemployment, but that the sensitivity of AFDC/TANF to unemployment has not risen or may have fallen over time. However, the evidence seems to be mixed. The authors' variable interacting the unemployment rate with a dummy for the postreform period has a positive coefficient in both the AFDC/TANF and the food stamp regressions, suggesting increased responsiveness of these programs, but it is statistically insignificant in both cases. The authors also interact classifications of the different state welfare reforms with unemployment. Such a classification is not an easy thing to do or one that can be done with confidence, given the multidimensional and qualitative changes in state welfare laws. In any case, only one of five coefficients in the AFDC/TANF caseload regressions is significantly different from zero at the 5 percent level or better, and the two that are significant in the food stamp caseload regressions are of conflicting sign. Thus, the evidence of decreased responsiveness is weak.

In the analysis using survey data on benefit receipt by program, the results are similarly inconclusive. The responsiveness of AFDC/TANF receipt to changes in unemployment more than doubles after reform, whereas that for food stamps does not quite double but is more precisely measured and significantly different from zero. These survey results should be interpreted with caution, however, given that the survey misses half of TANF and food stamp receipt.

Another interesting feature of the paper is its use of both administrative aggregate data and survey data. The authors suggest that similarities in the results in the two data sources may mean that the deficiencies of the survey data are not important. However, the differences in specifications, the large standard errors, and the lack of comparison of the magnitudes of the coefficients make this exercise unconvincing. One can easily compare in the survey and administrative data, however, the magnitude of the interaction coefficient on unemployment after reform relative to the main effect (the unemployment rate alone) in tables 4 and 7. The administrative data indicate that AFDC/TANF caseloads are about 20 percent more sensitive after reform, whereas the survey data indicate an increased responsiveness of 125 percent. The discrepancy for food stamps is also very large. This is not evidence that allows one to conclude that survey errors are unimportant.

In any case, it is not clear that one should conclude a great deal from such regressions about the likely changes in caseloads or benefit receipt in future recessions. Each recession is a little different. The responsiveness of poverty to unemployment has varied sharply across decades, as many authors have found (for example, Blank and Card 1993, Blank 2000, Haveman and Schwabish 2004, and Meyer and Sullivan forthcoming-a). In addition, changes in state welfare programs over time have been very large and are hard to summarize, and these might be confounding the relationship of caseloads and expenditure with unemployment.

AFDC/TANF receipt may be less sensitive now to unemployment than it has been historically, but the evidence is not there yet to show it. It would not be surprising if AFDC/TANF were not particularly sensitive to unemployment, because it is a program that serves a population with low historical employment rates. Past research has found that this sensitivity is indeed low and has changed over time (Blank 2001). If this sensitivity is lower in recent decades, it might reflect the fact that federal funding does not vary with unemployment under the block grant system introduced as part of welfare reform. Alternatively, it might be due to the program being more targeted at those who cannot work and thus are less sensitive to labor market conditions.

The paper's third set of results examines the effects of welfare reform on various well-being measures, principally poverty rates. The authors also look at living arrangements and "disconnectedness" (the condition of being effectively cut off from both work and welfare). For all outcomes, the authors examine the coefficient on the interaction of unemployment with welfare reform, essentially asking whether well-being declines more with higher unemployment after welfare reform than before. Before examining this interaction, or second-order effect, it is worth knowing a bit more about what happened overall after welfare reform. One might suspect that changes in caseloads provide limited information on well-being, given that AFDC/TANF caseloads fell from 5 million assistance units to under 2 million, yet the evidence is mixed on how families fared after welfare reform. James X. Sullivan and I looked extensively at this issue (Meyer and Sullivan 2004, 2008) and found that, overall, families' material well-being is apparently higher after welfare reform, but it is a complicated and mixed picture. Consumption by single mothers rose in all income deciles, and their income rose in all but the first. We argue that the decline in reported income for the bottom decile is likely due to misreporting. Housing characteristics (number of rooms, presence of air conditioning and appliances, and so forth) improved after welfare reform for those who were likely to be on welfare, but health insurance coverage fell for some groups of single mothers. Time spent in nonmarket activity (leisure time and time spent on housework) dropped substantially for single mothers, but this loss of time does not appear to have decreased their time with children (also see Gelber and Mitchell 2009); rather, it has come out of time spent cleaning and shopping and the like.

With the above as background, let me turn to the current results. The paper regresses several poverty measures, family structure, and a dummy variable for neither work nor welfare receipt on the unemployment rate after welfare reform as well as the unemployment rate for the entire period. These results are probably the most important findings of the paper. For only one of the outcomes is the key interaction coefficient significantly different from zero. That outcome is the share of people with income below

150 percent of the official poverty line. For the other cutoffs (100 percent and 50 percent of the poverty line), the coefficients are insignificant. Given that the official income definition used to determine the official poverty measure misses many of the most important parts of the safety net (food stamps, the EITC, the child tax credit, housing assistance), it is not an especially useful tool for evaluating the safety net. When the authors examine poverty measures that use alternative income definitions that account for taxes, food stamps, and other benefits, the changes are insignificant, as they are for other well-being outcomes. Even the alternative poverty numbers are questionable given that, as noted above, the survey that the authors rely on misses half of food stamps and TANF. I would urge the authors to look at changes in means and low percentiles of consumption in the Consumer Expenditure Survey.

The situation of families with children may be worse in high-unemployment areas than it was in the past under similarly high unemployment, but the data to determine if this is so are not yet available. Chairman Mao, when asked whether the French Revolution was a success, reportedly said that it was too early to tell. This sentiment applies even more strongly to the topic of this paper. In evaluating these analyses, we should be aware that it may be too early to determine how the safety net is affecting families in the Great Recession and its aftermath. The unemployment rate was 5.8 percent, equal to the median value over the full sample, in 2008, the next-to-last year of data examined in the principal analyses in the paper. Unemployment rose sharply in 2009, but one year of data with high unemployment is not a lot on which to base conclusions. There is substantial variation across states, but still it is too early to conclude how the new safety net will perform in recessions.

REFERENCES FOR THE MEYER COMMENT

Blank, Rebecca M. 2000. "Fighting Poverty: Lessons from Recent U.S. History." *Journal of Economic Perspectives* 14, no. 2: 3–19.

———. 2001. "What Causes Public Assistance Caseloads to Grow?" *Journal of Human Resources* 36, no. 1(Winter): 85–118.

———. 2009. "Economic Change and the Structure of Opportunity for Less-Skilled Workers." In *Changing Poverty, Changing Policies,* edited by Maria Cancian and Sheldon Danziger. New York: Russell Sage Foundation.

Blank, Rebecca M., and Alan S. Blinder. 1986. "Macroeconomics, Income Distribution, and Poverty." In *Fighting Poverty: What Works and What Does Not,* edited by Sheldon H. Danziger and Daniel H. Weinberg. Harvard University Press.

Blank, Rebecca M., and David Card. 1993. "Poverty, Income Distribution, and Growth: Are They Still Connected?" *BPEA,* no. 2: 285–339.

Gelber, Alexander M., and Joshua W. Mitchell. 2009. "Taxes and Time Allocation: Evidence from Single Women." Working Paper no. 15583. Cambridge, Mass.: National Bureau of Economic Research.

Haveman, Robert, and Jonathan Schwabish. 2000. "Has Macroeconomic Performance Regained Its Antipoverty Bite?" *Contemporary Economic Policy* 18, no. 4: 415–27.

Hellerstein, Judith K., and Melinda Morrill. 2010. "Booms, Busts, and Divorce." Working paper. University of Maryland and North Carolina State University.

Meyer, Bruce D. 2003. "Measuring the Well-Being of the Poor Using Income and Consumption." *Journal of Human Resources* 38S: 1180–1220.

———. 2004. "The Effects of Welfare and Tax Reform: The Material Well-Being of Single Mothers in the 1980s and 1990s." *Journal of Public Economics* 88, no. 7–8 (July): 1387–1420.

Meyer, Bruce D., and Robert M. Goerge. 2010. "The Analysis of Food Stamp Program Participation with Matched Administrative and Survey Data." Working paper. University of Chicago.

Meyer, Bruce D., and James X. Sullivan. 2008. "Changes in the Consumption, Income, and Well-Being of Single Mother Headed Families." *American Economic Review* 98, no. 5 (December): 2221–41.

———. Forthcoming-a. "Consumption and Income Poverty over the Business Cycle." *Research in Labor Economics.*

———. Forthcoming-b. "Further Results on Measuring the Well-Being of the Poor Using Income and Consumption." *Canadian Journal of Economics.*

Meyer, Bruce D., Wallace K. C. Mok, and James X. Sullivan. 2009. "The Under-Reporting of Transfers in Household Surveys: Its Nature and Consequences." Working Paper no. 15181. Cambridge, Mass.: National Bureau of Economic Research.

Moffitt, Robert A. 2003. "Introduction." In *Means-Tested Transfer Programs in the United States,* edited by Robert A. Moffitt. University of Chicago Press.

———. 2007. "Four Decades of Antipoverty Policy: Past Developments and Future Directions." *Focus* 25, no. 1 (Spring-Summer): 39–44.

Moffitt, Robert A., and John Karl Scholz. 2010. "Trends in the Level and Distribution of Income Support." Working Paper no. 15488. Cambridge, Mass.: National Bureau of Economic Research.

GENERAL DISCUSSION Donald Kohn wondered about possible interactions between welfare and unemployment insurance. Among the many advantages of having low-income individuals in the labor force rather than out of it is greater access to the UI system. Increased use of UI should damp the cyclicality of welfare by delaying any cyclical effects. This is particularly likely to occur with low-skilled people who have trouble reentering the labor force as extended benefits expire. One result is that any cyclical effects would tend to be seen at or after the end of a recession.

COMMENTS and DISCUSSION 143

Steven Davis was persuaded by the recent work of Bruce Meyer and many others arguing that the official poverty measures are too flawed to be useful as objects of research. A good alternative is to look at post-tax, post-transfer measures of income among the lower percentiles of the consumption distribution. He further wondered why many experts in this field had been wrong ex ante about the impact of welfare reform. Understanding this error would inform the theories and models used in evaluating the impact of changes in this and other policy programs. Christopher Jencks thought one reason the predictions had been so wrong was that AFDC payments made up a much smaller fraction of what people were living on before welfare reform than most researchers had assumed. Bruce Meyer added that the employment rate of single mothers, whose ability to work and be hired had been in question, rose more quickly than expected.

Helen Ladd asked whether it was correct that most of the increase in employment was in short-term or temporary jobs that did not lead to longer-term employment. Meyer noted that among high school dropout single mothers, employment went up by roughly 60 percent after reform. The increases for that group have persisted, but it remains a good question whether they have received wage increases over time that are typical for people with their skill level.

David Romer thought the critical question was whether the social safety net had been shredded to the point where a sizeable recession would cause an enormous amount of suffering. The tone of the paper and of the discussion implied that it had not, but quite a few of the individual indicators discussed in the paper suggested that the answer was not entirely clear. The authors find that poverty is now more cyclical, as is the number of disconnected women. And they find that both food insecurity and the postponing or forgoing of medical care rose substantially more in the most recent recession than previously.

Justin Wolfers noted that issues related to welfare, like the extension of unemployment insurance, are very much on the current policy agenda, making the discussion of direct contemporary policy relevance. He also perceived a puzzle in the paper's results. Since the beginning of the recent recession, the poverty rate was up by 1.8 percentage points, whereas the early-1980s recession had raised the poverty rate by 3.3 points. If welfare reform was what was different between the two periods, why wasn't the rise in the poverty rate even greater in the current downturn? In addition, almost everything that has been done to the social safety net over the past 20 years is not measured by the poverty rate. These two issues together suggest that the real puzzle of this recession is why the aggregate poverty rate has not risen much at all. It may be that UI is the answer and not welfare reform, which appears to have raised the cyclicality of poverty.

James Hines suggested thinking also about the cyclicality of the earned income tax credit, a policy that was motivated by many of the same ideas that had inspired welfare reform. It would be interesting to know whether the generosity of the EITC increases during recessions, effectively acting as a counterbalance to welfare reform. He conjectured that it may not increase, since virtually all of the EITC's benefits are conditioned on working, whereas unemployment rises in a recession. On the other hand, to the extent a recession causes some previously fully employed workers to become underemployed or to have to accept a lower wage, some of them might become newly eligible for the EITC.

Henry Aaron saw the discussion as highlighting that the most understudied subject in income distribution research is disability insurance. Over the period in question, the number of people on disability insurance tripled, and total expenditure on that program was probably larger than for any of the other programs under discussion. Disability insurance is not an income-tested program and thus goes at least in part to people who would not have been poor without the benefits. But a complete accounting of the effects of the recession on low-income Americans nonetheless calls for a discussion of what has happened with respect to disability insurance enrollments and expenditure.

Melissa Kearney thought that welfare reform, by essentially making it harder to enroll in and stay on a key form of government assistance, was important to the debates surrounding other assistance programs: about extending unemployment insurance, about making disability insurance harder to qualify for, and even about allowing stimulus payments to go to states' provision of these programs. She was interested in the role of the states, and in particular how much larger the welfare caseload increase would have been if states were not actively discouraging caseloads. She cited a paper by Jeffrey Kubik showing that in times of fiscal stress, states push more people from AFDC onto SSI, which suggests that states might be acting differently in the post-welfare reform era in terms of discouraging applications. Kearney proposed thinking about applications to all of these programs collectively as a better measure of the need for assistance. Many people are applying for these programs but not getting them, and long-term programs like disability insurance and SSI are more relevant to fiscal consequences.

Kristin Forbes wondered if it was accurate to interpret the paper's results as saying that welfare reform had significantly reduced the costs of a major U.S. entitlement program over time, while producing not only no large negative effects during normal times, but also no large general negative effects even during recessions. If this is true, are there lessons for reforming other major entitlement programs? In particular, a look back at what people were saying during the welfare reform debate of the 1990s might enlighten some of the current discussions about entitlement reforms.

Gary Burtless underscored that both the employment and the earnings of the population affected by welfare reform were much more resilient than most forecasters had expected: real wages at the bottom end of the earnings distribution improved after reform, for the first time in probably 20 years. He also found it striking that, unlike a lot of reforms, this one had been preceded by almost a decade of systematic randomized trials across the country, in which many of the elements of the reform were tested in local populations. None of these randomized trials had uncovered employment gains of the size witnessed after reform passed at the national level. It was and remains a mystery how much of that increase was due to possible social interaction effects (that is, individuals within a group influencing each other's behavior, for example by informing one another of new program rules and how best to respond to them), and to what extent the limitations of doing randomized trials for this kind of policy caused the effect of nationwide reform to be underestimated. It is hard to observe social interaction effects in a small-scale randomized trial, because only a small percentage of the affected population is enrolled in any one tested program.

Burtless also argued that welfare reform should have made overall unemployment rates slightly more cyclical, because a population that formerly had been largely insulated from the labor market, by being outside of it, was forced to enter the workforce. In a recession, a lot of disadvantaged single women are on the margin of being employed or unemployed rather than being solidly outside the workforce. However, this effect is likely small, as this population does not make up a large proportion of the working-age population.

Melissa Kearney picked up on Burtless' point about the possible social network effects of the 1996 reform. There have been some isolated policy studies but nothing in the models for cultural change. These sorts of cultural network effects are very well captured, however, in the agent-based models that are part of the Brookings Social Genome Project.

Ricardo Reis noted that recessions are times when discretionary fiscal spending is taking place, trying to channel more money toward a whole series of programs, including those that assist the poor. Much of the fiscal response to the recent crisis has taken the form of increasing transfers in almost every transfer program. Reis was curious to know more about how welfare money had been spent over the last 2 years and to what channels it was directed, because this might shed light on whether the outcomes are what might have been expected 15 or 20 years ago.

Robert Hall was interested in the relationship between unemployment and the TANF caseload, which has been shown to rise substantially in proportional terms but not nearly as much as unemployment during recessions. To take unemployment as the benchmark would suggest that each TANF unit depended largely on one person's earnings with the typical amount of unemployment. In reality, the matching of workers to TANF units is more complicated, and any given TANF unit may have zero, one, two, or more earners. Further, a model that makes the TANF caseload rise in proportion to unemployment neglects the high earnings replacement rate of UI for the population potentially eligible for TANF, and it neglects the relationship between unemployment in that population and the overall unemployment rate. Throughout the recession and its aftermath, real post-transfer income per capita has continued to rise. Households have responded to the recession by spending substantially less of their income and increasing their saving. The social loss associated with the recession is huge, but the loss at the household level is not as large because an effective system is in place to replace the income lost during a recession. This point is consistent with the finding by Parker and Vissing-Jorgensen in their paper for this conference, that everybody except the very rich is fairly well insulated from extreme income fluctuations.

Brian Jacob stressed the importance of individual state responses and perhaps also of the part of the federal response that takes place through other mechanisms besides transfers. It may be that the total costs of assistance have not really been reduced dramatically if these other things are included. Also, it might be that some states are being generous in other ways that minimize any negative effects of welfare reform.

Christopher Jencks observed, following on Jacob's point, that the federal government spends more on the EITC than was ever spent on AFDC, and so it would not be accurate to say that welfare reform has saved the government money. Rather, money was shifted away from cash welfare in order to make it pay to go to work. In some sense welfare reform can be called a success only if one ignores the effects on people's well-being and considers only the goal of getting people to work. Jencks also pointed out that the reason the EITC is the most effective program in raising people above the poverty line is not so much the generosity of the benefit but because it tends to help those already close to the poverty line.

Jencks noted that applying for benefits under TANF can be difficult. In many states, applicants are required to inquire about work from a list of firms before applying. Some who were probably eligible, in terms of genuine economic need, never come back. State welfare offices discourage people from applying, particularly when they do not want caseloads to rise. In the 1980s New York went so far as to close half its welfare offices. Simply counting applications can thus make it look like the need for welfare has collapsed even if actual eligibility has risen.

Bruce Meyer argued that it makes more sense to evaluate a program in terms of the reduction in the poverty gap it achieves. The effect of food stamps, for example, on the poverty gap is much more important than that of the EITC. Meyer suggested that in focusing on the interaction of welfare reform and unemployment, the paper was looking at a second-order effect. The main effect, namely, on consumption by single mothers, was an increase at almost all points of the distribution. For other outcomes like health insurance coverage, many single mothers toward the bottom have lost ground. They are also working more, which may have been the goal of the reform, but getting these single mothers into the workforce was itself costly.

THOMAS S. DEE
University of Virginia

BRIAN A. JACOB
University of Michigan

The Impact of No Child Left Behind on Students, Teachers, and Schools

ABSTRACT The controversial No Child Left Behind Act (NCLB) brought test-based school accountability to scale across the United States. This study draws together results from multiple data sources to identify how the new accountability systems developed in response to NCLB have influenced student achievement, school-district finances, and measures of school and teacher practices. Our results indicate that NCLB brought about targeted gains in the mathematics achievement of younger students, particularly those from disadvantaged backgrounds. However, we find no evidence that NCLB improved student achievement in reading. School-district expenditure increased significantly in response to NCLB, and these increases were not matched by federal revenue. Our results suggest that NCLB led to increases in teacher compensation and the share of teachers with graduate degrees. We find evidence that NCLB shifted the allocation of instructional time toward math and reading, the subjects targeted by the new accountability systems.

The No Child Left Behind (NCLB) Act of 2001 is arguably the most far-reaching education policy initiative in the United States over the last four decades. The hallmark features of this legislation compelled states to conduct annual student assessments linked to state standards, to identify schools that are failing to make "adequate yearly progress" (AYP), and to institute sanctions and rewards based on each school's AYP status. A fundamental motivation for this reform is the notion that publicizing detailed information on school-specific test performance and linking that performance to the possibility of meaningful sanctions can improve the focus and productivity of public schools.

NCLB has been extremely controversial from its inception. Critics charge that NCLB has led educators to shift resources away from important but nontested subjects, such as social studies, art, and music, and to focus instruction within mathematics and reading on the relatively narrow set of topics that are most heavily represented on the high-stakes tests (Rothstein, Jacobsen, and Wilder 2008, Koretz 2008). In the extreme, some suggest that high-stakes testing may lead school personnel to intentionally manipulate student test scores (Jacob and Levitt 2003). Although there have been hundreds of studies of test-based accountability policies in the United States over the past two decades, the evidence on NCLB is more limited, both because it is a newer policy and because the national scope of the policy makes it extremely difficult to find an adequate control group by which to assess the national policy.

This paper examines the impact NCLB has had on students, teachers, and schools across the country. We investigate not only how NCLB has influenced student achievement, but also how it has affected education spending, instructional practice, and school organization. Given the complexity of the policy and the nature of its implementation, we are skeptical that any single analysis can be definitive. For this reason we present a broad collage of evidence and look for consistent patterns.

Several findings emerge. First, the weight of the evidence suggests that NCLB has had a positive effect on elementary student performance in mathematics, particularly at the lower grades. The benefits appear to be concentrated among traditionally disadvantaged populations, with particularly large effects among Hispanic students. We do not find evidence that the policy has adversely affected achievement at either the top or the bottom end of the test-score distribution. Instead, the policy-induced gains in math performance appear similar across the test-score distribution. However, the available evidence suggests that NCLB did not have a comparable effect on reading performance.

A closer look at the potential mechanisms behind the observed improvement provides some additional insight. For example, we find evidence that NCLB increased average school district expenditure by nearly $600 per pupil. This increased expenditure was allocated both to direct student instruction and to educational support services. We also find that this increased expenditure was not matched by corresponding increases in federal support. The test-score gains associated with these expenditure increases fall short of the ambitious goals enshrined in NCLB. However, we present some qualified evidence suggesting that the size of the gains reflects a reasonable return on investment.

We also discuss evidence on how NCLB may have influenced alternative measures of educational practice and student outcomes. This evidence suggests that NCLB led to an increase in the share of teachers with master's degrees. We also find evidence that teachers responded to NCLB by reallocating instructional time from social studies and science toward key tested subjects, particularly reading. We also present evidence that NCLB led to distinct improvements in a teacher-reported index of student behaviors (which covers, among other things, attendance, timeliness, and intellectual interest) commonly understood as measuring "behavioral engagement" with school.

The paper proceeds as follows. Section I outlines the theoretical underpinnings of school accountability and provides background on the NCLB legislation. Section II examines the impact of NCLB on student achievement, marshaling evidence from a variety of different sources. Section III investigates potential mediating mechanisms, discussing how the policy affected educational expenditure, classroom instruction, and school organization, among other things. Section IV concludes with recommendations for future policy and research.

I. Background on School Accountability and NCLB

NCLB represented a bold new foray into education policy on the part of the federal government. However, the provisions it embodied built on a long history of reforms in standards and accountability at the state and local levels over several decades.

I.A. Theoretical Underpinnings of School Accountability

A basic perception that has motivated the widespread adoption of school accountability policies like NCLB is that the system of public elementary and secondary schooling in the United States is "fragmented and incoherent" (Ladd 2007, p. 2). In particular, proponents of school accountability reforms argue that too many schools, particularly those serving the most at-risk students, have been insufficiently focused on their core performance objectives, and that this organizational slack reflected weak incentives and a lack of accountability among teachers and school administrators. For example, Eric Hanushek and Margaret Raymond (2001, pp. 368–69) write that accountability policies are "premised on an assumption that a focus on student outcomes will lead to behavioral changes by students, teachers, and schools to align with the performance goals of the system" and that "explicit incentives . . . will lead to innovation, efficiency, and fixes to any observed performance problems."

The theoretical framework implicitly suggested by this characterization of public schools is a principal-agent model: the interests of teachers and school administrators, the agents in this framework, are viewed as imperfectly aligned with those of parents and voters. Furthermore, parents and voters cannot easily monitor or evaluate the input decisions made by these agents. The performance-based sanctions and rewards that characterize accountability policies are effectively output-based incentives that can be understood as a potential policy response to this agency problem. Similarly, some of the provisions in NCLB with regard to teacher qualifications can be construed as an agent selection approach to a principal-agent problem.

The principal-agent lens is also useful for understanding criticisms of accountability-based reforms. The assumption that the self-interest of teachers and administrators is misaligned implies that they may respond to accountability policies in unintentionally narrow or even counterproductive ways. For example, in the presence of a high-stakes performance threshold, schools may reallocate instructional effort away from high- and low-performing students and toward the "bubble kids"—those most likely, with additional attention, to meet the proficiency standard (see, for example, Neal and Schanzenbach 2010). Similarly, concerns about "teaching to the test" reflect the view that schools will refocus their instructional effort on the potentially narrow cognitive skills targeted by their high-stakes state assessment, at the expense of broader and more genuine improvements in cognitive achievement. Schools may also reallocate instructional effort away from academic subjects that are not tested, or even attempt to shape the test-taking population in advantageous ways.

I.B. Research on Accountability Reforms Adopted by States before NCLB

School accountability reforms similar to those brought about by NCLB were adopted in a number of states during the 1990s. Several studies have evaluated the achievement consequences of these reforms. Because of the similarities between NCLB and aspects of these pre-NCLB accountability systems, this body of research provides a useful backdrop against which to consider the potential achievement impacts of NCLB. In a recent review of this diverse evaluation literature, David Figlio and Helen Ladd (2007) suggest that three studies (Carnoy and Loeb 2002, Jacob 2005, and Hanushek and Raymond 2005) are the "most methodologically sound" (Ladd 2007, p. 9).

A study by Martin Carnoy and Susanna Loeb (2002), based on state-level achievement data from the National Assessment of Educational Progress (NAEP), found that the within-state improvement in math performance between 1996 and 2000 was larger in states with higher values on an accountability index, particularly for black and Hispanic students in eighth grade.[1] Similarly, Jacob (2005) found that, following the introduction of an accountability policy, math and reading achievement increased in the Chicago public schools, relative both to prior trends and to contemporaneous changes in other large urban districts in the region. However, Jacob (2005) also found that younger students did not experience similar gains on a state-administered, low-stakes exam and that teachers responded strategically to accountability pressures (for example, increasing special education placements).

Hanushek and Raymond (2005) evaluated the impact of school accountability policies on state-level NAEP math and reading achievement, as measured by the difference between the performance of a state's eighth-graders and that of fourth-graders in the same state 4 years earlier. This gain-score approach applied to the NAEP data implied that there were two cohorts of state-level observations in both math (1992–96 and 1996–2000) and reading (1994–98 and 1998–2002). Hanushek and Raymond (2005) classified state accountability policies as implementing either "report-card accountability" or "consequential accountability." States with report-card accountability provided a public report of school-level test performance, whereas states with consequential accountability both publicized school-level performance and could attach consequences to that performance. The types of potential consequences were diverse. However, virtually all of the systems in consequential accountability states included key elements of the school accountability provisions later enacted in NCLB (for example, identifying failing schools, replacing principals, allowing students to enroll elsewhere, and taking over, closing, or reconstituting schools). Hanushek and Raymond (2005, p. 307) note that "all states are now effectively consequential accountability states (at least as soon as they phase in NCLB)."

Hanushek and Raymond (2005) find that the introduction of consequential accountability within a state was associated with statistically significant

---

1. The accountability index constructed by Carnoy and Loeb (2002) ranged from 0 to 5 and combined information on whether a state required student testing and performance reporting to the state, whether the state imposed sanctions or rewards, and whether the state required students to pass an exit exam to graduate from high school.

increases in the gain-score measures. The achievement gains implied by consequential accountability were particularly large for Hispanic students and, to a lesser extent, white students. However, the estimated effects for the gain scores of black students were statistically insignificant, as were the estimated effects of report-card accountability. The authors argue that these achievement results provide support for the controversial school accountability provisions in NCLB, because those provisions are so similar to the consequential accountability policies that had been adopted in some states.

I.C. Key Features of the NCLB Legislation

The NCLB legislation was actually a reauthorization of the historic Elementary and Secondary Education Act (ESEA), the central federal legislation relevant to K-12 schooling. The ESEA, first enacted in 1965 along with other Great Society initiatives and previously reauthorized in 1994, introduced Title I, the federal government's signature program for targeting financial assistance to schools and school districts serving high concentrations of economically disadvantaged students. NCLB dramatically expanded the scope and scale of this federal legislation by requiring that states introduce school accountability systems that applied to *all* public schools and their students in the state. In particular, NCLB requires annual testing of public-school students in reading and mathematics in grades 3 through 8 (and at least once in grades 10 through 12), and that states rate each school, both as a whole and for key subgroups of students, with regard to whether they are making "adequate yearly progress" toward their state's proficiency goals.

NCLB also requires that states introduce "sanctions and rewards" relevant to every school and based on their AYP status. It mandates explicit and increasingly severe sanctions (from implementing public-school choice to staff replacement to school restructuring) for persistently low-performing schools that receive Title I aid. According to data from the Schools and Staffing Survey of the National Center for Education Statistics, 54.4 percent of public schools participated in Title I services during the 2003–04 school year. Some states applied these explicit sanctions to schools not receiving Title I assistance as well. For example, 24 states introduced accountability systems that threatened all low-performing schools with reconstitution, regardless of whether they received Title I assistance.[2]

---

2. Lynn Olson, "Taking Root," *Education Week*, December 8, 2004.

II. The Impact of NCLB on Student Achievement

The overarching goal of NCLB has been to drive broad and substantive improvements in student achievement. This section discusses the available empirical evidence on the achievement effects of NCLB, drawing on a variety of research designs and data sources including national time trends, comparisons between private and public schools, and comparisons across schools and states.

II.A. National Time Trends in Student Achievement

Because NCLB was introduced simultaneously throughout the United States, many observers have turned to state and national time-series trends in student achievement to assess its impact. For example, several studies have noted that student achievement, particularly as measured by state assessment systems, appears to have improved both overall and for key subgroups since the implementation of NCLB (Center on Education Policy 2008b). Others, however, argue that changes in student performance on high-stakes state tests can be highly misleading when states strategically adjust their assessment systems and teachers narrow their instructional focus to state-tested content (Fuller and others 2007).

Figure 1 presents data on national trends in student achievement from 1992 to 2007. These data are from the main NAEP and provide separate trends by grade (fourth and eighth), by subject (math and reading), and by race and ethnicity (white, black, and Hispanic).[3] These trends suggest that NCLB may have increased the math performance of fourth-graders. That is, these NAEP data suggest that fourth-grade math achievement has shifted noticeably higher during the NCLB era and may have also begun trending upward more aggressively. The trend data suggest similar gains in the math performance of black eighth-graders. However, the trends provide no clear suggestion that the onset of NCLB improved performance in

---

3. There are several different versions of the NAEP. The original NAEP, first administered in the early 1970s, is now called the Long-Term Trend (LTT) NAEP, because the Department of Education has made an effort to keep the content of this examination as consistent as possible over time in order to accurately gauge national trends. The LTT NAEP is administered to a small random sample of 9-, 13-, and 17-year-olds across the country and generally focuses on what many educators now think of as "basic" skills. What is now called the main NAEP was initiated in the early 1990s in an effort both to update the content and format of the national assessment so as test a broader domain of knowledge and skills, and to allow individual states to obtain their own, state-representative estimates. This exam is administered to fourth and eighth graders (and more recently to twelfth-graders).

Figure 1. Mean Scaled Scores on the Main NAEP, by Ethnicity, 1992–2007[a]

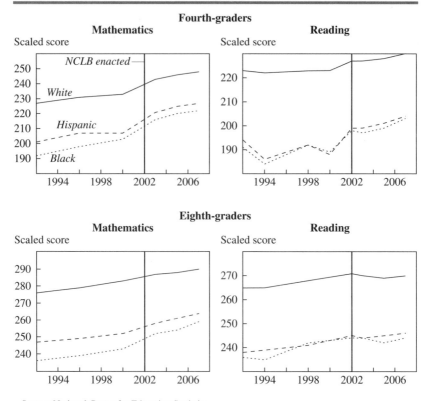

Source: National Center for Education Statistics.
a. Data are for all public schools.

the other three grade-subject combinations. Figure 2 shows achievement growth for 9- and 13-year-olds in math and reading, using data from the Long-Term Trend (LTT) NAEP, which has tracked student performance from the early 1970s. These data similarly suggest that the effects of NCLB on student achievement have been at best limited to certain groups.

II.B. Evidence from International Comparisons

Although these national achievement trends are suggestive, they do not necessarily provide the basis for reliable inferences about the impact of NCLB. Simple time-series comparisons may be biased by the achievement consequences of other time-varying determinants, such as the recession

Figure 2. Mean Scaled Scores on the Long-Term Trend NAEP, by Ethnicity, 1978–2004[a]

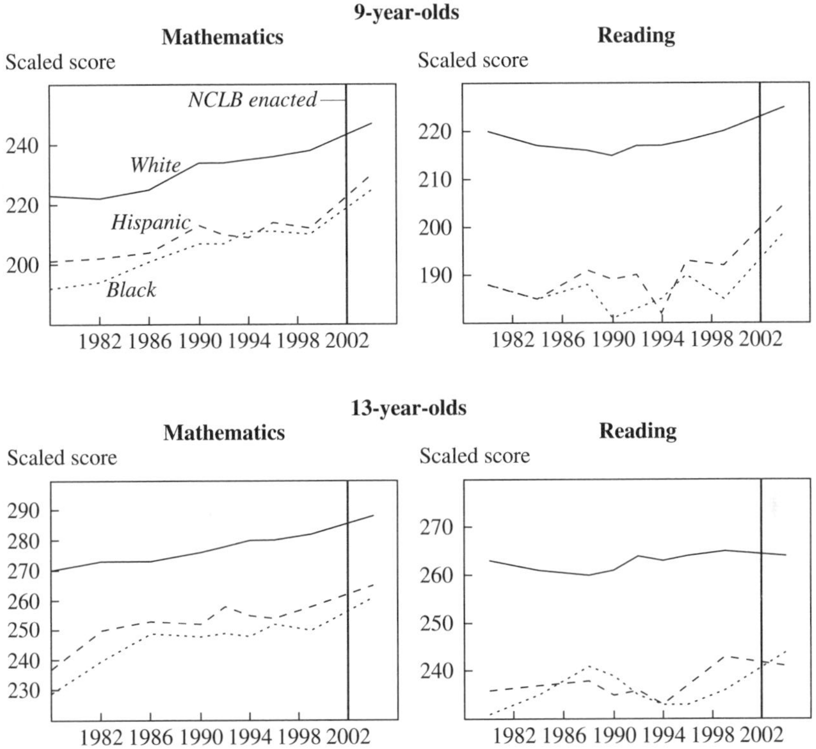

[Figure: Four panels showing NAEP scaled scores for 9-year-olds and 13-year-olds in Mathematics and Reading, by White, Hispanic, and Black ethnicity, from 1982 to 2002, with NCLB enactment marked.]

Source: National Center for Education Statistics.
a. Data are for all public schools.

that just preceded the introduction of NCLB. One straightforward way to benchmark the achievement trends observed in the United States is to compare them with the contemporaneous trends in other countries.

Because the time-series evidence in figure 1 suggests that any positive achievement effects from NCLB were likely to have been concentrated in fourth-grade math achievement, the comparative international achievement data from the Trends in International Mathematics and Science Study (TIMSS) are particularly relevant. The TIMSS collected trend data on fourth-grade math achievement for participating countries in 1995, 2003, and 2007. The top panel in figure 3 presents the fourth-grade scale scores in math from the TIMSS for the United States, for the 12 other countries that collected these performance data in each of these

Figure 3. Mean Scaled Scores of Fourth-Graders on the TIMSS and the PIRLS in the United States and Other Countries[a]

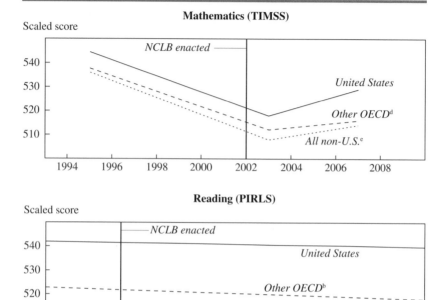

Source: National Center for Education Statistics.

a. The TIMSS (Trends in International Mathematics and Science Study) is an international assessment of the mathematics and science knowledge of fourth- and eighth-grade students, administered every 4 years since 1995. The PIRLS (Progress in International Reading Literacy Study) is an international assessment of the literacy achievement of fourth-grade students, administered every 5 years since 2001. Both studies are conducted by the International Association for the Evaluation of Educational Achievement.

b. Australia, England, Hungary, Japan, Netherlands, New Zealand, Norway, and Scotland.

c. Countries in note b plus Iran, Latvia, Singapore, and Slovenia.

d. England, France, Germany, Hungary, Italy, Kuwait, Netherlands, New Zealand, Norway, Scotland, Slovak Republic, and Sweden.

e. Countries in note d plus Bulgaria, Hong Kong, Iran, Israel, Latvia, Lithuania, Macedonia, Moldova, Morocco, Romania, Russia, Singapore, and Slovenia.

three study years, and for the subset of these comparison countries that are members of the Organization for Economic Cooperation and Development (OECD).

These trend data indicate that average math achievement on the TIMSS fell for all sets of countries by roughly equal amounts between the only available pre-NCLB year (1995) and the first academic year in which

NCLB was implemented (2002–03). Without additional years of data, we cannot assess the extent to which these comparative changes deviate from pre-NCLB trends. However, the available TIMSS data indicate that, by 2007, math achievement had comparatively improved in the United States, particularly with respect to the other OECD countries (an improvement of 11 scale points versus 4). These cross-country trends provide suggestive evidence consistent with the hypothesis that NCLB led to improvements in the math performance of younger students in the United States. However, the comparative test-score gain for the United States is relatively modest, amounting to only a 1.35 percent increase in average performance over pre-NCLB scores, and an 8 percent increase relative to the standard deviation in test scores.

Moreover, like the national time-series evidence, international comparisons provide no indication that NCLB improved the reading achievement of young students. The Progress in International Reading Literacy Study (PIRLS) reports data on the reading achievement of fourth-graders across a number of countries both in 2001 and in 2006. The bottom panel of figure 3 presents overall reading scores from the PIRLS by year for the United States, the group of 26 other countries that participated in both surveys, and the OECD members of this comparison group. On average, the United States outperformed these comparison countries. However, over the period that NCLB was implemented, all three sets of countries experienced quite similar and modest changes in PIRLS reading achievement.

Overall, then, the international evidence is at best suggestive. Contemporaneous changes within other countries may make them a poor comparison group for evaluating NCLB. The lack of multiple years of data also makes it difficult to distinguish possible policy effects from other trends or to identify any comparative differences with statistical precision. A subtler shortcoming of national and international time-series comparisons is that the presumption of a common, national effect ignores the possibility of heterogeneous effects of NCLB across particular types of states and schools.

II.C. Evidence from Accountability Risk Studies

However, several recent econometric studies have creatively leveraged this heterogeneity to identify the effects of NCLB. In particular, a widely used approach involves structuring comparisons across schools or students that face different risks of sanctions under NCLB. Derek Neal and Diane Schanzenbach (2010) present evidence that following the introduction of

NCLB in Illinois, the performance of Chicago public-school students near the proficiency threshold (that is, those in the middle of the distribution) improved while the performance of those at the bottom of the distribution remained the same or fell. Using data from the state of Washington, John Krieg (2008) finds that the performance of students in both tails of the distribution is lower when their school faces the possibility of NCLB sanctions.

Dale Ballou and Matthew Springer (2008), using data from a low-stakes exam fielded in seven states over a 4-year period, identify the achievement consequences of NCLB by constructing comparisons across grade-year cells that were included in AYP calculations and those that were not. Their approach takes advantage of the fact that between 2002–03 and 2005–06, states differed with respect to whether particular grades mattered for a school's accountability rating. Hence, their identification strategy leverages the fact that if the math scores of fourth-graders counted toward a school's accountability rating in one year but the math scores of fifth-graders in the same school did not count until the following year, one would expect student achievement to rise more quickly among fourth-graders relative to fifth-graders in the current year. Ballou and Springer find that the presence of AYP accountability modestly increased the math achievement of elementary-school students, particularly lower-performing students.

A recent study by Randall Reback, Jonah Rockoff, and Heather Schwartz (2010) adopts a similar approach, comparing student performance across elementary schools on the margin of making AYP. Using nationally representative data from the Early Childhood Longitudinal Study (ECLS), they find that reading and science scores on low-stakes tests improve by as much as 0.07 standard deviation when a school is on the margin for making AYP, but that the effects on math scores are smaller and statistically insignificant.

These accountability risk studies provide credible evidence on how NCLB-induced pressure influences the level and the distribution of student achievement. However, they have at least three potential limitations with respect to understanding the broad achievement consequences of NCLB. First, most of these studies have limited external validity because they do not rely on national data. Second, some rely on high-stakes assessments, which may not accurately reflect true student ability in the presence of strategic responses to NCLB (such as teaching to the test). Third, and perhaps most important, the treatment contrast in these studies may not approximate the full impact of NCLB because they rely on comparisons across schools or students, all of whom were observed in the post-NCLB policy regime. To the extent that NCLB had broad effects on public schools (that is, even on students and schools not under the direct threat of sanctions), these comparisons could understate the effects of interest.

II.D. Evidence from a Comparison of States over Time

To address some of the limitations described above and estimate what one might consider the "full" impact of NCLB, we utilize a strategy that compares changes in student performance within states over time (see Dee and Jacob forthcoming). We take advantage of the fact that NCLB was explicitly modeled on an earlier generation of state-level school accountability systems. In the decade before NCLB, about 30 states implemented consequential school accountability policies that were fundamentally similar to NCLB in that they mandated systematic testing of students in reading and math, public reporting of school performance on these exams, and the possibility of meaningful sanctions (including school takeover, closure, or reconstitution, replacing the principal, and allowing students to change schools) based on test-based school performance. In fact, some state officials argued that NCLB needlessly duplicates preexisting state accountability systems.[4]

The existence of these earlier NCLB-like accountability systems establishes natural treatment and control state groups. In our framework, states that adopted NCLB-like accountability before NCLB form our control group. Other states, for which NCLB catalyzed an entirely new experience with consequential school accountability, form our treatment group.[5] Of course, states that adopted accountability programs before NCLB were not randomly distributed. For this reason our "comparative interrupted time series" (CITS) strategy, described in more detail below, relies on within-state variation over time, allowing not only for different levels of

---

4. Michael Dobbs, "Conn. Stands in Defiance of Enforcing 'No Child.'" *Washington Post*, May 8, 2005.

5. We relied on a number of different sources to categorize pre-NCLB accountability policies across states, including prior studies of such policies (for example, Carnoy and Loeb 2002, Lee and Wong 2004, and Hanushek and Raymond 2005) as well as primary sources such as the Quality Counts series put out by *Education Week* ("Quality Counts '99," January 11, 1999, www.edcounts.org/archive/sreports/qc99/), the state-specific "Accountability and Assessment Profiles" assembled by the Consortium for Policy Research in Education (Goertz, Duffy, and Le Floch 2001), annual surveys on state student assessment programs fielded by the Council of Chief State School Officers, information from state education department websites, Lexis-Nexis searches of state and local newspapers, and conversations with academics and state officials in several states.

achievement across states before NCLB but also for different *trends* in achievement across states before NCLB.

GRAPHICAL EVIDENCE. We illustrate the logic of our identification strategy through a series of figures. This graphical evidence has the advantages of transparency and simplicity. We then present regression estimates that more clearly show the magnitude and statistical precision of our findings and allow us to demonstrate that the results are robust to a variety of alternative specifications and several falsification exercises.

Figure 4 shows the trends in NAEP scores for two groups: states that had adopted school accountability by 1998 (control states), and states that

Figure 4. Mean Scaled Scores on the Main NAEP, by Timing of Increased School Accountability, 1992–2007[a]

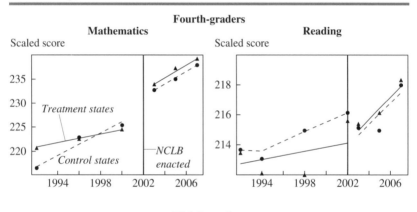

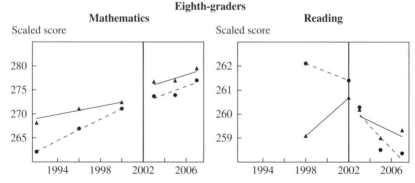

Source: National Center for Education Statistics and authors' calculations.

a. Data are for public schools only. Treatment states are those that did not adopt consequential school accountability policies before NCLB, and control states those that had adopted such policies before 1998. A small number of states that adopted accountability programs between 1999 and 2001 are excluded.

had not adopted school accountability before NCLB (treatment states).[6] The NAEP data are particularly well suited to this evaluation for several reasons. First, the NAEP is a technically well-developed assessment that covers a broad domain of knowledge and schools. Second, it provides consistent, state-representative measures of student performance for most states over the last two decades. Finally, the exam is a low-stakes exam for students, teachers, and schools.[7] Because teachers have no incentive to "teach to" the NAEP, it is likely to provide the most accurate measure of student achievement (Fuller and others 2007).

The figure plots the simple (unweighted) average scale score of each group of states in all years in which the exam was administered. Years are identified by the spring of the relevant academic year (for example, "1992" refers to the 1991–92 school year). The sample of states is consistent across years (that is, it is a balanced panel), and the state classification is a time-invariant characteristic. Data points to the left of the vertical line that indicates the enactment of NCLB are considered "pre-policy," and those to the right "post-policy."[8] To illustrate the pre- and post-NCLB achievement trends within each group, we also plot the fitted regression line from a simple linear regression conducted separately for each group × period (pre- or post-NCLB).

---

6. These figures exclude a small number of states that adopted state accountability programs between 1999 and 2001, in order to make a clear distinction between our treatment and comparison groups. However, the regression analysis described in the following section includes these "late adopter" states. Dee and Jacob (forthcoming) show that the inclusion of these late adopters does not change the findings in any substantive way.

7. That is, the NAEP is not used as the basis for student promotion or retention, teacher evaluation, or school accountability. Indeed, the NAEP is administered only to a small, random sample of fourth-, eighth-, and twelfth-grade students in each state.

8. When one dates the start of NCLB is a potentially important issue. NCLB secured final congressional approval on December 18, 2001, and was signed by President George W. Bush on January 8, 2002, both events thus occurring in the middle of the 2001–02 academic year. NCLB is often characterized as having been implemented during 2002–03 because states were required to use testing outcomes from the previous academic year as the starting point for determining whether a school was making adequate yearly progress (Palmer and Coleman 2003; Lynn Olson, "States Strive toward ESEA Compliance," *Education Week,* December 1, 2002). However, one could reasonably conjecture that the discussion and anticipation surrounding the adoption of NCLB would have influenced school performance during the 2001–02 school year. Alternatively, it could also be argued that NCLB should not be viewed as in effect until the 2003–04 academic year, when new state accountability systems were more fully implemented as well as more informed by guidance from and negotiations with the U.S. Department of Education (Lynn Olson, "States Strive toward ESEA Compliance," *Education Week,* December 1, 2002; Olson, "Taking Root," *Education Week,* December 8, 2004). For a more detailed discussion, see Dee and Jacob (forthcoming).

The top left panel of figure 4, which plots trends in fourth-grade math achievement, shows that in 1992, states that did not adopt accountability until NCLB scored roughly 5 scale points (0.18 standard deviation) higher on average than states that adopted school accountability policies by 1998. Although both groups of states made modest gains between 1992 and 2000, the group that adopted accountability policies before 1998 experienced more rapid improvement during this period.[9]

If the NCLB accountability provisions had an impact on student performance, one would expect achievement to increase more after 2002 in states with no prior accountability than in states with prior accountability. It is possible that NCLB led to a level shift in student achievement, which would be manifest as a shift in the intercept after NCLB. It is also possible that NCLB changed the *rate* of achievement growth, which would be manifest as a change in the *slope* of the achievement trend after NCLB.[10] Whether one considers a shift in the intercept or a change in the slope, our identification strategy relies on a comparison of treatment versus control states that accounts not only for the pre-NCLB levels of achievement in each group but also for the pre-NCLB achievement *trends* in each group.

The top left panel of figure 4 shows that the mean level of math achievement jumped noticeably in 2003 for both groups of states. However, relative to prior trends, this shift was larger among the "no prior accountability" group (the treatment states). Interestingly, there was little noticeable change in the growth *rate* across periods for the states with prior accountability (the control states): the slope of the achievement trend for this group is roughly the same before and after 2002. In contrast, achievement rose more rapidly in states with no prior accountability from 2003 to 2007 than from 1992 through 2000, such that the growth rates after 2002 were roughly equivalent across both groups of states. These trends suggest that NCLB had a positive impact on fourth-grade math achievement.

---

9. This visual evidence is consistent with the earlier evaluation literature that studied pre-NCLB state accountability reforms (for example, Carnoy and Loeb 2002, Jacob 2005, and Hanushek and Raymond 2005).

10. The rate of achievement growth might have increased after NCLB for several reasons. First, it may take states time to implement new curricula, instructional strategies, or other support services for students. Second, later cohorts of students will have been "exposed" to NCLB for a larger fraction of their school careers than earlier cohorts. Without imposing additional assumptions, we cannot cleanly distinguish between these effects. For this reason we focus on the "net" impact of NCLB in different years after the legislation was passed.

The trends for eighth-grade math (bottom left panel of figure 4) are similar to those for fourth-grade math, although less pronounced. The pattern for fourth-grade reading (top right panel of figure 4) is much less clear. The pre-NCLB reading trends for both groups are much noisier than the math trends. In particular, the two groups both experienced a decline in achievement in 1994 and then diverged in 1998, but both had made very large gains by 2002.[11] The states with prior accountability experienced a drop in achievement from 2002 to 2003, both in absolute terms and relative to trend. The other group experienced very little increase from 2002 to 2005. Perhaps most important, however, visual inspection of the data in these plots indicates that the earlier achievement trend was not linear, which is a central assumption of the linear CITS model. Similarly, the bottom right panel of the figure provides no evidence of an NCLB effect on eighth-grade reading achievement.

ESTIMATION STRATEGY. Perhaps the most straightforward approach to estimating the impact of NCLB in the framework described above is a simple difference-in-differences framework in which one compares the achievement levels of treatment and control states before and after the introduction of NCLB. However, a fundamental assumption of this model is that any preexisting trends in the outcome variables are equivalent across treatment and control groups. Figure 4 clearly showed that the control states (those that implemented consequential accountability before NCLB) realized more rapid improvements during the pre-NCLB period. For this reason we estimate a more flexible specification that allows for preexisting trends to differ across groups. Our model is the following:

$$(1) \quad Y_{st} = \beta_0 + \beta_1 YEAR_t + \beta_2 NCLB_t + \beta_3 \left(YR\_SINCE\_NCLB_t\right) \\ + \beta_4 \left(T_s \times YEAR_t\right) + \beta_5 \left(T_s \times NCLB_t\right) \\ + \beta_6 \left(T_s \times YR\_SINCE\_NCLB_t\right) + \beta_7 \mathbf{X}_{st} + \mu_s + \varepsilon_{st},$$

where Y_{st} is a measure of student achievement for state s in year t, $YEAR_t$ is a trend variable (defined as the year of the test minus 1989 so that it starts with a value of 1 in 1990), and $NCLB_t$ is a dummy variable equal to 1 for observations starting in the academic year 2002–03. $YR\_SINCE\_NCLB_t$ is defined as the year of the test minus 2002, so that this variable takes on a value of 1 for the 2002–03 year, which corresponds to the 2003 NAEP testing. $\mathbf{X}_{st}$ represents a vector of state × year covariates. In the main

---

11. The graph is scaled to accentuate what are really quite small absolute changes from year to year.

specification the only state-year covariates included are the fraction and its square of students who were tested but excluded from official reporting because of limited English proficiency or some type of learning disability. The variables μ_s and ε_{st} represent state fixed effects and a mean-zero random error, respectively.

T_s is a time-invariant variable that measures the treatment imposed by NCLB. In the most basic setup, T_s could be specified as a dummy variable, with a value of 1 indicating that a given state did not institute consequential accountability before NCLB. This is the approach implicitly taken in figure 4. However, it is more accurate to view the "treatment" provided by the introduction of NCLB in the framework of a dosage model. Slightly more than half of the states that introduced consequential school accountability before NCLB did so within the 4 years before NCLB's implementation. The simple binary definition of T_s above could lead to attenuated estimates of the NCLB effect, because the control group would include some states for which the effects of prior state policies and NCLB are closely intertwined.

For this reason we instead define T_s as the number of years during our panel period that a state did *not* have school accountability. Specifically, we define the treatment as the number of years *without* prior school accountability between the 1991–92 academic year and the onset of NCLB. Hence, states with no prior accountability have a value of 11. Illinois, which implemented its policy during the 1992–93 school year, has a value of 1; Texas has a value of 3, since its policy started in 1994–95; and Vermont has a value of 8, since its program started in 1999–2000. Our identification strategy implies that the larger the value of this treatment variable, the greater the potential impact of NCLB.

This regression specification allows for an NCLB effect that can be reflected in both a level shift in the coefficient on the outcome variable (β_5) and a shift in the coefficient on the achievement trend variable (β_6), each of which varies with treatment status, T_s. Specifications based on alternative functional forms generate results similar to those based on this canonical CITS design.[12] For the sake of parsimony, the impact estimate we report is the effect of NCLB by 2007 for states with no prior accountability relative to states that adopted school accountability in 1997 (the mean adoption

---

12. For example, we get similar results when we allow for a separate NCLB "effect" unique to each post-NCLB year. We also find similar results when we measure treatment status with multiple dummy variables, allowing the trend and shift variables to differ across groups of states that were early, middle, or late adopters of pre-NCLB accountability.

year among states that adopted accountability before NCLB).[13] For all models we present standard errors clustered by state to account for serial correlation and other forms of heteroskedasticity.

The primary threat to causal inference in our CITS design is the existence of time-varying unobservable factors that are coincident with the introduction of NCLB, affect treatment and control states differently, and independently affect student performance. One example is endogenous student mobility, such as might occur if NCLB caused families to leave or return to the public schools. Another problematic scenario would be one where either the treatment or the control states recovered from the 2001 recession more quickly. As discussed below, we examine the empirical relevance of these concerns in several ways and find no evidence that our findings are biased.

Other threats to the causal validity of this state-based research design are closely linked to exactly how the NCLB impact estimates from equation 1 should be interpreted. For example, our estimates will capture the impact of the accountability provisions of NCLB but *not* the effects of other NCLB provisions such as Reading First or the "highly qualified teacher" provision, which were unique nationwide. Second, under the maintained assumption that NCLB was effectively irrelevant in states with prior consequential accountability systems, our estimates will identify the effects of NCLB-induced school accountability provisions for a particular subgroup of states (those without prior accountability policies). To the extent that one believes that those states expecting to gain the most from accountability policies adopted them before NCLB, the results we report would understate the average treatment effects of school accountability. Similarly, our estimates will also understate the general effects of school accountability if NCLB amplified the effects of school accountability within the states that already had it. An alternative concern is that the accountability systems within control states may have been weakened as they were adjusted in response to NCLB. To the extent this occurred, our CITS approach would instead overstate the effects of NCLB. We suspect this concern is not empirically relevant because the school reporting and performance sanctions occasioned by NCLB (such as the possibility of school reconstitution or closure) were strong relative to prior state accountability policies. There is also direct empirical evidence

---

13. Specifically, the effect as of 2007 would be calculated as $\beta_5 + \beta_6(5)$ in the simple case where T_s is binary, but as $\beta_5(6) + \beta_6(6 \times 5)$ in our preferred specification where T_s is allowed to vary across states and the NCLB effect is identified relative to a state that implemented school accountability in 1997. As a practical matter, both approaches generate similar results (Dee and Jacob forthcoming, table 3).

consistent with this assumption: Dee and Jacob (forthcoming) find that states with preexisting school accountability systems did not change their proficiency thresholds after the onset of NCLB.

RESULTS. Table 1 presents estimates of regressions, based on equation 1, of the impact of NCLB on student performance in mathematics and reading. Overall, the results suggest that NCLB had uniformly positive effects on math performance among elementary students, particularly fourth-graders. The mean impact of 7.2 score points for fourth-grade math translates to an effect size of 0.23 standard deviation. The effects are even larger toward the left of the ability distribution. These estimates suggest that NCLB increased the proportion of fourth-graders reaching the basic level on NAEP by 10 percentage points, or a 16 percent increase relative to the control mean of 64 percent. Although the mean effects for eighth-graders are not statistically significant at conventional levels (a 0.10-standard-deviation effect, with a p-value of 0.12), the effects at the bottom tail are stronger. NCLB increased the fraction of eighth-graders reaching the basic level in math by 5.9 percentage points (9 percent).

Although we find that NCLB had larger impacts on the mathematics performance of lower-achieving students, we do not find any evidence that the introduction of NCLB harmed students at higher points on the achievement distribution. In contrast to some prior work within individual districts and states, we find that NCLB seems to have increased achievement at higher points on the achievement distribution more than one might have expected. For example, in fourth-grade math the impacts at the 75th percentile were only 3 scale points lower than those at the 10th percentile.

In contrast to the mathematics results, we do not find consistent evidence that NCLB influenced student achievement in reading. The NCLB impact estimates for the reading measures are smaller and, in most cases, statistically indistinguishable from zero. The one notable exception is the finding that NCLB improved the reading performance of higher-achieving fourth-graders (those at the 75th and the 90th percentiles) modestly but significantly. However, as noted earlier, a caveat to the reading results is the suggestive evidence that the pre-NCLB trends in reading achievement, which are noisy and nonlinear, poorly match the assumptions of the CITS design. Furthermore, the capacity of this research design to detect effects on the reading achievement of eighth-graders is attenuated by the fact that only 2 years of pre-NCLB NAEP data are available for this grade-subject combination.

To test the sensitivity of our results to some of the potentially time-varying unobservable factors described above, we conducted a series of falsification exercises in which we reestimated equation 1 with a variety of

Table 1. Regressions Estimating the Effect of NCLB on Fourth- and Eighth-Grade NAEP Mathematics and Reading Scores[a]

	Mathematics				Reading			
	Fourth grade (39 states, N = 227)		Eighth grade (38 states, N = 220)		Fourth grade (37 states, N = 249)		Eighth grade (34 states, N = 170)	
Dependent variable	Estimated effect	Mean pre-NCLB outcome in states without prior accountability	Estimated effect	Mean pre-NCLB outcome in states without prior accountability	Estimated effect	Mean pre-NCLB outcome in states without prior accountability	Estimated effect	Mean pre-NCLB outcome in states without prior accountability
Mean NAEP score	7.244** (2.240)	224	3.704 (2.464)	272	2.297 (1.441)	216	-2.101 (2.070)	261
Percent of pupils achieving at or above basic level	10.090** (3.145)	64	5.888** (2.680)	64	2.359 (1.592)	61	-3.763 (2.561)	73
75th-percentile NAEP score	6.634** (1.902)	244	4.340** (2.189)	296	2.258** (0.938)	240	1.289 (2.249)	282
90th-percentile NAEP score	5.205** (1.916)	259	2.537 (2.404)	314	2.097** (0.805)	258	1.172 (2.897)	299

Source: Authors' regressions.

a. Each reported coefficient is from a separate regression specified as in equation 1 in the text and is the sum of coefficients β_5 and β_6. Effects are as of 2007 for states with no prior accountability relative to states that adopted school accountability in 1997. See the text for details. Standard errors clustered by state are in parentheses. Asterisks indicate statistical significance at the ***1 percent, **5 percent, or *10 percent level.

Table 2. Regressions Estimating the Effect of NCLB on Fourth- and Eighth-Grade NAEP Mathematics Scores, by Ethnicity and Eligibility for Free School Lunch Program[a]

Dependent variable	Whites		Blacks	
	Estimated effect	Mean pre-NCLB outcome in states without prior accountability	Estimated effect	Mean pre-NCLB outcome in states without prior accountability
Fourth-graders				
Mean NAEP score				
OLS	5.953**	232	4.582	203
	(1.990)		(5.436)	
WLS	5.074**	233	15.378**	202
	(2.159)		(3.710)	
Percent of pupils achieving at or above basic level				
OLS	7.278**	76	8.431	35
	(3.016)		(6.693)	
WLS	7.597**	77	22.690**	33
	(3.531)		(6.199)	
Eighth-graders				
Mean NAEP score				
OLS	2.863	281	9.261	241
	(2.561)		(6.774)	
WLS	1.828	282	8.826	242
	(3.680)		(8.999)	
Percent of pupils achieving at or above basic level				
OLS	4.740*	74	9.977	28
	(2.639)		(7.886)	
WLS	4.253	76	10.004	28
	(3.134)		(11.955)	

Source: Authors' regressions.

a. Each reported coefficient is from a separate regression and estimates the effect of NCLB as of 2007. See table 1 and the text for details. OLS = ordinary least squares; WLS = weighted least squares (weighting by student enrollment). Standard errors clustered by state are in parentheses. Asterisks indicate statistical significance at the ***1 percent, **5 percent, or *10 percent level.

alternative outcome measures, including state-year poverty rates, median household income, employment-population ratios, and the fraction of students in the public schools. Across 40 regressions (10 models for each of the four grade × subject combinations), we find only one estimate significant at the 5 percent level and three estimates significant at the 10 percent level. These largely null findings suggest that the assumptions required for identification are indeed met. In Dee and Jacob (forthcoming), we also show that the results presented in table 1 are robust to a host of alternative specifications, including the inclusion of a variety of state-year covariates,

	Hispanics		Eligible for free school lunch		Not eligible for free school lunch	
Estimated effect	Mean pre-NCLB outcome in states without prior accountability	Estimated effect	Mean pre-NCLB outcome in states without prior accountability	Estimated effect	Mean pre-NCLB outcome in states without prior accountability
12.409**	204	6.934*	212	3.916	232
(4.540)		(3.604)		(3.102)	
11.625**	204	9.734**	212	2.603	234
(1.572)		(2.836)		(2.907)	
12.499*	40	11.186*	49	5.388	76
(6.334)		(5.769)		(4.435)	
25.883**	36	17.256**	49	6.832**	78
(2.779)		(4.986)		(3.118)	
20.031**	246	10.702*	257	2.199	279
(5.766)		(6.155)		(3.924)	
8.219**	247	15.761**	256	0.992	281
(4.135)		(5.631)		(4.171)	
22.006**	36	12.773*	47	3.152	72
(4.618)		(7.328)		(4.045)	
18.692**	36	23.432**	46	2.392	74
(4.666)		(6.398)		(3.478)	

the inclusion of state-specific time trends, the inclusion of a full set of year fixed effects, and weighting the data by the number of students enrolled in that state and year.[14] Moreover, the inclusion of 2009 NAEP data does not change the basic pattern of results presented here.

Table 2 reports regression estimates separately by subgroup, both unweighted and weighted by student enrollment. Interestingly, the positive

14. Dee and Jacob (forthcoming) show that these results are also robust to measuring the intensity of the treatment imposed by NCLB in terms of the stringency of the proficiency standards imposed by the state. Wong, Cook, and Steiner (2009) find this as well.

effects are particularly large among lower-income and minority students. For example, among fourth-graders, NCLB increased the math achievement of black and Hispanic students. Interestingly, the enrollment-weighted estimates are systematically larger than the unweighted estimates for low-income and black students. For example, the weighted estimate for African-American students is 15.4 points (roughly 0.5 standard deviation) compared with the unweighted estimate of 4.6 points. Taken at face value, this suggests an important source of treatment-effect heterogeneity, namely, that NCLB had a more positive effect on disadvantaged students in states with a greater number of such children (for example, NCLB was more effective for black students in Alabama than for black students in South Dakota). However, given the relatively small number of treatment states with large populations of black students, the possibility that this heterogeneity reflects other state-specific traits cannot be discounted. The effect of NCLB on Hispanic students was also quite large (roughly 12 points) and did not vary with weighting. The weighted impact on students eligible for subsidized lunches was 9.7 points (roughly 0.3 standard deviation).

II.E. Evidence from Public- and Private-School Comparisons

The above comparison of trends in student performance within states over time suggests that NCLB had a substantial impact on math achievement, particularly among disadvantaged students in fourth grade. As with any nonexperimental design, however, the findings rest on assumptions that cannot be fully tested. For this reason we present results from a complementary analysis that makes use of an alternative control group.

In this approach we assess the impact of NCLB by comparing trends over time in student performance in public versus Catholic schools.[15] Students in private schools are eligible to participate in a number of major programs under the ESEA, and NCLB's reauthorization of ESEA left these prior provisions largely intact (U.S. Department of Education 2007), implying that the NCLB reforms were comparatively irrelevant for private schools. The use of Catholic schools in this analysis improves upon international comparisons by providing a within-nation control group. However, as with the national and international time-series evidence, this approach

---

15. In earlier work (Dee and Jacob forthcoming) we identify several potential concerns with using Catholic schools to identify the impact of NCLB.

Figure 5. Mean Scaled Scores on the Main NAEP in Public and Catholic Schools, 1990–2007

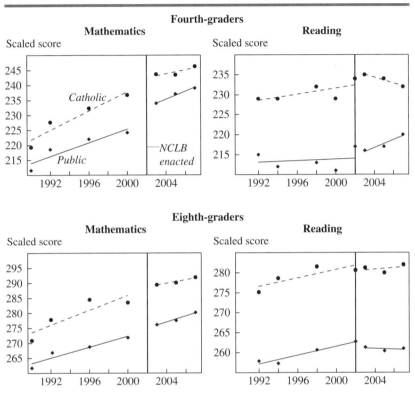

Source: National Center for Education Statistics.

also conflates the effects of NCLB across states and schools where its impact was heterogeneous.

Figure 5, which follows the same structure as figure 4 in comparing treatment and control states, shows pre- and post-NCLB achievement trends across public and Catholic schools. Although the performance of both public and Catholic students trended upward during the sample period, the latter consistently outperformed their public-school counterparts. However, following the implementation of NCLB, the math performance of public-school students converged somewhat toward that in the Catholic schools and entered a period of somewhat stronger trend growth. This comparative convergence is particularly pronounced for fourth-graders and is consistent with the other time-series evidence suggesting that NCLB improved math achievement, particularly among younger students. The reading achievement trends of eighth-graders are quite similar across public and Catholic schools, suggesting the absence of a meaningful NCLB impact. However, the reading achievement of public-school fourth-graders trended upward during the NCLB era, particularly relative to that of Catholic-school fourth-graders, which began a distinctive downward trend during the NCLB era.

These public-Catholic comparisons are broadly consistent with the state-based comparisons, suggesting that NCLB led to substantial gains in the mathematics achievement of fourth-graders and possibly of eighth-graders as well. These particular cross-sector comparisons also suggest that NCLB increased the reading achievement of fourth-graders. A recent study by Manyee Wong, Thomas Cook, and Peter Steiner (2009) includes regression estimates based on public-Catholic comparisons of this sort and draws similar conclusions. They also find similar, although less precisely estimated, results in comparisons of public schools and non-Catholic private schools.

II.F. Summary of Achievement Effects

Given the national scope of the policy, assessing the causal impact of NCLB on student performance is not straightforward. However, the body of evidence presented above seems to suggest that the federal school accountability policy did improve the math achievement of elementary students, particularly among socioeconomically disadvantaged groups. Comparable evidence that NCLB generated meaningful improvements in reading achievement is lacking, however. Moreover, the analysis presented above focuses exclusively on elementary schools. NCLB also requires AYP determinations for high schools, but here relatively little is known about NCLB's effects, in part because of data limitations: for example, no state-level data for secondary-school math achievement on the main NAEP are available after 2000.

What is the relevance for policy of the overall gains in math achievement that NCLB appears to have brought about? One way to benchmark a 7.2-point (0.23-standard-deviation) gain in fourth-grade math achievement is to compare this effect with achievement gaps that are of interest. For example, a test-score gain of this size is equivalent to approximately 24 percent of the black-white test-score gap observed in the 2000 NAEP data. Furthermore, because NCLB appears to have been more effective among disadvantaged subgroups, it may have contributed to closing some achievement gaps. For example, the effect of NCLB on the math achievement of

Hispanic fourth-graders was roughly 6 points larger than the corresponding effects on white students, implying that NCLB closed the white-Hispanic achievement gap by 19 percent.

III. Impact of NCLB on the Organization and Practice of Education

Given the encouraging effects on math achievement and the somewhat puzzling lack of effects for reading, it is natural to ask how NCLB affected the organization and practice of elementary education across the country. Such evidence on potential mediating mechanisms could not only guide revisions to the NCLB legislation, but also shed light on the education production function in ways that would inform other school reforms. To provide some coherence to the discussion that follows, we group nonachievement outcomes from a variety of sources into several broad categories: changes in educational resources, changes in instructional focus or methods or both, and changes in school organization, climate, or culture.

III.A. Impact on Education Expenditure

The direct costs of managing an accountability system are quite small on a per-pupil basis (Hoxby 2002). However, standards-based reforms have often been presented to the public as a trade: greater resources and flexibility for educators in exchange for greater accountability. One of the most strident criticisms of NCLB is that it failed to deliver on this bargain. However, there is surprisingly little research on the relationship between school accountability and spending, despite an extensive literature on education finance more generally.

One notable exception is an analysis of district-level expenditure data from 1991–92 to 1996–97 by Jane Hannaway, Shannon McKay, and Yasser Nakib (2002). Examining four states that implemented comprehensive accountability programs in the 1990s—Kentucky, Maryland, North Carolina, and Texas—they find that only two (Texas and Kentucky) increased educational expenditure more than the national average (but those two did so substantially). Hannaway and Maggie Stanislawski (2005) present evidence that the major pre-NCLB accountability reforms in Florida were associated with increased expenditure for instructional staff support and professional development, particularly in low-performing schools. Of course, it is difficult to determine whether the accountability policy caused the increased expenditure or whether both were merely parts of a broader reform agenda. Overall, the extant literature offers at best suggestive evidence on how accountability reforms may have influenced school spending.

To provide new evidence on how NCLB influenced local school finances, we pooled annual, district-level data on revenue and expenditure from U.S. Census surveys of school district finances (the F-33 Annual Survey of Local Government Finances) over the period from 1994 to 2008 (Dee, Jacob, and Schwartz 2010). Our analytical sample consists of all operational, unified school districts nationwide (roughly 10,000) for each survey year. To identify the effects of NCLB accountability on district finances, we utilize the same cross-state trend analysis described above, comparing within-state changes in school finance measures across states with and without pre-NCLB accountability programs.

Figure 6 shows trends in district expenditure over time separately for states that adopted consequential accountability before NCLB and those that did not. All results are reported in 2009 dollars and are weighted by district enrollment. As in the earlier figures, the trend lines are fitted linear regression lines.[16] The top left panel of figure 6 shows that total per-pupil expenditure rose more quickly from 1994 to 2002 in states that adopted pre-NCLB accountability policies. But following the introduction of NCLB, spending grew more slowly in these early-adopting states, suggesting that NCLB increased expenditure. The top right and bottom left panels of the figure show comparable results for the two largest categories of total expenditure, instructional and support service spending.

Table 3 presents regression estimates based on the model in equation 1, with the inclusion of the following district-year controls: enrollment, enrollment squared, the fraction of the student population that is black or Hispanic, the poverty rate (based on 2000 census data), the poverty rate squared, and the interaction between the poverty rate and the fraction black or Hispanic. As in earlier models, we present standard errors clustered by state. We report estimates of the impact of NCLB as of 2008 for states that did not have consequential accountability before NCLB relative to states that adopted consequential accountability in 1997.

The results indicate that NCLB increased total current expenditure by $570 per pupil, or by 6.8 percent from the 1999–2000 mean of $8,360. The increased expenditure was allocated to direct instruction and support ser-

---

16. Also as before, the figures omit states that adopted school accountability programs between 1999 and 2001, because the impacts of these state programs might be confounded with the introduction of NCLB in 2002. In the regression estimates discussed below, however, we include all states.

Figure 6. Expenditure per Pupil by Timing of Increased School Accountability, 1995–2008[a]

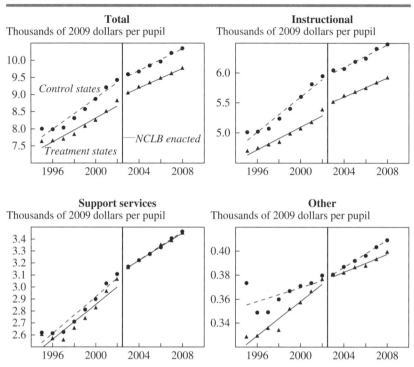

Source: Authors' calculations using data from the Common Core of Data's Local Education Agency (School District) Finance Survey.

a. All data are for elementary and secondary school expenditure. Sample is composed of all noncharter, unifed local education agency school districts, excluding Hawaii, the District of Columbia, and zero-enrollment districts. Estimates are weighted by district enrollment. Treatment and control states are defined as in figure 4.

vices in proportions roughly equivalent to average spending patterns, with effects of $430 (8.3 percent) and $155 (5.6 percent), respectively. Results presented in the bottom two rows of the table reveal that the increased expenditure was not matched by corresponding increases in federal support, consistent with allegations that NCLB constitutes an unfunded mandate. (However, the increase in spending on student support is not statistically significant at conventional levels.) In results not shown here, we find that the effects were fairly similar across districts with different baseline levels of student poverty, suggesting that NCLB did not meaningfully influence distributional equity. Moreover, in results reported elsewhere, we demonstrate that these findings are robust to the same falsification

Table 3. Regressions Estimating Effects of NCLB on Education Expenditure by Function and Revenue by Source
Constant (2009) dollars per pupil

Dependent variable	Mean for 1999–2000 school year	Estimated impact of NCLB[a]
Expenditure		
Total current expenditure, K-12	8,360	570**
	(2,061)	(237)
Instructional	5,209	430***
	(1,428)	(137)
Support services	2,786	155
	(772)	(112)
Other	365	−0.015
	(111)	(25)
Revenue		
Federal	660	42
	(473)	(31)
State and local	9,155	448
	(2,250)	(288)

Source: Authors' regressions.
a. Each reported coefficient is from a separate regression, based on roughly 140,000 district-year observations, that identifies the effect of NCLB as of 2008. See table 1 and the text for details. Standard deviations or standard errors clustered by state are in parentheses. Asterisks indicate statistical significance at the ***1 percent, **5 percent, or *10 percent level.

exercises and alternative specifications described earlier for the achievement analysis (Dee, Jacob, and Schwartz 2010).[17]

In light of the achievement effects discussed in the previous section, a natural and policy-relevant question is to ask how the monetized benefits of those test-score gains compare with the corresponding expenditure increases presented here. On the basis of prior estimates that a 1-standard-deviation increase in elementary math scores is associated with an 8 percent increase in adult earnings (Krueger 2003), the 0.23-standard-deviation impact of NCLB would translate into a lifetime earnings boost of 1.8 percent. Assuming a 3 percent discount rate, the present discounted value as of age 9 of such an increase beginning at age 18 is at least $13,300.[18] Hence, even if we assume that the increased expenditure due to NCLB is

---

17. As discussed in related work, we do not find substantial impacts on class size, suggesting that the increase in instructional expenditure due to NCLB may have been allocated to other functions (Dee, Jacob, and Schwartz 2010).

18. This calculation uses an age-earnings profile of 18- to 65-year-olds taken from the March 2007 Current Population Survey. Allowing for reasonable productivity-related growth in earnings of 2 percent a year increases the monetized benefit of the test-score gains due to NCLB to roughly $25,500.

sustained for all eight elementary-school years, the economic benefits of the corresponding test-score gains are at least twice as large. It should be stressed, however, that this exercise turns on multiple unstated assumptions. In particular, this back-of-the-envelope calculation ignores certain socially relevant benefits (such as the externalities of human capital improvements) and costs (such as the deadweight losses associated with raising government revenue to pay for the added spending). More generally, it is not clear that these expenditure increases were even a relevant mediating mechanism behind NCLB's achievement effects. Nonetheless, this calculation provides suggestive evidence that the achievement gains attributable to NCLB may compare favorably with the corresponding spending increases.

III.B. Impact on Teachers and Classrooms

One of the most prominent issues raised by NCLB concerns the intended and unintended ways in which it may have influenced classroom practice. In particular, test-based accountability policy creates a strong incentive for educators to focus on tested content and skills. Indeed, according to many, this is precisely the point of the reform. But at the same time, critics have worried that such incentives may cause schools to neglect important but nontested subjects, or to change instructional practice in a way that prioritizes narrow test preparation over broader learning. In this section we discuss the available evidence on how school accountability programs, including NCLB, influence classroom instruction.

The most consistent and compelling finding with regard to school accountability and classroom instruction involves the allocation of instructional time. A number of studies have documented that test-based accountability programs cause educators to reallocate instructional time toward tested subjects, to reallocate time within tested subjects toward specific content and skills covered on the exam, and to increase time devoted to narrow test preparation activities that may have little broader value (Hannaway and Hamilton 2008).

In 2001, for example, researchers at the National Board on Educational Testing and Public Policy surveyed a nationally representative sample of teachers, asking them a series of questions about how state-mandated testing programs influenced their practice (Pedulla and others 2003). Teachers in states where the exam results were used to hold teachers or schools accountable reported shifting instruction toward tested subjects more than did teachers in states where the exam results were used primarily for informational purposes. For example, 34 percent of teachers working in high-stakes testing regimes, but only 17 percent of teachers in moderate-stakes regimes, reported that the testing program had led them to increase the time spent in tested areas "a great deal." In addition, teachers in states with school accountability programs reported spending more time on a variety of activities designed to improve student test-taking skills, such as taking practice tests (Pedulla and others 2003). In states where the tests had important consequences for the schools, roughly 36 percent of elementary teachers reported spending more than 30 hours per year on test preparation activities, compared with only 12 percent of teachers in states where tests had few consequences for schools.[19]

Recent studies that focus on NCLB itself find similar results. In 2005, for example, researchers at the RAND Corporation collected data from teachers, principals, and superintendents in three states (California, Georgia, and Pennsylvania) to examine how they were responding to the introduction of NCLB (Hamilton and others 2007). Educators reported a narrowing of the curriculum and an emphasis on test preparation, particularly for "bubble kids" near the proficiency cut score for their state assessment system. In addition, educators responded to NCLB by increasing the alignment between the curriculum and state standards.

Studies of earlier school accountability programs found a similar increase in alignment. The programs led teachers to shift the content of their instruction within subjects (Stecher and others 1998, Koretz and others 1996, Jacob 2005, Koretz and Hamilton 2006). This literature emphasizes that the format and structure of the test itself can influence instruction. For example, Grace Taylor and others (2003) find that testing programs with short, open-ended items lead teachers to focus greater attention on problem-solving skills.

The Center on Education Policy (CEP) has studied the implementation and impact of NCLB since its inception (CEP 2006, 2007, 2008a, 2008b). As part of its work, CEP not only surveyed a nationally representative sample of school districts in 2005–06 and again in 2006–07, but also conducted more intensive case studies of selected school districts. District officials report that NCLB led them to increase the instructional time their schools devote to math or English language arts (ELA) or both. About 62 percent of districts reported that between 2001–02 and 2006–07 they increased instruction in these subjects in elementary schools, with the

---

19. Ladd and Zelli (2002) found similar results in a survey study of school principals in North Carolina during the period when the state was introducing its school accountability program. Principals reported devoting more resources to the high-stakes subjects of math, reading, and writing.

largest increases in districts with more schools in need of improvement (CEP 2007) and in urban and high-poverty districts (CEP 2006). Moreover, the reallocation reported by officials appears substantial. For example, 80 percent of districts that reported increasing ELA time did so by at least 75 minutes per week, and 54 percent reported doing so by at least 150 minutes per week (CEP 2008). Most districts that reported increased time for ELA or math reported cuts in time for other subjects or periods (such as social studies, art, music, gym, recess, or lunch) rather than increases in total time in school (CEP 2008).[20]

The CEP studies also suggest that NCLB influenced classroom practice in ways that may have attenuated teacher autonomy. For example, CEP (2006, 2007) reports that schools made a concentrated effort to align their curriculum with state standards in the wake of NCLB, thus changing the focus of their curriculum to put greater emphasis on tested content and skills. Many districts also became more prescriptive during this period about what and how teachers were supposed to teach (CEP 2006).

It is worth noting that the costs and benefits of these instructional changes depend on one's objectives and are not always clear even for a given objective. For example, many observers applaud the increasing emphasis on math and reading instruction, while others lament the decreasing attention on subjects such as art and music (Rothstein and others 2008).

Although these studies paint a consistent picture, they need to be interpreted with some caution. All of the research described thus far relies on self-reports from teachers or administrators. Moreover, the information is based on questions that ask respondents to retrospectively assess whether certain practices have changed over time. For this reason, one might be worried about the reliability and validity of the data (Bradburn and Sudman 1988).

Few studies have implemented regression-based research designs that attempt to isolate the effects of school accountability policies on district, school, and classroom practices from the potentially confounding effects of other determinants. One prominent exception is a recent study by Cecilia Elena Rouse and others (2007), which used a regression-discontinuity

---

20. A 2009 Government Accountability Office study based on teacher survey data (and supplemental interviews with state officials) finds that 90 percent of elementary teachers reported no change in instructional time for arts education between 2004–05 and 2006–07. At the same time, a larger fraction of teachers in schools identified as needing improvement under NCLB reported a decline in art instruction, relative to teachers in other schools. This study used data from the Department of Education's National Longitudinal Study of No Child Left Behind (NLS-NCLB).

design and data from surveys of principals in Florida to examine how schools responded to pressure from the state's accountability system. They find that accountability pressure leads to an increased emphasis on low-performing students (through grade retention, summer school, and tutoring, for example), increased overall instructional time, and reorganized school days. They also find suggestive evidence that accountability reduced principal control and increased the resources available to teachers. Furthermore, the school policies influenced by school accountability explain a meaningful fraction of student test-score gains, suggesting that schools responded to accountability pressure in specific ways that improved student achievement.

Although the work just summarized addresses some of the concerns raised in previous work, it has its own set of limitations. It does not address NCLB per se, and it estimates what one might describe as the partial impact of the Florida accountability system, comparing schools more or less affected by accountability pressure. However, it is possible that the accountability system in Florida, or NCLB more generally, led to changes across all schools.

In recent work we present new evidence on these issues using data from the nationally representative Schools and Staffing Survey (SASS) and the state-based CITS research design (Dee, Jacob, and Schwartz 2010). The SASS is a nationally representative survey of teachers and school administrators that has been conducted periodically since the early 1990s (in 1994, 2000, 2004, and 2008).[21] We use teacher responses from the survey to construct a variety of measures of classroom instruction and school organization. These data allow us to compare changes in teacher responses over time rather than rely on the teachers' retrospective judgments. They also provide more objective measures of some of the constructs: for example, the time-use questions ask about the actual number of hours per week a teacher devotes to math, rather than asking teachers to characterize their emphasis on math as "big" or "small" or whether it is greater or less than it was a certain number of years ago.

---

21. Because the pooled SASS data contain data from only two pre-NCLB periods, Dee, Jacob, and Schwartz (2010) also examined the robustness of the SASS-based models to the use of conventional difference-in-differences specifications. The results were quite similar to the CITS results, with the modest exception of one result discussed below. That paper also presents falsification exercises similar to those presented for the NAEP and F-33 models, the results of which generally suggest that the CITS specification based on the SASS data generates internally valid estimates.

Figure 7. School Resources by Timing of Increased School Accountability, 1994–2008

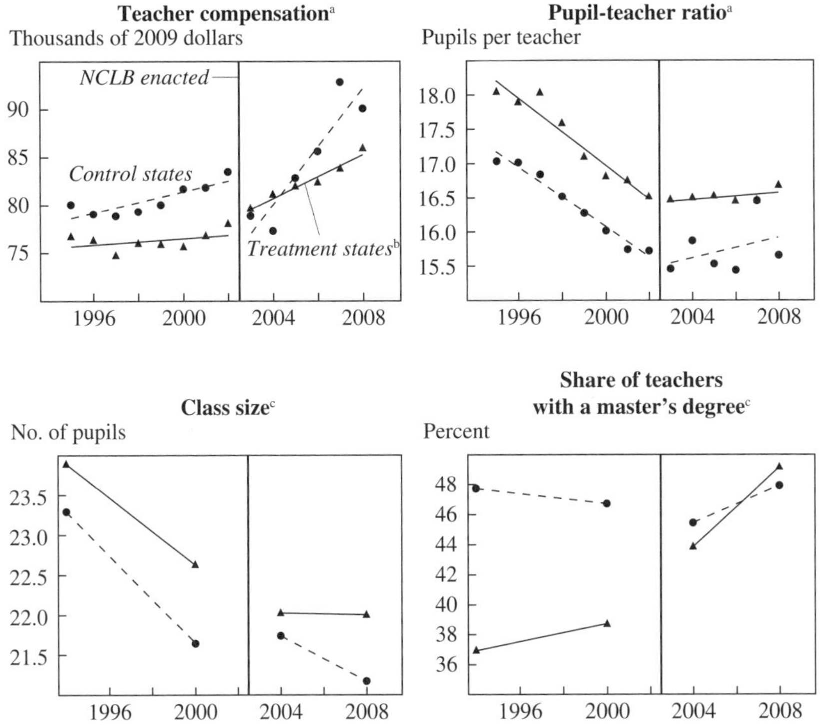

Teacher compensation[a]
Thousands of 2009 dollars

Pupil-teacher ratio[a]
Pupils per teacher

Class size[c]
No. of pupils

Share of teachers with a master's degree[c]
Percent

Source: Authors' calculations using data from the Common Core of Data (top panels) and the Schools and Staffing Survey (bottom panels).

a. Sample is composed of all noncharter, unifed local education agency school districts, excluding Hawaii, the District of Columbia, and zero-enrollment districts. Estimates are weighted by district enrollment. Teacher compensation includes the value of noncash employee benefits.

b. Treatment and control states are defined as in figure 4.

c. Sample consists of full-time elementary- and middle-school teachers with a main assignment in mathematics, English language arts, or general elementary instruction.

The top left panel of figure 7 shows the comparative trends in real teacher compensation by year across treatment and control states. As in the previous figures, we show the trends separately for states that did and did not adopt school accountability programs before NCLB. These district-level data indicate that, after the introduction of NCLB, average annual teacher compensation increased distinctly, from roughly $75,000 to over $80,000, in states that did not have prior school accountability. However, this graph also suggests an NCLB effect: this compensation growth was particularly large relative to the corresponding changes in states that had school accountability regimes before NCLB. The bottom right panel of figure 7 shows changes over time in the fraction of elementary- and middle-school teachers with a master's degree (based on the pooled SASS data) and similarly suggests an NCLB effect. In states with prior accountability programs, roughly 47 percent of teachers had a master's degree in 1994, compared with 37 percent of teachers in other states. Following the introduction of NCLB, the fraction of teachers with a master's degree jumped notably in states without prior accountability, so that in 2004 the rates were approximately equal across both groups of states. By 2008, teachers in states without prior accountability were slightly more likely to have a master's degree than their counterparts in other states. In contrast, the top right and bottom left panels of figure 7 provide no clear indication that NCLB influenced class sizes or pupil-teacher ratios, respectively (see also Dee, Jacob, and Schwartz 2010).

Table 4 presents regression estimates of these effects based on the CITS model in equation 1, adding a variety of controls for teacher, school, and district observed traits (Dee, Jacob, and Schwartz 2010). As above, standard errors are clustered by state. The results indicate that NCLB increased average teacher compensation by over $5,000, or by roughly 8 percent relative to the pre-NCLB mean of $79,577. The table also indicates that by 2008, NCLB had increased the fraction of teachers with a master's degree by roughly 0.056, from a baseline of 0.41, an increase of roughly 14 percent. Given that many districts require teachers to have a master's degree for permanent certification, it is possible that this effect reflects the response of states to the NCLB provision requiring schools to have "highly qualified" teachers in every classroom. The fact that states with prior accountability policies also had a substantially larger fraction of teachers with a master's degree suggests that programs adopted by states before NCLB may have contained some provisions regarding teacher qualifications.

The top right and bottom left panels of figure 8 show trends in time use for our sample of elementary-school teachers and principals for states that did and those that did not adopt school accountability programs before NCLB. The top right panel shows the amount of instructional time (in hours per week) that teachers report for core academic subjects. The bottom left panel shows the fraction of time during the week that self-contained teachers (those who provide instruction in multiple subjects to a single group of students) teach math and ELA, where the denominator is total time spent on the four core subjects (math, ELA,

Table 4. Estimated Effects of NCLB on School Resources, Allocation of Instructional Time, and Educational Climate

Dependent variable	Mean for 1999–2000 school year	Estimated impact of NCLB[a]
School resources		
Teacher compensation (dollars)[b]	79,577	5,067*
	(20,338)	(2,888)
Pupil-teacher ratio[b]	16.986	–0.151
	(2.692)	(0.491)
Class size	22.120	–0.328
	(4.990)	(0.500)
Fraction of teachers with master's degree	0.412	0.056**
	(0.492)	(0.028)
Instructional time		
Hours per week spent on core academic subjects[c]	21.758	–0.307
	(6.445)	(0.684)
Fraction of total hours spent on math and English	0.737	0.036***
	(0.130)	(0.012)
Fraction of total hours spent on English	0.476	0.023*
	(0.156)	(0.013)
Educational climate		
Fraction of schools where principal places highest priority on academic excellence or basic skill acquisition	0.875	–0.003
	(0.331)	(0.037)
Teachers' perceptions of school discipline	–0.003	0.074
	(0.989)	(0.115)
Teachers' perceptions of student engagement	0.059	0.220***
	(0.990)	(0.056)

Source: Authors' regressions.

a. Each reported coefficient is from a separate regression and identifies the effect of NCLB as of 2008. See table 1 and the text for details. Except where noted otherwise, estimates use pooled data from the Schools and Staffing Survey. Standard deviations or standard errors clustered by state are in parentheses. Asterisks indicate statistical significance at the ***1 percent, **5 percent, or *10 percent level.

b. Estimates use data from the Common Core of Data's Local Education Agency (School District) Finance Survey from the National Center for Education Statistics. Teacher compensation includes the value of noncash employee benefits.

c. Mathematics, English language arts, social studies, and science.

social studies, and science). The bottom right panel of the figure shows this ratio for ELA alone.

These figures suggest that NCLB did *not* lead to meaningful increases in the total amount of instructional time devoted to core subjects, but that instructional time allocated to math and ELA increased following the introduction of NCLB. Moreover, the effects seem to be larger in states that had not previously instituted school accountability, consistent with NCLB leading to this change.

Figure 8. School Allocation of Time, by Timing of Increased School Accountability, 1994–2008

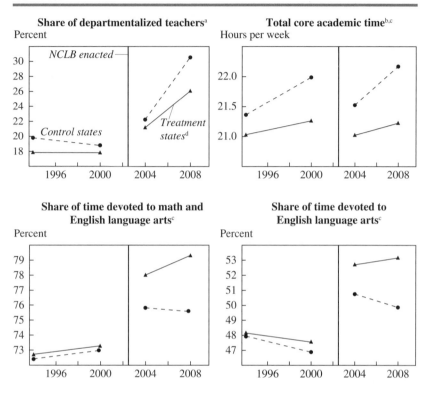

Source: Authors' calculations using data from the Schools and Staffing Survey.
a. Departmentalized teachers (those who instruct several classes of different students, usually in the same subject) as a share of all (departmentalized, self-contained, and team) teachers.
b. Time devoted to mathematics, English language arts, social studies, and science.
c. Sample consists of classes taught by self-contained and team teachers only.
d. Treatment and control states are defined as in figure 4.

Estimates reported in the middle panel of table 4 indicate that NCLB increased the fraction of time that teachers spend on math and ELA by 3.6 percentage points, relative to a baseline of 74 percent. This implies an additional 45 minutes per week of math and ELA instruction by teachers who spend 20 instructional hours on these two subjects. It appears that this increase was driven primarily by an increase in time devoted to ELA: table 4 indicates that NCLB increased the share of instructional time devoted to ELA by a weakly significant 2.3 percentage points. In contrast, we do not find that NCLB had statistically significant effects on the fraction of time devoted to math. This is particularly interesting given that we find substantial achievement effects in math but not in reading.

III.C. Impacts on School Organization, Climate, and Culture

The literature provides some evidence that test-based accountability policies, including NCLB, have spurred other useful changes in school-wide instructional practice. In the RAND study cited above (Hamilton and others 2007), for example, school and district administrators reported that NCLB increased the use of diagnostic assessment (exams used by teachers to determine a student's areas of strength and weakness) as an instructional tool and increased the technical assistance and professional development opportunities offered to schools. In earlier survey work, researchers found that teachers in high-stakes environments found test results more useful, and were more likely to use test information to inform their practice, than colleagues in low-stakes environments (Pedulla and others 2003). Similarly, teachers in the RAND study reported that their state's accountability system under NCLB led them to search for more effective teaching practices and, in nearly all cases, had led to positive changes in their schools (Hamilton and others 2007). Interestingly, for example, teachers reported that teaching practices and the general focus on student learning "changed for the better" under accountability. District officials in the CEP study reported an increase in the use of data to guide instruction (CEP 2006).

Unfortunately, the SASS has not routinely collected data on many of the school and teacher practices that are of interest, and this limits our capacity to isolate the effects of NCLB on some of these outcomes. However, the SASS has collected consistent data on several relevant school-level traits. For example, the principals who responded to the SASS were asked to choose their top three priorities from a list of nine educational goals. The top panel of figure 9 shows the comparative trend data for the share of principals who indicated that either academic excellence or acquisition of basic skills was their top goal. States with and without prior accountability did not converge on this measure of instructional focus after NCLB. This pattern suggests that NCLB did not generate a detectable increase in instructional focus, a result confirmed by the regression results in table 4.

Teachers surveyed in the SASS provided scaled responses to questions about whether principals and fellow teachers enforced rules for student conduct. The middle panel of the figure shows the comparative trends for the standardized responses to this question and suggests the lack of an

Figure 9. School Culture Outcomes by Timing of Increased School Accountability, 1994–2008

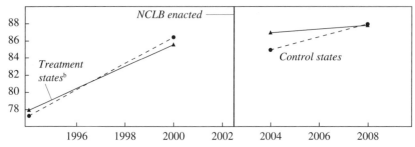

Principals place highest priority on academic excellence or basic skill acquisition[a]
Percent of schools

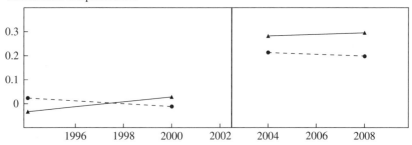

Teachers' perception of school discipline[c]
Standardized composite score[d]

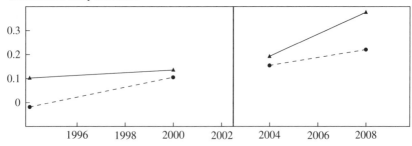

Teachers' perception of student engagement[c]
Standardized composite score

Source: Authors' calculations using data from the Schools and Staffing Survey.
a. Sample is limited to full-time elementary- and middle-school principals.
b. Treatment and control states are defined as in figure 4.
c. Sample is defined as in figure 7.
d. Higher scores indicate greater enforcement of rules or greater engagement.

NCLB effect (again confirmed by the results in table 4). The bottom panel shows the trend data for a standardized measure of how teachers viewed their students' school-relevant behavior and attitudes. This measure, an index of "behavioral engagement" with school, standardized to have a mean of zero and a standard deviation of 1, reflects the extent to which teachers feel that traits such as tardiness, absenteeism, and apathy are not a problem within their school. Here there seems to have been comparative improvement in this measure of student engagement for states that introduced school accountability because of NCLB. The regression results in table 4 indicate that the size of this increase is 0.22 base-year (1994) standard deviation.

This estimated effect on student engagement is over twice as large in high-poverty schools. However, Dee, Jacob, and Schwartz (2010) find that NCLB's estimated effects on this engagement measure are noticeably smaller (an effect size of 0.094) in a difference-in-differences specification, which does not condition on pretreatment trends unique to treatment status. We cannot definitively establish whether the CITS or the difference-in-differences specifications generate more accurate point estimates in this context. However, the differences in pre-NCLB student engagement trends across treatment and control states depicted in figure 9 are consistent with the motivation for the CITS specification. A very different caveat to this result is that NCLB's apparent effect on teacher-reported student engagement could simply be due to policy-induced changes in teacher expectations. For example, to the extent that NCLB increased the expectations for academic achievement in states without prior school accountability policies, it is possible that teachers simultaneously chose to benchmark the behavioral engagement of their students with school against a more lax standard. If this is true, our estimate of the impact on behavioral engagement is biased upward.

III.D. Summary

The evidence presented above suggests that NCLB has had both desirable and undesirable effects on school district spending, teachers, classroom practice, and school culture. Unfortunately, the lack of objective measures for several important instructional practices limits our ability to examine many of the most plausible mechanisms through which accountability may have operated to improve student achievement. Moreover, the analysis here does not allow us to identify which, if any, of the factors we identify as improving (for example, per-pupil spending, student engagement, teacher qualifications, or instruction time devoted to English) might explain the achievement effects we document. Nonetheless, this analysis provides important evidence on the policy-relevant, nonachievement consequences of NCLB (for example, its fiscal effects) as well as guideposts to the intended and unintended ways in which NCLB has shaped the available measures of educational practice.

IV. Conclusions

Eight years have passed since No Child Left Behind dramatically expanded the federal role in public schooling. Given the national scope of the policy, it is difficult to reach definitive conclusions about its impact. Nonetheless, evidence from a variety of data sources utilizing several plausible comparison groups suggests that NCLB has had a positive effect on elementary student performance in mathematics, particularly at the lower grades. The benefits appear to be concentrated among traditionally disadvantaged populations, with particularly large effects among Hispanic students. On the other hand, the existing evidence suggests that NCLB has not had a comparable effect on reading performance.

We find compelling evidence that NCLB increased per-pupil school district expenditure, particularly on direct instruction, a mediating mechanism that may explain the corresponding achievement gains. By 2008, for example, the policy appears to have increased annual spending per pupil by nearly $600 in states that did not have any school accountability program before NCLB; these increased outlays were not supported by corresponding increases in federal revenue. We also presented evidence that these expenditure increases may be modest relative to the present discounted value of the corresponding test-score gains. We also discussed evidence suggesting that NCLB influenced teachers and schools in several potentially important ways. It appears that NCLB has led elementary schools to increase instructional time devoted to math and reading, although the majority of evidence on this point comes from teacher and administrator survey data that are subject to potential bias. Similarly, teachers report that NCLB has encouraged schools to spend time on narrow test preparation activities. However, we also found evidence that NCLB led to increases in teacher-reported measures of students' behavioral engagement with school. Unfortunately, a lack of a richly detailed dataset that lends itself to credible identification strategies makes it difficult to assess whether NCLB influenced curriculum and instructional practices in more fundamental ways.

Nonetheless, the extant body of evidence can provide some guidance to the ongoing debate over the proposed reauthorization of NCLB. In March

2010 the Obama administration released an NCLB "blueprint" that outlined proposed features of a reauthorization (Klein and McNeil 2010). This proposal calls for continued annual reporting of school-level, test-based student assessments but allows for flexibility in how states calculate school effectiveness. The blueprint also calls for the use of nontest accountability indicators, especially measures of college and career readiness (such as attendance, course completion, and school climate). Another potentially critical feature of this proposal involves changing how measures of school performance are linked to consequences.

The blueprint also proposes to give states increased flexibility in how they might intervene in low-performing schools, mandating specific consequences only for the very lowest-performing schools and those with persistently large achievement gaps. It is not clear how states would respond to this added flexibility. However, the literature on pre-NCLB accountability policies suggests that simply reporting accountability measures that were unconnected to explicit consequences did not drive improvements in student achievement (Hanushek and Raymond 2005). This suggests that the targeted achievement gains attributable to NCLB could be at risk under state reforms that decouple performance measures from meaningful consequences.

ACKNOWLEDGMENTS We would like to thank Rob Garlick, Elias Walsh, Nathaniel Schwartz, and Erica Johnson for their research assistance. We would also like to thank Kerwin Charles, Robert Kaestner, Ioana Marinescu, and seminar participants at the Brookings Panel conference, a conference at the Harris School of Public Policy Studies at the University of Chicago, and at the NCLB: Emerging Findings Research Conference at the CALDER Center of the Urban Institute for helpful comments. An earlier version of this work was presented by Brian Jacob as the David N. Kershaw Lecture at the annual meeting of the Association of Public Policy Analysis and Management, November 2008. All errors are our own.

The authors report no relevant conflicts of interest.

References

Ballou, Dale, and Matthew Springer. 2009. "Achievement Trade-offs and No Child Left Behind." Washington: Urban Institute.

Bradburn, Norman M., and Seymour Sudman. 1988. *Polls and Surveys: Understanding What They Tell Us.* San Francisco: Jossey-Bass.

Carnoy, Martin, and Susanna Loeb. 2002. "Does External Accountability Affect Student Outcomes? A Cross-State Analysis." *Educational Evaluation and Policy Analysis* 24, no. 4 (Winter): 305–31.

Center on Education Policy. 2006. *From the Capital to the Classroom: Year 4 of the No Child Left Behind Act.* Washington.

———. 2007. "Choices, Changes, and Challenges: Curriculum and Instruction in the NCLB Era." A report in the series From the Capital to the Classroom: Year 5 of the No Child Left Behind Act. Washington.

———. 2008a. "Instructional Time in Elementary Schools: A Closer Look at Changes for Specific Subjects." A report in the series From the Capital to the Classroom: Year 5 of the No Child Left Behind Act. Washington.

———. 2008b. "Has Student Achievement Increased since 2002? State Test Score Trends through 2006–07." Washington.

Dee, Thomas, and Brian Jacob. Forthcoming. "The Impact of No Child Left Behind on Student Achievement." *Journal of Policy Analysis and Management.*

Dee, Thomas S., Brian A. Jacob, and Nathaniel L. Schwartz. 2010. "The Effect of No Child Left Behind on School Finance, Organization and Practice." Working paper. University of Virginia and University of Michigan.

Figlio, David N., and Helen F. Ladd. 2007. "School Accountability and Student Achievement." In *Handbook of Research in Education Finance and Policy,* edited by Helen F. Ladd and Edward B. Fiske. New York and London: Routledge.

Fuller, Bruce, Joseph Wright, Kathryn Gesicki, and Erin Kang. 2007. "Gauging Growth: How to Judge No Child Left Behind?" *Educational Researcher* 36, no. 5: 268–78.

Goertz, Margaret E., Mark C. Duffy, and Kerstin Carlson Le Floch. 2001. "Assessment and Accountability Systems in the 50 States: 1999–2000." CPRE Research Report no. RR-046. Philadelphia: Consortium for Policy Research in Education.

Hamilton, Laura S., Brian M. Stecher, Julie A. Marsh, Jennifer Sloan McCombs, Abby Robyn, Jennifer Lin Russell, Scott Naftel, and Heather Barney. 2007. *Standards-Based Accountability under No Child Left Behind: Experiences of Teachers and Administrators in Three States.* Santa Monica, Calif.: RAND Corporation.

Hannaway, Jane, and Laura Hamilton. 2008. "Performance-Based Accountability Policies: Implications for School and Classroom Practices." Washington: Urban Institute and RAND Corporation.

Hannaway, Jane, and Maggie Stanislawski. 2005. "Responding to Reform: Florida School Expenditures in the 1990s." Urban Institute and Colorado State University.

Hannaway, Jane, Shannon McKay, and Yasser Nakib. 2002. "Reform and Resource Allocation: National Trends and State Policies." In *Developments in School Finance, 1999–2000*, edited by William J. Fowler Jr. Washington: U.S. Department of Education, National Center for Education Statistics.

Hanushek, Eric A., and Margaret E. Raymond. 2001. "The Confusing World of Educational Accountability." *National Tax Journal* 54, no. 2: 365–84.

———. 2005. "Does School Accountability Lead to Improved Student Performance?" *Journal of Policy Analysis and Management* 24, no. 2: 297–327.

Hoxby, Caroline M. 2002. "The Cost of Accountability." In *School Accountability*, edited by Williamson M. Evers and Herbert J. Walberg. Stanford, Calif.: Hoover Institution Press.

Jacob, Brian A. 2005. "Accountability, Incentives and Behavior: The Impact of High-Stakes Testing in the Chicago Public Schools." *Journal of Public Economics* 89, no. 5–6: 761–96.

Jacob, Brian A., and Steven D. Levitt. 2003. "Rotten Apples: An Investigation of the Prevalence and Predictors of Teacher Cheating." *Quarterly Journal of Economics* 118, no. 3: 843–77.

Klein, Alyson, and Michele McNeil. 2010. "Administration Unveils ESEA Reauthorization Blueprint." *Education Week* (March 17).

Koretz, Daniel. 2008. *Measuring Up: What Educational Testing Really Tells Us*. Harvard University Press.

Koretz, Daniel M., and Laura S. Hamilton. 2006. "Testing for Accountability in K-12." In *Educational Measurement*, 4th ed., edited by Robert L. Brennan. Westport, Conn.: American Council on Education/Praeger.

Koretz, Daniel M., Sheila Barron, Karen J. Mitchell, and Brian M. Stecher. 1996. *The Perceived Effects of the Kentucky Instructional Results Information System (KIRIS)*. MR-792-PCT/FF. Santa Monica, Calif.: RAND Corporation.

Krieg, John M. 2008. "Are Students Left Behind? The Distributional Effects of the No Child Left Behind Act." *Education Finance and Policy* 3, no. 2: 250–81.

Krueger, Alan B. 2003. "Economic Considerations and Class Size." *Economic Journal* 113: F34–F63.

Ladd, Helen F. 2007. "Holding Schools Accountable Revisited." 2007 Spencer Foundation Lecture in Education Policy and Management. Washington: Association for Public Policy Analysis and Management. www.appam.org/awards/pdf/2007Spencer-Ladd.pdf (accessed November 8, 2009).

Ladd, Helen F., and Arnaldo Zelli. 2002. "School Based Accountability in North Carolina: The Responses of School Principals." *Education Administration Quarterly* 38, no. 4: 494–529.

Lee, Jaekyung, and Kenneth K. Wong. 2004. "The Impact of Accountability on Racial and Socioeconomic Equity: Considering Both School Resources and Achievement Outcomes." *American Educational Research Journal* 41, no. 4: 797–832.

Neal, Derek, and Diane Whitmore Schanzenbach. 2010. "Left Behind by Design: Proficiency Counts and Test-Based Accountability." *Review of Economics and Statistics* 92, no. 2: 263–83.

Palmer, Scott R., and Arthur L. Coleman. 2003. "The No Child Left Behind Act of 2001: Summary of NCLB Requirements and Deadlines for State Action." Washington: Council of Chief State School Officers (November). events. ccsso.org/content/pdfs/Deadlines.pdf (accessed November 13, 2009).

Pedulla, Joseph J., Lisa M. Abrams, George F. Madaus, Michael K. Russell, Miguel A. Ramos, and Jing Miao. 2003. *Perceived Effects of State-Mandated Testing Programs on Teaching and Learning: Findings from a National Survey of Teachers.* Chestnut Hill, Mass.: National Board on Educational Testing and Public Policy.

Reback, Randall, Jonah E. Rockoff, and Heather L. Schwartz. 2010. "The Effects of No Child Left Behind on School Services and Student Outcomes." Working paper. Barnard College and Columbia University.

Rothstein, Richard, Rebecca Jacobsen, and Tamara Wilder. 2008. "Grading Education: Getting Accountability Right." New York: Teachers College Press.

Rouse, Cecilia Elena, Jane Hannaway, Dan Goldhaber, and David Figlio. 2007. "Feeling the Florida Heat? How Low-Performing Schools Respond to Voucher and Accountability Pressure." Cambridge, Mass.: National Bureau of Economic Research.

Stecher, Brian M., Sheila Barron, Tessa Kaganoff, and Joy Goodwin. 1998. "The Effects of Standards-Based Assessment on Classroom Practices: Results of the 1996–97 RAND Survey of Kentucky Teachers of Mathematics and Writing." CSE Technical Report 482. National Center for Research on Evaluation, Standards, and Student Testing, University of California, Los Angeles.

Stullich, Stephanie, Elizabeth Eisner, Joseph McCrary, and Collette Roney. 2006. *National Assessment of Title I Interim Report to Congress,* Vol. I: *Implementation of Title I.* Washington: U.S. Department of Education, Institute of Education Sciences.

Taylor, Grace, Lorrie Shepard, Freya Kinner, and Justin Rosenthal. 2003. "A Survey of Teachers' Perspectives on High-Stakes Testing in Colorado: What Gets Taught, What Gets Lost." CSE Technical Report 588. National Center for Research on Evaluation, Standards, and Student Testing, University of California, Los Angeles.

U.S. Department of Education, Office of Planning, Evaluation and Policy Development, Policy and Program Studies Service. 2007. "Private School Participants in Federal Programs under the No Child Left Behind Act and the Individuals with Disabilities Education Act: Private School and Public School District Perspectives." Washington.

U.S. Government Accountability Office. 2009. "Access to Arts Education." Report to Congressional Requesters. GAO-09-286. Washington (February).

Wong, Manyee, Thomas D. Cook, and Peter M. Steiner. 2009. "No Child Left Behind: An Interim Evaluation of Its Effects on Learning Using Two Interrupted Time Series Each with Its Own Non-Equivalent Comparison Series." Working Paper no. WP-09-11. Institute for Policy Research, Northwestern University.

Comments and Discussion

COMMENT BY
CAROLINE M. HOXBY   Thomas Dee and Brian Jacob provide a review of existing empirical studies on how No Child Left Behind (NCLB) has affected student achievement. They also present original findings based on a difference-in-differences comparison of states that implemented school accountability only with NCLB and those that had implemented it previously. The difference-in-differences work relies on test scores from the National Assessment of Educational Progress (NAEP), the only examination regularly administered to samples of students representative of each state.

In their review of existing studies, Dee and Jacob concisely, yet accurately, summarize the most credible research on NCLB and the state accountability laws that preceded it. Much of the existing evidence is lacking in rigor or partial in nature, and the authors do an excellent job of differentiating between stronger and weaker results. However, Dee and Jacob's difference-in-differences work is the meat of their paper, and thus these comments focus on it.

Of all the areas within education in which the federal government plays a role, that in primary and secondary education is by far the most minor. Whereas each of the states has a responsibility for education written into its constitution and has a long history of financing and overseeing education, the federal government has traditionally confined itself to funding a small percentage of the education of poor and disabled students and those with limited knowledge of English. At no time before the Obama administration did the federal government account for more than 10 percent of public spending on primary and secondary education, and it has no formal role in the governance of any regular public school. Simply put, the federal government is a very junior partner in education policy; states and local school districts occupy the driver's seat.

This structure of financing and control has two important implications for all federal education policy. First, it is state governments and large school districts that set the pace and frontier in education policy. Second, the federal government has little ability to enforce its policy will: even when federal law mandates some education policy, it is states and districts that must implement it. And they are quite capable of implementing only the letter of the law, and none of its intent. These two implications are glaringly obvious in the history of NCLB.

Starting in the late 1980s, a number of states began to enact laws designed to hold their schools accountable for overall student outcomes. They instituted mandatory statewide exams and published the results prominently in the media and in "school report cards" sent to parents. They devised grading systems for their schools, which gave better grades to schools with higher test scores and graduation rates. The more sophisticated state grading systems incorporated value-added calculations for schools based on test scores, regression adjustments for sociodemographics, and weights on a variety of complex outcomes beyond scores. Schools that earned poor grades experienced interventions, sometimes welcome and sometimes not, from state departments of education. Chronically failing schools were reconstituted by some states. The states that led the accountability movement created powerful databases that allowed them to track students and teachers longitudinally, certified teachers through nontraditional routes (such as proficiency testing), rewarded teachers and schools they deemed successful, and established very modest forms of school choice.

The accountability movement was led by an informal but like-minded group of governors and chief state school officers, prominent among whom were Governor George W. Bush of Texas and Governor Jeb Bush of Florida. Both Bushes would later point to education accountability as their main legacy to the states they governed. Thus, it should come as no surprise that when NCLB was drafted as one of the first major policies of the George W. Bush presidency, the first draft looked a lot like Texas' and Florida's accountability policies. The final version, however, was a very dilute law, reflecting numerous political compromises and the federal government's negligible powers of enforcement.

NCLB was written in such a way that states antagonistic to school accountability could easily evade every aspect of the law. For instance, by choosing a test on which nearly all students did well from the start, a state could ensure that all its schools met the proficiency standard and thereby escaped all consequences of failure. (One state, Nebraska, got away with choosing no statewide test at all.) A state could comply with NCLB's reporting provisions by putting its school report cards on an obscure website with little or no functionality. Some websites deliberately prevented parents and journalists from comparing schools' reports. States could ensure that all their teachers met the "highly qualified" mandates of NCLB, which were meant to ensure subject area knowledge, simply by setting standards that automatically made all their existing teachers "highly qualified." For instance, some states declared all teachers who were experienced or certified to be highly qualified regardless of their proficiency or area of teaching. Districts that wished to evade the (very modest) school choice provisions of NCLB could refrain from notifying parents that their children were eligible to transfer to another public school and from telling parents that they could use their federal dollars for private tutoring services.

In short, NCLB was a peculiar law. It could have little effect on states antagonistic to school accountability. Rather, it was a nudge to states that supported accountability enough to welcome a nudge but not enough to have enacted accountability before NCLB. States that had already adopted pro-accountability measures viewed NCLB as a drag on their more ambitious, more sophisticated policies. For instance, Jeb Bush's Florida wrestled with the U.S. Department of Education, trying to get waivers from the federal school grading system, which was manifestly inferior to its own. Several states, especially Massachusetts, argued that NCLB gave them strong incentives to reduce the quality of their tests.

This is the backdrop to Dee and Jacob's analysis, and it is one that causes their difference-in-differences estimates to be quite unreliable. Their estimates almost certainly understate the effects in which policymakers are interested. My logic on this has three different components. First, Dee and Jacob's "control" states did not hold their policies constant, and so do not amount to true counterfactuals. Second, NCLB could be expected to have heterogeneous treatment effects depending on a state's willingness to implement it, and the difference-in-differences analysis does not account for this. Third, policymakers are interested in population-average effects, which the difference-in-differences analysis substantially understates. Let me take each of these in turn.

Dee and Jacob describe as "treated by NCLB" those states that had no school accountability program before the 2001 law. Their "control" states are those that had implemented their own accountability programs before 2001. Their difference-in-differences method identifies the effects of NCLB by comparing the pre-versus-post-NCLB achievement change in treated states with the pre-versus-post achievement change in control states. There are a few more details to the equation they estimate, but this comparison is the key to their identification strategy.

In a credible difference-in-differences exercise, the control states must reveal what would have occurred in the treated states had NCLB not been enacted. This they do not do in the Dee and Jacob exercise. The control states are the pro-accountability states that had already enacted more ambitious programs than NCLB and that continued to extend and improve their programs in the wake of its enactment. These states rolled out improved school grading systems, estimated the value added of individual teachers, and instituted rewards for individual students to excel (such as scholarships) and remedies for students who did not (such as summer school and grade retention). Many of the control states actually increased accountability more in the immediate aftermath of NCLB than did the treated states. Thus, the control states' achievement reflects not only the lagged effects of their pre-NCLB policies (since student achievement reacts gradually to policy) but also the effects of their post-NCLB increases in accountability. This makes the control states a very poor counterfactual for the treated states, most of which would have enacted no or only weak accountability programs had NCLB not existed. There is no guarantee that removing the pre-NCLB trend in the achievement of control states, as Dee and Jacob do, fixes the difference-in-differences strategy: such a fix would work only if the control states' pre- and post-NCLB policy changes just happened to produce a constant rate of change in achievement. This is possible but seems unlikely. Since the dynamics of how achievement reacts to accountability are unknown, one cannot even say whether removing a linear time trend over- or understates the true counterfactual.

Difference-in-differences strategies estimate a treatment effect that is local to the sort of states being "treated." If the effect of the NCLB was heterogeneous, which it surely was given states' variation in enthusiasm for implementing the law, the analysis requires treatment and control groups that are balanced in terms of their susceptibility to the treatment. Otherwise, the estimated effect does not reveal the population-average effect, which is largely what interests policymakers. That is, policymakers wish to know what the effect of NCLB would be in a state of average enthusiasm. Few if any policymakers have voiced a wish to know the effect of NCLB on *just* those states that balked at implementing accountability. Although a local effect of this kind might be interesting to a few people, it is not what policymakers think they are getting when they ask what the effect of school accountability is. In practice, estimation of a

COMMENTS and DISCUSSION

treatment effect that is local to the balky states almost certainly substantially understates the population-average effect. It is the econometrician's responsibility to insist that readers *not* interpret a local treatment effect as a population-average one when it is clear that the control and treatment groups were poorly balanced in terms of susceptibility to treatment.

In my experience, what interests voters is not even the population-average treatment effect that NCLB would have had. What interests them is the effect of a school accountability policy when implemented fairly faithfully by leaders who believe in it. The voters' choice is between, on the one hand, candidates who run on a platform of accountability and who would therefore attempt to implement it as intended, and on the other, candidates who run against accountability and would not implement it. So far, we have seen no candidates declare that they will implement an accountability program in a way that deliberately evades its intention.

Before summing up, I must say something about the mismatch between the empirical strategy the authors describe and the equation they use to implement it, which is

$$Y_{st} = \beta_0 + \beta_1 YEAR_t + \beta_2 NCLB_t + \beta_3 (YR\_SINCE\_NCLB_t) \\ + \beta_4 (T_s \times YEAR_t) + \beta_5 (T_s \times NCLB_t) \\ + \beta_6 (T_s \times YR\_SINCE\_NCLB_t) + \beta_7 \mathbf{X}_{st} + \mu_s + \varepsilon_{st}.$$

The authors describe their empirics in terms of *dosage:* essentially, they want to allow states that had no accountability program before NCLB to get the "full dose" of the 2001 law. They want to allow states that had already taken a full dose of accountability before 2001 to get little or nothing out of the law. This is reasonable as an explanation, but it suggests that they will measure dosage by indicators of the degree to which the state had already, by 2001, implemented the key features of NCLB (statewide testing, publication of school grades in report cards, highly qualified teachers, modest forms of school choice). One might also include enthusiasm for implementation as part of a state's dosage calculation.

Unfortunately, the estimating equation proxies dosage with T_s, the number of years a state was without school accountability between the 1991–92 academic year and the onset of NCLB. That is, the authors posit that dosage was linear in year of implementation, so that if a state's accountability program was implemented one year earlier, its NCLB dosage decreases by one unit. This specification does not match up with reality. First, states that implemented accountability earlier did not consistently have more ambitious accountability laws. For instance, most commentators would rate

Florida's program as easily the most ambitious, but it was not implemented until 1999–2000, making it a later-than-average implementer among the control states. Second, making the dose linear in year of implementation is very restrictive—so restrictive that the estimating equation is not plausibly eliminating differences in preexisting trends for control states based on their true dosage, which we have seen is crucial for avoiding bias in the difference-in-differences estimates. It would be preferable to have a proxy for dosage that is actually based on measures of the variety and stringency of the policies implemented.

NCLB, like most laws implemented nationwide, is very difficult to evaluate because no natural control group exists. What one would need to evaluate it perfectly is a "twin" United States without the law. Not having such a twin at their disposal, Dee and Jacob make a valiant effort to assess the effect of NCLB on student achievement. However, what they end up estimating is, even under the very optimistic assumption that their controls for preexisting trends and dosage work perfectly, an unusual parameter: the effect of school accountability on states that balk at implementing such laws and can evade them fairly easily. This effect may interest some, but it understates the effect that school accountability has with an average degree of rigor in implementation and probably greatly understates the effect with faithful implementation.

COMMENT BY

HELEN F. LADD Determining how the 2002 reauthorization of the federal Elementary and Secondary Education Act, commonly called No Child Left Behind (NCLB), has affected students, teachers, and schools poses a significant challenge because the program was implemented in all states at the same time. The most straightforward approaches, such as comparing trends in test scores before and after the introduction of NCLB, or comparing trends in the United States with those in other countries, generate conclusions that are at best suggestive because of the potential for confounding changes.

This paper by Thomas Dee and Brian Jacob makes an important contribution to the literature on NCLB. The authors have made a creative and valiant, if not completely successful, effort to use an innovative strategy to investigate the effects of NCLB not only on test scores but also on a number of mediating mechanisms such as spending and instructional practices. The authors' main conclusions are that NCLB generated some positive gains in mathematics, especially among disadvantaged fourth-graders, but

COMMENTS and DISCUSSION   201

no gains in reading, and that it induced higher state and local spending and a shift of attention toward math and reading within schools. These conclusions are generally plausible. At the same time, however, some perplexing timing patterns emerge that deserve further attention. In general, a stronger framing and a richer discussion of the policy implications would have made an excellent paper even more useful to the current policy debate.

THE STUDY DESIGN—AND A PERPLEXING FINDING FOR FOURTH-GRADE MATH. Central to the paper is the authors' interpretation of which states received the NCLB "treatment." Their innovation is to include in the treatment group only those states that did not have a prior, state-level accountability system at the time NCLB was introduced. The control group is then composed of the states that were early adopters of accountability systems, and the authors pay appropriate attention to when precisely these systems were adopted. The underlying logic is clear: only in states without existing accountability systems similar to that of NCLB would the introduction of NCLB represent a new treatment. Although this strategy is creative, it is not immune from criticism. Among my concerns are that the authors may have overstated the similarity of NCLB and the pre-NCLB accountability systems in many of the control states, and that in the post-NCLB period, such states may have responded to NCLB in ways that would render their outcome trends less than ideal measures of what the trends would have looked like in the treatment states in the absence of NCLB. (As an aside, I also wonder why the authors did not apply their treatment logic to their comparison of test scores between public schools and Catholic schools over time.) In any case, the authors' main analytical strategy is plausible—and better than most alternative approaches—but not perfect.

Using this strategy, the authors find the strongest test score gains for fourth-graders in math. The authors' analysis of test results is based on scores on the National Assessment of Educational Progress (NAEP), which is appropriate because the low stakes on this test make the scores far less subject to manipulation through teaching to the test than would be the case with the states' own high-stakes tests. The reliance on NAEP scores, however, means the authors are working with a small dataset: it includes only 39 states that had NAEP scores both before and after NCLB, and only a few years of data because the tests are not given every year. Their figure 4 shows a very big jump in fourth-grade NAEP scores from 2000 to 2003 in the treatment group relative to the control group, as well as some differential increase in the growth rates over time, and these patterns are confirmed by the authors' regression analysis. Such a large jump over that period seems highly implausible to me, however, given that 2003, which represents the 2002–03 school year, is the first year after the introduction of NCLB.

More framing is needed to help the reader evaluate the plausibility of this big jump and to provide more of a foundation for the rest of the paper. One perspective is that the accountability mechanism of NCLB was simply intended to reduce teacher shirking. Such a view is consistent with the brief principal-agent framing that the authors provide early in the paper. Within the context of such a perspective, teachers could conceivably raise student achievement quite quickly. Once teachers are put on notice that they are accountable for student test scores, for example, they might immediately stop shirking, and test scores might quickly rise. An alternative view is that NCLB is best interpreted as a catalyst for a variety of changes that may ultimately raise test scores but not immediately. Such changes might include, for example, increased state and local spending, more professional development for teachers, changes in instructional processes, or shifts in school schedules so that teachers can devote more effort to the tested subjects. All of these changes are likely to take some time to play out. This catalytic view is consistent with other findings in the paper, including, for example, the finding that states raised spending, but it is inconsistent with the empirical finding of a big gain in fourth-grade math scores in the first year of the program.

Two other considerations are also relevant to the expected timing of any effects. To the extent that education is a cumulative process, learning in fourth grade, for example, depends in part on how much children learned in earlier grades. For that reason, even if the teachers in the early grades understand the importance of their teaching for student test scores in subsequent grades and respond to NCLB by changing their practices in positive ways, it would take some time for those changes to show up in the achievement levels of fourth-graders. Moreover, the complexity of the implementation process should also have led to delayed effects on test scores. In response to NCLB, many states phased in the required testing and set up requirements in a way that backloaded the gains necessary to meet the 2013–14 proficiency goal, and sanctions were designed to be minimal at first and to increase over time. Such timing considerations make me suspicious of the estimated early gains in fourth-grade math test scores that emerge from Dee and Jacob's estimation strategy. Instead I would have expected at most very small effects in the initial year, with the effects increasing over time.

INTERPRETING THE MAGNITUDES. Even if we accept Dee and Jacob's estimates of the NCLB effects on test scores, it is reasonable to ask how one

Table 1. Gains in NAEP Test Scores in Massachusetts and Dee and Jacob's Estimated Effects of NCLB
Score points

	Fourth grade	Eighth grade
	Mathematics	
Massachusetts		
Average score, 2000	233	279
Average score, 2007	252	298
Change	+19	+19
National NCLB effect (Dee and Jacob)	+7.2	+3.7 (NS)[a]
	Reading	
Massachusetts		
Average score, 1998	223	269
Average score, 2007	236	273
Change	+13	+4
National NCLB effect (Dee and Jacob)	+2.3 (NS)	−2.1 (NS)

Sources: National Center for Education Statistics; Dee and Jacob, this volume, table 1.
a. NS = not statistically significant.

should interpret the magnitudes. The answer the authors themselves give is that the fourth-grade math effects are large enough to be policy relevant. They note, for example, that the estimated average gain of 7.2 scale points is about 24 percent of the black-white gap (but why that is a relevant comparison is not clear in this context), and that the gains for Hispanics relative to those for whites imply a 19 percent reduction in the Hispanic-white gap. An alternative, policy-motivated answer is that the gains are tiny relative to the gains needed to get all fourth-graders to 100 percent proficiency.

A third possible answer is that the effects are small relative to what might have been possible with an alternative, more comprehensive policy. This answer is given support by my table 1, which compares gains in NAEP scores in Massachusetts between 2000 and 2007 with the average NCLB "effect" estimated by Dee and Jacob on fourth- and eighth-grade math and reading scores. I have selected Massachusetts for the comparison because of the ambitiousness of its 1993 reform package and its highly touted success in raising test scores. The table shows that Dee and Jacob's estimated NCLB effects are far smaller than the actual gains achieved in Massachusetts. The estimated 7-point NCLB effect in fourth-grade math falls far short of the 19-point gain in Massachusetts, and the statistically insignificant 3.3-point effect in eighth-grade math is even further below the corresponding (also 19-point) gain in Massachusetts. In reading, Massachusetts experienced gains at both grade levels, whereas the NCLB effects are statistically indistinguishable from zero.

The nature of the Massachusetts reform package provides a possible explanation for the different patterns. In contrast to the NCLB reform, which was narrowly focused on test-based accountability, accountability was only one small part of a far more comprehensive reform effort in Massachusetts. This state's reform package included a substantial increase in funding (more than doubling in 10 years), new learning standards, revised student assessments based on clear curriculum frameworks, revised teacher licensing and professional development programs, and early childhood programs, as well as parental choice and the creation of new charter schools. Such a package is far closer to what in the education literature has been called standards-based reform than what was implemented under NCLB. Although NCLB is an outgrowth of the standards movement at the national level, it in fact incorporates only one part—the accountability part—of what was intended to be a far more positive, constructive, and comprehensive approach to raising the achievement of all students.

CONCLUSION AND IMPLICATIONS FOR POLICY. I draw several conclusions from Dee and Jacob's paper. First, any effects of NCLB on test scores are small at best. The positive effect of NCLB on average math scores that emerges from this study occurs too soon relative to what might have been reasonably predicted, and for that reason may be overstated. Moreover, even the reported effects are small relative to what Massachusetts has shown to be feasible. Further, whether there are positive effects on eighth-grade math is not clear, and no effects on reading emerge at either grade level. This latter fact is reported in the paper, but its implications are not discussed. On a brighter note, there may be some positive effects for black students in fourth-grade (although not in eighth-grade) math and for Hispanic students in math at both grade levels.

Among the authors' other findings is that NCLB appears to have induced additional state and local spending on education. My interpretation of this finding is that there is no free lunch. Stated differently, it is a mistake to believe that accountability systems can, by themselves and without associated funding, generate gains in student achievement. In addition, as most policy analysts would have predicted, NCLB appears to have shifted attention and resources away from other subjects toward math and reading. The thorny question, but one that an empirical study of this type cannot answer, is whether that shift is desirable or undesirable.

So what do such findings imply for policy? The answer is not fully clear, but my take differs quite sharply from the thoughts the authors present in the final section of the paper. First, the null findings for reading indicate to me that to the extent that higher reading scores are an important goal for the country, NCLB is clearly not the right approach. That raises the obvious follow-up question: what is? One possible answer, but one that goes far beyond the subject of this paper, is that policymakers need to pay attention to what goes on outside of schools as well as within schools. A second policy conclusion arises from the suggestive evidence that I have included here on Massachusetts, namely, that states may be in a better position to promote student achievement than the federal government. That raises the question of how the federal government can best encourage the states to engage in significant comprehensive reform efforts. My reading of Dee and Jacob's paper is that NCLB is far from the best approach for the federal government to pursue.

GENERAL DISCUSSION Brian Knight observed that although limited information is available on the paper's control group, the analysis would be improved by making the control and treatment groups as comparable as the data allow. He wondered whether there was any additional variation that could be exploited in choosing these groups. Knight was also struck by the reported increase in spending per pupil after NCLB and was curious whether there were heterogeneous effects, particularly at the state and local levels. He was interested in knowing more about the incidence of the spending increase, and in particular whether it fell mostly on state taxpayers or was paid for by cutting back other state spending.

Christopher Jencks found one of the paper's results, the effect of NCLB on fourth-grade mathematics scores in the first year of the policy change, to be implausibly large. Although math scores should have increased during this period, for the result to be convincing it was necessary to rule out other causes, such as differences in the content of the test over time. James Hines, however, found the results on fourth-grade math scores plausible and argued that it was not necessary to impose a linear trend.

Kristin Forbes found the different observed impacts of NCLB on math and reading scores interesting and wondered whether there was any theory that would have predicted this difference. Have any other countries undertaken similar reforms and observed this type of differential effect? An analysis of why NCLB has had a stronger impact on math than on reading could be important in understanding how NCLB has worked and what other types of educational reforms are likely to be the most effective.

Erik Hurst wondered what the proper way to specify the production function for human capital would be in this context. He was also interested in the effects of NCLB on other outcomes besides test scores, such as graduation rates and the incomes of graduates.

Caroline Hoxby spoke in defense of NCLB, noting that the law was intended to be similar to those previously implemented in reformist states. She thought most people would like to know what would have been the effect of NCLB on the average state—that is, on a state that had a typical amount of enthusiasm for implementing school accountability. This effect could be approximated by averaging two estimates: first, the estimated effect of school accountability laws in states that implemented them before NCLB (the enthusiastic implementer effect), and second, the estimated effect of NCLB in states that had no accountability law before NCLB (the unenthusiastic implementer effect). She observed further that math and reading are very different subjects, and that math is almost entirely taught at school whereas parents have a much bigger impact on reading, so that the disparate effects of NCLB on the two subjects were plausible.

Annette Vissing-Jorgensen noted that migration rates have differed across booms and recessions. These could affect the results for the impact of NCLB among Hispanic students. She also wondered about possible cohort effects, noting that such an effect could be occurring in the math results presented in the paper's figure 4. Students included at any year in the top panel would enter the bottom panel 4 years later.

Christopher Jencks agreed with the authors that NCLB is difficult to evaluate statistically since it was implemented all at once. However, some states set the standard for student proficiency quite high, so many students would have to learn more for a school's performance to be judged acceptable, while other states set low standards so that relatively few students would have to learn more for a school's performance to be judged acceptable. One would expect NCLB to have less of an impact in states where schools did not have to improve most students' performance. On the difference in results between math and reading, given that kids do not learn math on their own before going to school, as Hoxby had noted, one might have expected that family background would have more of an effect on reading than on math, but that prediction does not hold up in the authors' results.

Helen Ladd wondered whether the different results for reading than for math might have less to do with the differences between the subjects themselves than with the tests used to measure proficiency. State-level results using state tests have shown gains in reading that do not show up in the NAEP. If math curriculums are closer to what is tested on the NAEP than reading curriculums, the results might not come through as well for reading. Ladd also thought it worth noting that test scores are only part of the picture in evaluating NCLB. Costs are also a consideration, as are other measures of success besides achievement, such as graduation rates and college attendance, as Hurst had noted.

Adele Morris remarked that although the paper found no evidence that NCLB harmed students at the high end of the achievement scale, it might be worth taking a second look, particularly at the very highest level. One current debate about NCLB is the degree to which it could reduce the resources that schools devote to the education of gifted learners. To explore this, the authors could examine the dependent variable at the 95th percentile or higher for the NAEP score, as well as explore the effect of NCLB on expenditure on programs for the gifted.

Melissa Kearney commented that many observers have questioned whether the magnitude of the effect found for NCLB on fourth-grade math test scores is credible. Presumably there is a sizable empirical literature estimating the effects of earlier experimentation with accountability at the state level. Were the effects the authors found in line with those estimates? Or are previous estimates so small that there would have to be large general equilibrium effects in order for the paper's estimates to be right?

ROCHELLE M. EDGE
Board of Governors of the Federal Reserve System
REFET S. GÜRKAYNAK
Bilkent University

How Useful Are Estimated DSGE Model Forecasts for Central Bankers?

ABSTRACT Dynamic stochastic general equilibrium (DSGE) models are a prominent tool for forecasting at central banks, and the competitive forecasting performance of these models relative to alternatives, including official forecasts, has been documented. When evaluating DSGE models on an absolute basis, however, we find that the benchmark estimated medium-scale DSGE model forecasts inflation and GDP growth very poorly, although statistical and judgmental forecasts do equally poorly. Our finding is the DSGE model analogue of the literature documenting the recent poor performance of macroeconomic forecasts relative to simple naive forecasts since the onset of the Great Moderation. Although this finding is broadly consistent with the DSGE model we employ—the model itself implies that especially under strong monetary policy, inflation deviations should be unpredictable—a "wrong" model may also have the same implication. We therefore argue that forecasting ability during the Great Moderation is not a good metric by which to judge models.

Dynamic stochastic general equilibrium models were descriptive tools at their inception. They were useful because they allowed economists to think about business cycles and carry out hypothetical policy experiments in Lucas critique–proof frameworks. In their early form, however, they were viewed as too minimalist to be appropriate for use in any practical application, such as macroeconomic forecasting, for which a strong connection to the data was needed.

The seminal work of Frank Smets and Raf Wouters (2003, 2007) changed this perception. In particular, their demonstration of the possibility of estimating a much larger and more richly specified DSGE model (similar to that developed by Christiano, Eichenbaum, and Evans 2005), as well as their finding of a good forecast performance of their DSGE model relative to competing vector autoregressive (VAR) and Bayesian VAR (BVAR) models, led DSGE models to be taken more seriously by central bankers around the world. Indeed, estimated DSGE models are now quite prominent tools for macroeconomic analysis at many policy institutions, with forecasting being one of the key areas where these models are used, in conjunction with other forecasting methods.

Reflecting this wider use, in recent research several central bank modeling teams have evaluated the relative forecasting performance of their institutions' estimated DSGE models. Notably, in addition to considering their DSGE models' forecasts relative to time-series models such as BVARs, as Smets and Wouters did, these papers consider official central bank forecasts. For the United States, Edge, Michael Kiley, and Jean-Philippe Laforte (2010) compare the Federal Reserve Board's DSGE model's forecasts with alternative forecasts such as those generated in pseudo-real time by time-series models, as well as with official Greenbook forecasts, and find that the DSGE model forecasts are competitive with, and indeed often better than, others.[1] This is an especially notable finding given that previous analyses have documented the high quality of the Federal Reserve's Greenbook forecasts (Romer and Romer 2000, Sims 2002).

We began writing this paper with the aim of establishing the marginal contributions of statistical, judgmental, and DSGE model forecasts to efficient forecasts of key macroeconomic variables such as GDP growth and inflation. The question we wanted to answer was how much importance central bankers should attribute to model forecasts on top of judgmental or statistical forecasts. To do this, we first evaluated the forecasting performance of the Smets and Wouters (2007) model, a popular benchmark, for U.S. GDP growth, inflation, and interest rates and compared these forecasts with those of a BVAR and the Federal Reserve staff's Greenbook. Importantly, to ensure that the same information is used to generate our DSGE model and BVAR model forecasts as was used to formulate the Greenbook forecasts, we used only data available at the time of the corresponding Greenbook forecast (referred to hereafter as "real-time data") and reestimated the model at each Greenbook forecast date.

---

1. Other examples with similar findings include Adolfson and others (2007) for the Swedish Riksbank's DSGE model and Lees, Matheson, and Smith (2007) for the Reserve Bank of New Zealand's DSGE model. In addition, Adolfson and others (2007) and Christoffel, Coenen, and Warne (forthcoming) examine out-of-sample forecast performance for DSGE models of the euro area, although the focus of these papers is much more on technical aspects of model evaluation.

In line with the results in the DSGE model forecasting literature, we found that the root mean squared errors (RMSEs) of the DSGE model forecasts were similar to, and often better than, those of the BVAR and Greenbook forecasts. Our surprising finding was that, unlike what one would expect when told that the model forecast is better than that of the Greenbook, the DSGE model in an absolute sense did a very poor job of forecasting. The Greenbook and the time-series model forecasts similarly did not capture much of the realized changes in GDP growth and inflation in our sample period, 1992 to 2006. These models showed a moderate amount of nowcasting ability, but almost no forecasting ability beginning with 1-quarter-ahead forecasts. Thus, our comparison is not between one good forecast and another; rather, all three methods of forecasting are poor, and combining them does not lead to much improvement.

This finding reflects the changed nature of macroeconomic fluctuations in the Great Moderation, the period of lower macroeconomic volatility that began in the mid-1980s. For example, James Stock and Mark Watson (2007) have shown that since the beginning of the Great Moderation, the permanent (forecastable) component of inflation, which had earlier dominated, has diminished to the point where the inflation process has been largely influenced by the transitory (unforecastable) component. (Peter Tulip 2009 makes an analogous point for GDP.) Lack of data prevents us from determining whether the forecasting ability of estimated DSGE models has worsened with the Great Moderation. We do, however, examine whether these models' forecasting performance is in an absolute sense poor. We find that it is.

A key point, however, is that forecasting ability is not always a good criterion for judging a model's success. As we discuss in more detail below, DSGE models of the class we consider often imply that under a strong monetary policy rule, macroeconomic forecastability should be low. In other words, when there is not much to be forecasted in the observed out-of-sample data, as is the case in the Great Moderation, a "wrong" model will fail to forecast, but so will a "correct" model. Consequently, it is entirely possible that a model that is unable to forecast, say, inflation will nonetheless provide reasonable counterfactual scenarios, which is ultimately the main purpose of the DSGE models.

The paper is organized as follows. Section I describes the methodology behind each of the different forecasts that we will consider, including those generated by the Smets and Wouters (2007) DSGE model, the BVAR model, the Greenbook, and the consensus forecast published by Blue Chip Economic Indicators. We include the Blue Chip forecast primarily because there is a 5-year delay in the public release of Greenbook forecasts, and we want to consider the most recent recession. Section II then describes the data that we use, which, as noted, are those that were available to forecasters in real time, to ensure that the same information is used to generate our DSGE model and BVAR model forecasts as was used to formulate the Greenbook and Blue Chip forecasts. Section III describes and presents the results for our forecast comparison exercises, and section IV discusses these results. Section V considers robustness analysis and extensions, showing in particular that judgmental forecasts have adjusted faster than the others to capture developments during the Great Recession. Section VI concludes.

A contribution of this paper is the construction of real-time datasets using data vintages that match the Greenbook and Blue Chip forecast dates. The appendix describes the construction of these data in detail.[2]

I. Forecast Methods

In this section we briefly review the four different forecasts that we will later consider. These are a DSGE model forecast, a Bayesian VAR model forecast, the Federal Reserve Board's Greenbook forecast, and the Blue Chip consensus forecast.

I.A. The DSGE Model

The DSGE model that we use in this paper is identical to that of Smets and Wouters (2007), and the description given here follows quite closely that presented in section 1 of Smets and Wouters (2007) and section II of Smets and Wouters (2003). The Smets and Wouters model is an application of a real business cycle model (in the spirit of King, Plosser, and Rebelo 1988) to an economy with sticky prices and sticky wages. In addition to these nominal rigidities, the model contains a large number of real rigidities—specifically, habit formation in consumption, costs of adjustment in capital accumulation, and variable capacity utilization—that ultimately appear to be necessary to capture the empirical persistence of U.S. macroeconomic phenomena.

The model consists of households, firms, and a monetary authority. Households maximize a nonseparable utility function, with goods and labor effort as its arguments, over an infinite life horizon. Consumption enters the utility function relative to a time-varying external habit variable, and labor

---

2. All of the data used in this paper, except the Blue Chip median forecasts, which are proprietary, are available at www.bilkent.edu.tr/~refet/research.html.

is differentiated by a union. This assumed structure of the labor market enables the household sector to have some monopoly power over wages. This implies a specific wage-setting equation that, in turn, allows for the inclusion of sticky nominal wages, modeled following Guillermo Calvo (1983). Capital accumulation is undertaken by households, who then rent that capital to the economy's firms. In accumulating capital, households face adjustment costs—specifically, investment adjustment costs. As the rental price of capital changes, the utilization of capital can be adjusted, albeit at an increasing cost.

The firms in the model rent labor (through a union) and capital from households to produce differentiated goods, for which they set prices, which are subject to Calvo (1983) price stickiness. These differentiated goods are aggregated into a final good by different, perfectly competitive firms in the model, and it is this good that is used for consumption and accumulating capital.

The Calvo model in both wage and price setting is augmented by the assumption that prices that are not reoptimized are partially indexed to past inflation rates. Prices are therefore set in reference to current and expected marginal costs but are also determined, through indexation, by the past inflation rate. Marginal costs depend on the wage and the rental rate of capital. Wages are set analogously as a function of current and expected marginal rates of substitution between leisure and consumption and are partially determined by the past wage inflation rate because of indexation. The model assumes, following Miles Kimball (1995), a variant of Dixit-Stiglitz aggregation in the goods and labor markets. This aggregation allows for time-varying demand elasticities, which allows more realistic estimates of price and wage stickiness.

Finally, the model contains seven structural shock variables, equal to the number of observables used in estimation. The model's observable variables are the log difference of real GDP per capita, real consumption, real investment, the real wage, log hours worked, the log difference of the GDP deflator, and the federal funds rate. These series, and in particular their real-time sources, are discussed in detail below.

In estimation, the seven observed variables are mapped into 14 model variables by the Kalman filter. Then, 36 parameters (17 of which belong to the seven autoregressive moving average shock processes in the model) are estimated by Bayesian methods (5 parameters are calibrated). It is the combination of the Kalman filter and Bayesian estimation that allows this large (although technically called a medium-scale) model to be estimated rather than calibrated. In our estimations we use exactly the same priors as

Smets and Wouters (2007) as well as the same data series. Once the model is estimated for a given data vintage, forecasting is done by employing the posterior modes for each parameter. The model can produce forecasts for all model variables, but we use only the GDP growth, inflation, and interest rate forecasts.

I.B. The Bayesian VAR Model

The Bayesian VAR is, in its essence, a simple four-lag vector autoregression forecasting model, or VAR(4). The same seven observable series that are used in the DSGE model estimation are used. Having seven variables in a four-lag VAR leads to a large number of parameters to be estimated, which leads to overfitting and poor out-of-sample forecast performance. The solution is the same as for the DSGE model. Priors are assigned to each parameter (we again use those of Smets and Wouters 2007), and the data are used to update these in the VAR framework. Like the DSGE model, the BVAR is estimated at every forecast date using real-time data, and forecasts are obtained by utilizing the modes of the posterior densities for each parameter.

Both the judgmental forecast and the DSGE model have an advantage over the purely statistical model, the BVAR, in that the people who produce the Greenbook and Blue Chip forecasts obviously know a lot more than seven time series, and the DSGE model was built to match the data that are being forecast. That is, judgment also enters the DSGE model in the form of modeling choices. To help the BVAR overcome this handicap, it is customary to have a training sample, that is, to estimate the model with some data and use the posteriors as priors in the actual estimation. Following Smets and Wouters (2007), we also "trained" the BVAR with data from 1955 to 1965, but, in a sign of how different the early and the late parts of the sample are, we found that the trained and the untrained BVARs perform comparably. We therefore report results from the untrained BVAR only.

I.C. The Greenbook

The Greenbook forecast is a detailed judgmental forecast that until March 2010 (after which it became known as the Tealbook) was produced eight times a year by staff at the Board of Governors of the Federal Reserve System.[3] The schedule on which Greenbook forecasts are

---
3. The renaming of the Federal Reserve Board's main forecasting document in early 2010 reflected a reorganization and combination of the original Greenbook and Bluebook. Throughout this paper we will continue to refer to the Federal Reserve Board's main forecasting document as the Greenbook.

produced—and hence the data availability for each round—are somewhat irregular, since the Greenbook is made specifically for each Federal Open Market Committee (FOMC) meeting, and the timings of FOMC meetings are themselves somewhat irregular. Broadly speaking, FOMC meetings take place at approximately 6-week intervals, although they tend to be further apart at the beginning of the year and closer together at the end of the year. The Greenbook is generally closed about 1 week before the FOMC meeting, to allow FOMC members and participants enough time to review the document. Importantly—and unlike at several other central banks—the Greenbook forecast reflects the view of the staff and not the views of the FOMC members.

Greenbook forecasts are formulated subject to a set of assumed paths for financial variables, such as the policy interest rate, key market interest rates, and stock market wealth. Over time there has been some variation in the way these assumptions are set. For example, as can be seen from the Greenbook federal funds rate assumptions reported in the Philadelphia Federal Reserve Bank's Real-Time Data Set for Macroeconomists, from about the middle of 1990 to the middle of 1992, the forecast assumed an essentially constant path of the federal funds rate.[4] In other periods, however, the path of the federal funds rate has varied, reflecting a conditioning assumption about the path of monetary policy consistent with the forecast.

As with most judgmental forecasts, the maximum projection horizon for the Greenbook forecast is not constant across vintages but varies from 6 to 10 quarters, depending on the forecast round. The July-August round of each year has the shortest projection horizon of any, extending 6 quarters: from the current (third) quarter through the fourth quarter of the following year. In the September round, the staff extend the forecast to include the year following the next in the projection period. Since the third quarter is not yet ended at the time of the September forecast, that quarter is still included in the projection horizon. Thus, the horizon for that round is 10 quarters—the longest for any forecast round. The endpoint of the projection horizon remains fixed for subsequent forecasts until the next July-August round, as the starting point moves forward. In our analysis we consider a maximum forecast horizon of 8 quarters, because the number of observations of forecasts covering 9 and 10 quarters is very small. Of course, the number of observations for forecast horizons of 7 and 8 quarters (which we do consider) will be smaller than the number of observations for horizons of 6 quarters and shorter.

---

4. See www.philadelphiafed.org/research-and-data/real-time-center/greenbook-data/.

We use the forecasts produced for the FOMC meetings over the period from January 1992 to December 2004. Our start date represents the quarter when GDP, rather than GNP, became the key indicator of economic activity. This is not a critical limitation, since GNP forecasts could be used for earlier vintages. The end date was chosen by necessity: as already noted, Greenbook forecasts are made public only with a 5-year lag. Tables 1 to 13 in the online appendix provide detailed information on the dates of Greenbook forecasts we use and the horizons covered in each forecast.[5] (Appendix table A1 of this paper provides an example of how these tables look.) Note that the first four Greenbook forecasts that we consider fall during a period when the policy rate was assumed to remain flat throughout the projection period.

I.D. The Blue Chip Consensus Forecast

The Blue Chip consensus forecast is based on a monthly poll of forecasters at approximately 50 banks, corporations, and consulting firms and reports their forecasts of U.S. economic growth, inflation, interest rates, and a range of other key variables. The Blue Chip poll is taken on about the 4th or 5th of the month, and the forecasts are published on the 10th of that month. The consensus forecast, equal to the mean of the individual reported forecasts, is then reported along with averages of the top 10 and the bottom 10 forecasts for each variable. In our analysis we use only the consensus forecast.

As with the Greenbook, the Blue Chip forecast horizons are not constant across forecast rounds; in the case of the Blue Chip, the forecast horizons are uniformly shorter. The longest forecast horizon in the Blue Chip is 9 quarters. This is for the January round, for which a forecast is made for the year just beginning and the next, but since data for the fourth quarter of the previous year are not yet available, that quarter is also "forecast." The shortest forecast horizon in the Blue Chip is 5 quarters. This is for the November and December rounds, for which a forecast is made for the current (fourth) quarter and the following year.

We use the Blue Chip consensus forecasts over the period January 1992 to September 2009. The start date is chosen because it is the same as the start date for the Greenbook, and the end date is 1 year before the conference draft of this paper was written, so that the realized values of forecasted variables are also known.

---

5. Online appendices to papers in this issue may be found on the *Brookings Papers* webpage (www.brookings.edu/economics/bpea), under "Conferences and Papers."

II. Data and Sample

In this section we provide a brief overview of the data involved in the forecasting process and of our sample period. The appendix provides detail on our sources and information on how the raw data were converted to the form used in estimation.

The data we use for the estimation of the Smets and Wouters DSGE model and the BVAR model are the same seven series used by Smets and Wouters (2007), but only the real-time vintages of each series at each forecast date are used. Our forecast dates coincide with either the dates of Greenbook forecasts or those of the Blue Chip forecasts. That is, at each Greenbook or Blue Chip forecast date, we use only the data that were available as of that date to estimate the DSGE model and the BVAR.[6] We then generate forecasts out to 8 quarters. From the data perspective, the last known quarter is the previous one; therefore the 1-quarter-ahead forecast is the nowcast, and the n-quarter-ahead forecast corresponds to $n - 1$ quarters ahead, counting from the forecast date. This convention is also followed for the Greenbook and most Blue Chip forecasts.[7]

We evaluate the forecasts for growth in real GDP per capita, inflation as measured by the GDP deflator, and the short-term (policy) interest rate. GDP growth and inflation are expressed in terms of nonannualized, quarter-on-quarter rates, and interest rates are in levels. Our main focus will be on the inflation forecasts, because this is the forecast that is the most comparable across the different forecasting methods. The DSGE model and the BVAR produce continuous (and in very recent periods negative) interest rate forecasts, whereas the judgmental forecasts obviously factor in the discrete nature of interest rate setting and the zero nominal bound. The Blue Chip forecasts do not contain forecasts of the federal funds rate, and hence we cannot perform robustness checks for the interest rate forecast or use the longer sample for this variable.

---

6. See the appendix for exceptions. In a few instances, one of the variables from the last quarter had not yet been released on a Greenbook forecast date. In these instances we help the DSGE and BVAR forecasts by appending the Federal Reserve Board staff backcast of that data point to the time series. We verify that doing so does not influence our results by dropping these forecast observations from our analysis and rerunning our results.

7. The exceptions for the Blue Chip forecasts are the January, April, July, and October forecasts. These typically take place so early in the quarter that few or no data for the preceding quarter are available. For these forecasts the previous quarter is considered the nowcast.

A more subtle issue concerns GDP growth. The DSGE model is based on per capita values and produces a forecast of growth in GDP per capita, as does the BVAR. On the other hand, GDP growth itself is announced in aggregate, not per capita, terms, and the Greenbook and Blue Chip forecasts are expressed in terms of aggregate growth. Thus, one has to either convert the aggregate growth rates to per capita values by dividing them by realized population growth rates, or convert the per capita values to aggregate forecasts by multiplying them by realized population growth numbers.

The two methods should produce similar results, and the fact that the model uses per capita data should make little difference, as population growth is a smooth series with little variance. However, the population numbers reported by the Census Bureau and used by Smets and Wouters (and in subsequent work by others) have a number of extremely sharp spikes caused by the census picking up previously uncaptured population levels as well as by rebasings of the Current Population Survey. The spikes remain because the data are not revised backward; that is, population growth is assumed to have occurred in the quarter that the previously uncaptured population is first included, not estimated across the quarters over which it more likely occurred.

For this paper we used the population series used by Smets and Wouters in estimating the model, because we discovered the erratic behavior of the series only after our estimation and forecast exercise was complete. (We estimate the model more than 300 times, which took about 2 months, and did not have time to reestimate and reforecast using the better population series.) We note the violence that the unsmoothed series does to the model estimates and encourage future researchers to smooth the population series before using the data to obtain GDP per capita. Here we adjust the DSGE model and BVAR forecasts using the realized future population growth numbers to make them comparable to announced GDP growth rates and judgmental forecasts, but we again note that this is an imperfect adjustment, which likely reduces the forecasting ability of the DSGE model and the BVAR.[8]

---

8. We also experimented with converting the realized aggregate GDP growth numbers and Blue Chip forecasts to per capita values using the realized population growth rates, and converting the Greenbook GDP growth forecast into per capita values by using the Federal Reserve Board staff's internal population forecast. This essentially gives Blue Chip forecasts perfect foresight about the population component of GDP per capita, which improves their forecasting considerably because the variance of the population series is high, and weakens the Greenbook GDP forecast considerably because the Federal Reserve staff's population growth estimate is a smooth series. These results are available from the authors upon request.

We estimate the DSGE and BVAR models with data going back to 1965 and perform the first forecast as of January 1992. Because the Greenbook forecasts are embargoed for 5 years, our last forecast is as of 2004Q4, forecasting out to 2006Q3. There are two scheduled FOMC meetings per quarter, and thus all of our forecasts that are compared with the Greenbook are made twice a quarter. This has consequences for correlated forecast errors, as explained in the next section. For the Blue Chip forecasts, the forecasting period ends in 2010Q1, the last quarter for which we knew the realized values of the variables of interest at the time the conference draft of this paper was written. The Blue Chip forecasts are published monthly, and we produce a separate set of real-time DSGE and BVAR model forecasts coinciding with the Blue Chip publication dates.

We should note that our sample period for Greenbook comparisons, 1992 to 2004, is similar but not identical to those used in previous studies of the forecasting ability of DSGE models, such as Smets and Wouters (2007), who use 1990 to 2004, and Edge and others (2010), who use 1996 to 2002. Again, the sample falls within the Great Moderation period, after the long disinflation was complete, and most of the period corresponds to a particularly transparent period of monetary policymaking, during which the FOMC signaled its likely near-term policy actions with statements accompanying releases of its interest rate decisions.

III. Forecast Comparisons

We distinguish between two types of forecast evaluations. Given a variable to be forecasted, x, and its h-period-ahead forecast (made h periods in the past) by method y, $\hat{x}_{y,t}^h$, one can compute the RMSE of the real-time forecasts of each model:

(1) $$\text{RMSE} x_y^h = \sqrt{\frac{1}{T}\sum_{t=1}^{T}\left(x_t - \hat{x}_{y,t}^h\right)^2}.$$

Comparing the RMSEs across different forecast methods, a policymaker can then choose the method with the smallest RMSE to use. The RMSE comparison therefore answers the decision theory question: Which forecast is the best and should be used? To our knowledge, all of the forecast evaluations of DSGE models so far (Smets and Wouters 2007, Edge and others 2010, and those mentioned earlier for other countries) have used essentially this metric and concluded that the model forecasts do well.

Figure 1. Relative Root Mean Square Errors of DSGE Model, BVAR, and Greenbook Forecasts

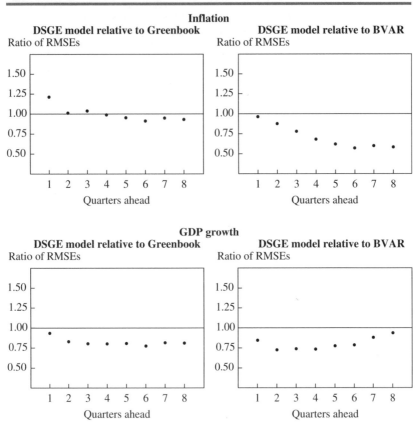

Source: Authors' calculations.

In figure 1 we show results of this exercise with real-time data and compare the RMSEs of the DSGE model forecasts for inflation and GDP growth with those of the Greenbook and BVAR forecasts at different horizons. This figure, which reports the ratios of the RMSEs from two models, visually conveys a result that Smets and Wouters and Edge and others have shown earlier: except for inflation forecasts at very short horizons (where the Greenbook forecasts are better), the DSGE model forecasts have the lower RMSE for both inflation and growth in all comparisons. The literature has taken this finding both as a vindication of the estimated medium-scale DSGE model, and as evidence that these models can be used for forecasting as well as for positive analysis of counterfactuals and for informing optimal policy.

Although figure 1 does indeed show that the DSGE model has the best forecasting record among the three methods we consider, it offers no clues about how good the "best" is. To further evaluate the forecasts, we first present, in figure 2, scatterplots of the 4-quarter-ahead forecasts (a horizon at which the DSGE model outperforms the Greenbook and BVAR) of inflation and GDP growth from the DSGE model and the realized values of these variables. The better the forecast performance, the closer the observations should fall to the 45-degree line.

Instead figure 2 shows that, for both variables, the points form clouds rather than 45-degree lines, suggesting that the 4-quarter-ahead forecast of the DSGE model is quite unrelated to the realized value. To get the full picture, we run a standard forecast efficiency test (see Gürkaynak and Wolfers 2007 for a discussion of tests of forecast efficiency and further references) and estimate the following equation:

$$(2) \qquad x_t = \alpha_y^h + \beta_y^h \hat{x}_{y,t}^h + \varepsilon_{y,t}^h.$$

A good forecast should have an intercept of zero, a slope coefficient of 1, and a high R^2. If the intercept is different from zero, the forecast has on average been biased; if the slope differs from 1, the forecast has consistently under- or overpredicted deviations from the mean, and if the R^2 is low, then little of the variation of the variable to be forecasted is captured by the forecast. Note that especially when the point estimates of α_y^h and β_y^h are different from zero and 1, respectively, the R^2 is a more charitable measure of the success of the forecast than the RMSE calculated in equation 1, as the errors in equation 2 are residuals obtained from the best-fitting line. That is, a policymaker would make errors of size $\varepsilon_{y,t}^h$ only if she knew the values of α_y^h and β_y^h and used them to adjust $\hat{x}_{y,t}^h$. The R^2 that is comparable to the RMSE measures calculated in equation 1 would be that implied by equation 2 with α_y^h and β_y^h constrained to zero and 1, respectively.

Tables 1, 2, and 3 show the estimation results of equation 2 for the DSGE model, BVAR, and Greenbook forecasts of inflation, GDP growth, and interest rates.[9] The tables suggest that forecasts of inflation and GDP

---

9. The standard errors reported are Newey-West standard errors for $2h$ lags, given that there are two forecasts made in each quarter. Explicitly taking into account the clustering at the level of quarters (since forecasts made in the same quarter may be correlated) made no perceptible difference. Neither did using only the first or the second forecast in each quarter.

Figure 2. Realized and Four-Quarters-Ahead DSGE Forecast Inflation and GDP Growth

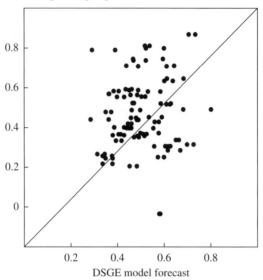

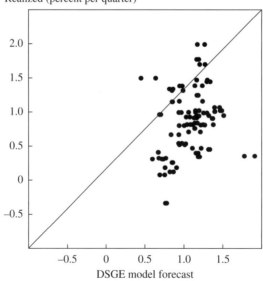

Source: Bureau of Economic Analysis data and authors' calculations.

Table 1. Inflation Forecast Accuracy: DSGE, BVAR, and Greenbook[a]

	Quarters ahead					
Forecast	1	2	3	4	5	6
DSGE model						
Slope	0.451**	0.089	0.031	0.209	0.167	0.134
	(0.108)	(0.149)	(0.250)	(0.261)	(0.216)	(0.174)
Intercept	0.261**	0.421**	0.446**	0.363**	0.386**	0.398**
	(0.051)	(0.082)	(0.122)	(0.128)	(0.112)	(0.112)
Adjusted R^2	0.13	0.00	0.00	0.02	0.01	0.01
BVAR model						
Slope	0.472**	0.205	0.224*	0.209	0.062	−0.033
	(0.096)	(0.133)	(0.104)	(0.121)	(0.094)	(0.119)
Intercept	0.216**	0.344**	0.322**	0.329**	0.430**	0.497**
	(0.052)	(0.091)	(0.066)	(0.085)	(0.069)	(0.097)
Adjusted R^2	0.17	0.03	0.04	0.04	0.00	0.00
Greenbook						
Slope	0.642**	0.288	0.268	0.209	−0.007	−0.386
	(0.084)	(0.161)	(0.188)	(0.245)	(0.306)	(0.253)
Intercept	0.138**	0.322**	0.332**	0.369**	0.477**	0.657**
	(0.048)	(0.091)	(0.106)	(0.130)	(0.157)	(0.136)
Adjusted R^2	0.48	0.08	0.05	0.02	0.00	0.06

Source: Authors' regressions.
a. Sample size is 104 observations in all regressions. Standard errors are in parentheses. Asterisks indicate statistical significance at the **1 percent or the *5 percent level.

growth have been very poor by all methods, except for the Greenbook inflation nowcast. The DSGE model inflation forecasts (table 1) have R^2s of about zero for forecasts of the next quarter and beyond, and slope coefficients very far from unity. The DSGE model forecasts of GDP growth (table 2) likewise capture less than 10 percent of the actual variation in growth, and point estimates of the slopes are again far from unity. Again except for the Greenbook nowcast, the results are very similar for the Greenbook and the BVAR forecasts.

All three forecast methods, however, do impressively well at forecasting interest rates (table 3). This is surprising since short-term rates should be a function of inflation and GDP and thus should not be any more forecastable than those two variables, except for the forecastability coming from interest rate smoothing by policymakers. The explanation here is that the interest rate is highly serially correlated, which makes it relative easy to forecast. (Indeed, in our sample the level of the interest rate behaves like a unit root process, as verified by an augmented Dickey-Fuller test not

Table 2. GDP Growth Forecast Accuracy: DSGE, BVAR, and Greenbook[a]

Forecast	Quarters ahead					
	1	2	3	4	5	6
DSGE model						
Slope	0.374*	0.485	0.477	0.507	0.485	0.553
	(0.174)	(0.249)	(0.321)	(0.303)	(0.312)	(0.279)
Intercept	0.419*	0.313	0.331	0.299	0.320	0.284
	(0.206)	(0.292)	(0.362)	(0.346)	(0.344)	(0.311)
Adjusted R^2	0.08	0.09	0.07	0.08	0.07	0.06
BVAR model						
Slope	0.041	−0.057	0.094	0.082	0.110	0.037
	(0.130)	(0.136)	(0.143)	(0.135)	(0.146)	(0.206)
Intercept	0.784**	0.894**	0.735**	0.754**	0.713**	0.815**
	(0.160)	(0.196)	(0.198)	(0.189)	(0.205)	(0.263)
Adjusted R^2	0.00	0.00	0.01	0.01	0.01	0.00
Greenbook						
Slope	0.641**	0.260	−0.081	−0.115	−0.416	−0.001
	(0.172)	(0.339)	(0.287)	(0.318)	(0.359)	(0.422)
Intercept	0.561**	0.721**	0.875**	0.893**	1.015**	0.852**
	(0.102)	(0.179)	(0.162)	(0.181)	(0.195)	(0.233)
Adjusted R^2	0.13	0.01	0.00	0.00	0.02	0.00

Source: Authors' regressions.
a. Sample size is 104 observations in all regressions. Standard errors are in parentheses. Asterisks indicate statistical significance at the **1 percent or the *5 percent level.

reported here.)[10] Thus, table 3 may be showing long-run cointegrating relationships rather than short-run forecasting ability. We therefore follow Gürkaynak, Brian Sack, and Eric Swanson (2005) in studying the change in the interest rate rather than its level.

Table 4 shows results for forecasts of changes in interest rates by the three methods. These results are now more comparable to those for the inflation and GDP growth forecasts, although in the short run there is higher forecastability in interest rate changes. The very strong nowcasting ability of the Greenbook derives partly from the fact that the Federal Reserve staff know that interest rate changes normally occur in multiples of 25 basis points, whereas, again, the BVAR and the DSGE model produce continuous interest rate forecasts.

---

10. Although nominal interest rates cannot theoretically be simple unit-root processes because of the zero nominal bound, they can be statistically indistinguishable from unit-root processes in small samples and pose the same econometric difficulties.

Table 3. Interest Rate Forecast Accuracy: DSGE, BVAR, and Greenbook[a]

	Quarters ahead					
Forecast	1	2	3	4	5	6
DSGE model						
Slope	1.138**	1.286**	1.373**	1.385**	1.381**	1.324*
	(0.031)	(0.085)	(0.181)	(0.305)	(0.416)	(0.538)
Intercept	−0.149**	−0.308**	−0.427**	−0.483	−0.528	−0.512
	(0.027)	(0.068)	(0.153)	(0.289)	(0.422)	(0.582)
Adjusted R^2	0.95	0.83	0.66	0.48	0.35	0.24
BVAR model						
Slope	0.924**	0.888**	0.867**	0.852**	0.828**	0.807**
	(0.020)	(0.041)	(0.076)	(0.126)	(0.191)	(0.262)
Intercept	0.056**	0.067	0.056	0.037	0.031	0.025
	(0.020)	(0.036)	(0.064)	(0.117)	(0.195)	(0.281)
Adjusted R^2	0.96	0.87	0.74	0.60	0.47	0.35
Greenbook						
Slope	0.993**	0.962**	0.904**	0.829**	0.735**	0.614**
	(0.006)	(0.025)	(0.057)	(0.098)	(0.148)	(0.194)
Intercept	0.001	0.012	0.049	0.112	0.200	0.316
	(0.006)	(0.025)	(0.056)	(0.096)	(0.150)	(0.205)
Adjusted R^2	1.00	0.96	0.87	0.72	0.54	0.36

Source: Authors' regressions.
a. Sample size is 104 observations in all regressions. Standard errors are in parentheses. Asterisks indicate statistical significance at the **1 percent or the *5 percent level.

Taken together, figure 2 and tables 1 through 4 show that although the DSGE model forecasts are comparable to and often better than the Greenbook and BVAR forecasts, this is a comparison of very poor forecasts with each other. To provide a benchmark for forecast quality, we introduce a forecast series consisting simply of a constant and another that forecasts each variable as a random walk, and we ask the following two questions. First, if a policymaker could have used one of the above three forecasts over the 1992–2006 period, or could have had access to the actual mean of the series over the same period and used that as a forecast (using zero change as the interest rate forecast at all horizons), how would the RMSEs compare? Second, how large would the RMSEs be if the policymaker simply used the last observation available on each date as the forecast for all horizons, essentially treating the series to be forecast as random walks?[11]

---

11. In the random walk forecasts we set the interest rate change forecasts to zero. That is, in this exercise the assumed policymaker treats the level of the interest rate as a random walk.

Table 4. Accuracy in Forecasting Changes in Interest Rates: DSGE, BVAR, and Greenbook[a]

	Quarters ahead					
Forecast	1	2	3	4	5	6
DSGE model						
Slope	0.498**	0.453*	0.560*	0.862*	1.127*	1.003
	(0.121)	(0.173)	(0.240)	(0.411)	(0.473)	(0.507)
Intercept	−0.012	−0.009	−0.017	−0.029	−0.041	−0.034
	(0.016)	(0.019)	(0.023)	(0.028)	(0.031)	(0.031)
Adjusted R^2	0.15	0.11	0.11	0.17	0.20	0.12
BVAR model						
Slope	0.724**	0.978**	1.202*	1.064*	1.025*	1.040*
	(0.133)	(0.274)	(0.459)	(0.489)	(0.476)	(0.482)
Intercept	−0.018	−0.027	−0.044	−0.043	−0.040	−0.038
	(0.014)	(0.019)	(0.028)	(0.033)	(0.033)	(0.033)
Adjusted R^2	0.30	0.17	0.16	0.16	0.17	0.18
Greenbook						
Slope	1.052**	1.191**	0.986**	0.588	0.423	−0.279
	(0.030)	(0.144)	(0.212)	(0.358)	(0.215)	(0.333)
Intercept	−0.006	−0.022	−0.023	−0.011	−0.006	0.005
	(0.003)	(0.013)	(0.022)	(0.023)	(0.024)	(0.022)
Adjusted R^2	0.96	0.50	0.14	0.03	0.02	0.01

Source: Authors' regressions.

a. Sample size is 104 observations in all regressions. Standard errors are in parentheses. Asterisks indicate statistical significance at the **1 percent or the *5 percent level.

The resulting RMSEs are depicted in figure 3. The constant forecast does about as well as the other forecasts, and often better, suggesting that the DSGE model, BVAR, and Greenbook forecasts do not contribute much information. It is some relief that the DSGE model forecast usually does better than the random walk forecast, an often-used benchmark.[12] However, the random walk RMSEs are very large. To put the numbers in perspective, observe that the RMSE of the 6-quarter-ahead inflation forecast of the DSGE model is about 0.22 in quarterly terms, or about

---

12. We also looked at how the DSGE model forecast RMSEs compare statistically with other forecast RMSEs (results available from the authors upon request). Results of Diebold-Mariano tests show that for inflation, the RMSE of the DSGE model is significantly lower than those of the BVAR and the random walk forecasts for most maturities, is indistinguishable from the RMSE of the Greenbook, and is higher than that of the constant forecast for some maturities; for GDP growth the DSGE model RMSE is statistically lower than those of the BVAR and the random walk forecasts and is indistinguishable from the RMSEs of the Greenbook and the constant forecasts.

Figure 3. Root Mean Square Errors of Alternative Forecasts

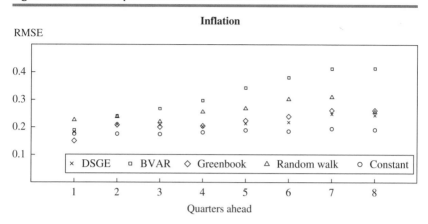

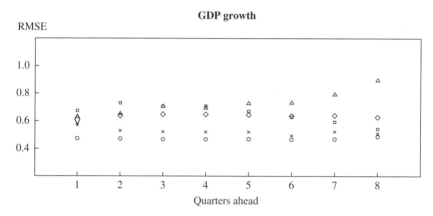

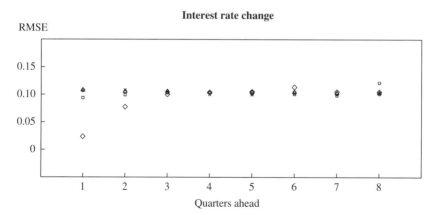

Source: Authors' calculations.

0.9 percent annualized, with a 95 percent confidence interval that is 3.6 percentage points wide. That is not very useful for policymaking.

IV. Discussion

Our findings, especially those for inflation, are surprising given the finding of Christina Romer and David Romer (2000) that the Greenbook is an excellent forecaster of inflation at horizons out to 8 quarters. Figure 4 shows the reason for the difference between their finding and ours. The Romer and Romer sample covers a period when inflation swung widely, whereas our sample—and the sample used in other studies for DSGE model forecast evaluations—covers a period when inflation behaved more like independent and identically distributed (i.i.d.) deviations around a constant. That is, there is little to be forecasted over our sample.

This finding is in line with Stock and Watson's (2007) result that after the Great Moderation began, the permanent (forecastable) component of inflation, which had earlier dominated, diminished in importance, and the bulk of the variance of inflation began to be driven by the transitory (unforecastable) component. It is therefore not surprising that no forecasting method does well. Bharat Trehan (2010) shows that a similar lack of forecastability is also evident in the Survey of Professional Forecasters (SPF) and the University of Michigan survey of inflation expectations. Andrew Atkeson and Lee Ohanian (2001) document that over the period 1984 to 1999, a random walk forecast of 4-quarter-ahead inflation out-

Figure 4. A Short History of Inflation

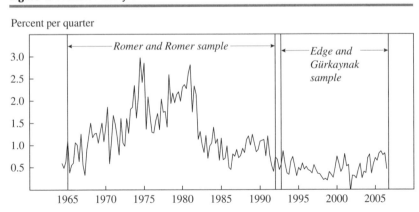

Source: BEA data.

performs the Greenbook forecast as well as Phillips curve models. (But our analysis finds that the DSGE model, with a sophisticated, microfounded Phillips curve, outperforms the random walk forecast.) Jeff Fuhrer, Giovanni Olivei, and Geoffrey Tootell (2009) show that this is due to the parameter changes in the inflation process that occurred with the onset of the Great Moderation. For forecasts of output growth, Tulip (2009) documents a notably larger reduction in actual output growth volatility following the Great Moderation relative to the reduction in Greenbook RMSEs, thus indicating that much of the reduction in output growth volatility has stemmed from the predictable component—the part that can potentially be forecast.

David Reifschneider and Tulip (2007) perform a wide-reaching analysis of institutional forecasts—those of the Greenbook, the SPF, and the Blue Chip, as well as forecasts produced by the Congressional Budget Office and the administration—for real GDP (or GNP) growth, the unemployment rate, and consumer price inflation. Although they do not consider changes in forecast performance associated with the Great Moderation, their analysis, which is undertaken for the post-1986 period, finds overwhelmingly that errors for all institutional forecasts are large. More broadly, Antonello D'Agostino, Domenico Giannone, and Paolo Surico (2006) also consider a range of time-series forecasting models, including univariate AR models, factor-augmented AR models, and pooled bivariate forecasting models, as well as institutional forecasts—those of the Greenbook and the SPF—and document that although RMSEs for forecasts of real activity, inflation, and interest rates dropped notably with the Great Moderation, time-series and institutional forecasts also largely lost their ability to improve on a random walk. Jon Faust and Jonathan Wright (2009) similarly note that the performance of some of the forecasting methods they consider improves when data from periods preceding the Great Moderation are included in the sample.

We would argue that DSGE models should not be judged solely by their absolute forecasting ability or lack thereof. Previous authors, such as Edge and others (2010), were conscious of the declining performance of Greenbook and time-series forecasts when they performed their comparison exercises but took as given the fact that staff at the Federal Reserve Board are required to produce Greenbook forecasts of the macroeconomy eight times a year. More precisely, they asked whether a DSGE model forecast should be introduced into the mix of inputs used to arrive at the final Greenbook forecast. In this case relative forecast performance is a relevant point of comparison. Another noteworthy aspect of central bank forecasting is that of "storytelling": not only are the values of the forecast variables important, but so, too, is the narrative explaining how present imbalances will be unwound as the macroeconomy moves toward the balanced growth path. A well-thought-out and much-scrutinized story accompanies the Greenbook forecast but is not something present in reduced-form time-series forecasts. An internally consistent and coherent narrative is, however, implicit in a DSGE model forecast, indicating that these models can also contribute along this important dimension of forecasting.

In sum, what do these findings say about the quality of DSGE models as a tool for telling internally consistent, reasonable stories for counterfactual scenarios? Not much. That inflation will be unforecastable is a prediction of basic sticky-price DSGE models when monetary policy responds aggressively to inflation. Marvin Goodfriend and Robert King (2009) make this point explicitly using a tractable model. If inflation is forecasted to be high, policymakers will increase interest rates and attempt to rein in inflation. If they are successful, inflation will never be predictably different from the (implicit) target, and all of the variation will come from unforecastable shocks. In models lacking real rigidities, the "divine coincidence" will be present,[13] which means that the output gap will have the same property of unforecastability. Thus, it is quite possible that the model is "correct" and therefore cannot forecast cyclical fluctuations but that the counterfactual scenarios produced by the model can still inform policy discussions.[14]

Of course, the particular DSGE model we employ in this paper does not have the divine coincidence, because of the real rigidities it includes, such as a rigidity of real wages due to having both sticky prices and sticky wages. Moreover, because this model incorporates a trade-off between stabilizing price inflation, wage inflation, and the output gap, optimal policy is not characterized by price inflation stabilization, and therefore price inflation is not unforecastable. Nonetheless, price inflation stabilization is a possible policy, which could be pursued even if not optimal, and this would imply unforecastable inflation. That said, this policy would likely not stabilize the output gap, thus implying some forecastability of the output gap. Ultimately, whether and to what extent the model implies fore-

---

13. The divine coincidence (see Blanchard and Galí 2007 for the first use of this term in print) refers to a property of New Keynesian models in which stabilizing inflation is equivalent to stabilizing the output gap, defined as the gap between actual output and the natural rate of output.

14. However, see Galí (2010) about the difficulties inherent in generating counterfactual scenarios using DSGE models.

castable or unforecastable fluctuations in inflation and GDP growth can be learned by simulating data from the model calibrated under different monetary policy rules and performing forecast exercises on the simulated data. We note the qualitative implication of the model that there should not be much predictability, especially for inflation, and leave the quantitative study to future research. Note also that our discussion here has focused on the forecastability of the output gap, not of output growth, which is ultimately the variable of interest in our forecast exercises. Unforecastability of the output gap need not imply unforecastability of output growth.

Finally, we would note that a reduced-form model with an assumed inflation process that is equal to a constant with i.i.d. deviations—in other words, a "wrong" model—will also have the same unforecastability implication. Thus, evaluating forecasting ability during a period such as the Great Moderation, when no method is able to forecast, is not a test of the empirical relevance of a model.

V. Robustness and Extensions

To verify that our results are not specific to the relatively short sample we have used or to the Greenbook vintages we employed, we repeated the exercise using Blue Chip forecasts as the judgmental forecast for the 1992–2010 period. (This test also has the advantage of adding the financial crisis and the Great Recession to our sample.) For this exercise we estimated the DSGE model and the BVAR using data vintages of Blue Chip publication dates and produced forecasts.

For the sake of brevity, we do not show the analogues of the earlier figures and tables but simply note that the findings are very similar when Blue Chip forecasts replace Greenbook forecasts and the sample is extended to 2010. (One difference is that the Blue Chip forecast has nowcasting ability for GDP as well as inflation.) The DSGE model forecast is similar to the judgmental forecast and is better than the BVAR, in terms of RMSEs, at almost all horizons, but all three forecasts are again very poor. (This exercise omits the forecasts of interest rates, since the Blue Chip forecasts do not include forecasts of the overnight rate.) The longer sample allows us to answer some interesting questions and provide further robustness checks.

Although we again use quarter-over-quarter changes and not annual growth rates for all of our variables, overlapping periods in long-horizon forecasting are a potential issue. In figure 5 we show the nonoverlapping, 4-quarter-ahead absolute errors of DSGE model forecasts made in January

Figure 5. Nonoverlapping DSGE Four-Quarters-Ahead Forecast Errors[a]

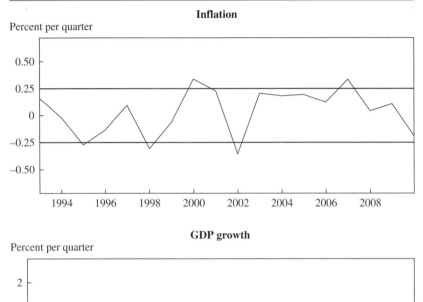

Source: Authors' calculations.
a. Horizontal lines at 0.25 and –0.25 indicate thresholds for errors exceeding 1 percentage point annualized.

of each year for the first quarter of the subsequent year. The horizontal lines at –0.25 and 0.25 indicate forecast errors that would be 1 percentage point in annualized terms. Most errors are near or outside these bounds. It is thus clear that our statistical results are not driven by outliers (a fact also visible in figure 2).

To provide a better understanding of the evolution of forecast errors over time, figure 6 shows 3-year rolling averages of RMSEs for 4-quarter-ahead forecasts, using all 12 forecasts for each year. Not surprisingly, these average forecast errors are considerably higher in the latter part of the sample, which includes the crisis episode. The DSGE model does

Figure 6. Three-Year Rolling Averages of Four-Quarters-Ahead RMSEs

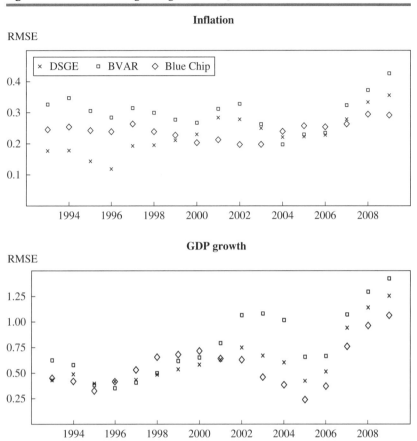

Source: Authors' calculations.

worse than the Blue Chip forecast once the rolling window includes 2008, for both the inflation and the GDP growth forecasts.

Lastly, we compare the forecasting performance of the DSGE and BVAR models with that of the Blue Chip forecasts during the recent crisis and recession. Figure 7 shows the forecast errors beginning with 4-quarter-ahead forecasts and ending with the nowcast for three quarters: 2007Q4, the first quarter of the recession according to the National Bureau of Economic Research dating; 2008Q3, when Lehman Brothers failed and growth in GDP per capita turned negative; and 2009Q1, when the extent of the contraction became clear (see Wieland and Wolters

Figure 7. Forecasts of Inflation and GDP Growth during the 2007–08 Crisis

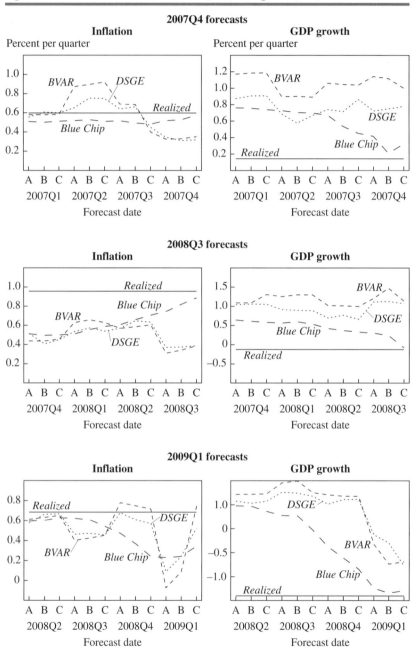

Sources: BEA data, Blue Chip Economic Indicators, and authors' calculations.

2010 for a similar analysis of more episodes). In all six panels in figure 7, the model forecast and the judgmental forecast are close to each other when the forecast horizon is 4 quarters. Although all the forecasts clearly first miss the recession, and then miss its severity, the Blue Chip forecasts in general fare better as the quarter to be forecasted gets closer, and especially when nowcasting.

An interesting point is that the judgmental forecast improves within quarters, especially the nowcast quarter, whereas the DSGE and BVAR model forecasts do not. As the quarter progresses, the DSGE model and the BVAR model have access only to more revised versions of data pertaining to previous quarters. Forecasters surveyed by the Blue Chip survey, however, observe within-quarter information such as monthly frequency data on key components of GDP and GDP prices as well as news about policy developments. Also, the Blue Chip forecasters surely knew of the zero nominal bound, whereas both of the estimated models (DSGE and BVAR) imply deeply negative nominal rate forecasts during the crisis.

It is not very surprising that judgmental forecasts fare better in capturing such regime switches. The DSGE model, lacking a financial sector and a zero nominal bound on interest rates, should naturally do somewhat better in the precrisis period. In fact, that is the period this model was built to explain. But this also cautions us that out-of-sample tests for DSGE models are not truly out of sample as long as the sample is in the period the model was built to explain. The next generation of DSGE models will likely include a zero nominal bound and a financial sector as standard features and will do better when explaining the Great Recession. Their real test will be to explain—but not necessarily to forecast—the first business cycle that follows those models' creation.[15]

VI. Conclusion

DSGE models are very poor at forecasting, but so are all other approaches. Forecasting ability is a nonissue in DSGE model evaluation, however, because in recent samples (over which these models can be evaluated using real-time data) there is little to be forecasted. This is consistent with

---

15. A promising avenue of research is adding unemployment explicitly to the model, as in Galí, Smets, and Wouters (2010). This will likely help improve the model forecasts, as Stock and Watson (2010) show that utilizing an unemployment gap measure helps improve forecasts of inflation in recession episodes.

the literature on the Great Moderation, which emphasizes that not only the standard deviation of macroeconomic fluctuations but also their nature has changed. In particular, cycles today are driven more by temporary, unforecastable shocks.

The lack of forecasting ability is not, however, evidence against the DSGE model. Forecasting ability is simply not a proper metric by which to judge a model. Indeed, the DSGE model's poor recent forecasting record can be evidence in favor of it. Monetary policy was characterized by a strongly stabilizing rule in this period, and the model implies that such policy will undo predictable fluctuations, especially in inflation. We leave further analysis of this point and of the forecasting ability of the model in pre- and post–Great Moderation periods to future work.

APPENDIX
Constructing the Real-Time Datasets

In this appendix we discuss how we constructed the real-time datasets that we use to generate all of the forecasts other than those of the Greenbook. To ensure that when we carry out our forecast performance exercises we are indeed comparing the forecasting ability of different methodologies (and not some other difference), it is critical that the datasets and other information that we use to generate our model forecasts are the same as those that were available when the Greenbook and Blue Chip forecasts were generated. For this we are very conscious of the timing of the releases of the data that we use to generate our model forecasts and how they relate to the Greenbook's closing dates and Blue Chip publication dates.

We begin by documenting the data series used in the DSGE model and in the other reduced-form forecasting models. Here relatively little discussion is necessary, since we employ essentially all of the same data series used by Smets and Wouters in estimating their model. We then move on to provide a full account of how we constructed the real-time datasets used to generate the model forecasts. We then briefly explain our construction of the "first final" data, which are ultimately what we consider to be the realized values of real GDP growth and the rate of GDP price inflation against which we compare the forecasts.

Data Series Used

To allow comparability with the results of Smets and Wouters (2007), we use exactly the same data series that they used in their analysis.

Because we will subsequently have to obtain different release vintages for all of our data series (other than the federal funds rate), we need to be very specific about not only which government statistical agency is the source of the data series but also which data release we use.

Four series used in our estimation are taken from the national income and product accounts (NIPA). These accounts are produced by the Bureau of Economic Analysis and are constructed at quarterly frequency. The four series are real GDP (GDPC), the GDP price deflator (GDPDEF), nominal personal consumption expenditures (PCEC), and nominal fixed private investment (FPI). The variable names that we use, except that for real GDP, are also the same as those used by Smets and Wouters. We use a different name for real GDP because whereas Smets and Wouters define real GDP in terms of chained 1996 dollars, in our analysis the chained dollars for which real GDP is defined change with the data's base year. (In fact, the GDP price deflator also changes with the base year, since it is usually set to 100 in the base year.)

Another series used in our estimation is compensation per hour in the nonfarm business sector (PRS85006103), taken from the Bureau of Labor Statistics' quarterly Labor Productivity and Costs (LPC) release. The variable name is that assigned to it by the data service (Macrospect) that Smets and Wouters used to extract their data.

Three additional series used in our estimation are taken from the Employment Situation Summary (ESS), which contains the findings of two surveys: the Household Survey and the Establishment Survey. These three series, which are produced by the Bureau of Labor Statistics and constructed at monthly frequency, are average weekly hours of production and nonsupervisory employees for total private industries (PRS85006023), civilian employment (CE16OV), and civilian noninstitutional population (LNSINDEX). The first of these series is from the Establishment Survey and the other two are from the Household Survey. Since our model is quarterly, we calculate simple quarterly averages of the monthly data.

The final series in our model, the federal funds rate, differs from the others in that it is not revised after the first release. This series is obtained from the Federal Reserve Board's H.15 release, published every business day, and our quarterly series is simply the averages of these daily data.

We transform all of our data sources for use in the model in exactly the same way as Smets and Wouters:

consumption = $\ln[(PCEC/GDPDEF)/LNSINDEX] \times 100$
investment = $\ln[(FPI/GDPDEF)/LNSINDEX] \times 100$

output = ln(GDPC/LNSINDEX) × 100
hours = ln[(PRS85006023 × CE16OV/100)/LNSINDEX] × 100
inflation = ln(GDPDEF/GDPDEF$_{-1}$) × 100
real wage = ln(PRS85006103/GDPDEF) × 100
interest rate = federal funds rate ÷ 4.

Obtaining the Real-Time Datasets Corresponding to Greenbook Forecasts

Appendix table A1 provides for the year 1997 what, in the vertical dimension, is essentially a timeline of the dates of all Greenbook forecasts and all release dates for the data sources that we use *and that revise*. The horizontal dimension of the table sorts the release dates by data source. The online appendix includes a set of tables for the whole 1992–2004 sample period. From these tables it is reasonably straightforward to understand how we go about constructing the real-time datasets that we use to estimate the models from which we obtain our model forecasts to be compared with the Greenbook forecasts. Specifically, for each Greenbook forecast the table shows the most recent release, or vintage, of each data source at the time that edition of the Greenbook closed. For example, for the June 1997 Greenbook forecast, which closed on June 25, the tables show that the most recent release of NIPA data was the preliminary release of 1997Q1, on May 30, and the most recent release of the LPC data was the final release of 1997Q1, on June 18.[16]

The ESS data require a little more explanation. These are monthly series for which the first estimate of the data is available quite promptly (within a week) after the data's reference period. Thus, for example, the last release of the ESS before the June 1997 Greenbook is that for May 1997, released on June 6. Each ESS release, however, includes not only the first estimate of the preceding month's data (in this case May) but also revisions to the two preceding months (in this case April and March). This means that from the perspective of thinking about quarterly data, the June 6 ESS release represents the second and final revision of 1997Q1 data.[17]

---

16. Until last year the three releases in the NIPA were called the advance release, the preliminary release, and the final release. Thus, the preliminary release described above is actually the second of the three. Last year, however, the names of the releases were changed to the first release, the second release, and the final release. We refer to the original names of the releases in this paper. Note also that there are only two releases of the LPC for each quarter. These are called the preliminary release and the final release.

17. Of course, the release also contains two-thirds of the data for 1997Q2, but we do not use this information at all. This is reasonably standard practice.

Table A1. Dates of Greenbook Forecasts and NIPA, LPC, and ESS Releases, 1997[a]

Month	Greenbook closed	Greenbook forecast horizon	Interim NIPA releases	Interim LPC releases	Interim ESS releases (monthly)	Interim ESS releases (quarterly)
January[†]	1/29/97	97Q1–98Q4	96Q3(F): 12/20/96		96Dec: 1/10/97[b]	96Q4: 1/10/97
			96Q4(A): 1/31/97 96Q4(P): 2/28/97	96Q4(P): 2/11/97 96Q4(F): 3/11/97[c]	97Jan: 2/7/97 97Feb: 3/7/97	96Q4(r1): 2/7/97 96Q4(r2): 3/7/97
March	3/19/97	97Q1–98Q4	96Q4(F): 3/28/97 97Q1(A): 4/30/97 97Q1(A, Err): 5/7/97	97Q1(P): 5/7/97	97Mar: 4/4/97 97Apr: 5/2/97	97Q1: 4/4/97 97Q1(r1): 5/2/97
May	5/15/97	97Q2–98Q4	97Q1(P): 5/30/97	97Q1(F): 6/18/97	97May: 6/6/97[d]	97Q1(r2): 6/6/97
June	6/25/97	97Q2–98Q4	97Q1(F): 6/27/97 97Q2(A): 7/31/97[c]	97Q2(P): 8/12/97[e]	97Jun: 7/3/97 97Jul: 8/1/97	97Q2: 7/3/97 97Q2(r1): 8/1/97
August	8/14/97	97Q3–98Q4	97Q2(P): 8/28/97	97Q2(F): 9/9/97	97Aug: 9/5/97	97Q2(r2): 9/5/97
September	9/24/97	97Q3–99Q4	97Q2(F): 9/26/97 97Q3(A): 10/31/97		97Sep: 10/3/97	97Q3: 10/3/97
November	11/6/97	97Q4–99Q4	97Q3(P): 11/26/97	97Q3(P): 11/13/97 97Q3(F): 12/4/97	97Oct: 11/7/97 97Nov: 12/5/97	97Q3(r1): 11/7/97 97Q3(r2): 12/5/97
December	12/11/97	97Q4–99Q4				

Sources: Board of Governors of the Federal Reserve System, Bureau of Economic Analysis, and Bureau of Labor Statistics.
a. NIPA = national income and product accounts; LPC = Labor Productivity and Costs; ESS = Employment Situation Summary; A = advance; P = preliminary; F = final; Err = corrected; r1 and r2, first and second revisions. Dagger indicates rounds for which one more quarter of employment data than of NIPA data are available.
b. Current Population Survey revisions also released on this date.
c. Annual revisions also released on this date.
d. Consumer Expenditure Survey revisions also released on this date.
e. Revision in response to the NIPA annual revisions also released on this date.

By looking up what vintage of the data was available at the time of each Greenbook, we can construct a dataset corresponding to each Greenbook that contains observations for each of our model variables taken from the correct release vintage. All vintages for 1992 to 1996 (shown in tables 1 to 5 in the online appendix) were obtained from ALFRED, an archive of Federal Reserve economic data maintained by the St. Louis Federal Reserve Bank. All vintages for 1997 to 2004 (shown in tables 6 to 13 in the online appendix and, for 1997, in table A1 in this paper) were obtained from datasets that since September 1996 have been archived by Federal Reserve Board staff at the end of each Greenbook round.

In the June 1997 example given above, the last observation that we have for each data series is the same: 1997Q1. This will not always be the case. For example, in every January Greenbook round, LPC data are not available for the preceding year's fourth quarter, ESS data are always available, and NIPA data are sometimes available, specifically, only in the years 1992–94. This means that in the January Greenbook for all years other than 1992–94, there is one more quarter of employment data than of NIPA data. This is also the case in the October 2002 and 2003 Greenbooks; all Greenbooks for which this is an issue are marked with a dagger (†) in table A1 of this paper and in tables 1 to 13 of the online appendix.

Differences in data availability can also work the other way. For example, in the Greenbooks marked with an asterisk (*) in table A1 of this paper and tables 1 to 13 of the online appendix, there is always one less observation of the LPC data than of the NIPA data. We use the availability of the NIPA data as what determines whether data are available for a given quarter or not. Thus, if we have an extra quarter of ESS data (as we do in the rounds indicated by †), we ignore those data, even those for HOURS, in making our first quarter-ahead forecasts. If instead we have one less quarter of the LPC data (as we do in the rounds indicated by *), we use the Federal Reserve Board staff's estimate of compensation per hour for the quarter, which is calculated based on the ESS's reading of average hourly earnings. This is always available in real time, since the ESS is very prompt. Of course, this raises the question of why (given its timeliness) we do not just use the ESS's estimate for wages (that is, average hourly earnings for total private industry) instead of the LPC's compensation per hour for the nonfarm business sector series. One reason is our desire to stay as close as possible to Smets and Wouters, but another is that real-time data on average hourly earnings in ALFRED extend back only to 1999. Also, there are much more elegant ways to deal with the lack of uniformity in data availability that we face. In particular, the Kalman filter, which is present in our DSGE model, represents one way to make use of data that are available for only some series. We leave this to future work.

Obtaining the Real-Time Datasets Corresponding to Blue Chip Forecasts

Tables 14 though 31 of the online appendix provide a timeline of the dates for all Blue Chip forecasts and the release dates of all our data sources. These tables are exactly analogous to tables 1 to 13 of the online appendix for the Greenbook except that they extend further in time to September 2009, one year before the conference draft of this paper was written. Note also that there are 12 Blue Chip forecasts per year.

As with the Greenbook, there are instances where the last observation in time differs across series. Indeed, this is more frequent for the Blue Chip, because its survey of forecasters occurs at the beginning of the month, close to the time when the ESS is released, whereas the preliminary release of the LPC is usually at the beginning of February, May, August, and November. The timing of the ESS's release means that for every January, April, July, and October edition of the Blue Chip forecasts, there is an extra quarter of employment data that we do not use in the estimation. Again, these rounds are marked with a dagger in tables 14 to 31 of the online appendix. Blue Chip rounds marked with an asterisk denote those for which we have one less quarter of LPC data than of NIPA data. In these cases, however, the LPC data are released only a day or so later, so we make the assumption that forecasters do have these data over the relevant quarters. As with the Greenbook forecast, we use the availability of NIPA data to determine whether data are available for a quarter.

Constructing the First Final Data

The data release tables also give some indication of how we construct the "first final" data series, the series against which the Greenbook, Blue Chip, and model forecasts are evaluated. Every third release of the NIPA data and every second release of the LPC data is marked with an "F," indicating that it is the final release of the data before they are revised in either an annual or a comprehensive revision. For ESS releases, the final release for any quarter is indicated by "r2." This denotes the second revision to the data, which is the last revision before any annual revision or benchmarking is made. Note that even when considering our economic growth forecasts, we are in fact considering real GDP growth per capita, and for this reason we must also pay attention to the "first final" releases of the ESS.

We construct the first final data by simply extracting the first final observation—always the last one—from each final (F) or second revision (r2) vintage. We must, however, extract not the *levels* of these observations but rather the *growth rates*. The reason is that whenever there is a comprehensive revision, the base year of real GDP and the GDP price deflator changes, so that if we were to construct our first final series in levels, the series would have large jumps at quarters where a comprehensive revision takes place. Deriving our first final series in growth rates overcomes this problem.

ACKNOWLEDGMENTS We are grateful to Burçin Kısacıkoğlu for outstanding research assistance that went beyond the call of duty. We thank Harun Alp, Selim Elekdağ, Jeff Fuhrer, Marvin Goodfriend, Fulya Özcan, Jeremy Rudd, Frank Smets, Peter Tulip, Raf Wouters, and Jonathan Wright, as well as seminar participants at Bilkent University, the Brookings Panel, the Central Bank of Turkey, the Geneva Graduate Institute, George Washington University, the Johns Hopkins University, Middle East Technical University, and the Paris School of Economics for very useful comments and suggestions. We thank Ricardo Reis, Chris Sims, and the editors for several rounds of detailed feedback, and Volker Wieland and Maik Wolters for allowing us to cross-check our data with theirs. This paper uses Blue Chip Economic Indicators and Blue Chip Financial Forecasts: Blue Chip Economic Indicators and Blue Chip Financial Forecasts are publications owned by Aspen Publishers. Copyright © 2010 by Aspen Publishers, Inc. All rights reserved. http://www.aspenpublishers.com. The views expressed here are our own and do not necessarily reflect the views of the Board of Governors or the staff of the Federal Reserve System.

The authors report no relevant potential conflicts of interest.

References

Adolfson, Malin, Michael K. Andersson, Jesper Lindé, Mattias Villani, and Anders Vredin. 2007. "Modern Forecasting Models in Action: Improving Macroeconomic Analyses at Central Banks." *International Journal of Central Banking* 3, no. 4: 111–44.

Atkeson, Andrew, and Lee E. Ohanian. 2001. "Are Phillips Curves Useful for Forecasting Inflation?" Federal Reserve Bank of Minneapolis *Quarterly Review* 25, no. 1 (Winter): 2–11.

Blanchard, Olivier, and Jordi Galí. 2007. "Real Wage Rigidities and the New Keynesian Model." *Journal of Money, Credit and Banking* 39, no. 1: 35–65.

Calvo, Guillermo A. 1983. "Staggered Prices in a Utility-Maximizing Framework." *Journal of Monetary Economics* 12, no. 3: 383–98.

Christiano, Lawrence J., Martin Eichenbaum, and Charles L. Evans. 2005. "Nominal Rigidities and the Dynamic Effects of a Shock to Monetary Policy." *Journal of Political Economy* 113, no. 1: 1–45.

Christoffel, Kai, Günter Coenen, and Anders Warne. Forthcoming. "Forecasting with DSGE Models." In *Handbook of Forecasting*, edited by M. Clements and D. Hendry. Oxford University Press.

D'Agostino, Antonello, Domenico Giannone, and Paolo Surico. 2006. "(Un) Predictability and Macroeconomic Stability." ECB Working Paper no. 605. Frankfurt: European Central Bank.

Edge, Rochelle M., Michael T. Kiley, and Jean-Philippe Laforte. 2007. "Documentation of the Research and Statistics Division's Estimated DSGE Model of the U.S. Economy: 2006 Version." FEDS Working Paper 2007-53. Washington: Board of Governors of the Federal Reserve System.

———. 2010. "A Comparison of Forecast Performance between Federal Reserve Staff Forecasts, Simple Reduced-Form Models, and a DSGE Model." *Journal of Applied Econometrics* 25: 720–54.

Faust, Jon, and Jonathan H. Wright. 2009. "Comparing Greenbook and Reduced Form Forecasts Using a Large Realtime Dataset." *Journal of Business and Economic Statistics* 27, no. 4: 468–79.

Fuhrer, Jeff, Giovanni Olivei, and Geoffrey M. B. Tootell. 2009. "Empirical Estimates of Changing Inflation Dynamics." FRB Boston Working Paper no. 09-4. Federal Reserve Bank of Boston.

Galí, Jordi. 2010. "Are Central Banks' Projections Meaningful?" CEPR Discussion Paper 8027. London: Centre for Economic Policy Research.

Galí, Jordi, Frank Smets, and Rafael Wouters. 2010. "Unemployment in an Estimated New Keynesian Model." Working paper. Barcelona: Centre de Recerca en Economia Internacional.

Goodfriend, Marvin, and Robert G. King. 2009. "The Great Inflation Drift." Working Paper no. 14862. Cambridge, Mass.: National Bureau of Economic Research.

Gürkaynak, Refet S., and Justin Wolfers. 2007. "Macroeconomic Derivatives: An Initial Analysis of Market-Based Macro Forecasts, Uncertainty, and Risk." *NBER International Seminar on Macroeconomics* 2005, no. 2: 11–50.

Gürkaynak, Refet, Brian Sack, and Eric T. Swanson. 2005. "Market-Based Measures of Monetary Policy Expectations." *Journal of Business and Economic Statistics* 25, no. 2: 201–12.

Kimball, Miles S. 1995. "The Quantitative Analytics of the Basic Neomonetarist Model." *Journal of Money, Credit and Banking* 27, no. 4, part 2: 1241–77.

King, Robert G., Charles I. Plosser, and Sergio T. Rebelo. 1988. "Production, Growth and Business Cycles I." *Journal of Monetary Economics* 21, no. 2–3: 195–232.

Lees, Kirdan, Troy Matheson, and Christie Smith. 2007. "Open Economy DSGE-VAR Forecasting and Policy Analysis: Head to Head with the RBNZ Published Forecasts." Discussion Paper no. 2007/01. Wellington: Reserve Bank of New Zealand.

Reifschneider, David, and Peter Tulip. 2007. "Gauging the Uncertainty of the Economic Outlook from Historical Forecasting Errors." FEDS Working Paper no. 2007-60. Washington: Board of Governors of the Federal Reserve.

Romer, Christina D., and David H. Romer. 2000. "Federal Reserve Information and the Behavior of Interest Rates." *American Economic Review* 90, no. 3: 429–57.

Sims, Christopher A. 2002. "The Role of Models and Probabilities in the Monetary Policy Process." *BPEA*, no. 2: 1–40.

Smets, Frank, and Raf Wouters. 2003. "An Estimated Dynamic Stochastic General Equilibrium Model of the Euro Area." *Journal of the European Economic Association* 1, no. 5: 1123–75.

———. 2007. "Shocks and Frictions in US Business Cycles: A Bayesian DSGE Approach." *American Economic Review* 97, no. 3: 586–606.

Stock, James H., and Mark W. Watson. 2007. "Why Has U.S. Inflation Become Harder to Forecast?" *Journal of Money, Credit and Banking* 39, no. 1: 3–33.

———. 2010. "Modeling Inflation after the Crisis." Paper presented at the Federal Reserve Bank of Kansas City Economic Policy Symposium, Jackson Hole, Wyo., August 26–28.

Trehan, Bharat. 2010. "Survey Measures of Expected Inflation and the Inflation Process." FRBSF Working Paper Series no. 2009-10. Federal Reserve Bank of San Francisco.

Tulip, Peter. 2009. "Has the Economy Become More Predictable? Changes in Greenbook Forecast Accuracy." *Journal of Money, Credit and Banking* 41, no. 6: 1217–31.

Wieland, Volker, and Maik H. Wolters. 2010. "The Diversity of Forecasts from Macroeconomic Models of the U.S. Economy." Working paper. Goethe University.

Comments and Discussion

COMMENT BY
RICARDO REIS[1]   Progress in the study of short-run economic fluctuations seems to come in three stages. First, macroeconomists become excited by the arrival of a new theoretical approach, a new set of principles to organize knowledge, or some new modeling tools. Second come the refiners, who explore how to apply the idea to an increasing number of markets and to tease out all of its implications. Third, a synthesis emerges, bringing together the progress in different areas into one large model that tries to capture many features of an aggregate economy. This last stage is always technically challenging and involves considerable ingenuity at fine tuning models to match the subtleties of the data.

One example of this evolution is the progress from Keynes's ideas on the role of aggregate demand, disequilibrium, and rigidities, to the refining work on the investment accelerator, the consumption function, money demand, and the Phillips curve, finally leading to the synthesis of these ideas in the large-scale MPS and Brookings models. Similarly, over the last 30 years, the ideas of Finn Kydland and Edward Prescott (1982) and Gregory Mankiw and David Romer (1991) were applied and refined, culminating in the 2000s in the dynamic stochastic general equilibrium (DSGE) synthesis of Lawrence Christiano, Martin Eichenbaum, and Charles Evans (2005) and Frank Smets and Raf Wouters (2003). For a subgroup of macroeconomists, work in the last few years has been solidly in the third, synthesis stage.

The DSGE approach has never lacked for criticism (for a recent critique, see Caballero 2010), but until recently these models seemed successful at empirically matching business cycle facts and producing short-run forecasts that were as good as those from vector autoregressions (VARs). However,

---

1. I am grateful to Betsy Feldman, Dylan Kotliar, and Benjamin Mills for comments.

the Great Recession dealt this body of work a heavy blow. The models not only failed to predict the crisis but also were unable to provide an interpretation of the events after the fact, because for the most part they omitted a financial sector. It is too early to tell whether this failure will lead to this class of DSGE models being refined or abandoned, but already it is clear that their empirical performance must be judged more carefully.

This is what Rochelle Edge and Refet Gürkaynak set out to do in this paper: to reassess empirically the forecasting performance of the Smets and Wouters DSGE model. They explore how this model would have forecasted, from 1 to 8 quarters ahead, movements in inflation, output growth, and interest rates between 1997 and 2006. Importantly, they do not give the model the unfair advantage of 20-20 hindsight. In 2000Q1, for example, their fictional econometrician produces estimates and forecasts using only the data available at the time.

The conclusions of their exercise are surprising, at least to this reader. On the positive side, the DSGE model's forecasts beat those from a Bayesian VAR as well as the Greenbook forecasts compiled by the staff of the Federal Reserve, and its forecasts are precise, as demonstrated by their small root mean squared errors (RMSEs). On the negative side, the forecasts themselves are terrible, worse than a simple naïve forecast of constant inflation (or constant output growth), and worse than a forecast that simply assumes that inflation equals its last available observation. In addition, the model's low RMSEs are much less impressive once one realizes that the variance of inflation was also quite small during this period. Rather, the forecasting power is close to zero, and trying to improve the forecasts through some second-stage "cleaning" regressions makes almost no difference.

Contemplating this outcome, the authors see the glass as half full. They argue that according to the model, if monetary policy was effective, then inflation *should* be difficult to predict and should have a low variance. I am considerably more skeptical of this point of view in light of the events of the last 2 years. Inflation and output growth have not been stable since 2008, but rather have fallen quite dramatically. At the same time, the model's forecast errors for 2008–10 are large and persistent, as figures 5 and 6 of the paper demonstrate. If the authors' explanation is correct, these two facts would have been highly unlikely, unless monetary policy suddenly became particularly ineffective during these last 2 years. I would argue instead that larger shocks during this period simply exposed the model's faults.

Beyond this general assessment, I will offer two comments on the paper, as well as on the broader literature on DSGEs and forecasting. First, I will quibble somewhat with the authors' methodology, in particular with their peculiar mix of Bayesian and frequentist elements. Second, I will argue more generally that by setting themselves the goal of unconditional forecasting of aggregate variables, macroeconomists are setting such a high bar that they are almost sure to fail. Instead I will argue, through reference to a practical example, that DSGE models can be useful at making predictions even when they fail at making forecasts.

FORECASTING METHODOLOGY. The problem of estimation and forecasting with a DSGE model (or indeed with most models) can be expressed in the following setup. Assume that a researcher has a model or structure, S, that postulates some relationships among variables. The model has a vector of parameters, θ, and some prior information is available about what their values might be, captured in a probability density function $p(\theta|S)$. The sample of data that one is trying to explain at some date t, including current and past observations of many variables, is denoted by y_t, and its density is $p(y_t|S)$. Finally, the likelihood of having observed these data is the density $L(y_t|S,\theta)$, which is typically known and easy to calculate given certain assumptions about the normality of the distribution of shocks.

Edge and Gürkaynak use Bayes's rule to estimate the parameters:

$$(1) \qquad p(\theta|y_t, S) = \frac{L(y_t|S, \theta) p(\theta|S)}{p(y_t|S)}.$$

The output is a posterior density that reflects the uncertainty about the parameters through the whole posterior distribution. Although conceptually simple, this estimation work can be computationally exhausting. Fortunately, there has been much progress on algorithms in this area, as evidenced by the fact that Edge and Gürkaynak's paper contains more than 300 estimates of the model for different subsamples.

BAYESIAN ESTIMATION BUT NOT BAYESIAN FORECASTING. When it comes to forecasting, the authors take a distinctly non-Bayesian approach. First, they pick the mode of the posterior density at a date t: $\theta_t^* = \arg\max_\theta p(\theta|y_t, S)$. Next, they use the model's law of motion to obtain the probability density for the variable to be forecasted j periods ahead: $p(y_{t+j}|y_t, S, \theta^*)$. Finally, they take the average over this density to represent their model forecast as an expectation:

$$(2) \qquad m_{t+j}(\theta_t^*, S) = \int y_{t+j}\, p(y_{t+j}|y_t, S, \theta_t^*)\, dy_{t+j}.$$

The common approach when taking a frequentist perspective is to take the mode of the density (akin to the maximum-likelihood estimator) and produce the unbiased point forecast. But this is unnatural to the Bayesian, who is careful to take into account parameter uncertainty in the estimation stage, and so does not want to ignore it by focusing on the mode when it comes to forecasting. Likewise, it is awkward for a Bayesian to focus on one average forecast rather than report that there is a distribution of possible forecasts, each with some probability of occurring.

As I see it, asked what the model predicts for inflation or output j periods out, the Bayesian forecaster would perform the following computation:

$$(3) \qquad b(y_{t+j}|y_t, S) = \int p(y_{t+j}|y_t, S, \theta) p(\theta|y_t, S) d\theta.$$

That is, she would consider both the uncertainty about the future due to the possible arrival of shocks, captured as a density, $p(y_{t+j}|y_t, S, \theta)$, and the uncertainty on the parameter estimates, captured as a posterior, $p(\theta|y_t, S)$. Instead of producing a single average forecast, the Bayesian forecaster would integrate over all the possible parameter combinations, θ, and report not a single number but rather a density function of possible forecasts, $b(y_{t+j}|y_t, S)$, given the current data and the model at hand. To assess whether the model is good at forecasting, this econometrician might then ask, How often does the actual realization of y_{t+j} fall within the interquartile range of its prediction, $b(y_{t+j}|y_t, S)$? If this happens much less often than 75 percent of the time, then the model is not giving good forecasts.

WHAT IS IN THE MODEL, WHAT IS IN THE PARAMETERS? Another difficulty with the authors' methodology is that although they try very hard to keep future information from influencing their past forecasts, one can only push this pseudo-forecasting exercise so far. The authors are careful to try to use only data available up to date t to produce forecasts for date $t + j$. This care is evident in two ways. First, the forecast, $m_{t+j}(\theta_t^*, S)$, depends on the posterior estimate of parameters, θ_t^*, which used only data up to date t. Second, the data are not the revised data that we have today for that period, but rather the data that forecasters had available at the time.

However, Edge and Gürkaynak use the model structure S at all dates, as given to them by Smets and Wouters (2007). As the opening paragraph of Smets and Wouters (2003) makes clear, this structure did not arise purely from theory. Rather, it assumes a particular utility function with a very peculiar habit term and a very specific law of motion. The Smets and Wouters model assumes adjustment costs for some actions but not for others, and it has sporadic updating, not of prices, but of prices relative to a backward-looking index. All of these elements and more arose because the Smets and Wouters model is the result of an iterative process between theorists and the data over the previous 20 years. Thus, even if the authors' estimates of the parameters in 1992Q1 use only information available then, the structure brought to the data was arrived at by researchers looking continuously at the data all the way into the 2000s and adjusting that structure to improve its fit and forecasting performance.

Moreover, the distinction between S and θ is ultimately arbitrary. The Smets and Wouters model has a Cobb-Douglas production function (the S) for which the parameter is the labor share (the θ). But one can also see this as a production function with a constant elasticity of substitution (the S) and with the labor share and this elasticity of substitution (the θ) as parameters. Researchers used data covering all of the sample to agree on a strict prior that the elasticity of substitution is exactly equal to 1, and this knowledge has become embedded in the structure of the model, transitioning from θ to S. In short, Edge and Gürkaynak make forecasts from the perspective of the 1990s using the structure S that researchers arrived at from interacting with the data in the 2000s.

THE HIGH, AND PERHAPS UNREALISTIC, EXPECTATIONS OF MACROECONOMISTS. Turning more generally to the goal of the broad literature that uses DSGE models in forecasting, I wonder whether macroeconomists are being unrealistically ambitious. At the same session of the Brookings Panel conference at which Edge and Gürkaynak presented this paper, two other papers were presented. In one, Thomas Dee and Brian Jacob build a regression model of educational outcomes to identify the effects of the No Child Left Behind policy. In the other, Gary Gorton and Andrew Metrick offer a theory of the role of shadow banks in the financial system and use it to justify a form of regulation. One could ask the authors of both papers, What are your unconditional forecasts for student achievement and total financial assets, respectively, in the United States for 2010–12?

If one attempted, literally, to use the models in those papers to make such forecasts, the results would likely be terrible. But it is not hard to guess that the authors would be puzzled that I would even be asking the question, and almost surely they would not endorse the forecasts thus arrived at. Nor, I would venture, would most, if not all, labor and financial economists. Most economists write models to capture some particular trade-offs and to make some limited predictions about what would happen if a particular policy were followed. To many economists, it is hard to imagine that one could know enough about any given market to

Figure 1. Federal Funds Rate: DSGE Model Forecast and Actual, 2001Q3–2003Q2

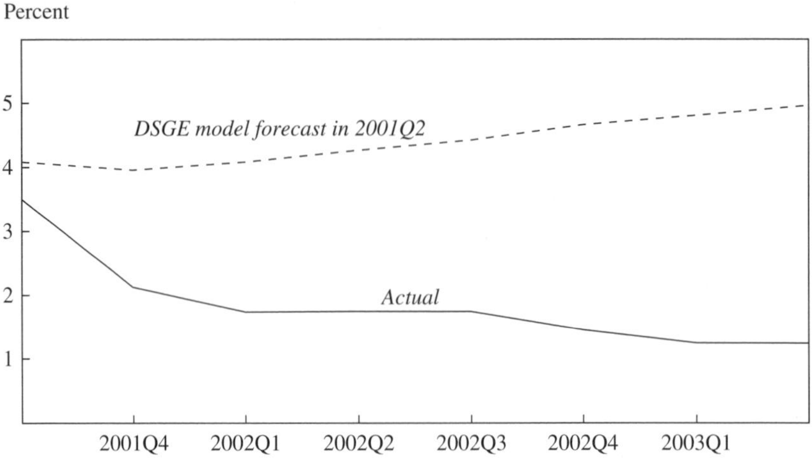

[Figure: Line chart showing DSGE model forecast in 2001Q2 remaining near 4–5 percent while the Actual federal funds rate drops from about 3.5 percent in 2001Q4 to about 1.2 percent by 2003Q1.]

Source: Federal Reserve data and author's calculations.

make the type of unconditional forecasts sought in the question posed in the previous paragraph.

Some macroeconomists, however, do not shy away from producing unconditional forecasts. On the one hand, this is puzzling. If anything, our ability to forecast many aggregate variables at once is likely smaller than our ability to forecast outcomes in particular education or financial markets. On the other hand, it is understandable that macroeconomists produce these forecasts because there is an enormous demand for them from policymakers and the public at large. One consequence of this ambition to produce unconditional forecasts is that, with some regularity, the forecasts fail, sometimes in spectacular fashion. Forecasting is, simply put, a very hard thing to do.

PREDICTION INSTEAD OF FORECASTING. Even if unconditional forecasting may be too hard a task, a model can still make sharp *predictions* that are useful to policymakers. As an interesting illustration, consider the challenge facing the Federal Reserve at the start of 2001Q3. The economy was hit by a shock that economists did not predict (and, I would add, should not have predicted): the September 11 terrorist attacks. Imagine that the Federal Reserve at the time was using the Smets and Wouters model estimated by Edge and Gürkaynak to consider two possible policy responses to this shock. One response would be to ignore the shock, keeping to the same course of action as planned beforehand. This is displayed in my figure 1 as

COMMENTS and DISCUSSION

Figure 2. Inflation: DSGE Model Forecast, Actual, and Post–September 11 Counterfactual, 2001Q3–2003Q2

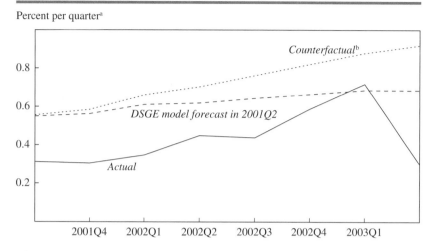

Source: Bureau of Economic Analysis data and author's calculations.
a. Inflation is measured as the quarter-to-quarter change in the GDP deflator.
b. Inflation rate that would have prevailed had the Federal Reserve not changed its federal funds rate target after September 11, 2001.

the forecasted path for nominal interest rates before the terrorist attack. The other response would be to cut nominal interest rates aggressively. This is captured in the figure by the actual path of interest rates that the Federal Reserve followed. Figure 2 shows the effect of the two policies for inflation, and figure 3 for GDP. I obtained these by substituting the differences between the two paths in figure 1 and treating those as innovations that were then fed through the model. Because the solved Smets and Wouters model is linear, this delivers the right partial effect from considering what discretionary policy response to follow.

The model predicts that by aggressively cutting interest rates, the Federal Reserve generated higher inflation throughout the next 2 years, cumulating to a difference of almost 0.3 percentage point. That implies that whereas actual inflation in the United States was 0.3 percent in 2003Q2, if the Federal Reserve had not reacted to the shock, it would have been close to zero. Similarly, according to the model, GDP growth, instead of being close to zero between 2001Q3 and 2003Q2, would have been between −0.2 and −0.3 percent for most of 2002 and 2003.

This is the type of prediction that, I would conjecture, policymakers want from a model. It answers the following question: If some policy course is

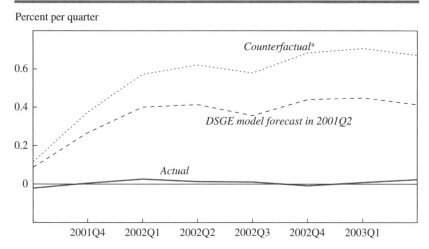

Figure 3. GDP Growth: DSGE Model Forecast, Actual, and Post–September 11 Counterfactual, 2001Q3–2003Q2

Source: Bureau of Economic Analysis data and author's calculations.
a. GDP growth rate that would have prevailed had the Federal Reserve not changed its federal funds rate target after September 11, 2001.

followed, what will happen? Moreover, the DSGE model can confidently answer two further questions. First, why is the model predicting this? The impulse responses to monetary policy shocks in the model, and the trade-offs that agents face within it, provide a clear answer to this question. Second, how confident can we be about these predictions? This could be easily assessed by using the Bayesian approach I described in the previous section, rather than taking the modal estimate as I did for these plots.

This is where DSGE models excel. Indeed, few other types of models in economics can compete with them at answering these types of questions. DSGE models allow the researcher to provide precise quantitative predictions, to quantify the uncertainty around them, and to attach to the forecasts an internally coherent economic narrative. Considering more alternative scenarios is easy within the model, and more broadly, the information presented this way can be supplemented with that from other models as well as other subjective inputs.

If the models are going to be used this way, then one would like to know how good these predictions are. Unconditional forecasts do not answer this question, even if they give a strong hint (and the poor performance of the forecasts found by the authors suggests that the predictions may not be very trustworthy). As an alternative, researchers can (and do) compare the model's predictions with identified impulse responses from VARs or from natural experiments. Or they can use individual studies of the different mechanisms that the model is synthesizing, to see if the different parts of the story hold up on their own. I hope that more effort will go into refining the tests of models along this dimension. This would help in judging other DSGE models as well as in ultimately deciding whether the whole DSGE research agenda is useful.

REFERENCES FOR THE REIS COMMENT

Caballero, Ricardo J. 2010. "Macroeconomics after the Crisis: Time to Deal with the Pretense-of-Knowledge Syndrome." *Journal of Economic Perspectives* 24, no. 4: 85–102.

Christiano, Lawrence J., Martin Eichenbaum, and Charles L. Evans. 2005. "Nominal Rigidities and the Dynamic Effects of a Shock to Monetary Policy." *Journal of Political Economy* 113: 1–45.

Kydland, Finn E., and Edward C. Prescott. 1982. "Time to Build and Aggregate Fluctuations." *Econometrica* 50, no. 6: 1345–70.

Mankiw, N. Gregory, and David Romer. 1991. *New Keynesian Economics,* vols. 1 and 2. MIT Press.

Smets, Frank, and Raf Wouters. 2003. "An Estimated Dynamic Stochastic General Equilibrium Model of the Euro Area." *Journal of the European Economic Association* 1, no. 5: 1123–75.

———. 2007. "Shocks and Frictions in US Business Cycles: A Bayesian DSGE Approach." *American Economic Review* 97, no. 3: 586–606.

COMMENT BY

CHRISTOPHER A. SIMS   It is important from time to time to look at the forecasting records of models used for policy analysis. This is how forecasters and users of models learn which ones are more reliable and discover ways to improve model specifications. Doing these evaluations is harder than it might appear. Data revisions are of the same order of magnitude as forecast errors, so it is essential to take a consistent view of what is to be forecast and to make sure that forecasts being compared are based on the same data. This is a formidable task if done carefully, and this paper by Rochelle Edge and Refet Gürkaynak has indeed done it carefully.

The paper says that the forecasts of dynamic stochastic general equilibrium models, like the other forecasts it considers, have been "poor" and "not very useful for policymaking" and that the DSGE model forecasts "do not contribute much information." But there is in fact no support for these conclusions in the data the paper displays.

The only way to justify a claim that a forecast is poor is to show that some other feasible way to forecast was, or would have been, better. The period covered by most of the authors' tables and figures, running through 2006, was one of unusual macroeconomic stability. Previous studies of forecast accuracy have shown that the margin of superiority of sophisticated forecasting methods over naive methods was small in this period, as is to be expected when the variables being forecast make small and smooth movements. Yet the paper's figure 3 shows that the DSGE model forecasts had, for the most part, root mean square errors as good as or better than every other feasible forecast the paper considers. In some cases the "forecast" that the paper labels as a "constant" forecast does better, but this is not a feasible alternative—it uses data from the future in "forecasting" the future, so as to automatically eliminate bias in the forecast. What is more remarkable is that the margin by which the DSGE model forecasts improve on the other forecasts is not statistically small. The paper points out (in a footnote!) that statistical tests show the DSGE model forecasts to have better RMSEs than feasible purely statistical alternatives (the Bayesian VAR and random walk forecasts) by a statistically significant margin for inflation and GDP growth. One would like to know what the corresponding results for forecasts of interest rates or interest rate changes are. It might appear from figure 3 that the RMSEs are essentially the same after the first 2 quarters for interest rates, but because the nowcast of interest rates by the Greenbook is so much more accurate than the others, the scale in figure 3 is spread out, and the apparent similarity of the RMSEs in that plot for later quarters may be misleading.

The paper also presents another approach to evaluating forecast accuracy, based on regressions of actual values on their forecasts. An ideal forecast would have a coefficient of 1 in such a regression and a constant term of zero. In comparing forecasts meeting this ideal, the higher the R^2 for the regression, the better, and a higher R^2 would imply a lower RMSE. For inflation, the paper's table 1 shows that all the forecasts have low R^2s with actual values and statistically significant constant terms. They are very far from "ideal." Since the R^2s are low, the differences among the forecasts in RMSE must be determined by their degree of bias and by the scale of the random variation in the forecast around a constant. It is clear, then, why the constant forecast does well, in terms of RMSEs, for inflation: in a contest where bias is a major determinant of accuracy, it has simply eliminated bias after seeing the future data. But for forecasts like these, the regression results give little direct insight into accuracy. The BVAR and DSGE regression results look quite similar, even in the sizes of their estimated coefficients, yet the DSGE model's RMSE is considerably better, by a statistically significant margin, than that of the BVAR at all horizons beyond the first.

The results for GDP growth in table 2 show a clear difference between the DSGE model and the other two forecasts. Although one cannot be sure, because the paper does not present the results of such tests, it looks as if the DSGE model forecasts would pass a test of "rationality" (a slope of 1 and an intercept of zero) at least at the 3-quarter horizon and beyond, whereas the other two forecasts clearly would not. The picture that results is somewhat puzzling: the regression results suggest that there is little evidence that using the longer-horizon DSGE model GDP forecasts in unmodified form was a mistake, whereas there is strong evidence in the regression that doing so with the Greenbook forecast of GDP was a mistake. This corresponds to the clear margin of superiority in terms of RMSE for the DSGE model over the Greenbook and the BVAR in figure 3 for GDP, but leaves it a bit mysterious why the Greenbook forecasts emerge as statistically indistinguishable in terms of RMSE from the DSGE forecasts. Possibly this is a matter of using 95 percent confidence levels to define "indistinguishable" when a difference would have emerged at the 90 percent level, but one cannot be sure from the paper's brief footnote discussion of formal RMSE-difference tests.

The results for interest rates in tables 3 and 4 show a very different picture. The R^2s of the forecasts of interest rate levels (table 3) using actual data are high, and it appears that tests of rationality might be passed at longer horizons for all the models. (In saying such tests "might be passed," I am looking at whether the coefficients lie within 2 standard errors of the ideal-forecast values. This is not foolproof, because the estimated coefficients could be correlated.) Table 4 shows that this good performance is not simply a consequence of making "no change" forecasts for interest rate levels. The R^2s are statistically significantly positive at the 10 percent level for forecasts of interest rate changes at most long horizons for both the BVAR and the DSGE forecasts, and again it appears that at these horizons, in most cases, these forecasts would pass tests of rationality. It is not surprising that the Greenbook does not do so well at long-horizon forecasting of changes in interest rates, because for most of this period the Greenbook forecasts assumed constant interest rates.

The message from tables 3 and 4 is that although the DSGE interest rate forecasts were not clearly better than those of a BVAR, there was a substantial amount of predictable variation in interest rates, and both the BVAR and the DSGE forecasts succeeded in capturing it.

Where does this pattern of results leave us? Certainly not with a conclusion that the DSGE forecasts were "poor." This is especially true when one considers that the DSGE model is known, through published research on its impulse responses, to imply strong reactions of the economy to interest rate changes generated by policy. If the DSGE model had misestimated these reactions, therefore, it would have produced, in a period with substantial, predictable variation in interest rates, mistaken forecasts of GDP and inflation. Rather, the DSGE model produced forecasts of stable inflation and GDP growth by correctly modeling the response of monetary policy to the state of the economy, thereby producing good interest rate forecasts, and then by correctly modeling the stabilizing effects of these interest rate policy reactions on GDP growth and inflation.

A few less central aspects of the paper also deserve comment. First, the paper observes that a 2-standard-error confidence band for inflation 6 quarters ahead would be, according to the authors' calculations, 4 percentage points wide and says that such a confidence interval is "not very useful for policymaking." But this is the actual level of the uncertainty. The paper gives no evidence that some other way of forecasting could reduce this uncertainty. It should certainly be "useful" to policymakers to know the actual level of uncertainty. And this level of uncertainty would not in fact look unreasonable to most policymakers. Central banks that produce regular inflation reports usually display forecasts of inflation and output as fan charts, with clear error bands that widen over time. Policymaking in these countries is based on these projections and error bands, and the fan charts show forecast uncertainty consistent with the degree of forecast accuracy shown in figure 3 for the DSGE model forecasts. For example, the Swedish Riksbank's October 2010 *Monetary Policy Report* shows a fan chart for inflation in which the 90 percent band for annualized consumer price inflation 6 quarters ahead is about 4.8 percentage points wide, and of course a 95 percent band would be considerably wider. The error bands are said to be based on the historical record of Riksbank forecast accuracy, and the fan charts seem informative about expected future inflation, as well as realistic about the uncertainty surrounding these expectations.

The paper describes its priors, both for the DSGE model itself and for the BVAR naive standard of comparison, only by reference to Smets and Wouters (2003). It is unfortunate that the seminal Smets and Wouters paper used a prior for the BVAR that is highly simplified relative to any that would be used in a serious forecasting application of BVARs. The

"Minnesota prior" family of which this paper's BVAR prior is a member has a number of parameters that in any particular application have to be tuned, either by a formal Bayesian procedure that would integrate over a prior on these parameters, or informally by experimenting with a few settings of them, to be sure that the default settings are not far out of sync with the data. Smets and Wouters set these parameters at default values without checking whether the default values were reasonable for their data. The claim in the original Smets and Wouters papers that their DSGE model specification fits better than their BVAR comparison model is itself fragile if the parameters of the prior are handled more realistically. The BVAR might have been a stronger competitor to the DSGE model in this paper's analysis if the BVAR prior had been handled more carefully.

Finally, one of the main advantages of DSGE models estimated by Bayesian methods over previous vintages of econometric policy models is that the DSGE models provide usable measures of postsample uncertainty about parameters, and hence of uncertainty about forecasts. We are therefore interested at least as much—maybe more—in whether the model's characterization of the *distribution* of forecast errors is correct as we are in the accuracy of the point forecasts. This paper could have cited measures of this distributional accuracy, reporting, for example, how often actual values lay outside the model's implied 68 percent or 90 percent error bands as computed at the forecast date. That the paper did not seems to me a lost opportunity.

REFERENCE FOR THE SIMS COMMENT

Smets, Frank, and Raf Wouters. 2003. "An Estimated Dynamic Stochastic General Equilibrium Model of the Euro Area." *Journal of the European Economic Association* 1, no. 5: 1123—75.

GENERAL DISCUSSION   Justin Wolfers noted that the Bayesian setup means that the authors have a probability distribution over likely forecast errors, and hence he suggested that the authors use the full set of model posteriors to compare the size of the average forecast errors with those implied by the model.

Annette Vissing-Jorgensen remarked that the stock market should be useful in forecasting, since it is a valuable predictor of consumption growth. She was not sure how valuable an addition it would be in forecasting inflation, but it could be a useful indicator for GDP.

David Romer noted the paper's emphasis on the fact that, in baseline New Keynesian models like the DSGE model they use, inflation is not forecastable. In fact, those models imply that when the output gap has an important predictable component—which it appears to, based on its lagged values—inflation has an important forecastable component as well. He also commented that the paper's characterization of the model as predicting little variation in inflation during the sample period was somewhat of an exaggeration, and that the paper's figure 2 showed nontrivial variation in predicted inflation.

Donald Kohn expressed the hope that the recent period would turn out to be an outlier not worth including in the analysis. He noted that the DSGE model is not useful when policymakers need it most. Nor does it have a financial sector, which is a problematic omission given that sector's central role in the crisis. The Federal Reserve's FRB-US model has a rich financial sector, which could be adapted in an ad hoc way. As it is, however, the model is not useful for policy when interest rates are at their zero lower bound. Whatever the virtues and limitations of the various models, policymakers still have to know when to abandon the model and recognize the story that is unfolding around them.

Robert Gordon objected to the so-called New Keynesian Phillips curve embedded in all DSGE models, including that in the paper. By omitting the impact on inflation of supply shocks, including changes in the relative price of energy and of imports, as well as the impact of changes in trend productivity growth and of the imposition and then termination of the Nixon price controls in 1971–74, the models' inflation equations omit significant variables that give rise to a negative correlation between inflation and output. As a result, all New Keynesian Phillips curves report coefficients of inflation on the output gap that are biased toward zero.

Christopher Sims noted that models do sometimes forecast interest rates, and thus it is not hard to condition on interest rates not going below zero. Observing that GDP had been somewhat better forecasted by the DSGE model than inflation, Sims thought the zero lower bound should be imposed on the model either by building it in or by throwing out simulations with forecasted paths implying negative rates.

William Nordhaus thought that, in some sense, oranges were being compared to tangerines. There is a difference between a true forecast and a forecast that allows itself a peek at the future. The Blue Chip and Greenbook forecasts are true forecasts, but the DSGE forecasts are not. True forecasts will probably come from DSGE models in the future, but as of yet this has not happened. All forecasts are indeed quite poor, as the paper recognizes, and we often do not remember how poor they were after the fact. Nordhaus wondered what would be revealed by surveying a wider sample of forecasters, as has been done by the *Wall Street Journal,* especially about the extent to which forecasters' predictions tend to cluster together.

Ricardo Reis noted that recent research on the Smets-Wouters model interprets some of its residuals as being accounted for by the missing financial sector. However, he thought that where the model was most deficient was in its treatment of fiscal policy, and specifically its assumptions that government purchases are exogenous and that taxes are lump sum and neutral.

Robert Hall closed the discussion by reminding the Panel that Paul Samuelson had once said, at a Brookings Papers conference years ago, "If you have to forecast, forecast often."

GARY GORTON
Yale University

ANDREW METRICK
Yale University

Regulating the Shadow Banking System

ABSTRACT The shadow banking system played a major role in the recent financial crisis but remains largely unregulated. We propose principles for its regulation and describe a specific proposal to implement those principles. We document how the rise of shadow banking was helped by regulatory and legal changes that gave advantages to three main institutions: money-market mutual funds (MMMFs) to capture retail deposits from traditional banks, securitization to move assets of traditional banks off their balance sheets, and repurchase agreements (repos) that facilitated the use of securitized bonds as money. The evolution of a bankruptcy safe harbor for repos was crucial to the growth and efficiency of shadow banking; regulators can use access to this safe harbor as the lever to enforce new rules. History has demonstrated two successful methods for regulating privately created money: strict guidelines on collateral, and government-guaranteed insurance. We propose the use of insurance for MMMFs, combined with strict guidelines on collateral for both securitization and repos, with regulatory control established by chartering new forms of narrow banks for MMMFs and securitization, and using the bankruptcy safe harbor to incentivize compliance on repos.

After the Great Depression, by some combination of luck and genius, the United States created a bank regulatory system that oversaw a period of about 75 years free of financial panics, considerably longer than any such period since the founding of the republic. When this quiet period finally ended in 2007, the ensuing panic did not begin in the traditional system of banks and depositors, but instead was centered in a new "shadow" banking system. This system performs the same functions as traditional banking, but the names of the players are different, and the regulatory structure is light or nonexistent. In its broadest definition, shadow banking includes such familiar institutions as investment banks, money-market mutual funds (MMMFs), and mortgage brokers; some rather old contractual forms, such as sale-and-repurchase agreements (repos); and more esoteric instruments such as asset-backed securities (ABSs), collateralized debt obligations (CDOs), and asset-backed commercial paper (ABCP).[1]

Following the panic of 2007–09, Congress passed major regulatory reform of the financial sector in the Dodd-Frank Wall Street Reform and Consumer Protection Act of 2010. Dodd-Frank includes many provisions relevant to shadow banking; for example, hedge funds must now register with the Securities and Exchange Commission (SEC), much over-the-counter derivatives trading will be moved to exchanges and clearinghouses, and all systemically important institutions will be regulated by the Federal Reserve. Retail lenders will now be subject to consistent, federal-level regulation through the new Consumer Financial Protection Bureau housed within the Federal Reserve.

Although Dodd-Frank takes some useful steps in the regulation of shadow banking, there are still large gaps where it is almost silent. Three important gaps involve the regulation of MMMFs, securitization, and repos. Fortunately, the law also created a council of regulators, the Financial Stability Oversight Council, with significant power to identify and manage systemic risks, including the power to recommend significant changes in regulation, if deemed necessary for financial stability.[2] We will argue that the above three areas played the central role in the recent crisis and are in need of further regulation.

MMMFs, securitization, and repos are key elements of what has been called off-balance-sheet financing, which differs from the on-balance-sheet financing of traditional banks in several important ways. Figure 1 is the classic textbook depiction of the financial intermediation of loans on bank balance sheets in the traditional banking system. In step A depositors transfer money to the bank in return for credit on a checking or savings account, from which they can withdraw at any time. In step B the bank lends these funds to a borrower and holds this loan on its balance sheet to maturity.

---

1. Some of the important shadow banking terms are defined later in the paper and in the appendix. In other work (Gorton and Metrick 2010, forthcoming), we refer to the specific combination of repos and securitization as "securitized banking." Since this paper takes a broader view to include activities beyond repos and securitization, we use the more common but less precise term "shadow banking."

2. This power, crucial for the future regulation of shadow banking, is granted in section 120 of the Dodd-Frank legislation. Although any new regulations cannot exceed current statutory authority, this authority would still allow for significant new regulation of MMMFs, repos, and securitization without the need for new legislation.

Figure 1. Traditional On-Balance-Sheet Intermediation

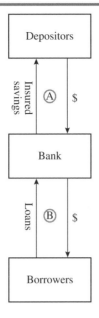

Historically, the traditional system was subject to bank runs, but these were ended in the United States in 1934 through the introduction of federal deposit insurance. With deposits thus insured, depositors have little incentive to withdraw their funds when the solvency of the bank comes into question. Deposit insurance works well for retail investors but leaves a challenge for institutions with large cash holdings. With deposit insurance capped at $100,000 per account, institutions such as pension funds, mutual funds, states and municipalities, and cash-rich nonfinancial companies lack easy access to safe, interest-earning, short-term investments. The shadow banking system of off-balance-sheet lending (figure 2) provides a solution to this problem.

Step 2 in figure 2 is the analogue to step A in figure 1, but with one important difference. To achieve protection similar to that provided by deposit insurance, an MMMF or other institutional investor receives collateral from the bank. In practice, this transaction takes the form of a repo: the institutional investor deposits $X and receives some asset from the bank as collateral; the bank agrees to repurchase the same asset at some future time (perhaps the next day) for $Y. The percentage $(Y - X)/X$ is called the repo rate and (when annualized) is analogous to the interest rate on a bank deposit.

Figure 2. Off-Balance-Sheet Intermediation in the Shadow Banking System

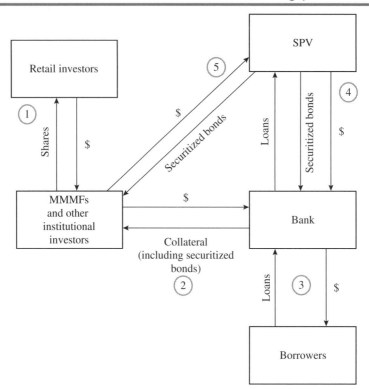

Typically, the total amount deposited will be some amount less than the value of the asset used as collateral; the difference is called a "haircut." For example, if an asset has a market value of $100 and a bank sells it for $80 with an agreement to repurchase it for $88, the repo rate is 10 percent (= [88 − 80]/80) and the haircut is 20 percent ([100 − 80]/100). If the bank defaults on its promise to repurchase the asset, the investor keeps the collateral.[3]

The step that moves this financing off the balance sheet of the bank is step 4, where loans are pooled and securitized. We will discuss this step in

---

3. As we discuss later, repos are carved out of the Chapter 11 bankruptcy process: They are not subject to the automatic stay rule. If one party to the repo transaction fails, the other party can unilaterally terminate the transaction and keep the cash or sell the bond, depending on which side of the transaction that party has taken.

Figure 3. Money Market Mutual Funds, Mutual Funds, Demand Deposits, and Bank Assets, 1975–2008

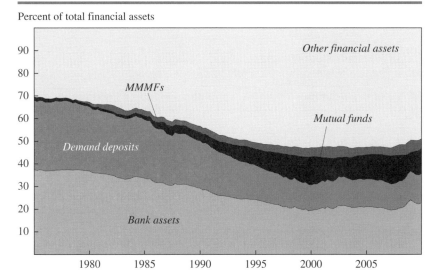

Source: Federal Reserve Flow of Funds data.

detail in section I. For now, the key idea is that the outputs of this securitization are either purchased directly by institutional investors in step 5 or used as collateral for other loans in step 2. In effect, the bonds created by securitization are often the main source of collateral that provides insurance for large depositors.

Each of the components in this off-balance-sheet financing cycle has grown rapidly since 1980. The most dramatic growth has been in securitization: Federal Reserve Flow of Funds data show that the ratio of off-balance-sheet to on-balance-sheet loan funding grew from zero in 1980 to over 60 percent in 2007. To illustrate the growth in MMMFs, figure 3 shows total bank assets, bank demand deposits, mutual fund assets, and MMMF assets as percentages of total financial assets: the bank share of total assets fell by about 20 percentage points from 1980 to 2008.

As we discuss later, there are no comprehensive data measuring the repo market. However, an indication of its growth is the growth in the balance sheets of the institutions that play the role of banks in repo transactions as depicted in figure 2. Before the crisis, these were essentially the investment banks, or broker-dealers. In order for these institutions to act as banks and offer repos, they needed to hold bonds that could be used as collateral. The

Figure 4. Assets of Broker-Dealers, Commercial Banks, Households, and Nonfinancial Corporations, 1958–2010

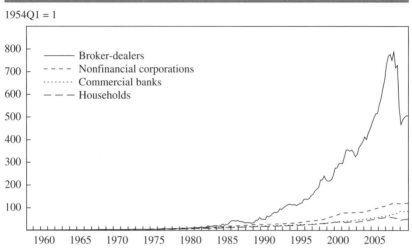

Source: Federal Reserve Flow of Funds data.

yield on the collateral accrues to the bank, which pays the repo rate. So, for example, if the bond is an asset-backed security with a coupon rate of 6 percent, and the repo rate is 3 percent, the bank earns the difference. This required that their balance sheets grow significantly as the repo market grew. Figure 4 shows that broker-dealer assets indeed grew rapidly after about 1990, while commercial bank assets grew at a rate much closer to that of GDP.

Why did shadow banking grow so much? We address this question in section I. One force came from the supply side, where a series of innovations and regulatory changes eroded the competitive advantage of banks and bank deposits. A second force came from the demand side, where demand for collateral for financial transactions gave impetus to the development of securitization and the use of repos as a money-like instrument. Both of these forces were aided by court decisions and regulatory rules that allowed securitization and repos special treatment under the bankruptcy code. A central idea of this paper is that the bankruptcy safe harbor for repos has been crucial to the growth of shadow banking, and that regulators can use access to this safe harbor as the lever to enforce minimum repo haircuts and control leverage.

If the growth of shadow banking was central to the crisis and was facilitated by regulatory changes, then why not simply reverse all these changes? Would such reversals bring us back to a safer system dominated by traditional banks? We do not believe that such a radical course is possible even if it were desirable, which it is not, in our view. The regulatory changes were, in many cases, an endogenous response to the demand for efficient, bankruptcy-free collateral in large financial transactions: if repos had not been granted this status, the private sector would have sought a substitute, which likely would have been even less efficient. In any case, we will not try in this paper to justify the existence of the shadow banking system. Instead we take the broad outlines of the system as given and ask how the current regulatory structure could be adapted to make the system safer without driving its activity into a new unregulated darkness.

In section II we discuss how the shadow banking system broke down in the crisis. The features of this breakdown are similar to those from previous banking panics: safe, liquid assets suddenly appeared to be unsafe, leading to runs. MMMFs, which appeared to be as safe as insured deposits to many investors, suddenly appeared vulnerable, leading to runs on those funds. Securitization, which investors had trusted for decades as creating a form of "information-insensitive" securities free of adverse selection problems, suddenly lost the confidence of investors: hundreds of billions of dollars of formerly information-insensitive triple-A-rated securities became information-sensitive.[4] Since the cost of evaluating all this newly suspect paper was high, investors simply exited all securitizations. In this new environment the high-quality collateral necessary for repos no longer existed. In Gorton and Metrick (forthcoming), we claim that the resulting run on repos was a key propagation mechanism in the crisis.

Section III applies lessons from the successful regulation of traditional banking to infer principles for the regulation of shadow banking. History has demonstrated two methods for reducing the probability of runs in a system. The first, standardized collateralization, was introduced after the Panic of 1837, when some states passed free banking laws under which state bonds were required to back paper bank notes. Free banking laws were the basis for the National Bank Acts, which created national bank notes backed by

---

4. The "information-sensitive" and "information-insensitive" nomenclature comes from Dang, Gorton, and Holmström (2010a, 2010b). "Information-insensitive" roughly means that the cost of producing private information about the payoff on the security is not worth bearing by potentially informed traders. Such securities do not face adverse selection when sold or traded. But a crisis occurs when a shock causes production of such private information to become profitable.

U.S. Treasury securities as collateral; these notes were the first currency in the United States to trade at par against specie. The second method, government insurance, was tried at the state level without great success before the Civil War and again in the first decades of the 20th century. Success finally came when, during the Great Depression, the Federal Deposit Insurance Corporation (FDIC) was created to insure demand deposits. This innovation stopped the cycle of runs on demand deposits and allowed them to be used safely as money.

Today, repos have emerged as a new monetary form, and history offers the same two methods to consider for stabilizing their use. As discussed in detail in section IV, which describes our specific proposals, we believe that insurance would be workable for MMMFs, but that collateralization would be preferable for repos and securitization. For MMMFs the problems are straightforward and have already been well addressed by other authors. We adopt the proposal of the Group of Thirty (2009): MMMFs would have the choice of being treated either as narrow savings banks (NSBs) with stable net asset values, or as conservative investment funds with floating net asset values and no guaranteed return. Under this system, the former would fall clearly within the official financial safety net, but the latter would not.[5]

The narrow banks proposed by the Group of Thirty for MMMFs provide a model for regulating securitization based on the chartering of "narrow funding banks" (NFBs) as vehicles to control and monitor securitization, combined with regulatory oversight of acceptable collateral and minimum haircuts for repos. Under this regime the rules for acceptable collateral would allow that collateral to play a role analogous to that of the state bonds backing bank notes in the free banking period, or the U.S. Treasury securities backing greenbacks during the national banking era; minimum repo haircuts would play a role analogous to capital ratios for depository institutions. The danger of exit from this system and the creation of yet another shadow banking system would be mitigated by allowing only licensed NFBs and repos the special protections provided under the bankruptcy code.

Section V concludes with a discussion of related topics in regulation and monetary policy. The appendix supplements the text with a glossary of shadow banking terminology used in the paper.

---

5. The Group of Thirty (2009) proposal uses the term "special purpose banks" for what we call "narrow savings banks" for terminological consistency with other parts of our proposal.

I. The Rise of Shadow Banking

Shadow banking is the outcome of fundamental changes in the financial system in the last 30 to 40 years, as a result of private innovation and regulatory changes that together led to the decline of the traditional banking model. Faced by competition from nonbanks and their products, such as junk bonds and commercial paper, on the asset side of their balance sheets, and from MMMFs on the liability side, commercial banks became less profitable and sought new profit opportunities.[6] Slowly, traditional banks exited the regulated sector. In this section we review in more detail the three important changes in banking discussed briefly above: MMMFs, securitization, and repos.

I.A. Money-Market Mutual Funds

Since the 1970s there has been a major shift in the preferred medium for deposit-like transactions away from demand deposits toward MMMFs.[7] MMMFs were a response to interest rate ceilings on demand deposits (Regulation Q). In the late 1970s the assets of MMMFs totaled around $4 billion. In 1977 interest rates rose sharply and MMMFs grew in response, by more than $2 billion per month during the first 5 months of 1979 (Cook and Duffield 1979). The Garn-St. Germain Act of 1982 authorized banks to issue short-term deposit accounts with some transaction features but no interest rate ceiling. These were known as "money-market deposit accounts." Michael Keeley and Gary Zimmerman (1985) document that these accounts attracted $300 billion in the 3 months after their introduction in December 1982, and they argue that the result was a substitution of wholesale for retail deposits, and of direct price competition for nonprice competition, both responses resulting in increased bank deposit costs. MMMFs really took off in the mid-1980s, their assets growing from $76.4 billion in 1980 to $1.8 trillion by 2000, an increase of over 2,000 percent. Assets of MMMFs reached a peak of $3.8 trillion in 2008, making them one of the most significant financial product innovations of the last 50 years.

An important feature of MMMFs that distinguishes them from other mutual funds is that they seek to maintain a net asset value of $1 per share.

---

[6]. These changes have been much noted and much studied, so we only briefly review them here. See Keeley and Zimmerman (1985), Bryan (1988), Barth, Brumbaugh, and Litan (1990, 1992), Boyd and Gertler (1993, 1994), Edwards and Mishkin (1995), and Berger, Kashyap, and Scalise (1995), among many others.

[7]. MMMFs are registered investment companies that are regulated by the SEC in accordance with Rule 2a-7, adopted pursuant to the Investment Company Act of 1940.

It is this feature that enables MMMFs to compete with insured demand deposits. MMMFs are closely regulated; they are required, for example, to invest only in high-quality securities that would seem to have little credit risk. The SEC has recently proposed a series of changes to MMMF regulation; these regulations, part of the Investment Company Act of 1940 (as amended), have come under review by a working group of regulators, but none of the recent proposals would change the fact that MMMFs are not explicitly insured. The maintenance of the $1 share price was almost universally successful in the decades leading up to the crisis. This may have instilled a false sense of security in investors who took the implicit promise as equivalent to the explicit insurance offered by deposit accounts. The difference, of course, is that banks pay for deposit insurance (and pass that cost along to depositors), whereas the promise to pay $1 per share costs the MMMFs nothing. In the crisis, the government made good on the implicit promise by explicitly guaranteeing MMMFs, and in the wake of that move it may not be credible for the government to commit to any other strategy. As long as MMMFs have implicit, cost-free government backing, they will have a cost advantage over insured deposits. We return to this point in section IV, where we adopt the proposals of the Group of Thirty (2009) for MMMFs to either pay for explicit insurance or drop the fiction of stable value.

I.B. Securitization

Securitization is the process by which traditionally illiquid loans are packaged and sold into the capital markets. This is accomplished by selling large portfolios of loans to special purpose vehicles (SPVs), which are legal entities that in turn issue rated securities linked to the loan portfolios. Figure 5 illustrates how securitization works. An originating firm lends money to a number of borrowers. A number of these loans are then pooled into a portfolio, which is sold to an SPV, a master trust in the figure. The SPV finances these purchases by selling securities in the capital markets. These securities are classified into tranches, which are ranked by seniority and rated accordingly. The whole process thus takes loans that traditionally would have been held on the balance sheet of the originating firm and creates from them marketable securities that can be sold and traded via the off-balance-sheet SPV.

Securitization is a large and important market. Figure 6 shows the annual issuance since 1990 of all securitized products, including nonagency mortgage-backed securities, the major nonmortgage categories (credit card receivables, auto loans, and student loans), and other asset classes; for

Figure 5. The Securitization Process

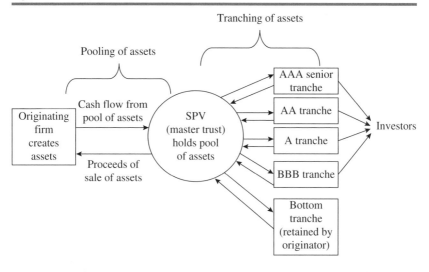

Figure 6. Issuance of Corporate Debt and Asset-Backed Securities, 1990–2009

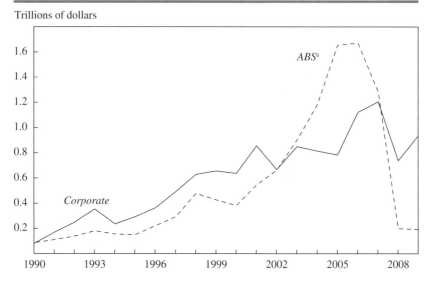

Source: Thomson Reuters.
a. Excludes debt issued by federal government agencies and government-sponsored enterprises.

comparison, the figure also shows the annual issuance of corporate bonds (including convertible debt). Starting at about the same level, the two series rise roughly in parallel until around 2000, when securitization begins to grow explosively. Securitization peaks in 2006 and then falls precipitously in the crisis.

To understand the potential economic efficiencies of securitization, it is important to understand how the SPV structure works. An SPV has no purpose other than the transaction or transactions for which it was created; it can make no substantive decisions. The rules governing SPVs are set down in advance and carefully circumscribe their activities. Indeed, no one works at an SPV, and it has no physical location.[8]

Two other essential features of an SPV concern bankruptcy. First, SPVs are "bankruptcy remote"; that is, the insolvency of the sponsor (the bank or firm originating the loans) has no impact on the SPV. In particular, creditors of a bankrupt sponsor cannot claw back assets from the SPV. Second, the SPV itself is designed so that it can never, as a practical matter, become legally bankrupt. The most straightforward way to achieve this would be for the SPV to waive its right to file a voluntary bankruptcy petition, but this is legally unenforceable. So the way to minimize the risk of either voluntary or involuntary bankruptcy is to design the SPV in a way that makes the risk of bankruptcy very small.[9]

Why would a bank choose to move some assets off its balance sheet through securitization? There are several costs and benefits of this decision, all of which have been changing rapidly over the last several decades.

BANKRUPTCY. The most important design feature of securitization is that the ABSs issued by an SPV do not trigger an event of default in the case where the underlying portfolio does not generate enough cash to make the contractual coupon payments on the outstanding bonds.[10] Instead there is an early amortization event: the cash that is available is used to make principal payments early, rather than coupon payments.

---

8. This description of securitization and SPVs is based on Gorton and Souleles (2006).
9. See Klee and Butler (2002) for some details on how SPVs are structured to avoid bankruptcy.
10. The LTV Steel case (In re LTV Steel, Inc., No. 00-43866, 2001 Bankr. LEXIS 131 (Bankr. N.D. Ohio Feb. 5, 2001)) threatened the bankruptcy remoteness concept, but the parties settled before a court decision was handed down, and the parties agreed that there had been a "true sale" of the assets to the SPV. Although the outcome was ambiguous, it did not hamper the growth of securitization. There have been no other cases challenging bankruptcy remoteness. See, for example, Kettering (2008), Schwarcz (2002), and Stark (2002).

Avoiding Chapter 11 bankruptcy is valuable. Thomas Plank (2007, p. 654) compares securitization with what happens to a secured creditor in bankruptcy and concludes that "securitization reduces the bankruptcy tax on secured lenders to originators and owners of mortgage loans and other receivables, and therefore has reduced the bankruptcy premiums charged to the obligors of mortgage loans and other receivables." Gorton and Nicholas Souleles (2006) show empirically that this is an important source of value to securitization.

TAXES. Debt issued off the balance sheet does not have the advantageous tax benefits of on-balance-sheet debt. For profitable firms this can make a large difference. Consider a bank that is deciding how to finance a portfolio of mortgage loans that has the same risk properties as the rest of the bank's assets. Profitable firms with little chance of bankruptcy have a high likelihood of being able to treat the interest on that debt as a deductible expense, and so for these firms it is optimal to finance on the balance sheet. For firms that are less profitable and closer to bankruptcy, which therefore have a lower likelihood of using this tax shield, it will be relatively more advantageous to finance off the balance sheet. Gorton and Souleles (2006) find this to be true empirically, in a study of credit card securitizations. Using credit ratings as a measure of profitability and bankruptcy risk, Moody's (1997a, 1997b) also reaches this conclusion.

MORAL HAZARD. Because the rules governing SPVs permit them very little discretion, once a portfolio of loans has been transferred to an SPV, there is no danger of other activities of the SPV imposing costs on the holders of the securitized bonds. In contrast, the expected bankruptcy costs to the holder of a bank's bonds are affected by the other actions of bank management.

Given the fiduciary responsibilities of corporate directors toward equity holders, and given the familiar principal-agent problems among shareholders, directors, and managers, moral hazard will always be a potential concern for bank bondholders. But this concern can be mitigated by the existence of bank "charter value." As discussed by Alan Marcus (1984), a positive charter value gives a bank an incentive to avoid risk taking that might lead to bankruptcy and the loss of the charter. Bank regulations and positive charter values are complementary in that banks tend to abide by regulations—that is, they internalize risk management—when charter values are high. There is persuasive evidence that, historically, such charter value at banks did improve risk management, but that this value and the protection it provided have decreased over time. The competition from junk bonds and MMMFs, together with deregulation (for example, of interest rate ceilings), caused bank charter values to decline, which in turn led banks to increase their risk and reduce their capital.[11]

Given the decline in charter values and the resulting increase in bank risk taking, bank bondholders would face higher moral hazard costs for on-balance-sheet financing and demand higher returns as compensation. This provides a cost advantage to securitization that has been growing over time.

REGULATORY COSTS. One regulatory response to increased risk taking by banks has been the introduction of specific capital requirements. In 1981 regulators announced explicit capital requirements for the first time in U.S. banking history: all banks and bank holding companies were required to hold primary capital of at least 5.5 percent of assets by June 1985. Virtually all banks did meet these capital requirements by 1986, but it is interesting how this was accomplished: banks that were capital deficient when the new requirements were announced tended to grow more slowly than capital-rich banks (Keeley 1988).[12]

If bank regulators impose capital requirements that are binding (that is, that require banks to hold more capital than they would voluntarily in equilibrium), then, when charter value is low, bank capital will exit the regulated bank industry. One way to do this is through off-balance-sheet securitization, which has no requirements for regulatory capital.

ADVERSE SELECTION. It is sometimes alleged that an investor in securitized bonds faces an adverse selection problem: loan originators who have better information about the loans than the investor has might try to put the worst loans into the portfolio being sold to the SPV. Aware of this problem, investors and sponsoring firms have designed several structural mitigants. First, loan originators are allowed limited discretion in selecting loans for the portfolio to be securitized. The loans are subject to detailed eligibility criteria and specific representations and warranties. Once eligible loans have been specified, either they are selected for the portfolio at random,

---

11. This process is documented by Keeley (1990), Gorton and Rosen (1995), Demsetz, Saidenberg, and Strahan (1996), Galloway, Lee, and Roden (1997), and Gan (2004), among others.

12. Another important change occurred in 1999, when Congress passed the Gramm-Leach-Bliley Act. This act permitted affiliations between banks and securities firms; it created a special type of bank holding company, called a financial holding company, which is allowed to engage in a wider range of activities (such as insurance underwriting and merchant banking) or under less stringent regulations (for example, on securities underwriting and dealing) than traditional bank holding companies. Before then, the ability of banks to engage in such activities had been strictly constrained by the 1933 Glass-Steagall Act and the Bank Holding Company Act of 1956.

or all the qualifying loans are put into the portfolio. Second, originators of securitizations retain a residual interest (essentially the equity position) in them. In principle, these features align the interests of securitization investors and loan originators (Gorton 2010), and indeed, except in the case of subprime mortgages, securitization has worked well. When an entire asset class turns out to be suspect, as happened with subprime mortgage securitization, there is clearly a problem, but it is not adverse selection. With respect to subprime securitizations, the evidence on adverse selection remains ambiguous.[13]

TRANSPARENCY AND CUSTOMIZATION. Evaluation of the creditworthiness of any bank requires analyses of its balance sheet, operations, management, competitors, and so on. Information on each of these elements is at best only partly disclosed to bank investors, and even in the absence of moral hazard problems, creditworthiness can vary over time from changes in ordinary business operations.[14] In comparison, an SPV's portfolio is completely known, and any changes over time are noted in the trustee reports. Although the underlying SPV portfolio may contain thousands of individual assets and is by no means simple to evaluate, it is considerably more transparent than a corresponding bank balance sheet, which may have many such collections of assets and zero disclosure of individual loans.

With the ability to disclose specific assets underlying securitized bonds, off-balance-sheet financing can allow customization of such bonds for any niche of investors. Investors desiring exposure to (or hedges against) mortgages, auto loans, or credit card receivables can purchase exactly what they want through securitized bonds without having to take on exposure to any other type of asset. Furthermore, although banks can and do offer their own debt at different levels of seniority, the transparency of SPV portfolios allows for easier evaluation of the different tranches. One specific type of customization is used to create safe senior tranches that can trade as information-insensitive, triple-A-rated securities. The production of these senior tranches was in part an endogenous response to a rising demand for safe collateral in repos and other financial transactions. We discuss this special case in the next subsection.

---

13. The recent allegations about the Goldman Sachs Abacus transactions (see the SEC complaint at Securities and Exchange Commission v. Goldman Sachs & Co. and Fabrice Tourre, www.sec.gov/litigation/complaints/2010/comp21489.pdf) concern synthetic CDOs, not traditional securitization. Synthetic securitizations were not quantitatively large.

14. Indeed, Morgan (2002) provides evidence that banks are more opaque than nonfinancial firms.

Figure 7. Financial Assets of Institutional Investors in Five Countries, 1980–2008

Percent of GDP

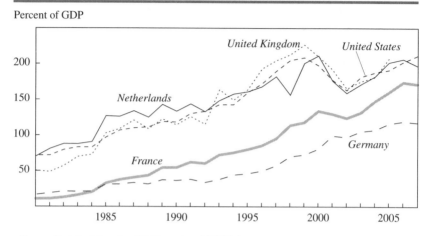

Source: Bank for International Settlements and OECD data.

I.C. Repos

One key driver of the increased use of repos is the rapid growth of money under management by institutional investors, pension funds, mutual funds, states and municipalities, and nonfinancial firms. These entities hold cash for various reasons but would like to have a safe investment that earns interest, while retaining flexibility to use the cash when needed—in short, a demand deposit-like product. In the last 30 years these entities have grown in size and become an important feature of the financial landscape. For example, according to the Bank for International Settlements (BIS 2007, p. 1, note 1), "In 2003, total world assets of commercial banks amounted to USD 49 trillion, compared to USD 47 trillion of assets under management by institutional investors." Figure 7 shows this increase as a ratio of GDP in five large economies: the median ratio more than tripled from 1980 to 2007.

For large depositors like these, repos can act as a substitute for insured demand deposits because repo agreements are explicitly excluded from Chapter 11: that is, they are not subject to the automatic stay. Instead, repos, like derivatives, have a special status under the U.S. Bankruptcy Code. The repo contract allows either party to unilaterally enforce the termination provisions of the agreement as a result of a bankruptcy filing by the other party. A depositor, for example, can unilaterally terminate its repo with a bank when the bank becomes insolvent and sell the collateral. Without this protection, a party to a repo contract would be just another creditor waiting for the bankruptcy proceedings to conclude in order to be repaid.[15]

Repo collateral can be rehypothecated; that is, the collateral received in a repo deposit can be freely reused in another transaction with an unrelated third party. For example, bonds received as collateral can be posted to a third party as collateral in a derivatives transaction; that party can then borrow against the same collateral, and so on. As the BIS (1999, pp. 7–8) has pointed out, this results in "high levels of 'velocity' in repo markets. This occurs when a single piece of collateral is used to effect settlement in a number of contracts on the same day. It allows the daily repo trading volume of a particular note issue to exceed the outstanding amount of the issue, as participants are able to borrow and lend a single piece of collateral repeatedly over the course of a day." Manmohan Singh and James Aitken (2010) argue that measures of repos are significantly larger when rehypothecation is taken into account.[16]

The legal infrastructure facilitating the use of repos as money has evolved as their volume has grown. Since 1978, the year a new bankruptcy code was adopted, both the U.S. Bankruptcy Code and the Federal Deposit Insurance Act have provided exemptions for certain kinds of financial contracts. It was in 1984 that the bankruptcy code was amended to allow parties to a repo to liquidate collateral without the counterparty going into bankruptcy.[17] But this applied only to repos based on Treasury securities, agency securities, bank certificates of deposit, and bankers' acceptances.[18] In 2005 the Bankruptcy Reform Act expanded the definition of a repo to

---

15. See, for example, Johnson (1997) and Schroeder (1996). The safe harbor provision for repo transactions was recently upheld in a court lawsuit brought by American Home Mortgage Investment Corp. against Lehman Brothers. See Schweitzer, Grosshandler, and Gao (2008).

16. Rehypothecation creates a multiplier process for collateral, similar to the more familiar money multiplier. Since there are no official data on repos, the size of this multiplier is not known. Fegatelli (2010) looks at this issue using data from Clearstream, a Luxembourg-based clearinghouse. See also Adrian and Shin (2008), who link the use of repos to monetary policy.

17. The amendment was motivated by the Lombard-Wall decision (see Lombard-Wall, Inc. v. Columbus Bank & Trust Co., No. 82 B 11556 (Bankr. S.D.N.Y. 1982)), which held that an automatic stay provision prevented the depositor who held the collateral from selling the collateral without court permission. See, for example, Garbade (2006) and Krimminger (2006).

18. It is not clear that actual market practice was limited to this set of securities. In fact, the evidence is that it was not. For example, according to Liu (2003), "In recent years market participants have turned to money market instruments, mortgage and asset-backed securities, corporate bonds and foreign sovereign bonds as collateral for repo agreements." No court cases have tested this.

make transactions based on any stock, bond, or other security eligible for bankruptcy safe harbor protection.[19]

The unfortunate reality is that no official data on repos exist other than what the Federal Reserve collects with regard to the amounts transacted by the 18 primary dealer banks. According to these data, primary dealers reported financing $4.5 trillion in fixed-income securities with repos as of March 4, 2008. However, these data are known to cover only a fraction of the U.S. market.[20] BIS economists Peter Hördahl and Michael King (2008, p. 37) report that repo markets doubled in size from 2002 to 2007, "with gross amounts outstanding at year-end 2007 of roughly $10 trillion in each of the US and euro repo markets, and another $1 trillion in the UK repo market." They also report that the U.S. repo market exceeded $10 trillion in mid-2008, including double counting.[21] The European repo market, generally viewed as smaller than the U.S. market, was €4.87 trillion in June 2009, having peaked at €6.78 trillion in June 2007, according to the International Capital Market Association (ICMA) European Repo Market Survey (2010). According to figures published in ICMA's June 2009 survey, the repo market globally grew at an average annual rate of 25 percent between 2001 and 2007. Although the available evidence strongly suggests that the repo market is very large, it is impossible to say how large it is in the United States.

We have described the repo market as essentially a deposit market, but repos have a number of other significant uses as well. They are used to hedge derivative positions and to hedge primary security issuance. Repos are also important for maintaining "no arbitrage" relationships between cash and synthetic instruments. A very important use of repos is in taking "short" positions in securities markets. By using a repo, a market participant can sell a security that he or she does not own by borrowing it from another party in the repo market. Without a repo market (or an analogous

---

19. See Krimminger (2006), Garbade (2006), Smith (2007), Sissoko (2010), Johnson (1997), Schroeder (1996), and Walters (1984).

20. Federal Reserve Flow of Funds data cover only the U.S. primary dealers and thus show an even lower figure than the Federal Reserve's other numbers.

21. "Double counting" refers to counting both repo and reverse repo (see the appendix) in the same transaction. The extent of this issue is unclear, as no data exist on the extent of involvement of nonfinancial firms in repos; only financial firms have been counted, estimated, or surveyed. Again, anecdotally, many nonfinancial firms' treasury departments (for example, Westinghouse, IBM, and Microsoft) invest in repos, as do institutional investors and states and municipalities, as discussed above.

market transaction using collateral), this would be impossible. Repos are also an important mechanism for obtaining leverage, especially for hedge funds. There are many such examples. It is for all these reasons that repos have been described as the core of the financial system (Comotto 2010).

II. The Role of Shadow Banking in the Financial Crisis

The chronology of events in the financial crisis of 2007–09 is well known, and a growing number of papers address various aspects of the crisis.[22] In this section we briefly summarize the crisis as a run on various forms of "safe" short-term debt.

A proximate cause of the crisis was a shock to home prices, which had a large detrimental effect on subprime mortgages. In turn, ABSs linked to subprime mortgages quickly lost value. The shock spread quickly to other asset classes as entities based on short-term debt were unable to roll over the debt or faced withdrawals. Essentially, there was a run on short-term debt. The epicenters were the repo market, the market for ABCP, and MMMFs. We briefly discuss each in turn.

Gorton and Metrick (2010, forthcoming) and Gorton (2010) have argued that the core problem in the financial crisis was a run on repos. The panic occurred when depositors in repo transactions with banks feared that the banks might fail and they would have to sell the collateral in the market to recover their money, possibly at a loss given that so much collateral was being sold at once. In reaction, investors increased repo haircuts. Tri Vi Dang, Gorton, and Bengt Holmström (2010a, 2010b) argue that a haircut amounts to a tranching of the collateral to recreate an information-insensitive security in the face of the shock, so that it is again liquid.

An increase in a repo haircut is tantamount to a withdrawal from the issuing bank. Think of a bond worth $100 that was completely financed in the repo market with a zero haircut. A 20 percent haircut on the same bond would require that the bank finance $20 some other way. In effect,

---

22. Among many others, Brunnermeier (2009), Adrian and Shin (2010), Krishnamurthy (2010), He, Khang, and Krishnamurthy (2010), Gorton and Metrick (2010a, 2010b), and Gorton (2010) document and analyze the crisis. Some examples of theory-oriented papers are Acharya, Gale, and Yorulmazer (2009), Brunnermeier and Pedersen (2009), Geanakoplos (2009), Dang, Gorton, and Holmström (2010a, 2010b), He and Xiong (2009), Pagano and Volpin (2009), Shleifer and Vishny (2009), Uhlig (2009), and Martin, Skeie, and von Thadden (2010).

$20 has been withdrawn from the bank. If no one will provide financing to the bank through new security issuance or a loan, the bank will have to sell assets. In the crisis, withdrawals in the form of increased repo haircuts caused deleveraging, spreading the subprime crisis to other asset classes.

It was not only in the repo market that problems occurred. There were also runs on other types of entities that were heavily dependent on short-term debt and held portfolios of ABSs. ABCP conduits and structured investment vehicles (SIVs) are operating companies that purchased long-term ABSs and financed them with short-term debt, largely commercial paper. Just before the crisis began, ABCP conduits had about $1.4 trillion in total assets (Carey, Correa, and Kotter 2009). Most ABCP programs were sponsored by banks. Daniel Covits, Nellie Liang, and Gustavo Suarez (2009, p. 7) report that "more than half of ABCP daily issuance has maturities of 1 to 4 days [referred to as "overnight"], and the average maturity of outstanding paper is about 30 days" (see also Carey, Correa, and Kotter 2009). Our reform proposals below also address ABCP conduits and SIVs.

MMMFs were also hit hard during the crisis. MMMFs are not just a retail product; they managed 24 percent of U.S. business short-term assets in 2006 (Brennan and others 2009). At that time, just before the crisis, these funds held liabilities of ABCP conduits, SIVs, and troubled financial firms such as Lehman Brothers. Upon Lehman's failure, concern that these funds would have trouble maintaining their implicit promise of a $1 net asset value induced some investors to withdraw their funds. Faced with a run, these entities were forced to sell assets at fire-sale prices (Brennan and others 2009). There was a flight to quality: investors moved assets out of MMMFs that invested mainly in private sector debt and into MMMFs that primarily invested in U.S. Treasury debt. From September to December 2008, the former suffered a net cash outflow of $234 billion while the latter received a net inflow of $489 billion (Brennan and others 2009). On September 29, 2008, the government announced its Temporary Guarantee Program for Money Market Funds; this temporarily guaranteed certain account balances in MMMFs that qualified.

In summary, the financial crisis was centered in several types of short-term debt (repos, ABCP, MMMF shares) that were initially perceived as safe and "money-like" but later found to be imperfectly collateralized. In this way the crisis amounted to a banking panic, structurally similar to centuries of previous panics involving money-like instruments such as bank notes and demand deposits, but with the "banks" taking a new form. To regulate this new form of banking, we turn next to the lessons of history.

III. Lessons from History and Principles for Reform

Bank regulation has been at the forefront of public policy issues in finance since the founding of the United States. The essential feature of banking is the provision of "money," that is, a medium that can be easily used to conduct transactions without losses to insiders (that is, the better-informed party). Throughout U.S. history, a central aim of government involvement has been to provide a regulatory structure that ensures the existence of such a safe medium of exchange and avoids systemic banking crises. Before the creation of federal deposit insurance in 1934, the government's efforts to ensure the safety of bank-produced media of exchange took two primary forms. The first was safe and transparent collateral backing for bank money. The idea was that instead of backing bank money with opaque long-term loans, it should be backed by specified government securities. The second was various kinds of insurance schemes tried by the states. It is also worth commenting briefly on the role of private bank clearinghouses, which developed into institutions that sought to safeguard the credibility of bank money. In this section we briefly review these regulatory attempts.

Before the Civil War the predominant form of bank money was privately issued bank notes. These were issued by banks at par, but when used at some distance from the issuing bank, they were accepted only at a discount (see, for example, Gorton 1996, 1999). This early period of banking in the United States was plagued with difficulties, and various solutions were proposed. For the sake of brevity, we start our examination with the Panic of 1837.[23]

The Panic of 1837 disclosed the defects of the New York Safety Fund System and ushered in that state's Free Banking Act of 1838.[24] The Safety Fund had been established in New York in 1829 as an insurance system. Each member bank was required to make periodic contributions, as a percentage of its capital, to a fund for the payment of the debts of any insolvent member after its own assets had been exhausted. Of course, the problem was that the bank had to be insolvent in order for claims to be made on the fund, but at least in principle the note holders would not suffer losses. The Panic of 1837 was the first test of the Safety Fund. Banks suspended convertibility of notes and deposits into specie in May of that year. Later that year came the first calls on the Safety Fund. In the end, the fund was

---

23. For a history of U.S. banking before this period, see, among others, Knox (1900).
24. We focus here on New York, which was the most important state in this history in many ways. For more general treatments, see, for example, Dewey (1910), Golembe (1960), and Rockoff (1974).

not adequate to meet all the demands made on it from the debt of insolvent banks, even with an extra tax on member banks. The fund was basically abandoned: although it continued for chartered banks until 1866, very few banks participated.

New York's Free Banking Act, imitated by many (but not all) other states, introduced a fundamental idea into the design of banking: the use of explicit and mostly transparent collateral to back the issuance of private money.[25] Free banking laws had the following standard features: entry was relatively easy, requiring no special state legislation (previously a state banking charter had required a specific act of the legislature); free banks were required to post eligible state bonds with the state auditor as collateral for notes issued (some states allowed federal bonds also); free banks were required to pay specie on demand or would (after a grace period) forfeit their charter; free banks were organized as limited liability firms. Our concern is with the bond collateral. The eligible bonds were publicly known, and what bonds were posted by each bank was also known. The state auditor kept the bank's printing plates and printed the notes.

The bond backing system worked in principle, but in practice the collateral—the state bonds—was not riskless. Arthur Rolnick and Warren Weber (1984) show that free banks failed when the value of the bonds they posted as collateral fell. The Panic of 1857, which largely involved another bank liability that had grown enormously, namely, demand deposits, revealed the deficiencies of a system that backed note issuance with bank bonds.

The use of bond collateral for note issuance under the free banking laws was the basis for the most successful financial legislation in U.S. history, the National Bank Acts. According to Andrew Davis (1910, p. 7), "The success of [free banking] suggested that a uniform national currency might in the same way be provided through the emissions of special associations [national banks], which should secure their notes by the pledge of government securities." Partly as a way of financing the Civil War, Congress passed the National Bank Acts in 1863 and 1864 to create a uniform federal currency. National bank notes were liabilities of a new category of banks, called "national banks." They could issue notes upon depositing U.S. Treasury securities with the federal government equal in face value to 111 percent (later reduced to 100 percent) of the value of notes issued. After the Panic of 1873, banks were further required to make deposits into

---

25. Connecticut, Florida, Illinois, Indiana, Iowa, Louisiana, Massachusetts, New Jersey, Ohio, Pennsylvania, Tennessee, Vermont, Virginia, and Wisconsin adopted free banking laws before the Civil War.

a Treasury-run redemption fund. As Milton Friedman and Anna Schwartz (1963, p. 21) summarized, "Though national bank notes were nominally liabilities of the banks that issued them, in effect they were indirect liabilities of the federal government thanks to both the required government bond security and the conditions for their redemption." National bank notes circulated at par, and there were none of the problems that had plagued the antebellum period. But although these notes remained safe, panics did occur during the national banking period, in 1873, 1884, 1893, 1907, and 1914. It was these panics, centered on demand deposits rather than bank notes, that eventually led to the creation of federal deposit insurance through the FDIC.

Deposit insurance has a long history in the United States, dating back to the New York Safety Fund System briefly discussed above. Before the FDIC was created, there were numerous state-organized insurance schemes. Before the Civil War, in addition to New York, Indiana, Iowa, Michigan, Ohio, and Vermont organized such systems. These had different designs, and whereas some can be described as successful (Indiana, Iowa, and Ohio), others were not. Although deposits were not insured under the national banking system, the National Bank Acts were followed by a halt to state insurance programs for almost 50 years. After the Panic of 1907, however, some states again introduced deposit insurance programs, notably Oklahoma, which was then followed by a number of other states, including Kansas, Mississippi, Nebraska, North Dakota, South Dakota, Texas, and Washington. All collapsed during the 1920s, when agricultural prices fell (see Golembe 1960, Calomiris 1989, 1990).

During the national banking era, private bank clearinghouses in various cities undertook the role of monitoring banks, and in the Panics of 1893 and 1907 they provided a kind of insurance. When suspension of convertibility occurred, organized by the clearinghouse, the clearinghouses would not exchange currency for checks. But they did issue clearinghouse loan certificates, in small denominations that could be used as money, in both 1893 and 1907. These certificates were the joint liability of all members of that clearinghouse that were located in its city. Thus, claims on an individual bank that might be insolvent were replaced with claims on the group of banks (see Gorton and Mullineaux 1987, Gorton 1985).

To summarize, after the Civil War, collateral backing by specified eligible bonds under the National Bank Acts solved the problems with bank notes but left demand deposits vulnerable to panic. The problem of demand deposit panics was solved only in 1934 with the creation of federal deposit insurance.

IV. Some Proposals for the Regulation of Shadow Banking

Our proposals are based on two themes developed in the paper:

—An important cause of the recent panic was that seemingly safe instruments like MMMF shares and triple-A-rated securitized bonds suddenly seemed unsafe. New regulation should seek to make it clear, through either insurance or collateral, which instruments are truly safe and which are not.

—The rise of shadow banking was facilitated by a demand-driven expansion in the bankruptcy safe harbor for repos. This safe harbor has real value to market participants and can be used to bring repos under the regulatory umbrella.

We use these themes to develop our specific proposals for MMMFs, securitization, and repos.

IV.A. MMMFs: Narrow Savings Banks or Floating Net Asset Values

The central regulatory problem for MMMFs is simple: MMMFs compete in the same space as depository banks, but differ from them in providing an implicit promise to investors that they will never lose money. This promise, for which the MMMFs do not have to pay, was made explicit by the government in the recent crisis. This problem is well understood and has been discussed for many years by academics and regulators. To solve it, we adopt the specific proposal of the Group of Thirty (2009), which is concise enough that we quote it in full:

> a. Money market mutual funds wishing to continue to offer bank-like services, such as transaction account services, withdrawals on demand at par, and assurances of maintaining a stable net asset value (NAV) at par should be required to reorganize as special-purpose banks, with appropriate prudential regulation and supervision, government insurance, and access to central bank lender-of-last-resort facilities.
>
> b. Those institutions remaining as money market mutual funds should only offer a conservative investment option with modest upside potential at relatively low risk. The vehicles should be clearly differentiated from federally insured instruments offered by banks, such as money market deposit funds, with no explicit or implicit assurances to investors that funds can be withdrawn on demand at a stable NAV. Money market mutual funds should not be permitted to use amortized cost pricing, with the implication that they carry a fluctuating NAV rather than one that is pegged at US$1.00 per share.

The logic of this proposal—the elimination of "free" insurance for MMMFs—seems powerful. So why has it not been adopted? One reason is that the MMMF industry is reluctant to part with free insurance, and a $4 trillion industry can make for a powerful lobby. A second reason is that 2010 still seems a dangerous time to be disrupting such a large short-term credit market. We certainly are sympathetic to this second reason, but we believe that any changes can be decided now and implemented after the credit markets have recovered.

Our only tweak on the Group of Thirty proposal is that we call their special-purpose banks "narrow savings banks," or NSBs. We do this to underline the analogy to our "narrow funding banks" (NFBs) for securitization, as described in the next subsection.

IV.B. Securitization: Narrow Funding Banks

The basic idea of NFBs is to bring securitization under the regulatory umbrella. What may seem radical at first glance becomes less so when it is recognized that securitization is just banking by another name, and that it makes sense to regulate similar functions with similar rules. Indeed, the logic is the same as that for the creation of NSBs in place of MMMFs. NFBs would be genuine banks with charters, capital requirements, periodic examinations, and access to the Federal Reserve's discount window. Under the proposal, all securitized products *must* be sold to NFBs; no other entity would be allowed to buy ABSs. (NFBs could also buy other high-grade assets, such as U.S. Treasury securities.) NFBs would be new entities located between securitizations and final investors. Instead of buying ABSs, final investors would buy the liabilities of NFBs.

An NFB regulator would design and monitor the criteria for NFB portfolios. It would determine what classes of ABSs are eligible for purchase by NFBs and would determine the criteria governing the allowed proportions of different asset classes in the portfolio and the proportions of assets of different ratings. With these rules, the regulator would be setting collateral requirements for NFBs in the same way that the National Bank Acts set collateral requirements for bank notes in the 19th century, and in the same way that bank regulators set capital requirements in the 21st century.

Note that under the Group of Thirty's proposal, the government would offer explicit government insurance for what we are calling NSBs, just as it does today for depository banks. Such insurance would be workable for NSBs because all holdings of these banks would have the same seniority, and the entire portfolio would be required to have low risk. Securitization is different. Because ABSs typically have multiple tranches, we do not believe that insurance would be a practical solution: the subordinated components would have some risk and could not be insured, and insurance on the senior components would exacerbate the information problems in the subordinated components. It would defeat the purpose of our proposed regulatory structure to create a new form of government guarantee only to create a new form of adverse selection. Thus, we have proposed collateralization combined with supervision, but we acknowledge that this combination cannot provide the same 100 percent protection as government insurance. For that reason NFB liabilities can never be considered perfect substitutes for government debt, and the Federal Reserve would need to ensure a sufficient supply of non-NFB collateral. We return to this important point in section V.

Our proposal does place new burdens on the regulatory system. The NFB regulator would have to monitor NFB portfolios and perhaps take corrective action. Would it be up to the task? We believe that this task is no different from that faced by traditional bank regulators. The NFB regulator would need to assess the risks of each NFB's activities and evaluate the amount of capital it needed. If the regulatory system is incapable of performing this activity for NFBs, it will be equally challenged if these activities remain on the balance sheets of traditional banks.

NFBs would be a different category of bank because their activities would be so narrowly circumscribed; they would be rules-driven, transparent, stand-alone, newly capitalized entities that could buy only ABSs and other low-risk securities and issue liabilities. They would not be allowed to take deposits, make loans, engage in proprietary trading, or trade derivatives. These limitations would result in a much lower risk profile than traditional banks have, with lower earnings volatility and a much lower return on equity.[26]

NFBs can be viewed as regulated collateral creators or repo banks. They would be allowed to fund themselves through repos. They could engage in repo transactions with private depositors, as could other entities as discussed below. Since all ABSs would have to be sold to NFBs, NFBs would subsume the function of ABCP conduits, SIVs, and related limited-finance companies. These other entities could become NFBs but would have to sever ties with bank sponsors and meet the other NFB requirements. NFBs would therefore complement traditional banks' origination and securitization activities. As in the precrisis economy, traditional banks could fund

---

26. For greater concreteness we provide an abbreviated sample term sheet indicating the main features of a NFB at the *Brookings Papers* website. As the sample term sheet indicates, if capital or other triggers are hit, the NFB would automatically go into a limited, "no growth mode," and if it does not recover, it would automatically go into wind-down, in a process we call "natural amortization." This would be a form of living will governing all the points of transition between operating states. There would be no bailouts of NFBs.

loans through securitization, but the resulting ABSs would have to be purchased by NFBs.

IV.C. Repos: Licenses, Eligible Collateral, and Minimum Haircuts

There are two sides to a repo contract: the depositor, who provides cash to the bank in exchange for interest and receives collateral (the transaction is a "reverse repo" from the depositor's perspective), and the bank, which receives the money and initially holds the bonds used as collateral. In the crisis the problem was that the housing price shock caused securitized products to become information-sensitive, leading to withdrawals from the repo market, which in turn forced banks to liquidate collateral. This would suggest that we focus our proposals for new regulation on the banks, the providers of collateral, rather than on the depositors. Indeed, we want to provide a safe, deposit-like account for the bulk of repo depositors. The problem is that, as discussed above, repos have many other uses as well, including the short selling of bonds for hedging purposes and the conducting of arbitrage to keep derivative prices in line with prices on the underlying assets. So any regulation of repos must make them safe for depositors while at the same time allowing for these other uses. This is the basis for our repo proposal, which distinguishes the treatment of banks from that of other entities that can use repos:

—*Banks* (NFBs, NSBs, and commercial banks) would be allowed to engage in repo financing, that is, the activity of borrowing money, paying interest, and providing collateral.

—*Nonbank entities* would also be allowed to engage in repos, but only with a license, and would face other constraints as discussed below.

—*Eligible collateral for banks* in repo transactions would be restricted to U.S. Treasury securities, liabilities of NFBs, and such other asset classes as the regulator deems appropriate.

—*Eligible collateral for nonbank entities* could be any type of security, but the transaction would be subject to minimum haircuts and position limits as specified below.

—*Minimum haircuts* would be required on all collateral used in repos and could be specific to the two parties and the collateral offered.

—*Position limits* would be set for nonbank entities, in terms of gross notional amounts issued or held, as a function of firm size and the collateral used.

—*Rehypothecation* would be limited automatically by the minimum haircuts.

Eligible collateral for banks would be any bond that the regulators approve for their portfolios; this would include approved ABSs, government bonds, and possibly the debt of government-sponsored entities. As with the regulations on NFBs, the rules for eligible collateral would be analogous to 19th-century rules for collateral on bank notes.

Because of position limits and possibly higher minimum haircuts, repos outside of banks would be constrained. The advantage thus conferred on being a bank would keep this type of money creation mostly within the regulated sector but would not prevent the use of repos for a broader range of purposes other than as a deposit.

NFBs would not be required to finance all, or even part, of their portfolios using repos. Indeed, we would expect that NFBs would issue some longer-term debt, for purchase by institutional investors, and use some repo financing as well, with the relative proportions determined by supply and demand.

Nonbank licensed entities allowed to engage in repos would include, for example, hedge funds, which have usually financed themselves in the repo market. In doing so they would be borrowing against securities posted as collateral; they would not act as repo depositors. On the other side of the transaction would be a bank or other entity lending against the collateral and possibly borrowing from a third entity against this same collateral.

If none of these three entities is a bank, position limits with regard to total repos outstanding (regardless of direction) on each of the three entities would constrain this type of transaction. Haircuts would depend on the identities of the parties to a repo, in a bilateral repo, and on the type of collateral. Minimum haircuts may not be binding on some transactions, but they are likely to be meaningful because of the restriction to eligible collateral. Minimum haircuts would not prevent all runs; they would, however, limit leverage and reduce rehypothecation.

In summary, our proposed rules would create two types of allowable repo. The first type, offered by commercial banks and NFBs, would capture the monetary function of repos and would be regulated in a manner analogous to the regulation of bank notes (with regard to collateral) in the 19th century and depository institutions in the 21st (using minimum haircuts as an analogue to capital requirements). The second type could be offered by any institution with a license and would be regulated so as to be more expensive than the first. Policymakers and the judiciary could prevent a third type, totally unregulated repos, by making clear that only the first two types receive the special bankruptcy protections. The repo market owes much of its existence to these protections; by offering them only to regulated repos, leakage from the regulated system could be minimized.

V. Discussion

Repos and securitization should be regulated because they are, in effect, new forms of banking, but with the same vulnerability as other forms of bank-created money. Like previous reforms of banking, our proposals seek to preserve banking and bank-created money but eliminate bank runs. Our proposals are aimed at creating a sufficient amount of high-quality collateral that can be used safely in repo transactions. NFBs would be overseen to ensure the creation of safe collateral, and repos would mostly be restricted to banks. Our proposals are built on the idea that these activities are efficient, in part because of the safe harbor from bankruptcy, the maintenance of which is the incentive for agents to abide by the proposed rules.

As we showed in section III, the vulnerability of bank-created money to banking panics has a long history, and the history of attempts to eliminate this problem is almost as long. Collateralization has been one successful approach. Off-balance-sheet banking has become the major source of collateral and needs to be overseen. We propose that NFBs become the entities that transform ABSs into government-overseen collateral. Repos then can be backed by this high-quality collateral.

In this paper we have not provided all the details necessary for determining acceptable collateral or for setting minimum haircuts. These details would need to be worked out in conjunction with rules for bank capital, with which they would be closely intertwined. Although it is clear that setting rules for shadow banking would make new demands on regulators, these demands would be analogous to those that arise when setting rules for banks. Whether risks are retained on the balance sheet or allowed to go off the balance sheet, there is no escaping the need for regulators to evaluate these risks. We do not see any pure private sector solutions to ensure the safety of the banking system, and so the role of regulators will remain essential. If today's regulators are found not to be up to the task, they should be better trained and better paid. If instead the task is simply impossible, then either we are destined to have more crises, or we will be forced to live with a greatly constrained financial system.

Space constraints prevent us from discussing a number of important related issues, but we will close by briefly focusing on two. The first is whether our proposals would lead to a shortage of suitable collateral, as apparently has happened in the past. As the crisis showed, if the volume of U.S. Treasury securities outstanding is insufficient for use as collateral, the private sector will have an incentive to try to create substitutes, such as triple-A-rated bonds. The problem is that the substitutes cannot always be information-insensitive. In 2005 the idea of the U.S. Treasury providing a backstop facility, a "securities lender of last resort," was broached (see Garbade and Kambhu 2005, U.S. Treasury 2005). Our view is that such a facility might need to be available on a regular basis, but that it should be run by the Federal Reserve, which might also need to issue its own securities to be used exclusively as repo collateral. The Federal Reserve needs to focus more carefully on the provision (and measurement) of liquidity, and it is the job of the Fed to provide collateral.

A second issue concerns monetary policy generally. Because no measure presently exists of the whole of the repo market, we do not know its full size or the extent of rehypothecation. It seems that U.S. Treasury securities are extensively rehypothecated (Krishnamurthy and Vissing-Jorgensen 2010) and therefore should be viewed as money. This means that open market operations are simply exchanging one kind of money for another, rather than exchanging money for "bonds." Open market operations may need to be rethought.

APPENDIX

Glossary of Shadow Banking Terms

Asset-backed commercial paper (ABCP): Short-term debt issued by a bankruptcy-remote *special purpose vehicle,* or conduit, which uses the proceeds to purchase *asset-backed securities.* Such vehicles are set up by a bank or other sponsor but owned and actively managed by a management company legally separate from the sponsor. See Fitch Ratings (2001).

Asset-backed security (ABS): A bond backed by the cash flows from a pool of specified assets in a *special purpose vehicle* rather than by the general credit of a corporation or other entity. The asset pool may contain residential mortgages, commercial mortgages, auto loans, credit card receivables, student loans, aircraft leases, royalty payments, or any of a variety of other types of asset.

Collateralized debt obligation (CDO): An instrument issued by a *special purpose vehicle* that buys a portfolio of fixed-income assets, financing the purchase by issuing CDOs in tranches, whose risk ranges from low (senior tranches, rated triple-A) through medium (mezzanine tranches, rated double-A to Ba/BB), to high (equity tranches, unrated).

Rehypothecation: In the repo context, the right to freely use the bonds received as collateral for other purposes.

Narrow funding bank (NFB): A proposed new type of bank that may buy only asset-backed securities and certain other high-quality assets, as approved by a regulator. The regulator sets the portfolio criteria with respect to the proportions of asset types and their ratings. NFBs would be able to issue any nondeposit liability and would have access to the discount window but could not engage in other activities. As regulated banks, NFBs would have charters, capital requirements, and regulatory examinations.

Narrow savings bank (NSB): A proposed new type of insured depository institution into which existing MMMFs seeking deposit insurance protection could be transformed. As insured entities, NSBs would have charters, capital requirements, and regulatory examinations.

Sale-and-repurchase agreement (repo): A contract in which an investor places money with a bank or other entity for a short period and receives (and takes physical possession of) collateral valued at market prices, as well as interest. The bank or other entity simultaneously agrees to repurchase the collateral at a specified price at the end of the contract. From the perspective of the bank, the transaction is a "repo," and from the perspective of the depositor, the same transaction is a "reverse repo."

Securitization: The process of financing a portfolio of loans by segregating specified cash flows from those loans and selling securities in the capital markets that are specifically linked to those flows. The firm originating the loans (the "sponsor") sets up a *special purpose vehicle* to which it then sells the specified cash flows, and which issues the (rated) linked securities. The sponsor continues to service the cash flows; that is, it makes sure that the cash flows are arriving and performs certain other tasks associated with traditional lending.

Special purpose vehicle (SPV): An SPV (also called a special purpose entity, SPE) is a legal entity set up for a specific, limited purpose by a sponsoring firm. An SPV can take the form of a corporation, trust, partnership, or limited liability company, but it is not an operating company in the usual sense. It has no employees or physical location and is strictly bound by a set of rules so that it can only carry out some specific purpose or circumscribed transaction, or a series of such transactions. An essential feature of an SPV is that it is "bankruptcy remote," that is, incapable of becoming legally bankrupt and unaffected by the bankruptcy of its sponsor. See Gorton and Souleles (2006).

Tranche: From the French for "slice," a portion of a portfolio ordered by seniority and sold separately from other portions; for example, a triple-A-rated tranche is more senior than a triple-B-rated tranche of the same portfolio.

ACKNOWLEDGMENTS We thank Stefan Lewellen, Marcus Shak, and Lei Xie for research assistance; Darrell Duffie, Victoria Ivashina, Robert Merton, Stephen Partridge-Hicks, Eric Rasmusen, Nicholas Sossidis, David Scharfstein, Andrei Shleifer, Carolyn Sissoko, Jeremy Stein, Phillip Swagel, David Swensen, Daniel Tarullo, the editors, participants at the Brookings Panel conference, and seminar participants at MIT for many helpful comments and discussions; E. Philip Davis, Ingo Fender, and Brian Reid for assistance with data; and Sara Dowling for help with the figures.

Gary Gorton was a consultant to AIG Financial Products from 1996 to 2008. Andrew Metrick served in the Obama administration during the debate and passage of the Dodd-Frank legislation. In addition, he has served as a consultant for various financial institutions.

References

Acharya, Viral, Douglas Gale, and Tanju Yorulmazer. 2009. "Rollover Risk and Market Freezes." Working paper. New York University.

Adrian, Tobias, and Hyun Song Shin. 2010. "The Changing Nature of Financial Intermediation and the Financial Crisis of 2007–09." Staff Report no. 439. Federal Reserve Bank of New York.

Bank for International Settlements. 1999. "Implications of Repo Markets for Central Banks: Report of a Working Group Established by the Committee on the Global Financial System of the Central Banks of the Group of Ten Countries." Basel.

————. 2007. "Institutional Investors, Global Savings and Asset Allocation." Report submitted by a Working Group established by the Committee on the Global Financial System. Basel (February).

Barth, James R., R. Dan Brumbaugh, and Robert E. Litan. 1990. "The Banking Industry in Turmoil: A Report on the Condition of the U.S. Banking Industry and the Bank Insurance Fund." Report of the Subcommittee on Financial Institutions Supervision, Regulation and Insurance of the House Banking Committee. Washington: Government Printing Office.

————. 1992. *The Future of American Banking*. London: Sharpe.

Berger, Allen N., Anil K Kashyap, and Joseph M. Scalise. 1995. "The Transformation of the U.S. Banking Industry: What a Long, Strange Trip It's Been." *BPEA*, no. 2: 55–201.

Boyd, John H., and Mark Gertler. 1993. "U.S. Commercial Banking: Trends, Cycles, and Policy." In *NBER Macroeconomics Annual 1993*, edited by Olivier Blanchard and Stanley Fischer. MIT Press.

————. 1994. "Are Banks Dead? Or Are the Reports Greatly Exaggerated?" In *The Declining Role of Banking?* Federal Reserve Bank of Chicago.

Brennan, John J., and others. 2009. "Report of the Money Market Working Group." Washington: Investment Company Institute (March 17).

Brunnermeier, Markus K. 2009. "Deciphering the Liquidity and Credit Crunch 2007–2008." *Journal of Economic Perspectives* 23, no. 1: 77–100.

Brunnermeier, Markus K., and Lasse Heje Pedersen. 2009. "Market Liquidity and Funding Liquidity." *Review of Financial Studies* 22, no. 6: 2201–38.

Bryan, Lowell L. 1988. *Breaking Up the Bank: Rethinking an Industry under Siege*. Homewood, Ill.: Dow Jones-Irwin.

Calomiris, Charles. 1989. "Deposit Insurance: Lessons for the Record." Federal Reserve Bank of Chicago *Economic Perspectives* (May–June): 10–30.

————. 1990. "Is Deposit Insurance Necessary? A Historical Perspective." *Journal of Economic History* 50, no. 2: 283–95.

Carey, Mark, Ricardo Correa, and Jason Kotter. 2009. "Revenge of the Steamroller: ABCP as a Window on Risk Choices." Working paper. Washington: Board of Governors of the Federal Reserve System.

Comotto, Richard. 2010. "A White Paper on the Operation of the European Repo Market, the Role of Short-Selling, the Problem of Settlement Failures and the

Need for Reform of the Market Infrastructure." Zurich: International Capital Market Association, European Repo Council.

Cook, Timothy Q., and Jeremy G. Duffield. 1979. "Money Market Mutual Funds: A Reaction to Government Regulations or a Lasting Financial Innovation?" Federal Reserve Bank of Richmond *Economic Review* (July–August): 15–31.

Covitz, Daniel M., Nellie Liang, and Gustavo A. Suarez. 2009. "The Evolution of a Financial Crisis: Panic in the Asset-Backed Commercial Paper Market." Finance and Economics Discussion series no. 2009–36. Washington: Federal Reserve Board.

Dang, Tri Vi, Gary Gorton, and Bengt Holmström. 2010a. "Financial Crises and the Optimality of Debt for Liquidity Provision." Working paper. University of Mannheim, Yale University, and Massachusetts Institute of Technology.

———. 2010b. "Repo Haircuts." Working paper. University of Mannheim, Yale University, and Massachusetts Institute of Technology.

Davis, Andrew McFarland. 1910. *The Origin of the National Banking System*. National Monetary Commission, 61 Cong. 2 sess. Document no. 582. Washington: Government Printing Office.

Demsetz, Rebecca S., Marc R. Saidenberg, and Philip E. Strahan. 1996. "Banks with Something to Lose: The Disciplinary Role of Franchise Value." Federal Reserve Bank of New York *Economic Policy Review* 2, no. 2: 1–14.

Dewey, Davis R. 1910. *State Banking before the Civil War*. Washington: Government Printing Office.

Edwards, Franklin R., and Frederic S. Mishkin. 1995. "The Decline of Traditional Banking: Implications for Financial Stability and Regulatory Policy." Federal Reserve Bank of New York *Economic Policy Review* 1, no. 2: 27–45.

Fegatelli, Paolo. 2010. "The Role of Collateral Requirements in the Crisis: One Tool for Two Objectives?" Working Paper 44. Banque Centrale du Luxembourg.

Fitch Ratings. 2001. "Asset-Backed Commercial Paper Explained." *Structured Finance* (November 8).

Friedman, Milton, and Anna Jacobson Schwartz. 1963. *A Monetary History of the United States, 1867–1960*. Princeton University Press.

Galloway, Tina M., Winson B. Lee, and Dianne M. Roden. 1997. "Banks' Changing Incentives and Opportunities for Risk Taking." *Journal of Banking and Finance* 21, no. 4: 509–27.

Gan, Jie. 2004. "Banking Market Structure and Financial Stability: Evidence from the Texas Real Estate Crisis in the 1980s." *Journal of Financial Economics* 73: 567–601.

Garbade, Kenneth D. 2006. "The Evolution of Repo Contracting Conventions in the 1980s." Federal Reserve Bank of New York *Economic Policy Review* (May): 27–42.

Garbade, Kenneth D., and John E. Kambhu. 2005. "Why Is the U.S. Treasury Becoming a Lender of Last Resort for Treasury Securities?" Staff Report no. 223. Federal Reserve Bank of New York.

Geanakoplos, John. 2010. "The Leverage Cycle." In *NBER Macroeconomics Annual 2009*, vol. 24, edited by Daron Acemoglu, Kenneth Rogoff, and Michael Woodford. University of Chicago Press.

Golembe, Carter H. 1960. "Deposit Insurance Legislation of 1933: An Examination of Its Antecedents and Its Purposes." *Political Science Quarterly* 75, no. 2: 181–200.

Gorton, Gary. 1985. "Clearinghouses and the Origin of Central Banking in the United States" *Journal of Economic History* 45: 277–83.

———. 1996. "Reputation Formation in Early Bank Note Markets." *Journal of Political Economy* 104, no. 2: 346–97.

———. 1999. "Pricing Free Bank Notes." *Journal of Monetary Economics* 44: 33–64.

———. 2010. *Slapped by the Invisible Hand: The Panic of 2007*. Oxford University Press.

Gorton, Gary B., and Andrew Metrick. 2010. "Haircuts." Federal Reserve Bank of St. Louis *Review* 92, no. 6.

———. Forthcoming. "Securitized Banking and the Run on Repo." *Journal of Financial Economics*.

Gorton, Gary, and Donald J. Mullineaux. 1987. "The Joint Production of Confidence: Endogenous Regulation and Nineteenth Century Commercial-Bank Clearinghouses." *Journal of Money, Credit and Banking* 19, no. 4: 457–68.

Gorton, Gary, and Richard Rosen. 1995. "Corporate Control, Portfolio Choice, and the Decline of Banking." *Journal of Finance* 50, no. 5 (December): 1377–1420.

Gorton, Gary B., and Nicholas S. Souleles. 2006. "Special Purpose Vehicles and Securitization." In *The Risks of Financial Institutions*, edited by René M. Stulz and Mark Carey. University of Chicago Press.

Group of Thirty. 2009. "Financial Reform: A Framework for Financial Stability." Washington. www.group30.org/pubs/recommendations.pdf.

He, Zhiguo, and Wei Xiong. 2009. "Dynamic Debt Runs." Working paper. Princeton University.

He, Zhiguo, In Gu Khang, and Arvind Krishnamurthy. 2010. "Balance Sheet Adjustments in the 2008 Crisis." Working Paper 15919. Cambridge, Mass.: National Bureau of Economic Research.

Hördahl, Peter, and Michael R. King. 2008. "Developments in Repo Markets during the Financial Turmoil." *BIS Quarterly Review* (December): 37–53.

International Capital Market Association. 2010. "European Repo Market Survey: Number 18—conducted December 2009." Zurich.

Johnson, Christian A. 1997. "Derivatives and Rehypothecation Failure: It's 3:00 p.m., Do You Know Where Your Collateral Is?" *Arizona Law Review* 39: 949–1001.

Keeley, Michael C. 1988. "Bank Capital Regulation in the 1980s: Effective or Ineffective?" Federal Reserve Bank of San Francisco *Economic Review*, no. 1 (Winter): 3–20.

———. 1990. "Deposit Insurance, Risk, and Market Power in Banking." *American Economic Review* 80, no. 5: 1183–1200.

Keeley, Michael C., and Gary C. Zimmerman. 1985. "Competition for Money Market Deposit Accounts." *Federal Reserve Bank of San Francisco Economic Review* 2: 3–27.

Kettering, Kenneth C. 2008. "Securitization and Its Discontents: The Dynamics of Financial Product Development." *Cardozo Law Review* 29, no. 4: 1553–1728.

Klee, Kenneth N., and Brendt C. Butler. 2002. "Asset-Backed Securitization, Special Purpose Vehicles and Other Securitization Issues." *Uniform Commercial Code Law Review* 35, no. 2: 23–67.

Knox, John Jay. 1900. *A History of Banking in the United States*. New York: Bradford Rhodes & Company.

Krimminger, Michael. 2006. "The Evolution of U.S. Insolvency Law for Financial Market Contracts." Washington: Federal Deposit Insurance Corporation.

Krishnamurthy, Arvind. 2010. "How Debt Markets Have Malfunctioned in the Crisis." *Journal of Economic Perspectives* 24, no. 1: 3–28.

Krishnamurthy, Arvind, and Annette Vissing-Jorgensen. 2010. "The Aggregate Demand for Treasury Debt." Working paper. Kellogg School, Northwestern University.

Liu, Henry C. K. 2003. "The Global Economy in Transition." Invited lecture at the ERC/METU International Conference on Economics, Ankara, Turkey, September 6. www.henryckliu.com/page181.html.

Marcus, Alan. 1984. "Deregulation and Bank Financial Policy." *Journal of Banking and Finance* 8: 557–65.

Martin, Antoine, David Skeie, and Ernst-Ludwig von Thadden. 2010. "Repo Runs." Staff Report no. 444. Federal Reserve Bank of New York.

Moody's Investors Service. 1997a. "Alternative Financial Ratios for the Effects of Securitization." (Reprinted in *Securitization and Its Effect on the Credit Strength of Companies: Moody's Perspective 1987–2002, Special Comments*. New York: Moody's, 2002).

———. 1997b. "The Costs and Benefits of Supporting 'Troubled' Asset-Backed Securities: Has the Balance Shifted?" (Reprinted in *Securitization and Its Effect on the Credit Strength of Companies: Moody's Perspective 1987–2002, Special Comments*. New York: Moody's, 2002).

Morgan, Donald P. 2002. "Rating Banks: Risk and Uncertainty in an Opaque Industry." *American Economic Review* 92, no. 4: 874–88.

Pagano, Marco, and Paolo Volpin. 2008. "Securitization, Transparency, and Liquidity." Working paper. Universitá di Napoli Federico II and London Business School.

Plank, Thomas E. 2007. "Toward a More Efficient Bankruptcy Law: Mortgage Financing under the 2005 Bankruptcy Amendments." *Southern Illinois University Law Review* 31, no. 3: 641–68.

Rockoff, Hugh. 1974. "The Free Banking Era: A Reexamination." *Journal of Money, Credit and Banking* 6, no. 2: 141–67.

Rolnick, Arthur, and Warren Weber. 1984. "The Causes of Free Bank Failures: A Detailed Examination." *Journal of Monetary Economics* 21: 47–71.

Schroeder, Jeanne L. 1996. "Repo Madness: The Characterization of Repurchase Agreements under the Bankruptcy Code and the U.C.C." *Syracuse Law Review* 46: 999–1050.

Schwarcz, Steven L. 2002. "Impact of Bankruptcy Reform on 'True Sale' Determination in Securitization Transactions." *Fordham Journal of Corporate and Financial Law* 7: 353–64.

Schweitzer, Lisa, Seth Grosshandler, and William Gao. 2008. "Bankruptcy Court Rules That Repurchase Agreements Involving Mortgage Loans Are Safe Harbored under the Bankruptcy Code, but That Servicing Rights Are Not." *Journal of Bankruptcy Law* (May–June): 357–60.

Shleifer, Andrei, and Robert W. Vishny. 2009. "Unstable Banking." Working Paper no. 14943. Cambridge, Mass.: National Bureau of Economic Research.

Singh, Manmohan, and James Aitken. 2010. "The (Sizable) Role of Rehypothecation in the Shadow Banking System." IMF Working Paper WP/10/172. Washington: International Monetary Fund.

Sissoko, Carolyn. 2010. "The Legal Foundations of Financial Collapse." *Journal of Financial Economic Policy* 2, no. 1: 5–34.

Smith, Edwin E. 2008. "Financial Contracts under the Bankruptcy Code." *ABI Committee News* 5, no. 2 (May): 536–41.

Stark, Robert. 2002. "Viewing the LTV Steel ABS Opinion in Its Proper Context." *Journal of Corporation Law* 27: 211–30.

Uhlig, Harald. 2009. "A Model of a Systemic Bank Run." *Journal of Monetary Economics* 57, no. 1: 78–96.

U.S. Treasury. 2005. "TBAC Discussion Charts, November 1, 2005." Washington. www.treas.gov/offices/domestic-finance/debt-management/adv-com/minutes/dc-2005-q4.pdf.

U.S. Treasury, Securities and Exchange Commission, and Board of Governors of the Federal Reserve System. 1992. *The Joint Report on the Government Securities Market*. Washington. www.ustreas.gov/offices/domestic-finance/debt-management/gsr92rpt.pdf.

Walters, Gary. 1984. "Repurchase Agreements and the Bankruptcy Code: The Need for Legislative Action." *Fordham Law Review* 52: 828–49.

Comments and Discussion

COMMENT BY
ANDREI SHLEIFER This fascinating paper by Gary Gorton and Andrew Metrick provides an extremely useful overview of the shadow banking system, puts it into historical perspective, explains how it is responsible for the financial crisis, and makes a proposal for how to fix it. Yet the paper is much more than an overview, and in some crucial ways it provides a highly distinctive perspective. This perspective consists of four propositions.

First, starting with the widely accepted notion that the defining feature of the shadow banking system is securitization, the paper goes on to argue that the essential aspect, indeed the raison d'être, of securitization is maturity transformation, that is, the transformation of long-term financial instruments, such as mortgages, into short-term securities, such as repos and commercial paper. Securitization became so massive, in the authors' view, not so much to create allegedly safe long-term securities through diversification and the tranching of risky debt, as many economists have argued, but rather to use these securities to provide fodder for short-term finance. Long-term securities, in this view, served mainly as collateral for short-term borrowing instruments. It is the demand for short-term securities from money market mutual funds and other short-term investors that made securitization possible.

Second, the paper argues that the abrupt withdrawal of short-term finance was responsible for the financial crisis. Because investors in short-term securities expected complete safety, the realization that these securities might be at risk caused them to withdraw financing on very short notice. This withdrawal took the form of rapidly rising haircuts on repo transactions or even runs. When the dealer banks that engineered the maturity transformation faced this withdrawal of short-term finance, they had to liquidate the positions they had financed with short-term debt, triggering massive losses, declines in their balance sheets, and reductions in their ability to finance either their existing holdings or other investments.

Third, among the several different forms of short-term finance associated with the maturity transformation, the real culprit for the increase in financial fragility, in the authors' view, is the repo. Repo financing of asset-backed securities (ABS) holdings was particularly aggressive because by law repos are bankruptcy remote: the parties extending such collateralized finance do not become part of the bankruptcy estate should the borrower default. Such regulatory protection of repo finance, Gorton and Metrick maintain, caused it to grow to gigantic levels. Its withdrawal, or the sharp increase in its cost, is therefore primarily responsible for the crisis.

Fourth, in the light of the above three points, the paper argues that the route to financial stability is to regulate repo financing of ABS holdings. This would be done by, first, forcing all ABSs to be rated by a government-regulated agency and sold to specialized narrow banks; second, restricting the quantity of ABSs that can be financed with repos and the terms of that financing; and third, more closely regulating the lenders in the repo market, particularly the money market mutual funds.

As I explain below, all four of these distinctive propositions are, to varying degrees, controversial. I am not suggesting that I know that they are wrong. Rather, my goal is to point out that information is extremely limited even today about exactly who were the various buyers of ABSs, what was the extent of maturity transformation, and even what were the main sources of financial fragility. We do know by now that the Federal Reserve did not collect the information that would today, 2 years later—let alone in 2008—enable us to answer these questions with confidence. We also know that neither the Federal Reserve nor many of the major market participants, such as AIG and Citibank, understood the vulnerability of shadow banking at the time of the crisis. What really happened is still largely a matter of guesswork. It may well turn out that Gorton and Metrick's assessments are correct, and then in retrospect they will look like geniuses, but my intention is to identify the areas of extreme uncertainty in our knowledge today.

To begin, the fundamental assumption of the Gorton and Metrick narrative is that securitization was, to a first approximation, all about providing fodder for short-term riskless finance. For this to be the case, it must be that nearly all ABSs, or at least the lion's share, were financed short-term by their holders. It is surely the case that a good deal of ABSs went into structured investment vehicles (SIVs) or were held by dealer banks themselves, and in these instances, short-term finance was common. Yet at least some, and possibly a good part, of ABSs were acquired by pension funds, insurance companies, and even government-sponsored enterprises. For those buyers, short-term financing was probably much less important. The reason this observation is of some consequence is that Gorton and Metrick's regulatory proposal would require that all ABSs be maturity transformed, which presumably would prevent their being sold to investors in long-term securities. I am far from certain that this would be desirable.

Gorton and Metrick's second assumption is that the withdrawal of this short-term finance was responsible for the crisis. This assumption seems plausible, since sharp reductions in short-term financing did occur around the time of Lehman Brothers' failure, but even here there are some issues. First, the reductions in short-term financing of long-term positions in ABSs began in the summer of 2007, as the market for asset-based commercial paper dried up. This withdrawal of short-term financing was countered by several liquidity interventions from the Federal Reserve, which successfully delayed the collapse of the markets until the fall of 2008.

Second, and more important, it is far from clear whether the withdrawal of short-term financing in August and September 2008 actually precipitated the collapse or was, alternatively, its consequence. After all, bad news about both housing and commercial real estate was coming into the market throughout 2008, making it increasingly clear that several of the major financial institutions were insolvent. Was the withdrawal of short-term finance a response to this realization of insolvency, or did it actually precipitate the insolvency? Following Douglas Diamond and Philip Dybvig (1983), economists often use the term "run" to describe a multiple-equilibrium situation, in which a bad equilibrium with a run can occur despite solid fundamentals. Such a run does not seem to be a good description of what happened to Lehman and other banks in 2008. The withdrawal of short-term finance surely undermined bank balance sheets, but it seems to me at least as plausible that this withdrawal was a response to an already incurable situation rather than its cause. And if that is the case, regulating short-term finance might not be as high a priority as Gorton and Metrick indicate.

Gorton and Metrick's third assumption, namely, that repo financing of ABSs was the source of instability in the financial system, is the most controversial. Dealer banks relied on a variety of short-term financing mechanisms, including not only repo but also prime brokerage and commercial paper. Prime brokerage enabled dealer banks to use the assets they held on

COMMENTS and DISCUSSION

Figure 1. Overnight Repos and Commercial Paper of Financial Institutions Outstanding, 1994–2009

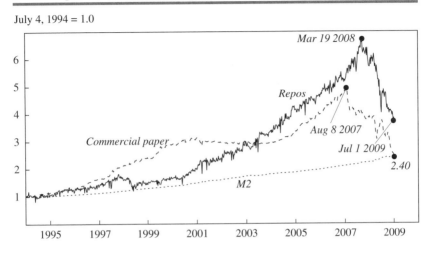

Source: Adrian and Shin (2010).

behalf of their brokerage clients as collateral for their own borrowing. The withdrawal of those accounts was apparently extremely costly to Bear Stearns and perhaps other dealer banks. Commercial paper is, of course, the most traditional form of short-term financing and was hugely important in the years before the crisis. Indeed, the SIVs, which were the institutions most centrally involved in the maturity transformation, financed themselves with commercial paper, and not with repos. My figure 1, taken from Tobias Adrian and Hyun Song Shin (2010), shows outstanding volumes of repos and commercial paper around the time of the crisis. The two series show extremely similar patterns of extraordinary growth before the crisis, followed by a rapid collapse. How do Gorton and Metrick know that, even assuming that the withdrawal of short-term finance in August and September 2008 was at the heart of the crisis, it was repos rather than commercial paper that tipped the balance? Lehman, after all, defaulted on its commercial paper. This issue is critical since commercial paper is not an innovation but a very old financial instrument (the Federal Reserve's 1913 charter gives it responsibility for that market), and in particular it does not enjoy the legal advantages with respect to bankruptcy that repos do. It would seem a bit audacious to lay the blame on repos' bankruptcy remoteness when commercial paper financing follows a nearly identical pattern of growth and decline.

There are some further reasons to doubt that repos were the straw that broke the camel's back. Most fixed-income repo financing uses government or agency bonds as collateral. ABSs are used as collateral in only a relatively small share of the repo market, and it seems highly doubtful to me that repo financing of their own ABS holdings was important for dealer banks. There is no evidence that the repo market in government or agency paper malfunctioned badly during the crisis. Moreover, many dealer banks are just intermediaries in repo financing: they borrow securities from hedge funds and provide them with short-term financing, and then lend these securities on to cash-rich, often foreign, banks and borrow cash from them. So long as the dealer banks can count on getting the hedge funds to cough up additional cash when the haircuts on loans rise, the situation is stable. To elevate ABS repos to the prominence in the crisis that Gorton and Metrick wish to assign to it, they need to provide a good deal more evidence.

These reservations bring me to their policy proposal, which of course would require a major regulatory overhaul of the whole shadow banking system. Let me not focus on the question of whether, if the underlying assumptions of the Gorton and Metrick analysis are correct, their proposal would be a good idea. I understand that the Federal Reserve Bank of New York considered a similar proposal a while ago and decided against it because it was impractical. Let me instead come back to the three assumptions.

First, if implemented, the proposal to allow only narrow funding banks to purchase ABSs would deprive buyers of ABSs not interested in short-term instruments of access to these securities. If, as the authors believe, securitization reduces the cost of capital for desirable investment projects, and if much of the demand comes from investors uninterested in short-term finance of their positions, shutting off this demand might not promote efficiency.

Second, if short-term finance was not the culprit during this crisis, but instead the problem was, for example, the failure of financial intermediaries to understand the risks of the securities they were holding, it is not clear how the proposal addresses the central problem. Would the world be a safer place if dealer banks maintained large holdings of ABSs, or provided guarantees to SIVs, without relying on short-term finance? Presumably, when these institutions are subject to capital requirements and other regulations, they still face huge pressure to shrink their balance sheets when they suffer losses.

Third, and perhaps most important, if ABS repos do occupy the central position in the crisis to which Gorton and Metrick have elevated them, then the singular focus on this market might leave the system as a whole just as fragile as it was before. If the government raises the cost of one form of short-term financing and does nothing else, presumably the dealer banks will turn to other forms. I agree wholeheartedly with Gorton and Metrick that the existing financial infrastructure failed miserably during the crisis, but I would wish to have a bit more confidence that we are wrecking and replacing the parts of it that are actually rotten rather than the ones that are not.

In this regard, let me make one final point, to which I have already alluded. It seems to me that the fundamental cause of the financial crisis is that market participants, as well as the regulators, did not understand the risks inherent in ABSs and other new types of securities. They did not expect that home prices could fall so much and so fast and in so many places at once. They did not understand correlations in home prices and defaults. They used incorrect models. It is not just the ratings agencies that messed things up, but the whole market misunderstood the risks, as is clear from the fact that the price of risk was extremely low in the summer of 2007 and did not rise much in the months after that.

As long as market participants do not understand the risks of the securities they are buying, whether these securities are ABSs or prime money market fund shares or something that will be invented in the future, and see profit opportunities in places where there are none, the financial system will adjust to meet their demand (see Gennaioli, Shleifer, and Vishny 2010). One implication of this is the standard point that providing the intermediaries with bigger cushions of capital and liquidity is desirable. But perhaps a deeper point is that in such environments where important risks are misunderstood, shutting down one mechanism whereby investors and intermediaries pursue their profits is unlikely to work. They will try to realize their dreams through other instruments instead. Regulating a particular instrument, or a particular segment of the market, to solve a more fundamental problem is highly unlikely to work.

REFERENCES FOR THE SHLEIFER COMMENT

Adrian, Tobias, and Hyun Song Shin. 2010. "The Changing Nature of Financial Intermediation and the Financial Crisis of 2007–2009." *Annual Review of Economics* 2: 603–18.

Diamond, Douglas W., and Philip H. Dybvig. 1983. "Bank Runs, Deposit Insurance, and Liquidity." *Journal of Political Economy* 91, no. 3: 401–19.

Gennaioli, Nicola, Andrei Shleifer, and Robert W. Vishny. Forthcoming. "Neglected Risks, Financial Innovation, and Financial Fragility." *Journal of Financial Economics*.

COMMENT BY
DANIEL K. TARULLO Broadly speaking, threats to financial stability can arise in two ways: first, through the rapid deterioration or failure of a large institution with leverage sufficient to have widespread knock-on effects, and second, through the breakdown of a significant market in which large numbers of leveraged actors depend upon similar sources of liquidity and, importantly, backup liquidity in periods of stress. These two sources of systemic risk can be, and usually are, related. In fact, the severity of the recent crisis might be explained as an explosive combination of the two. But the different origins of risk call for different or, perhaps more precisely, complementary, policy responses.[1]

To date, reform in financial regulation and supervision has focused mainly on large regulated institutions. Three examples are the just-announced Basel III capital rules, much of the Dodd-Frank Act, and the Federal Reserve's revamping of its supervision of large holding companies. Of course, attention has also been paid to the second source of systemic risk, notably in Dodd-Frank's provisions for prudential supervision of payments, clearing, and settlement systems. But more will need to be done in this area, particularly as new constraints applicable to large regulated institutions push more activity into the unregulated sector.

This paper by Gary Gorton and Andrew Metrick fits squarely within this enterprise. It builds on two important insights from work that Gorton was pursuing well before the financial crisis began. The first was that the enormous growth of the shadow banking system generally, and the repurchase agreement, or "repo," market specifically, depended on the engineering of triple-A-rated securities that led participants to believe they did not need to inquire into the soundness of the underlying collateral. This financial engineering largely succeeded in insulating participants from idiosyncratic risk. But when the value of whole classes of the underlying collateral was drawn into serious question, initially by the collapse of the subprime housing market, participants' lack of information about the collateral they held led to a shattering of confidence in all the collateral.

In the absence of the regulation and government backstop that have applied to the traditional banking system since the Depression, a run on assets in the entire repo market ensued. The resulting forced sale of assets into an illiquid market turned many illiquid institutions into insolvent ones.

---

1. The views presented here are my own and not necessarily those of other members of the Board of Governors of the Federal Reserve System or the Federal Open Market Committee. Tom King and Michael Palumbo of the Board staff contributed to these remarks.

The fallout has been such that, to this day, the amount of repo funding available for nonagency residential mortgage-backed securities, commercial mortgage-backed securities, high-yield corporate bonds, and other instruments backed by assets with any degree of risk remains substantially below its pre-September 2008 levels.

The second insight of Gorton's on which this paper builds is the importance of statutory franchise value for the business model viability of at least some kinds of regulated financial entities. Where competition from unregulated entities is permitted, whether explicitly or de facto, capital and other requirements imposed on regulated firms may shrink margins enough to make them unattractive to investors. The result, as in the past, will be some combination of regulatory arbitrage, assumption of higher risk in permitted activities, and exit from the industry. Each of these outcomes at least potentially undermines the original motivation for the regulation.

Gorton and Metrick provide a concrete, although rather skeletal, proposal to remedy the information problem in the repo market through creation of statutory franchise value for what they call narrow funding banks (NFBs). These banks would be "narrow" in that their only assets would be asset-backed securities (ABSs) and very high quality instruments such as Treasury securities. They would, it appears, make their money from the income streams associated with the ABSs. They would raise the funds to purchase ABSs through debt issuance and, most significantly for the proposal, the repo market, in which the collateral offered would be liabilities of the NFBs. The government would regulate the NFBs directly, as it does all banks, but also by setting requirements for the ABSs that could be bought by the NFBs. This regulation is intended to provide market confidence in the liabilities of the NFBs, which would be further buttressed by NFB access to the discount window.

A key feature of the proposal is that, by law, *only* NFBs could buy securitized assets. The consequent franchise value would compensate NFBs for the costs they incur because they can hold only high-quality securities, are subject to supervision and prudential requirements, and have to operate in a highly transparent fashion. In essence, ABS-backed repo funding would be limited to NFBs.

The first two questions I would pose about this creative policy proposal are the most basic: What problem is it supposed to solve, and how does the breadth of the remedy align with that problem? Given their analysis of the breakdown of the repo market, Gorton and Metrick's answer might be self-evident: Their proposal aims to solve the information problems that increased the risk from maturity transformation associated with ABS repo funding. This, of course, is not a solution for the entire shadow banking system, although an effective plan for reforming the ABS repo market would be a major accomplishment in itself.[2]

But the solution that Gorton and Metrick propose to this problem would significantly restrict *all* asset-backed securitization. Although it is obvious that too much credit was created through ABSs and associated instruments in the years preceding the crisis, it seems at least reasonable to question whether the best policy response is this dramatic a change in the regulatory environment. One wonders, for example, if it is desirable to forbid anyone but NFBs from buying ABSs, particularly if there are investors interested in holding these assets regardless of their utility in repo arrangements. The severe problems now associated with ABSs began with assets held by mismatched entities like structured investment vehicles or financial institutions engaged in capital arbitrage under Basel II, not those held by end investors.

A variant on this initial question is how much the legal environment for securitization should be changed in order to provide a source of stable short-term liquidity in wholesale funding markets. Limiting securitization purchases to NFBs would surely result in some tailoring of ABSs to the business models of NFBs, an outcome that might not be identical to a securitization market tailored to the funding needs of lenders providing credit to businesses and consumers. Also, as I will explain later, Gorton and Metrick's proposal would require nontrivial changes in bank regulatory policy, as well as the significant extension of discount window access to a new kind of institution. All this would be in pursuit of a mechanism for generating large amounts of liquidity. A cost-benefit discussion is probably needed at the outset, with careful specification of the benefits of the repo market that the authors are trying to save, weighed against the likely impact on, among other things, the securitization market and the regulatory system.

A second set of questions concerns how the NFBs would operate in practice. As a threshold matter, it is worth noting that policymakers may find the proposal to have a certain binary quality. That is, it would structurally change the entire securitization market and a large portion of the repo market essentially overnight. In effect, Gorton and Metrick put all securitization eggs into one basket. If the new system worked well, the benefits presumably would be significant, and perhaps quickly realized. Indeed, the new system might succeed in helping to restart, on a sounder basis, various ABS submarkets that remain largely dormant 3 years after

---

2. For a survey of the entire shadow banking system, see Pozsar and others (2010).

the crisis began to unfold.³ If, on the other hand, the new system encountered major difficulties, there might be materially reduced adaptive capacity in other financial actors, possibly for a considerable period.

One obvious source of difficulty is the possibility, well recognized by Gorton and Metrick, that the business model mandated for NFBs might not be viable and stable. Like all forms of narrow banks proposed over the years, NFBs as a group would seem likely to generate relatively low revenue, given the low risk of the securities in which they would have to invest. Gorton and Metrick propose to counter this problem by granting franchise value through the statutory monopoly on securitization mentioned earlier and through access to the Federal Reserve's discount window. Picking up on their analogy to the creation of deposit insurance in the 1930s, the monopoly on securitization is intended to help offset the regulatory costs imposed on NFBs in the same way that the monopoly on the "business of banking" was intended to offset the regulatory costs imposed on insured depository institutions.

Unlike the business environment for banks in the 1930s, however, securitization and repo lending are national, if not international, activities, with little to suggest that any advantage would be derived from local knowledge. It seems quite possible that the economies of scale associated with the NFB model are sufficiently high that the industry structure would tend toward oligopoly, or even monopoly. That is, too *much* franchise value might be created. In that event there would be significant additions to the cost side of the proposal's ledger, in the form of the price and quantity effects that result from noncompetitive industry structures.

Regardless of the eventual structure of the industry, NFBs essentially would be monolines, with highly correlated risk exposures. They could be particularly vulnerable to funding difficulties in times of deteriorating credit conditions. Yet by the terms of Gorton and Metrick's proposal, they apparently would not be able to hedge interest rate or other risks. The authors propose giving NFBs access to the discount window to forestall liquidity problems and runs on the NFBs, presumably in the same way that deposit insurance stopped runs on traditional banks. Here again, though, the analogy is not a perfect one. Whereas banks and their depositors are assured that the Federal Deposit Insurance Corporation will keep the latter

---

3. The relative dormancy of these markets is also due in part to the limited supply of the loans needed to feed the securitization process.

whole in the event of the former's failure, the Federal Reserve does not make binding commitments to lend to any institution and actively discourages reliance on the window for regular funding. In this regard, it is noteworthy that the haircuts imposed on collateral presented at the discount window rose during the recent crisis, although to a lesser extent than in the repo market itself.

A third question about the Gorton and Metrick proposal arises because of the significant changes in current law and practice that it would require. The prohibition on ABS holdings by anyone other than NFBs is the obvious and major example. But there are several others. In addition to the possibly problematic features of discount window lending in general for the proposal, the Federal Reserve has traditionally opened the window to nondepository institutions only in particularly stressed conditions. Under the Dodd-Frank Act, any use of credit ratings in federal regulations will be prohibited, an obvious complication to the proposal. This part of Dodd-Frank has accelerated and expanded the efforts already under way at the federal banking agencies to lessen regulatory reliance on ratings. In truth, it may pose no greater challenge for this proposal than for many existing capital rules.[4] Still, it may require extension of the authors' confidence that the regulator could adequately oversee ABS ratings to confidence that it could assign ratings in the first place. I would observe that the substantial effort expended by staff at the Board and at the Federal Reserve Bank of New York to evaluate the creditworthiness of a relatively small number of securitizations in the Term Asset-Backed Securities Loan Facility (TALF) suggests the enormity of that task. Furthermore, the wisdom of having a government agency—even the independent central bank—assume such a permanent, central role in credit allocation is at least subject to debate.

A final regulatory issue is raised by another feature of Gorton and Metrick's proposal prompted by their expectation that equity returns for NFBs will be lower than for traditional banks. In place of the equity capital requirements generally applicable to banking organizations, they propose that NFBs issue capital notes that would be debt-like except in periods of stress, when they would convert to equity. In essence, all of an NFB's capital would be contingent capital. Although contingent capital is an item on the financial regulatory agenda, it is considered a possible supplement to

---

4. For a discussion of some of the issues raised in the context of capital requirements, see Board of Governors of the Federal Reserve System (2010).

common equity, not a substitute for it. In this respect, the proposal moves in the opposite direction from Basel III, which has followed markets in making common equity the centerpiece of capital evaluation and requirements.[5]

These inconsistencies with current law and practice in the Gorton and Metrick proposal do not themselves argue against its soundness. They do, however, underscore the degree to which the NFBs would require development of a new financial regulatory approach, as well as a restructuring of the ABS and repo markets.

More generally, the existence of costs or problems with the proposal is not sufficient grounds to reject it. In the face of very real flaws in the precrisis state of these markets, and the failure of some ABS markets to recover, even where it seems they could function sensibly, there is a very good case for such a policy initiative. So let me consider briefly whether variants on Gorton and Metrick's basic approach might retain its core benefits while addressing some of its potential problems.

One possibility would be to broaden the permissible ownership of NFBs to include bank holding companies. This modification would make the most sense if one believed that the proposal's basic approach was promising but that the risks of either an untenable business model or high industry concentration, and consequent anticompetitive effects, were high. It is possible that a number of large, diversified financial holding companies would find an NFB a viable part of their operations. Gorton and Metrick would require, however, that NFBs be stand-alone entities, and they would specifically prohibit ownership by commercial banks, in an effort to avoid implicit contractual guarantees. This is a legitimate concern, to be sure, but one that might be at least imperfectly addressed through specific restrictions on relationships between affiliates in a bank holding company. The relevant comparison is thus between the residual costs of the regulated relationship and the effects of an anticompetitive industry structure.

A second variant, also motivated by industry structure problems, would be to turn NFBs from what in Gorton and Metrick's proposal are essentially privately owned public utilities into actual public utilities. However, the extent to which this change in ownership structure would ameliorate the anticompetitive problems is uncertain. Moreover, the concerns mentioned earlier with respect to government judgments on credit allocation

---

5. It also seems likely that the kinds of quantitative liquidity requirements currently under development by the Basel Committee on Banking Supervision would be difficult for NFBs to satisfy.

would remain, even if they are provided another layer of insulation through the device of a government corporation. In addition, of course, the history of Fannie Mae and Freddie Mac is a cautionary tale of the potential for a government monopoly with a conservative mandate to expand its operation into much riskier activities.

At first glance, then, it is not at all clear that structural modifications to Gorton and Metrick's basic approach would be preferable to the proposal as they have described it. Options that depart from their approach would need to find different ways of solving the information problems that they identify. Let me briefly note some possible alternatives that would use regulatory requirements to create a class of ABSs in which markets could, without inquiry into the nature and quality of the underlying assets, have confidence even in periods of stress. One way, of course, would be to follow more closely the deposit insurance analogy by establishing an insurance system, a proposal that Gorton and Metrick endorse with respect to money market funds. They suggest, however, that an insurance system for securitization markets would be impractical because of the existence of multiple tranches, at least some of which would be uninsurable and thus would, in their view, exacerbate rather than ameliorate information problems.

Another alternative would begin with an important idea that the paper mentions, but which is not at the center of the proposal: making the repo bankruptcy exception available only where the collateral conforms to certain criteria established by law or regulation. Given the demand for repo funding, it seems worth considering whether this device could be used to create the franchise value necessary to sustain a sizable wholesale funding market subject to safety and soundness regulation. Indeed, if this approach has promise, it might be feasible for a regulatory body to establish the requisite criteria without providing insurance. With or without insurance, the "franchise value" might attach more to the instrument than to an institution.

It is beyond the scope of this comment to enumerate the potential difficulties with these ideas, but they are not hard to discern. In common with the authors' proposal, they would require a level of expertise and involvement in credit rating by the government that could pose practical and, in some conceivable versions, policy concerns. In any case, these are thoughts for further discussion, rather than developed options. Gorton and Metrick have, in setting forth this proposal, continued to shape our understanding of the role and risks of the shadow banking system, while adding a specific proposal to our menu of possible responses.

REFERENCES FOR THE TARULLO COMMENT

Board of Governors of the Federal Reserve System. 2010. "Advance Notice of Proposed Rulemaking Regarding Alternatives to the Use of Credit Ratings in the Risk-Based Capital Guidelines of the Federal Banking Agencies." Joint Advance Notice of Proposed Rulemaking. Washington (August 10). www.federalreserve.gov/newsevents/press/bcreg/bcreg20100810a1.pdf.

Pozsar, Zoltan, Tobias Adrian, Adam Ashcraft, and Hayley Boesky. 2010. "Shadow Banking." Federal Reserve Bank of New York Staff Reports no. 458 (July). www.newyorkfed.org/research/staff_reports/sr458.pdf.

GENERAL DISCUSSION Jonathan Parker noted that runs on highly rated securities had also happened in money market mutual funds. Under current regulation, the quality of a money market fund cannot easily be discerned, and the structure of the fund gives fund managers little incentive to become informed about the quality of highly rated assets. Thus, there is often a trade-off between higher returns and an unknown amount of additional risk. Given the short-term nature of these investments, there is not only little incentive to gather information, but often little time to gather it when it becomes clear that information is needed. There is thus a trade-off in regulation between liquidity—the speed with which money can be withdrawn (or not rolled over)—and information creation. If something goes wrong and the asset is withdrawable on demand or in the short term, I can get out, but I will not be able to process whether that was the right decision. The solution then seems to be to increase the terms of lending to promote stability, so information can be gathered, but this comes at the cost of liquidity. Parker also noted, with respect to the securitization model, that there is no reason originators cannot be required to sell systemic securitized risk to be insured against a macro crisis, while at the same time holding the idiosyncratic risk of their loans for incentive reasons.

Robert Hall observed that the financial world has a thirst to hold wealth with a zero probability of negative nominal return. The issue raised by the paper is the value of creating institutions that cannot go bankrupt. In a low-inflation economy, this issue of preventing negative nominal returns is an important one, suggesting a simple change: rather than raise inflation, depositors should get a lower return in exchange for a lower probability of a negative return, while still allowing for the possibility.

Kristin Forbes suggested that the paper was in effect saying that the shadow banking system arose to compensate for shortcomings in the bankruptcy system, and especially the length of time to resolve a bankruptcy case. If that is so, one would expect that countries with stronger bankruptcy regimes and faster bankruptcy resolution would have smaller shadow banking systems. Do the cross-country data support this? Her prior was that they did not. Countries such as the United States have fairly strong and effective bankruptcy systems yet have the largest shadow banking systems.

Phillip Swagel thought that Andrei Shleifer's concern over the authors' proposal involving nationalization of the nonagency repo market was misplaced. The proposal would remove some of the existing legal protection for repo transactions that do not involve high-quality collateral. Thus, it would reduce government coverage, not increase it. This seemed to Swagel a reasonable way to provide an incentive for the use of better collateral. On the other hand, there should be greater understanding of the limits to which high-quality collateral matters. The week after Lehman Brothers failed, the U.S. Treasury offered insurance for money market mutual funds. What was striking was that essentially all of these funds—even those that invested only in securities that were already government-guaranteed, such as Treasury and agency bonds—chose to buy the insurance. These funds already had the highest-quality collateral, yet it didn't matter; they wanted to provide even more reassurance to investors. The lesson Swagel drew was that in a true crisis, even the best collateral is not good enough.

Steven Davis argued that it was not obvious how the authors' proposal flowed from their interpretation of the crisis. Excessive leverage was what contributed in many ways to the crisis, facilitating the housing bubble, among other things. Thus, the regulatory system needs to be able to regulate leverage, for example through haircuts. For Davis, this implied a different solution: that banks be required to hold more capital, since the world is riskier than previously thought.

Ricardo Reis was interested in the idea of repos as a way around bankruptcy. He raised three issues. First, in the cross section of countries, do we see more use of repos (or similar instruments) in countries with the least efficient bankruptcy procedures? Second, across industries, are repos used more in industries where finances are more opaque? And third, if the problem was the delays caused by bankruptcy proceedings, why not reform the bankruptcy code?

JAMES R. HINES JR.
University of Michigan

State Fiscal Policies and Transitory Income Fluctuations

ABSTRACT State and local expenditure and tax revenue respond less to the business cycle than do federal spending and revenue, thereby reducing the countercyclicality of total government expenditure and revenue. This paper considers forces responsible for the cyclical pattern of state expenditure and revenue. Annual fluctuations in state personal income are associated with small changes in state spending and significant changes in tax receipts; receipt of federal grants is associated with greater state spending. Tax collections, and to a lesser degree expenditure, of larger states are more closely associated with annual income fluctuations than are the tax collections and expenditure of smaller states. These state size differences may proxy for other state characteristics, such as the extent to which a state faces interstate competition for mobile businesses and individuals, and the quality of state government. The spending and tax revenue of states with less mobile populations closely track income fluctuations, as does spending in states where convictions of public officials for federal corruption crimes are more common. In small states, and in states with more mobile populations and better corruption records, government expenditure and revenue appear to rise and fall less with income, and in that respect more closely resemble the federal government.

In the United States, fiscal policy is the province not only of the federal government but also of 50 state governments and their local governments. Collectively, these nonfederal governments accounted for roughly 40 percent of total government expenditure in 2007, and an even larger fraction of total government revenue. Since states and municipalities operate independently of the federal government and of each other, it follows that a significant portion of U.S. fiscal policy is uncoordinated. As a result, any deliberate countercyclical fiscal policy conducted by the federal government has the potential to be affected, possibly even undermined, by the actions of state and local governments.

The federalist structure of U.S. fiscal policy would be of little macroeconomic consequence if states and localities behaved just like smaller versions of the federal government, but there is little reason to expect them to, and considerable evidence that they do not. States and localities differ from the federal government and from each other in the economic functions they serve, their average level and composition of expenditure, the extent to which they are subject to national economic shocks, and their beliefs about the role of government in managing the economy. Perhaps most important, state and local decisionmaking is driven by interests and constraints that differ from those of the federal government: states have incentives to pursue policies that benefit their own stakeholders, and they are subject to competition from other states.

The aggregate evidence for the postwar period suggests that during economic downturns, state and local tax collections decline less than do federal tax collections, and state government spending expands less than does federal spending. This general pattern has been mirrored in the recent U.S. experience. For example, in 2007 the federal government collected $1.638 trillion in taxes other than social insurance contributions, a figure that declined substantially in the recent recession, to $1.142 trillion in 2009. State and local tax collections also declined, but much more gradually: from $1.314 trillion in 2007 to $1.267 trillion in 2009. Federal government spending of $3.458 trillion in 2009 was $558 billion greater than in 2007, whereas state and local spending of $2.026 trillion in 2009 exceeded 2007 spending by just $115 billion.[1] Changes in federal expenditure and in state and local expenditure reflect policy changes as well as the changing incomes of the population. In addition, federal grants-in-aid to state and local governments rose by $104 billion between 2007 and 2009; removing this component leaves self-financed aggregate state expenditure only $11 billion larger in nominal terms, and smaller in real terms, during 2009 than in 2007. It is clear that state and local governments reacted to the recession that began at the end of 2007 very differently than did the federal government.

There are reasons to expect states not to expand their spending during recessions. Almost all state governments have annual balanced budget requirements, with only limited exceptions for bad economic times, so the declining tax revenue that characterizes most economic downturns is

---

1. The state and local totals are the sum of state, county, city, and other local taxes and spending. Federal and aggregate state and local government tax and expenditure data, both at annual and quarterly frequencies, are drawn from the U.S. national income and product accounts.

likely to be accompanied by reduced spending. These balanced budget requirements certainly do not prevent states from financing additional spending with greater borrowing, as evidenced by the fact that many states do borrow, but the requirements raise the political and administrative costs of running deficits, since they commonly require that state legislatures enact extraordinary measures to undertake the necessary borrowing. States with balanced budget requirements can maintain or expand spending across the cycle by running budget surpluses during good economic times, which can then be drawn down during bad economic times, but in practice it has proved difficult for many states to conduct their fiscal affairs that way. Finally, the adoption of balanced budget requirements reflects a shared expectation among states that they will not make extensive use of debt finance to combat adverse economic developments.

A second reason why state governments might fail to increase expenditure during economic downturns is that the tax revenue reductions that accompany economic contractions generally discourage spending even in the absence of a requirement that budgets be balanced. It has been widely documented that the expenditure of subnational governments is significantly affected by cash windfalls, whether positive or negative; this is known as the "flypaper effect": money tends to stick where it hits. The flypaper effect was first observed in the context of intergovernmental grants, typically those from the federal government to state governments, which appeared to have a much greater impact on state spending than can be easily reconciled with the actual income and substitution effects of the grants.

There is considerable controversy over the origins of the flypaper effect, its magnitude, and whether it reflects political dynamics or more fundamental aspects of the way that individuals make decisions.[2] But whatever its sources, the flypaper effect describes an empirical regularity: money in hand and available is more likely to be spent than is money that is not quite as readily available, even though it is fully obtainable. Although the flypaper effect is often interpreted narrowly to apply to specific categories of revenue and expenditure, a more general view (see, for example, Hines and Thaler 1995) is that it reflects a feature of human nature that applies broadly to many revenue sources and expenditure categories, and results from the difficulty that people have in not spending resources that are

---

2. See, for example, Hines and Thaler (1995), Strumpf (1998), and Baicker (2005). Knight (2002), Gordon (2004), and Lutz (2010) offer evidence and interpretations that the magnitude of the flypaper effect may be overstated by earlier studies that fail to control properly for the endogeneity of grant receipts to spending levels, although even the data presented by Lutz (2010) appear to be consistent with significant flypaper effects.

available to them. Thus, for example, Olivier Blanchard, Florencio Lopez-de-Silanes, and Andrei Shleifer (1994) report that firms obtaining cash windfalls from victorious lawsuits significantly increased their expenditure on acquisitions of other firms; and in the context of state reactions to economic fluctuations, Douglas Holtz-Eakin, Whitney Newey, and Harvey Rosen (1989) find that local revenue shocks are associated with subsequent spending increases by municipal governments. Any natural tendency of state governments to spend money that they have on hand reduces the likelihood that states will pursue countercyclical fiscal policies.[3]

Against these considerations, however, must be set the potential benefits of greater spending, including the avoidance of draconian budget cuts, during economic downturns. To the extent that tax cuts and greater government spending during recessions facilitate the employment of underutilized resources within a state, they have the potential to promote the welfare of state residents.[4] Apart from any desire to put underutilized resources to work, states that can avoid damaging, cash flow–driven budget cuts during bad economic times have the potential to improve their own business conditions and property values. This may matter more for smaller (that is, less populous) states than for larger states: since they tend to face the most elastic populations of businesses and individuals, they may have the strongest incentives to avoid boom-and-bust fiscal cycles that, to the extent that they are inefficient or reduce welfare, could result in declining populations, incomes, and property values.

---

3. An additional reason why states might reduce expenditure during recessions is that state spending becomes more expensive, on an after-federal-tax basis, to the degree that fewer taxpayers itemize deductions or that those who do itemize face lower marginal tax rates. The ability of taxpayers who itemize on their federal income tax returns to take deductions for state and local income and property tax payments generally reduces the after-tax cost of state spending, and thereby encourages state governments to spend more than they would were state taxes nondeductible (Feldstein and Metcalf 1987). Given that only roughly one-third of American taxpayers itemize their deductions, however, and that the fraction itemizing does not appear to fall systematically during recessions (the numbers of taxpayers itemizing deductions rose during the 1980, 1991–92, and 2001 recessions, according to IRS data: "SOI Bulletin Historical Table 7," www.irs.gov/taxstats/article/0,,id=175812,00.html), the effect of tax deductibility on state expenditure is unlikely to account for significant expenditure reactions to economic downturns.

4. There is enormous controversy over the extent to which countercyclical fiscal policy influences the employment of resources during economic downturns. See, for example, Auerbach, Gale, and Harris (2010), Auerbach and Gorodnichenko (2010), Barro and Redlick (2009), Blanchard and Perotti (2002), Cogan and others (2010), Hall (2009), Romer and Romer (2010), and Woodford (2010). Gramlich (1997) identifies circumstances in which state governments might benefit from expanding the employment of underutilized resources through expansionary fiscal policies, and Bahl (1984) reviews older evidence of the association of state tax and spending policies and business cycle fluctuations.

States differ in the extent to which their levels of expenditure and taxation vary over the business cycle. Changes in the expenditure and tax revenue of larger states are more positively correlated with state income fluctuations than are those of smaller states. This fiscal pattern of large versus small states may reflect the pressures that all governments face to spend money during the good times when it is available, and reduce expenditure at other times; the somewhat greater immobility of population and business activity in large states arguably makes it more feasible for their governments to follow such spending patterns than it is for smaller jurisdictions. Expenditure and tax revenue in states with less mobile populations (where mobility is measured by the fraction of adults born in a state who subsequently reside there), and in states whose public officials are frequently convicted of federal corruption crimes, exhibit correlations with income fluctuations similar to those of large states. This suggests that state size might proxy in these regressions for other attributes of larger states, such as relatively more captive populations of individuals and businesses, and perhaps lower quality of government.

Section I of this paper uses quarterly national income accounts data (available for states only as an aggregate) from 1947 to 2010 to identify the extent to which state and local tax revenue and spending change during national income fluctuations. This evidence suggests that the 2007–09 experience is unusual only in its magnitude: real federal tax collections per capita tend to decline in years in which the economy performs poorly, whereas state and local tax collections are much more stable; furthermore, federal government spending tends to rise more rapidly during bad economic times than it does during good times, a pattern that is much less evident among state and local governments.

Section II of the paper uses Census of Governments data to identify the determinants of state tax and spending patterns, distinguishing between large and small states. States exhibit marked propensities to spend out of federal grant dollars, and larger states display tax revenue and expenditure patterns that are more closely associated with income fluctuations than are those of smaller states. Section III concludes.

I. Aggregate Patterns of Federal and State Taxes and Spending

Expenditure by the federal government accounts for about 20 percent of aggregate national expenditure in virtually every year since World War II. Figure 1 depicts ratios of real federal spending and of real state and local

Figure 1. Federal Spending and State and Local Spending, 1947Q1–2010Q1[a]

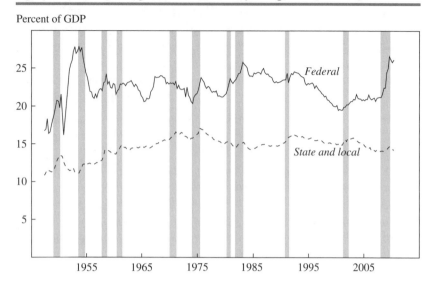

Source: National income and product accounts.
a. Shading indicates recessions as identified by the Business Cycle Dating Committee of the National Bureau of Economic Research.

spending to real U.S. GDP, as reported in quarterly national income account data from 1947Q1 to 2010Q1.[5] It is noteworthy that federal spending as a fraction of GDP appears to rise with the onset of recessions, particularly since the 1960s. Doubtless recessions have this effect for multiple reasons, including not only that the federal government pursues a deliberately countercyclical fiscal policy, but also that a sluggish responsiveness of federal expenditure to changes in income means that the ratio rises when GDP fails to grow as rapidly as anticipated. Ratios of state and local expenditure to GDP appear to exhibit a similar pattern of rising in recessions, although from visual inspection it is not clear whether they do so to the same degree as federal expenditure. Certainly state and local spending

---

5. GDP, federal taxes, and state and local taxes are deflated using the GDP deflator. Government consumption and investment expenditures are separately deflated using the corresponding deflators, and all other categories of government expenditure (transfer payments, interest payments, and others) are deflated using the GDP deflator.

during the 2007–09 recession did not rise as sharply as federal spending.[6] But since the latest recession is just one of several postwar recessions, it is useful to consider how state and local spending and federal spending have responded in others.

Table 1 presents averages of quarterly growth rates of real federal government and aggregate state and local government tax revenue and spending per capita.[7] These growth rates are calculated as first differences of the logarithms of seasonally adjusted quarterly values. Table entries are cell means; thus, for example, the first column indicates that, in quarters in which the output gap declined, the log of real federal income tax collections per capita rose by an average of 0.0177. Strictly speaking, this corresponds to a growth rate of 1.79 percent, but as a convenient approximation, these log differences are commonly interpreted as percentage growth rates. The output gap is the difference between the economy's potential GDP and actual GDP, divided by potential GDP, as reported by the Congressional Budget Office.

The evidence in table 1 suggests that the cyclical patterns of U.S. federal tax and spending policies differ from those of state and local governments. In quarters during which the economy is expanding and the output gap is narrowing, the mean growth rate of real federal tax revenue per capita is 1.77 percent, whereas in quarters during which the output gap is widening, the mean growth rate of this revenue measure is –1.16 percent. State and local tax collections, by contrast, show a more muted difference, growing at a quarterly average rate of 1.13 percent when the output gap narrows and 0.27 percent when it widens. The last three columns of table 1 show that during recession quarters (as identified by the Business Cycle Dating Committee of the National Bureau of Economic Research), the mean growth rate of real federal tax revenue per capita is –2.91 percent, whereas at other times the mean growth rate is 1.08 percent; state and local tax revenue grew by an average of –0.02 percent during recession

---

6. Aizenman and Pasricha (2010) compare recent levels of certain (nontransfer) state and federal spending categories with levels predicted from a simple time-series model and argue that discretionary state fiscal policy is by this measure so contractionary that it roughly offsets the recent federal expansion. This conclusion appears to depend critically on the model used to predict discretionary spending; but almost any measure shows that state spending failed to expand during the 2007–09 recession, which suggests that states did not pursue active countercyclical policies.

7. Variables are converted to per capita terms using quarterly interpolations of annual population data from the U.S. Census.

Table 1. Growth in Real Federal and Aggregate State and Local Spending and Tax Revenue per Capita under Differing Economic Conditions

Expenditure or revenue measure	Average quarterly growth rate[a]									
	Output gap			Output gap			Recession quarter?[d]		
	Narrowing[b]	Widening	Difference	Negative[c]	Positive	Difference	No	Yes	Difference
Expenditure									
Federal nondefense	0.61	1.07	−0.45	−0.01	1.49	1.50	0.77	1.74	−0.98
	(0.46)	(0.36)	(0.59)	(0.52)	(0.33)	(0.61)	(0.37)	(0.62)	(0.72)
State and local	0.58	0.57	0.01	0.57	0.60	−0.03	0.52	0.91	−0.39
	(0.09)	(0.10)	(0.13)	(0.11)	(0.09)	(0.14)	(0.07)	(0.19)	(0.20)
Difference	0.03	0.49	−0.46	−0.58	0.89	−1.47	0.25	0.84	−0.59
	(0.45)	(0.38)	(0.59)	(0.52)	(0.32)	(0.61)	(0.36)	(0.66)	(0.75)
Tax revenue									
Federal	1.77	−1.16	2.93	1.01	−0.22	1.22	1.08	−2.91	3.99
	(0.38)	(0.38)	(0.53)	(0.33)	(0.43)	(0.54)	(0.28)	(0.64)	(0.70)
State and local	1.13	0.27	0.86	0.79	0.67	0.11	0.93	−0.02	0.95
	(0.08)	(0.12)	(0.14)	(0.11)	(0.11)	(0.15)	(0.07)	(0.21)	(0.22)
Difference	0.64	−1.43	2.07	0.22	−0.89	1.11	0.15	−2.89	3.04
	(0.36)	(0.36)	(0.51)	(0.30)	(0.41)	(0.51)	(0.27)	(0.62)	(0.68)
No. of observations	125	119		106	139		200	52	

Source: Author's calculations.
a. Reported values are simple averages of quarterly growth rates of real spending or real tax revenue per capita from 1949Q1 to 2010Q1, calculated as approximations based on first differences in the logarithms of seasonally adjusted values as reported in the national income and product accounts. Standard errors are in parentheses.
b. Quarters during which the output gap (difference between potential and actual GDP, divided by potential GDP, as defined by the Congressional Budget Office) was declining.
c. Quarters during which the output gap was negative (actual GDP exceeded potential GDP).
d. Recession quarters are those identified by the Business Cycle Dating Committee of the National Bureau of Economic Research as recession months. Data are from 1947Q1 through 2010Q1.

quarters, and 0.93 percent at other times. As the table indicates, these differences between federal and state and local tax revenue growth are statistically as well as quantitatively significant.

Federal spending tends to rise more rapidly when the economy is performing poorly than when it is performing well; state and local spending exhibits a similar pattern, but to a much smaller degree. Table 1 presents figures for federal nondefense expenditure, a portion of the federal budget that is less subject than total expenditure to exogenous shocks and more amenable to deliberate adjustment in response to changing macroeconomic conditions. Real federal nondefense spending per capita rose by a mean of 1.49 percent during quarters in which potential GDP exceeded actual, and at other times fell by an average of 0.01 percent. State and local government real expenditure per capita rose by an average of 0.60 percent during quarters in which potential GDP exceeded the actual; it also rose, by an average of 0.57 percent, at other times. As indicated in table 1, the relationship between federal expenditure growth and the output gap differs statistically from that between the growth of state and local spending and the output gap. The differences between federal and state and local spending growth during rising and falling output gaps, and during NBER-defined recessions, are not significant but point in the same direction: federal spending generally expands more than does state and local spending during difficult economic times.

In interpreting the evidence in table 1, it is important to bear in mind that these patterns reflect not only the degree to which the state of the economy may influence government tax and expenditure choices, but also the impact of taxes and government expenditure on economic performance. The federal government is larger, in terms of both revenue and spending, than the 50 state governments combined, and it is more likely to coordinate fiscal and monetary policy; as a result, federal actions have greater potential to influence the course of the economy. A simple interpretation of the means in table 1 might take the output gap and the cyclical status of the economy to be unaffected by government tax and spending changes, which is inaccurate if federal economic management is effective, and particularly if taxes and spending are coordinated with other government policies. To the extent that federal tax reductions and spending increases reduce the severity of economic downturns, simple interpretations of the statistics in table 1 understate the extent to which the federal government actively manages taxation and spending in response to underlying economic conditions. The same argument applies to state and local governments, although their smaller aggregate size gives it somewhat less significance. Furthermore, one way in which the federal government actively manages aggregate demand during downturns is by using federal grant dollars and other inducements to encourage states to spend money; thus, some federal spending is effectively channeled through the states and appears as state expenditure even though it is largely federally determined.

Differences between federal fiscal policy and the fiscal policies of state and local governments reflect many considerations, including the federal government's explicit mandate to manage the economy over the business cycle, and the ability and desire of state governments to react to changing economic circumstances. Since states are heterogeneous, it is potentially instructive to compare the fiscal policies of states with differing characteristics, in order to identify factors that may contribute to the determination of overall state policies.

II. Understanding State Fiscal Policy

In the absence of countervailing policy action, tax revenue generally increases as incomes rise, creating opportunities for states to fund greater expenditure. A close connection between income changes and expenditure changes could, of course, constitute efficient state fiscal policy, although it also is characteristic of the flypaper effect as applied to state finances. To the extent that the flypaper effect is behavioral, fiscal policies driven by flypaper considerations are potentially costly from an efficiency standpoint. Small jurisdictions generally have the most elastic tax bases (Bucovetsky 1991, Kanbur and Keen 1993, Wilson and Wildasin 2004) and therefore face significant costs of adopting suboptimal policies that may chase away their business and individual populations. The very fact that adopting inefficient policies is so expensive has the potential to discipline politics in these smaller states to avoid some of the behavioral inefficiencies that could persist among their larger neighbors whose tax bases are more secure.

In evaluating state fiscal policy, then, it is instructive to distinguish between smaller and larger states in analyzing the impact of income fluctuations on taxes and expenditure. For that purpose it is necessary to use data from the Census of Governments. These data are available from 1951 to 2007 for the lower 48 states and the District of Columbia; coverage of Alaska and Hawaii is more limited, both in years and in data items, and so these states are omitted from the analysis. The data include information on state government expenditure, state personal incomes, populations, receipts of grants from the federal government, and collections of major sources of revenue.[8] It is worth emphasizing that the present analysis does not use data on city, county, or other local taxes and spending, since the purpose is to analyze the determinants of taxes and spending at the state level. Personal income and state tax collections are converted to real 2005 dollars using the GDP deflator, and state government expenditure is converted to real 2005 dollars using the Bureau of Economic Analysis price index for state and local government consumption expenditure and gross investment; all variables are measured in per capita terms.

The state regressions include interactions between balanced budget requirements and changes in state incomes. Every state except Vermont has a formal requirement that its budget be balanced on an annual basis. However, these requirements vary considerably in their ability to constrain state legislatures, a fact that has permitted analysts to evaluate their impact by comparing the experiences of states with strict balanced budget laws with those that have more leeway to run deficits. Earlier research (for example, Poterba 1994, Alt and Lowry 1994) finds that states with more binding balanced budget requirements react to fiscal crises (variously defined) differently than do states with less binding requirements, although the reactions appear to be idiosyncratic in that they are influenced by local politics.

Poterba (1994, 1997), Von Hagen (1991), and numerous other studies use the characterization of state budget stringency from the now-defunct Advisory Commission on Intergovernmental Relations as their source of variation in state budget rules. In the simplest of these classifications, roughly half of the states are classified as having "strict" rules, with requirements that entail, if necessary, mid-year budget adjustments and actions by state executive agencies that make it politically costly (although by no means impossible) to run deficits. The regressions reported in tables 2, 3, and 4 include this variable interacted with changes in real state income per capita.

Columns 2-1 and 2-2 of table 2 report regressions in which the dependent variable is the first difference of the log of real state expenditure. The regressions include a complete set of year and state dummy variables. State population is entered as the difference between a state's share of the U.S. population and the sample mean of 0.0204; all other independent variables are entered as first differences in time. The estimated

---

8. Data on detailed categories of state government expenditure are not available for 2007. Annual state populations are available from the Census.

Table 2. Regressions Explaining Annual Changes in State Spending and Tax Revenue

	Dependent variable[a]			
	Δ log spending		Δ log tax revenue	
Independent variable[b]	2-1	2-2	2-3	2-4
Δ income[c]	−0.0159	0.119**	0.368***	0.367***
	(0.0695)	(0.0588)	(0.0836)	(0.0836)
Δ income$_{-1}$	0.0691	0.101*	0.299***	0.304***
	(0.0598)	(0.0593)	(0.0551)	(0.0591)
Balanced budget req.[d] × Δ income	0.00715	−0.0160	−0.0644	−0.0618
	(0.0798)	(0.0709)	(0.107)	(0.107)
Balanced budget req. × Δ income$_{-1}$	0.0186	0.00722	0.0796	0.0769
	(0.0988)	(0.0935)	(0.0723)	(0.0726)
Population[e] × Δ income	−2.261	−0.740	9.975***	10.30***
	(1.953)	(1.751)	(2.636)	(2.757)
Population × Δ income$_{-1}$	4.714**	4.778**	4.881***	4.847**
	(2.066)	(2.237)	(1.795)	(1.888)
Population	−1.374	1.170	−8.162**	−8.534**
	(3.788)	(3.194)	(3.998)	(4.140)
Population$_{-1}$	1.675	−0.941	8.235**	8.600**
	(3.768)	(3.133)	(3.965)	(4.114)
Δ grants-income ratio[f]		4.862***		0.100
		(0.809)		(0.447)
Δ grants-income ratio$_{-1}$		0.606*		0.00611
		(0.311)		(0.361)
Population × Δ grants-income ratio		98.88**		17.53
		(39.82)		(20.58)
Population × Δ grants-income ratio$_{-1}$		−2.500		−14.55
		(9.095)		(12.44)
R^2	0.279	0.348	0.270	0.270

Source: Author's regressions.
a. Dependent variables are annual log changes in real state government spending or tax revenue per capita. All regressions include state and year fixed effects. Sample size is 2,695 in all regressions. Standard errors clustered at the state level are in parentheses.
b. Variables subscripted "−1" are one-year lags.
c. Annual change in the log of real state personal income per capita.
d. Dummy variable equal to 1 for states with a strict annual balanced budget requirement, and zero otherwise.
e. Difference between the state's population as a fraction of total U.S. population and the sample mean of 0.0204.
f. Annual change in the ratio of federal grants to state personal income.

coefficients on the differences in log real income per capita (−0.0159), and its one-year lag (0.0691), in the regression in column 2-1, together imply that a 1 percent increase in income (measured as a deviation from the national average) in a state with population equal to the sample mean and no strict balanced budget requirement is accompanied by a 0.0532 percent rise in state spending. This is a very small effect, and statistically indistinguishable from zero, suggesting that short-term income changes have little average effect on state spending. The small size of the association may reflect a combination of deliberate countercyclical policy and sluggishness in adjusting spending to genuine income changes, together with any measurement error in state personal income. The positive coefficients on the interactions of the balanced budget requirement with the change in income in column 2-1 are consistent with expenditure by states with strict budgetary rules tracking state income changes more closely than does expenditure by other states. However, the small magnitudes and statistical insignificance of the coefficients suggest that balanced budget rules do not have powerful average effects over the sample period.

The coefficient on the interaction between (de-meaned) state population and the one-year-lagged change in income in column 2-1 (4.714) indicates that government spending by larger states is more positively associated with once-lagged income fluctuations than is government spending by smaller states. The negative coefficient on contemporaneous income changes in the same column (−2.261) implies, however, that this association is mitigated by effects in the first year; the sum of these coefficients is 2.453, with a standard error of 2.689. The regression reported in column 2-2 adds as explanatory variables the first difference of the ratio of grants received from the federal government to state personal income, the interaction of this variable with de-meaned state population, and lags of these two variables. The effect on spending of population interacted with lagged income changes continues to be positive, although the sum of this coefficient and the unlagged corresponding term is 4.038, with a standard error of 2.938 that makes it insignificant.

Intergovernmental grants have the expected positive effect in the regression reported in column 2-2, the coefficients together implying that a state with mean population increases its expenditure by 5.468 percent as grants increase by 1 percent of state income. One way to interpret the impact of intergovernmental grants is to specify the change in state spending as a function of the change in state personal income and grant receipts:

(1) $$\Delta \ln S_t = \beta \Delta \ln(y_t + \gamma g_t),$$

in which S_t is state expenditure in year t, y_t is state personal income in year t, g_t is government grant receipts in year t, and Δ is the first difference operator. The parameter γ reflects the fact that government grants may not affect spending to the same extent that personal income does; values of

$\gamma > 1$ correspond to larger effects of government grants. Equation 1 can be rewritten as

(2) $$\Delta \ln S_t = \beta \Delta \ln y_t + \beta \Delta \ln\left(1 + \gamma \frac{g_t}{y_t}\right).$$

Using a first-order Taylor approximation to the second term on the right side of equation 2, evaluated at the mean value of $\frac{g_t}{y_t}$, denoted $\left(\frac{g}{y}\right)$, produces

(3) $$\Delta \ln S_t = \beta \Delta \ln y_t + \beta \frac{\gamma}{\left[1 + \gamma\left(\frac{g}{y}\right)\right]} \Delta \frac{g_t}{y_t}.$$

Column 2-2 presents estimated coefficients from a state spending regression that includes $\Delta \frac{g_t}{y_t}$ as an explanatory variable. Equation 3 implies that the ratio of the sum of grant effects (5.468) for a state with mean population to the sum of income effects for a state without a strict balanced budget requirement (0.22), which is 24.9, should equal $\frac{\gamma}{\left[1 + \gamma\left(\frac{g}{y}\right)\right]}$, or (given the very small size of government grants relative to income) approximately γ. The estimates therefore imply that a dollar of grant receipt has about the same impact on state government spending as $25 in additional state personal income per capita, which, if taken literally, implies that the marginal propensity to spend out of grant income is in the neighborhood of 80 percent.[9] This clearly reflects not only the significant effects that grants have on spending levels, but also that grant receipts are influenced by state spending levels, sometimes on a one-for-one basis. It is noteworthy, however, that the 98.88 coefficient on the interaction of state population and federal grants suggests that whatever the process is that determines the association of state spending and federal grants, this process appears to operate more strongly for large states than for small states. This is consistent with a greater willingness of large states to spend out of transitory income, although it may also reflect aspects of the grant allocation process

---

9. The 0.220 estimated income elasticity in column 2-2, together with the 0.1475 mean ratio of state spending to state personal income, implies that, evaluated at the mean, the marginal propensity to spend by state government out of a dollar of personal income is $(0.22)(0.15) = 0.033$. Then $(25)(0.033) = 0.825$.

that somehow reward expenditure by large states more than expenditure by small states.

Columns 2-3 and 2-4 of table 2 present estimated coefficients from regressions in which the dependent variable is the first difference of the log of state tax revenue, and the independent variables are the same as those used in the regressions reported in columns 2-1 and 2-2. State tax revenue rises with income: the sum of the first two coefficients in column 2-3 indicates that for a state with mean population and no strict balanced budget requirement, income growth by 1 percent is associated with 0.667 percent tax revenue growth. The significant positive coefficients on the interactions of population and the change in state personal income (current and lagged) imply that rising income is more strongly associated with increased tax collections in larger than in smaller states. This is consistent with the less statistically powerful evidence in columns 2-1 and 2-2 that expenditure of larger states exhibits stronger income associations than does expenditure of smaller states. The coefficients imply that increasing the size of an average state by 1 percent of the U.S. population increases the estimated tax revenue change associated with a 1 percent income fluctuation by 22 percent (from 0.667 percent to 0.816 percent). Including federal grants as explanatory variables in the regression reported in column 2-4 has little effect on these estimates, and the coefficients on grants are much smaller in magnitude than are the corresponding coefficients in column 2-2, notably failing to indicate that the spending effects of grants are crowded out through tax reductions.

It is possible to estimate state-specific income sensitivities of government expenditure and tax collections using a modified version of the specification reported in columns 2-2 and 2-4 that substitutes for the terms Δ income, Δ income$_{-1}$, population $\times$ Δ income, and population $\times$ Δ income$_{-1}$ a complete set of state dummy variables interacted with the sum of the change in log state personal income and its lag. The estimated coefficients on these interactions, plotted against state population in the top panel of figure 2, capture the extent to which the expenditures of different states respond to income changes. California, Massachusetts, Virginia, and Wisconsin exhibit the greatest sensitivity of state government spending to state personal income, and Delaware and Kansas the least. The bottom panel of figure 2 reveals that California, Michigan, Pennsylvania, and Virginia exhibit the greatest sensitivity of tax collections to state personal income, and Delaware and Nebraska are the least sensitive. The figure shows considerable variation across states for both revenue and spending sensitivity but suggests a general positive relationship between both and

Figure 2. State Size and Income Sensitivity of State Spending and Tax Revenue

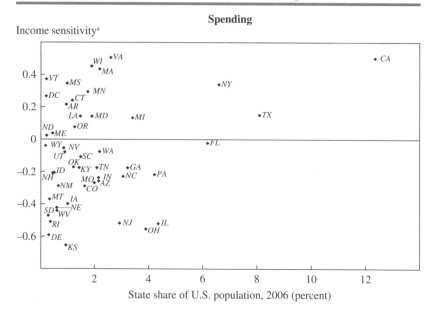

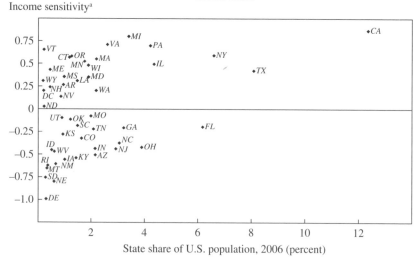

Source: Authors' calculations.
a. State-specific coefficient on the change in real state personal income per capita in a regression in which the dependent variable is the quarterly change in log state expenditure (top panel) or in log state tax revenue (bottom panel). The regression uses the same specification as in column 2-2 of table 2 but substitutes state-specific interactions with the change in income variable for the terms Δ income, Δ income$_{-1}$, population $\times$ Δ income, and population $\times$ Δ income$_{-1}$.

state population, with no obvious outliers responsible for the estimation results. As a robustness check, the regressions reported in columns 2-2 and 2-4 were rerun dropping potentially important single states, including California, but the impact on the size and significance of the regression estimates was small.

Further evidence comes from distinguishing state expenditure by function and state tax revenue by source. The first five columns of table 3 report estimated coefficients from regressions in which the dependent variables are log changes in real expenditure per capita on education, health and hospitals, public welfare, highways and roads, and unemployment insurance. These are the five largest state government spending categories; education and public welfare alone accounted for more than half of total state spending in 2006. In these regressions there is a mild association of spending and intergovernmental grants, particularly in the categories of health and hospitals, public welfare, and highways, for which the federal government makes available substantial matching grants. However, the grants variable used in these regressions is total grants received by states; the grants are not distinguished by category, in an effort to avoid the most obvious sources of endogeneity.

The coefficients reported in these first five columns of table 3 imply that interactions of state population shares and income changes have sizable positive effects on the growth rates of education and health and hospital spending, and large but statistically insignificant effects on the growth rate of public welfare spending. In the case of education, the sum of the coefficients on current and lagged income changes interacted with population share is 12.863 (with a standard error of 3.846), which implies that increasing the size of an average state by 1 percent of the U.S. population is associated with roughly one-third greater income sensitivity of education spending. In the case of health and hospitals, the sum of the population and income interaction coefficients is 12.331 (with a standard error of 5.987), which, together with the income coefficients, implies that increasing the size of an average state by 1 percent of the U.S. population is associated with a 26 percent greater income sensitivity of health and hospital expenditure. The sums of the estimated coefficients on the population-income interaction are negative (but insignificant) in the case of highway spending and unemployment insurance, the latter of which expands during economic downturns. In the interpretation that larger states display greater spending responsiveness to transitory income fluctuations, it might be expected that changes in unemployment insurance expenditure, which are negatively associated with income changes, should react with greater magnitude in large states.

Table 3. Regressions Explaining Annual Changes in State Spending by Category and Tax Revenue by Source

	Dependent variable[a]								
	Δ log spending					Δ log tax revenue[c]			
Independent variable[b]	Education	Health and hospitals	Public welfare	Highways	Unemployment insurance	Individual income tax	Corporate income tax	Sales tax	Property tax
Δ income	0.258***	0.308***	0.257***	0.247**	−1.038*	0.414**	0.616**	0.107	0.708
	(0.0885)	(0.107)	(0.0780)	(0.114)	(0.563)	(0.178)	(0.253)	(0.0995)	(0.539)
Δ income$_{-1}$	0.127	0.164	−0.0738	0.347*	−1.294***	−0.0244	0.538***	0.257**	0.0425
	(0.0939)	(0.115)	(0.107)	(0.201)	(0.301)	(0.187)	(0.191)	(0.0857)	(0.632)
Balanced budget req. × Δ income	−0.0285	0.179	−0.0197	0.188	−0.725	−0.232	−0.0862	0.0109	−0.499
	(0.0970)	(0.111)	(0.0952)	(0.167)	(0.732)	(0.236)	(0.303)	(0.112)	(0.716)
Balanced budget req. × Δ income$_{-1}$	0.0755	−0.115	0.0726	−0.0621	0.0607	0.523*	−0.328	0.0717	0.425
	(0.114)	(0.129)	(0.115)	(0.218)	(0.322)	(0.302)	(0.283)	(0.0962)	(0.781)
Population × Δ income	7.186**	7.470	7.551***	−10.88**	−24.46	14.68**	17.79**	4.279	0.361
	(3.286)	(5.132)	(2.731)	(4.921)	(21.16)	(8.654)	(10.29)	(2.951)	(17.16)
Population × Δ income$_{-1}$	5.677*	4.861*	0.559	1.953	−23.90**	5.829	5.974	2.851	10.23
	(3.230)	(2.876)	(4.417)	(4.954)	(10.38)	(6.085)	(8.307)	(2.389)	(23.43)
Population	2.646	0.122	−8.374	1.458	29.49*	−27.64	31.07	−14.54**	−9.934
	(4.691)	(7.133)	(8.949)	(9.406)	(16.16)	(18.03)	(20.55)	(7.149)	(74.12)
Population$_{-1}$	−2.574	−0.277	9.196	−0.493	−28.97*	28.21	−31.13	14.74**	6.595
	(4.644)	(6.968)	(9.021)	(9.210)	(16.08)	(18.24)	(20.76)	(7.142)	(71.09)
Δ grants-income ratio	1.512**	3.028**	8.379***	11.16***	5.000**	−1.135	−1.591	−0.212	6.357**
	(0.681)	(1.210)	(1.103)	(1.560)	(2.286)	(1.443)	(1.627)	(0.536)	(3.268)
Δ grants-income ratio$_{-1}$	0.413	0.466	1.713***	0.952	0.186	−0.536	−2.398	−0.155	6.740*
	(0.509)	(0.793)	(0.541)	(1.289)	(1.047)	(1.658)	(1.575)	(0.494)	(3.612)
Population × Δ grants-income ratio	27.84	46.09	213.0***	−82.00	151.5**	1.785	66.85	0.430	296.8
	(41.81)	(38.94)	(49.60)	(73.35)	(59.79)	(55.76)	(65.95)	(26.74)	(186.0)
Population × Δ grants-income ratio$_{-1}$	−29.74*	−6.594	−18.58	−11.51	−145.0**	−6.432	7.299	−22.06	51.11
	(17.15)	(33.60)	(20.48)	(32.84)	(71.77)	(46.23)	(71.28)	(22.49)	(149.2)
No. of observations	2,646	2,646	2,646	2,646	2,646	2,191	2,249	2,695	2,345
R^2	0.214	0.087	0.312	0.209	0.705	0.132	0.216	0.204	0.027

Source: Author's regressions.
a. All regressions include state and year fixed effects. Standard errors clustered at the state level are in parentheses.
b. See table 2 for definitions.
c. States not collecting tax revenue from the indicated source are omitted from the sample for that regression.

The last four columns of table 3 report coefficients from regressions in which the dependent variables are log changes in real individual income tax collections per capita, corporate tax collections, sales tax collections, and property tax collections. Not all states use all of these taxes—a fact reflected in the varying sample sizes. Among these taxes, corporate and sales tax collections display significant associations with income fluctuations, although the point estimate of income effects on property taxes is large, with a very large standard error. Only in the individual income tax regression is there a significant effect of the interaction between population size and current plus lagged income changes (the sum of current and lagged coefficients is 20.51, with an associated standard error of 8.00); corporate income tax revenue also has a large estimated effect (23.76) but with a large standard error (15.70). As a practical matter, the differing income sensitivities associated with different state taxes make it feasible for state governments to select revenue sources that tailor their revenue streams, within limits, to desired tax collections as incomes fluctuate.

The associations of state size with expenditure and tax responsiveness to changes in state incomes (and changes in federal grant receipts) raise the possibility that other variables correlated with state size may be responsible for this pattern. To the extent that state size matters because larger states have less mobile populations, direct measures of U.S. population mobility might be used in place of state size; and if larger states tend to have more dysfunctional governments, then measures of state government corruption might also be used. D'Vera Cohn and Rich Morin (2008) report the fractions of adult Americans born in each state who continued to live in their state of birth during 2005–07; their figures are reproduced as appendix table 1. (The figures should be interpreted to mean that, for example, 69 percent of current American adults who were born in California continued to live there during 2005–07.) Edward Glaeser and Raven Saks (2006) report average annual convictions of state public officials for federal corruption-related crimes per 100,000 state residents between 1976 and 2002; these data do not include figures for the District of Columbia.

Table 4 presents regressions with the same specifications as those in table 2 but adding as independent variables interactions of measures of population mobility and state corruption with income fluctuations. (Mobility and corruption are time-invariant measures for each state and therefore not included as independent variables.) The results suggest that the results reported above for state size may partially reflect the impact of

Table 4. Regressions Investigating the Effect of Population Mobility and Corruption on State Spending and Tax Revenue

	Dependent variable[a]			
	Δ log spending		Δ log tax revenue	
Independent variable	4-1	4-2	4-3	4-4
Δ income	−0.00499	0.145**	0.480***	−0.482***
	(0.0607)	(0.0592)	(0.0666)	(0.0712)
Δ income$_{-1}$	0.165*	0.165*	0.305	0.306***
	(0.0843)	(0.0849)	(0.0646)	(0.0690)
Balanced budget req. × Δ income	−0.0142	−0.0372	−0.133*	−0.132*
	(0.0689)	(0.0638)	(0.0761)	(0.0764)
Balanced budget req. × Δ income$_{-1}$	−0.0528	−0.0454	0.0619	0.0600
	(0.0939)	(0.0922)	(0.0735)	(0.0742)
Population[c] × Δ income	−5.297	−3.840	3.236	3.354
	(3.245)	(2.932)	(2.350)	(2.420)
Population × Δ income$_{-1}$	−1.157	0.307	4.170*	4.115
	(3.134)	(3.145)	(2.368)	(2.490)
Immobility[b] × Δ income	1.269**	0.920**	1.983***	2.016***
	(0.520)	(0.453)	(0.385)	(0.386)
Immobility × Δ income$_{-1}$	1.617***	0.894	0.363	0.341
	(0.580)	(0.608)	(0.418)	(0.450)
Corruption[c] × Δ income	0.616**	0.592**	−0.320	−0.327
	(0.245)	(0.224)	(0.284)	(0.285)
Corruption × Δ income$_{-1}$	−0.158	−0.251	−0.0226	−0.0159
	(0.334)	(0.357)	(0.281)	(0.282)
Population	−1.956	1.478	−7.909*	−8.298*
	(4.000)	(3.304)	(4.060)	(4.205)
Population$_{-1}$	2.437	−1.068	8.147**	8.537**
	(4.019)	(3.250)	(4.036)	(4.188)
Δ grants-income ratio		5.703***		0.121
		(0.572)		(0.528)
Δ grants-income ratio$_{-1}$		0.743**		−0.0774
		(0.290)		(0.431)
Population × Δ grants-income ratio		56.63**		15.45
		(28.26)		(22.60)
Population × Δ grants-income ratio$_{-1}$		−3.067		−17.70
		(10.09)		(13.80)
R^2	0.304	0.372	0.278	0.278

Source: Authors' regressions.

a. Dependent variables are annual log changes in real state government spending or tax revenue per capita. All regressions include state and year fixed effects. Sample size is 2,640 in all regressions. Standard errors clustered at the state level are in parentheses. See table 2 for definitions of variables not defined below.

b. Difference between the fraction of adults born in the state who lived there in 2005–07 and the sample mean of 0.5741.

c. Difference between the average annual number of federal corruption convictions of state government officials per 100,000 state residents during 1976–2002 and the sample mean of 0.2709.

population mobility; the evidence is weaker in the case of state government performance. In the regression reported in column 4-1, the estimated effect of the interaction of state mobility and income fluctuations is large and statistically significant (the sum of the coefficients is 2.89, with a standard error of 0.51), indicating that expenditure by states with less mobile populations is more closely associated with income fluctuations than is expenditure by states with more mobile populations. The interaction of corruption and income changes is positive and significant for contemporaneous income changes, but not for the sum of current and lagged changes; the sum of the coefficients on contemporaneous and lagged interactions of population and income changes is also insignificant. Similar results appear with the introduction of the grants variables in the regression reported in column 4-2 and for the tax regressions reported in columns 4-3 and 4-4.

Measured immobility as reported in appendix table 1 has a correlation of 0.53 with state population shares, which in part explains why the population mobility effects in the regressions reported in table 4 look similar to those reported for state size in table 2. Since population mobility is potentially influenced by state fiscal policies, it may be problematic to treat these variables as strictly exogenous—but the same is true of state population. In both cases there is reason to expect these variables to be related to the underlying mobility of the population, but it is very difficult to distinguish the effect of state size per se from the effects of any other variables that are strongly correlated with state size.

III. Conclusion

Tax revenue of state and local governments is more robust in economic downturns than is federal tax revenue, whereas state and local government spending grows at a slower rate in downturns than does federal spending. It is tempting to attribute much of this pattern to choices made long ago about the respective tax bases of federal and subfederal governments. States and localities rely to a much greater extent than does the federal government on property taxes and expenditure-type taxes such as sales and excise taxes, whereas the federal government depends more on income and payroll taxes. State and local revenue might as a result be more stable over the business cycle, and although this does not explain differences in expenditure patterns, it offers a plausible explanation of patterns of tax receipts. One difficulty with this interpretation is that property taxes, which are used almost exclusively by state and local governments, do not appear to be less sensitive to income fluctuations than are income taxes; a second is that local, state, and federal governments are entitled to change their funding models at any time if they are dissatisfied with the revenue streams they produce.

It is perhaps surprising that larger states do not have spending and tax policies that more closely resemble those of the federal government, since they are closer in size to the nation as a whole than are smaller states, and their governments may be closer in character to the federal government. Also, as Edward Gramlich (1997) and others note, states—particularly large states—may be able to internalize a large share of the benefits of stimulating their economies when there are underutilized resources. To the extent that larger states have less mobile populations, they are less subject to the point raised by Blanchard and Lawrence Katz (1992) that interstate worker mobility quickly mitigates adverse state economic outcomes (however, see Rowthorn and Glyn 2006 for a contrary interpretation of the evidence). The logic of this argument implies that states with more mobile populations might get smaller returns from trying to increase demand for local factors. Yet the evidence suggests otherwise and therefore may reflect either additional economic considerations or a failure of government optimization.

To the extent that there are national externalities associated with state and local fiscal policies, the federal government has instruments at its disposal that can influence patterns of state and local taxes and spending. The most powerful of these is the provision of grants to state governments. There is ample evidence that state spending is influenced by federal grants, so a carefully tailored countercyclical grant policy has the potential to encourage states, acting on their own behalf, to behave in a manner that effectively incorporates the interests of other states in stimulating the economy when resources are otherwise underutilized.

ACKNOWLEDGMENTS I thank Molly Saunders-Scott and Daniel Schaffa for outstanding research assistance, and Kathryn Dominguez, Bill Gale, Lutz Kilian, Brian Knight, the editors, and participants at the Brookings Panel conference for extremely helpful comments on earlier drafts.

The author reports no relevant potential conflicts of interest.

APPENDIX

Table A1. Interstate Population Mobility, 2005–07

State	Percent of adults born in the state now living there	State	Percent of adults born in the state now living there
Alabama	63.7	Montana	47.1
Alaska	28.2	Nebraska	50.2
Arizona	61.5	Nevada	48.7
Arkansas	54.5	New Hampshire	52.8
California	69.0	New Jersey	55.6
Colorado	54.7	New Mexico	53.5
Connecticut	57.1	New York	55.5
Delaware	54.0	North Carolina	71.4
District of Columbia	13.0	North Dakota	40.4
Florida	66.0	Ohio	65.1
Georgia	69.6	Oklahoma	55.6
Hawaii	57.3	Oregon	59.2
Idaho	48.6	Pennsylvania	63.8
Illinois	59.0	Rhode Island	53.9
Indiana	62.8	South Carolina	66.0
Iowa	54.0	South Dakota	43.4
Kansas	50.2	Tennessee	66.7
Kentucky	62.6	Texas	75.8
Louisiana	64.4	Utah	66.1
Maine	55.3	Vermont	52.5
Maryland	61.1	Virginia	61.9
Massachusetts	58.7	Washington	64.3
Michigan	67.5	West Virginia	48.9
Minnesota	66.3	Wisconsin	68.6
Mississippi	54.9	Wyoming	35.7
Missouri	61.9		

Source: Cohn and Morin (2008).

References

Aizenman, Joshua, and Gurnain Kaur Pasricha. 2010. "On the Ease of Overstating the Fiscal Stimulus in the US, 2008–9." Working Paper no. 15784. Cambridge, Mass.: National Bureau of Economic Research (February).

Alt, James E., and Robert C. Lowry. 1994. "Divided Government, Fiscal Institutions, and Budget Deficits: Evidence from the States." *American Political Science Review* 88, no. 4: 811–28.

Auerbach, Alan J., William G. Gale, and Benjamin H. Harris. 2010. "Activist Fiscal Policy." *Journal of Economic Perspectives* 24, no. 4: 141–64.

Auerbach, Alan J., and Yuriy Gorodnichenko. 2010. "Measuring the Output Responses to Fiscal Policy." Working Paper no. 16311. Cambridge, Mass.: National Bureau of Economic Research (August).

Bahl, Roy. 1984. *Financing State and Local Government in the 1980s.* Oxford University Press.

Baicker, Katherine. 2005. "Extensive or Intensive Generosity? The Price and Income Effects of Federal Grants." *Review of Economics and Statistics* 87, no. 2: 371–84.

Barro, Robert J., and Charles J. Redlick. 2009. "Macroeconomic Effects from Government Purchases and Taxes." Working Paper no. 15369. Cambridge, Mass.: National Bureau of Economic Research (September).

Blanchard, Olivier Jean, and Lawrence F. Katz. 1992. "Regional Evolutions." *BPEA*, no. 1: 1–61.

Blanchard, Olivier, and Roberto Perotti. 2002. "An Empirical Characterization of the Dynamic Effects of Changes in Government Spending and Taxes on Output." *Quarterly Journal of Economics* 117, no. 4: 1329–68.

Blanchard, Olivier Jean, Florencio Lopez-de-Silanes, and Andrei Shleifer. 1994. "What Do Firms Do with Cash Windfalls?" *Journal of Financial Economics* 36, no. 3: 337–60.

Bucovetsky, S. 1991. "Asymmetric Tax Competition." *Journal of Urban Economics* 30, no. 2: 167–81.

Cogan, John F., Tobias Cwik, John B. Taylor, and Volker Wieland. 2010. "New Keynesian versus Old Keynesian Government Spending Multipliers." *Journal of Economic Dynamics and Control* 34, no. 3: 281–295.

Cohn, D'Vera, and Rich Morin. 2008. "American Mobility: Who Moves? Who Stays Put? Where's Home?" Social and Demographic Trends Report. Washington: Pew Research Center (December).

Dahlberg, Matz, Eva Mörk, Jørn Rattsø, and Hanna Ågren. 2008. "Using a Discontinuous Grant Rule to Identify the Effect of Grants on Local Taxes and Spending." *Journal of Public Economics* 92, no. 12: 2320–35.

Feldstein, Martin S., and Gilbert E. Metcalf. 1987. "The Effect of Federal Tax Deductibility on State and Local Taxes and Spending." *Journal of Political Economy* 95, no. 4: 710–36.

Glaeser, Edward L., and Raven E. Saks. 2006. "Corruption in America." *Journal of Public Economics* 90, no. 6–7: 1053–72.

Gordon, Nora. 2004. "Do Federal Grants Boost School Spending? Evidence from Title I." *Journal of Public Economics* 88, no. 9–10: 1771–92.

Gramlich, Edward M. 1997. "Subnational Fiscal Policy." In *Financing Federal Systems: The Selected Essays of Edward M. Gramlich.* Cheltenham, U.K.: Edward Elgar.

Hall, Robert E. 2009. "By How Much Does GDP Rise if the Government Buys More Output?" *BPEA*, no. 2: 183–231.

Hines, James R., Jr., and Richard H. Thaler. 1995. "The Flypaper Effect." *Journal of Economic Perspectives* 9, no. 4: 217–26.

Holtz-Eakin, Douglas, Whitney Newey, and Harvey S. Rosen. 1989. "The Revenues-Expenditures Nexus: Evidence from Local Government Data." *International Economic Review* 30, no. 2: 415–29.

Kanbur, Ravi, and Michael Keen. 1993. "Jeux sans Frontières: Tax Competition and Tax Coordination When Countries Differ in Size." *American Economic Review* 83, no. 4: 877–92.

Knight, Brian. 2002. "Endogenous Federal Grants and Crowd-Out of State Government Spending: Theory and Evidence from the Federal Highway Aid Program." *American Economic Review* 92, no. 1: 71–92.

Lutz, Byron. 2010. "Taxation with Representation: Intergovernmental Grants in a Plebiscite." *Review of Economics and Statistics* 92, no. 2: 316–32.

Poterba, James M. 1994. "State Responses to Fiscal Crises: The Effects of Budgetary Institutions and Politics." *Journal of Political Economy* 102, no. 4: 799–821.

———. 1997. "Do Budget Rules Work?" In *Fiscal Policy: Lessons from Economic Research,* edited by Alan J. Auerbach. MIT Press.

Rowthorn, Robert, and Andrew J. Glyn. 2006. "Convergence and Stability in U.S. Employment Rates." *Contributions to Macroeconomics* 6, no. 1: article 4. www.bepress.com/bejm/contributions/vol6/iss1/art4.

Romer, Christina D., and David H. Romer. 2010. "The Macroeconomic Effects of Tax Changes: Estimates Based on a New Measure of Fiscal Shocks." *American Economic Review* 100 no. 3: 763–801.

Strumpf, Koleman S. 1998. "A Predictive Index for the Flypaper Effect." *Journal of Public Economics* 69, no. 3: 389–412.

Von Hagen, Jürgen. 1991. "A Note on the Empirical Effectiveness of Formal Fiscal Restraints." *Journal of Public Economics* 44, no. 2: 199–210.

Wilson, John Douglas, and David E. Wildasin. 2004. "Capital Tax Competition: Bane or Boon?" *Journal of Public Economics* 88, no. 6: 1065–91.

Woodford, Michael. 2010. "Simple Analytics of the Government Expenditure Multiplier." Working Paper no. 15714. Cambridge, Mass.: National Bureau of Economic Research (January).

Comments and Discussion

COMMENT BY
WILLIAM G. GALE   The Great Recession and the associated fiscal policy responses in many countries have renewed research interest in the effects of activist fiscal stabilization and stimulus policies (Auerbach, Gale, and Harris 2010). This paper by James Hines addresses an important but often underanalyzed component of that issue, the role of subnational governments.

In the United States, state and federal governments can have important influences on overall fiscal stimulus for at least three reasons. First, these governments' spending and taxes, which equaled 14 percent and 9 percent of GDP, respectively, in 2009, are sizable relative to those of the federal government. Second, almost all states have balanced budget rules. When revenue falls during a recession, states must either draw down their rainy-day funds, raise taxes, or cut spending; the latter two options are likely to act as procyclical policies that could exacerbate the downturn. James Poterba (1994), for example, finds strong evidence that states contract spending and raise taxes when faced with a negative fiscal shock. He also finds that states with stricter budget rules (for example, those that apply to the enacted budget, rather than just the proposed budget) respond to unexpected deficits by reducing spending much more than other states.

Third, one federal stimulus option—besides raising government purchases, raising transfers to individuals or businesses, or cutting taxes—is to provide transfers to the states, which could ease their balanced budget constraints and reduce the need for contractionary state responses. Although the argument that transfers to states are stimulative is plausible, there is surprisingly little evidence on their countercyclical effects.[1]

Edward Gramlich (1978, 1979) and Robert Reischauer (1978) evaluate the effects of three federal grant programs undertaken in response to the 1973–75 recession. One program offered countercyclical revenue to the states in the form of block grants, another paid the salaries of state and local government workers, and a third contributed funding for capital improvements. The general finding was that states' short-run response to this federal aid was primarily to bolster their rainy-day funds; increases in outlays and reductions in taxes were modest in the short run. The long-run response—particularly in the form of decreased income tax revenue—was substantial but materialized after the recession had ended. It is unclear how relevant these findings are to the current economic downturn, however, given the dated nature of the evidence, differences between the 1975 economy and today's, and differences between the states' economic situations then and now: in the current downturn, states have been hurt both by the recession and by the housing crisis, which heightened the need for state transfers to local governments due to reduced municipal property tax revenue.

Concerns that state and local government responses to their budget difficulties might undermine federal stimulus efforts are also highlighted by historical considerations.[2] The classic paper by Cary Brown (1956) shows that states did not conduct countercyclical policy during the Great Depression. Subfederal governments still accounted for the majority of government spending during that era, and in the aggregate they tightened their budgets between 1931 and 1933 and provided no net stimulus between 1933 and 1942.

Likewise, Kenneth Kuttner and Adam Posen (2001) show that during Japan's "lost decade," fiscal efforts at the national level were inconsistent, smaller than commonly thought, and undercut by a variety of factors. Among these was that Japan's announced public spending initiatives turned out to be significantly larger than what ended up being implemented, because many of the announced federal programs required partial local

---

1. In an analysis of provisions included in the 2009 federal stimulus package, the Congressional Budget Office (2010) estimates output multipliers between 1.0 and 2.5 for transfers to state governments for infrastructure spending, and between 0.7 and 1.8 for transfers for other purposes.

2. The following two paragraphs are based on Auerbach and Gale (2010).

government funding that did not materialize. Also, coordination issues with local government limited effective planning and implementation.

Hines's paper begins with a demonstration that state activities in the recent downturn through 2009 provided virtually no net stimulus in the aggregate, after accounting for federal grants. Other researchers have reported similar findings for the recent downturn (for example, Aizenman and Pasricha 2010).

With this finding as background, the paper then investigates how state policy has varied over the business cycle in the past, and reaches several major conclusions. First, state-level fiscal policy is less countercyclical than federal policy. This result is as expected, and although the results do not show states running actively procyclical policies as suggested by the simple balanced budget rule analysis above, they still imply that the impact of federal countercyclical policies is smaller than it would be if states acted exactly like the federal government.

Second, large states tend to have more procyclical policies than smaller states. This result may seem backward at first: one might expect larger states to act more like the federal government (which can be thought of as an aggregation of all states) and therefore to behave more countercyclically than small states. However, Hines explains that because smaller states face more elastic populations of taxpayers and businesses, they need to be more responsive to local needs during downturns, and hence need to run more countercyclical policies. In particular, state spending on education and health, and revenue collected through the income tax, are more sensitive to income fluctuations in large states than in small states.

Third, most of the cyclical variation at the state level occurs through changes in revenue rather than in spending. Aggregate state spending is not particularly sensitive to income fluctuations, but taxes are.

The fourth main result is that states have a high propensity to spend federal grants, and this propensity is higher in large states than in small. This is important given the key issue of whether federal grants to states are stimulative. However, the extent to which grant levels are endogenous with respect to state spending levels is difficult to ascertain, which muddies the interpretation.

Policymakers were seeking answers on these issues as they were constructing the American Recovery and Reinvestment Act of 2009, the main federal stimulus package in the recent recession. If and when another stimulus package is debated, whether and in what form to extend aid to the states will continue to be a critical question. At the same time, several other issues would be worth exploring further. The first is the sensitivity of

Hines's overall results to his use of the whole 1951–2007 time period. The nation experienced only two recessions in the 20 years preceding 2007, and the nature of the aggregate fiscal response to the business cycle changed over that period (Auerbach, Gale, and Harris 2010). It would be interesting to know how robust the results are to a divided sample period.

Second, if the focus is on understanding state responses during economic downturns, it would be interesting to know whether the response to rises versus falls in income is asymmetric because of inertia or political constraints. It is certainly plausible that the response of states to a recession is not the exact opposite of their response to an expansion.

Another issue of interest is how, precisely, states run countercyclical policies, given their balanced budget rules. Do they exploit built-in features of the rules (for example, a requirement that the budget be balanced, but only on an ex ante basis)? Do they exploit the fact that such rules typically apply only to the operating budget, so that debt-financed capital expenditures, one classic type of countercyclical policy, are still possible? Are they running budget surpluses on average, building up reserves, and then draining their rainy-day funds during hard times? Do federal grants in fact enhance their ability to run countercyclical policies? Hines's paper provides a foundation from which future research could explore all of these issues.

REFERENCES FOR THE GALE COMMENT

Aizenman, Joshua, and Gurnain Kaur Pasricha. 2010. "On the Ease of Overstating the Fiscal Stimulus in the US, 2008–9." Working Paper no. 15784. Cambridge, Mass.: National Bureau of Economic Research.

Auerbach, Alan J., and William G. Gale. 2009. "Activist Fiscal Policy to Stabilize Economic Activity." In *Financial Stability and Macroeconomic Policy*. Federal Reserve Bank of Kansas City.

Auerbach, Alan J., William G. Gale, and Benjamin H. Harris. 2010. "Activist Fiscal Policy." *Journal of Economic Perspectives* 24, no. 4: 141–64.

Brown, E. Cary. 1956. "Fiscal Policy in the 'Thirties: A Reappraisal." *American Economic Review* 46, no. 5: 857–79.

Congressional Budget Office. 2010. "Estimated Impact of the American Recovery and Reinvestment Act on Employment and Economic Output from July 2010 through September 2010." Washington (November).

Gramlich, Edward M. 1978. "State and Local Budgets the Day after It Rained: Why Is the Surplus So High?" *BPEA*, no. 1: 191–216.

———. 1979. "Stimulating the Macro Economy through State and Local Governments." *American Economic Review* 69, no. 2: 180–85.

Kuttner, Kenneth N., and Adam S. Posen. 2001. "The Great Recession: Lessons for Macroeconomic Policy from Japan." *BPEA*, no. 2: 93–185.

Poterba, James M. 1994. "State Responses to Fiscal Crises: The Effects of Budgetary Institutions and Politics." *Journal of Political Economy* 102, no. 4: 799–821.

Reischauer, Robert D. 1978. "Federal Countercyclical Policy—the State and Local Role." Prepared for the Seventy-first Annual Conference on Taxation of the National Tax Association–Tax Institute of America, Philadelphia, Pa., November 13.

COMMENT BY

BRIAN KNIGHT   In this paper, James Hines investigates differences between state and federal fiscal responses to business cycle fluctuations and delves into cross-state differences in fiscal policy over the business cycle. This is obviously an important topic given both the current economic climate and the fiscal challenges facing both the federal government and state and local governments. Given this importance, I was surprised to learn that Hines's was the first systematic comparison of federal and state-local fiscal policy and thus was delighted to see him tackle this issue. I will first summarize his key findings before turning to some comments on the analysis and a discussion of the results.

The paper's analysis is divided into two parts. The first is a national analysis of quarterly national income and product accounts data covering 1947–2010. Hines finds that federal spending and taxes exhibit the expected countercyclical pattern, with spending rising and taxes falling during recessions identified by the National Bureau of Economic Research (NBER). This result is robust to using the output gap, as defined by the Congressional Budget Office, as an alternative measure of recessions. Hines's corresponding subnational measures of revenue and spending are based on national aggregate data and combine the state and local sectors into one. Using this measure, Hines finds some evidence of a countercyclical pattern in state and local fiscal policy, but one that is smaller in magnitude than the results for the federal government. The state and local results are also less robust than the corresponding federal patterns to measures based on the output gap. Taken together, the key finding from this first analysis is that federal fiscal policy is more countercyclical than state and local fiscal policy.

The second part of the paper is based on annual state-level Census data covering the years 1951–2007. Thus, unlike the aggregate analysis, this analysis excludes data from the most recent recession. Also, this analysis incorporates spending and taxes from state governments alone and thus excludes data on fiscal policy at the local level. The key findings here can be summarized as follows. First, fiscal policy does not differ between states with and states without strict balanced budget rules. Second, there is a strong flypaper effect: the marginal propensity of states to spend from federal grants is close to 1, and about 25 times the marginal propensity to spend from other sources of income. Third, state policy is more countercyclical in states with small populations than in more populous states. Hines interprets this finding as reflecting the fact that large states face less competitive pressure, since voters in these states are less likely to vote with their feet. That is, this pattern of procyclical policy in large states may reflect the suboptimal propensity of politicians to spend, rather than save, budget surpluses during economic booms, and pressures to save any surpluses may be less relevant in large states. As corroborating evidence for this "political failure" interpretation, Hines shows that, conditional on population, fiscal policy is more procyclical in states with less mobile populations, where voting with one's feet is arguably more costly, and in states with high levels of corruption, where these political failures are presumably more salient.

I found the results from the first analysis to be quite convincing in terms of documenting that federal fiscal policy tends to be more countercyclical than fiscal policy at the state and local level. This is certainly consistent with normative principles, as outlined by Wallace Oates (1999), who argues that, in most cases, stabilization policy is best carried out at the central level. This result follows from the fact that state and local governments have open economies and thus neither the means nor the incentives to counteract economic downturns with expansionary fiscal policy. Although this is the conventional wisdom in the federalism literature, Edward Gramlich (1987), as discussed in more detail below, puts forward a case for a more active macroeconomic stabilization policy at the state and local level.

Given Hines's finding of a difference in countercyclicality between the federal government and state and local governments, a natural question is what the root causes of this difference might be. One possible answer is that nearly all states have balanced budget rules, which, by limiting borrowing during recessions, may constrain their ability to conduct countercyclical fiscal policy. One weakness of this interpretation, however, is that it is seemingly inconsistent with another of Hines's findings, cited above, that state fiscal policy is independent of the presence of strict balanced budget rules at the state level. A second possibility derives from the fact that federal taxation is largely based on income, whether individual or corporate, whereas state and local tax bases are more based on sales and property. To the extent that income is more volatile than either consumption or land and housing values, then, holding tax rates fixed, federal tax revenue will automatically exhibit more volatility over the business cycle than do state and local tax revenues. Hines provides some evidence in favor of this hypothesis in table 3, but the standard errors in these regressions are quite large, making it difficult to reject the hypothesis that revenues from income, sales, and property tax systems at the state level exhibit similar patterns over the business cycle.

A third possibility, mentioned above, is that because states are less able than the federal government to prevent the benefits of their countercyclical policy from spilling over to other jurisdictions, they have neither the means nor the incentive to counteract a weak economy. But this idea is inconsistent with Hines's finding, also described above, that fiscal policy is more countercyclical in less populous states, which presumably have more open economies and thus less control over economic activity within their borders than do larger states.

A final possibility, not explored in the paper, is that federal tax systems may be more progressive than state tax systems on average, and that this greater progressivity builds greater countercyclicality into federal fiscal policy. All else equal, reductions in individual income under a progressive system tend to move taxpayers into tax brackets with lower tax rates and hence lower tax payments.

As mentioned above, Hines also finds strong evidence of a flypaper effect. In interpreting this result, however, some lessons from the existing literature on the flypaper effect are worth noting. First, many federal grant programs have matching provisions. For example, the federal share of Medicaid spending varies across states from a minimum of 50 percent, consistent with a dollar-for-dollar federal match of state spending, to around 75 percent, consistent with a 3-to-1 federal match. These substantial matching provisions introduce significant substitution effects, and consequently one should not expect the marginal propensity to consume from grants to equal the marginal propensity to consume from income. That is, the standard theoretical prediction of equivalence between grant income and private income is based upon a model with purely lump-sum federal grants. Indeed, Robert Moffitt (1984) investigates this issue in the context of the Aid to Families with Dependent Children program (the predecessor of today's Temporary Assistance for Needy Families) and shows that the flypaper effect can be explained entirely by the program's matching provisions. Second, several recent papers, such as Brian Knight (2002), Nora Gordon (2004), and Byron Lutz (2010), argue that the flypaper effects documented in the literature might be explained by endogeneity problems. That is, if federal funds tend to flow to jurisdictions with strong preferences for public spending, then the observed flypaper effects may reflect the presence of this third factor. Moreover, results using exogenous variation in grant receipts tend to exhibit significantly weaker flypaper effects.

I found Hines's results on the differences in fiscal policy between small and large states to be quite interesting, and the idea that political failures of fiscal policy are more salient in large states to be compelling. On the other hand, when one combines this finding with the finding that federal fiscal policy is more countercyclical, one is left with the puzzling result that it is fiscal policy in small states rather than in large states that more closely resembles federal fiscal policy. If differences between small states and large states reflect the differing ability to vote with one's feet, why is the inability to save surpluses during booms not even more of an issue at the federal level, where the population is even less mobile? This issue of differences in fiscal policy between small and large states certainly deserves further exploration.

Regarding this comparison, a potential statistical issue that is not discussed in the paper involves measurement error: any error associated with measuring economic activity may be more pronounced in small states than in large states. This might explain why state taxes and spending more closely track state income in large states than in small states. Although this differential measurement error seems unlikely to entirely explain the differences in fiscal policy that Hines documents, it may lead to their being overstated.

A related fiscal institution not explored in the paper is the rainy-day fund, which, in the context of the author's "political failure" story, can be interpreted as a mechanism through which state governments can commit to saving during economic booms for use during economic contractions. Indeed, many of these funds have provisions designed to address political failure. For example, some states require deposits into the rainy-day fund during favorable economic times, and many allow withdrawals only during downturns. Consistent with the idea that states are unable to commit to saving during booms, Knight and Arik Levinson (1999) document that contributions to these rainy-day funds tend to increase overall state savings on a dollar-for-dollar basis and, moreover, that funds with stricter rules regarding contributions and withdrawals tend to have higher overall savings than funds with more lax rules.

A final issue that this paper raises involves regional business cycles. The first part of the paper is framed around the national business cycle and the associated differences in responses to national shocks by the federal government and state and local governments. Yet because some shocks are industry-specific, many recessions have important regional components or might even be limited to one region. Consideration of such spatial variation in business cycles gives rise to a number of interesting issues that are relevant to the paper's results. First, states and localities may be in a better position to respond to local economic shocks than the federal government: state officials may have better information about local economic conditions, or, perhaps for political reasons, the federal government may be unable to respond to highly localized economic shocks. Whatever the reason, the better ability of states and localities to respond to local shocks suggests an important role for state and local governments in macroeconomic stabilization policy (Gramlich 1987).

Second, any federal response to localized economic downturns raises moral hazard considerations. The expectation of increased federal funding for states and localities in fiscal distress may provide incentives for them to run excessive deficits and engage in other risky fiscal practices. To the extent that the federal government cannot commit to not bailing out state and local governments, strict balanced budget rules may be a necessary ingredient of fiscal policy at the state and local level.

Third, federal automatic stabilizers provide a type of insurance against regional contractions: relatively vibrant regions cross-subsidize regions suffering from economic downturns, with the expectation that these roles will be reversed when the economic conditions are reversed. In a careful examination of this issue, Pierfederico Asdrubali, Bent Sørensen, and Oved Yosha (1996) document that about 13 percent of shocks to gross state product are smoothed by federal fiscal policy, with federal taxes, transfers, and grants all providing significant contributions.

In summary, I found this to be a very interesting paper that makes a significant contribution to the literature on stabilization policy and federalism. I hope that this paper will help to stimulate research in this area in the coming years.

REFERENCES FOR THE KNIGHT COMMENT

Asdrubali, Pierfederico, Bent E. Sørensen, and Oved Yosha. 1996. "Channels of Interstate Risk Sharing: United States 1963–1990." *Quarterly Journal of Economics* 111, no. 4 (November): 1081–1110.

Gordon, Nora. 2004. "Do Federal Grants Boost School Spending? Evidence from Title I." *Journal of Public Economics* 88, no. 9–10 (August): 1771–92.

Gramlich, Edward M. 1987. "Subnational Fiscal Policy." *Perspectives on Local Public Finance and Public Policy* 3: 3–27.

Knight, Brian. 2002. "Endogenous Federal Grants and Crowd-Out of State Government Spending: Theory and Evidence from the Federal Highway Aid Program." *American Economic Review* 92, no. 1 (March): 71–92.

Knight, Brian, and Arik Levinson. 1999. "Rainy Day Funds and State Government Savings." *National Tax Journal* 52, no 3 (September): 459–72.

Lutz, Byron. 2010. "Taxation with Representation: Intergovernmental Grants in a Plebiscite Democracy." *Review of Economics and Statistics* 92, no. 2 (May): 316–32.

Moffitt, Robert. 1984. "The Effects of Grants-in-aid on State and Local Expenditures: The Case of AFDC." *Journal of Public Economics* 23, no. 3 (April) 279–305.

Oates, Wallace E. 1999. "An Essay on Fiscal Federalism." *Journal of Economic Literature* 37, no. 3 (September): 1120–49.

GENERAL DISCUSSION Alan Auerbach noted the lack of a distinction in the paper between automatic and discretionary responses. Presumably some state programs, like some federal programs, are automatically cyclical in their expenditure. It would be interesting to know whether the variation found by Hines relates to differences in these types of programs across states. Are states behaving differently because some but not others are deliberately responding to recessions, or is everything on automatic pilot, and do the differences across states have to do with different compositions of expenditure across these program types? Henry Aaron agreed that the distinction is important, and he suggested that the hypothesis that discretionary tax policy is almost unambiguously procyclical would soon be tested in an effort by the Center on Budget and Policy Priorities to monitor virtually every proposed state tax increase.

Jonathan Parker argued that state income might not be the right dependent variable. A state that cuts back a lot on spending may see a much bigger rebound in income than one that cuts back little or not at all. Also, very high income households account for a large amount of tax revenue in some states. In New York, Wall Street bonuses alone accounted for about $30 billion of state income in 2007, so that when bonuses fell by more than half in 2008, it blew a multibillion-dollar hole in the state budget. This raises the question of whether the recent high cyclicality of high incomes is responsible. Parker noted that that would be the case only for states and localities that rely on the income tax: a state that derives most of its revenue from a progressive income tax is going to have higher revenue cyclicality than one that relies on a flat consumption tax.

Benjamin Friedman was struck by the differential effect that Hines found between larger and smaller states. Because of spillover effects, one might have thought a priori that countercyclical spending policy, and especially discretionary spending, would be more effective in larger than in smaller states. But then the differential would be in the opposite direction from Hines's finding, leading to the question: is the expected effect offset by other factors?

Steven Davis wanted to see more evidence supporting the theory that smaller states are more efficient in their spending. For example, Hines's argument suggests that smaller states would have more efficient court systems. Is this in fact the case? If the theory is correct, smaller states should perform better on average than larger states on other attributes, too, even the choice of tax base and the quality of public services.

Laurence Ball argued that it might be beneficial to consider a more continuous measure of the business cycle, such as unemployment, rather than a binary indicator like NBER recession dating. He suspected that the results could be quite different. Justin Wolfers added that NBER recessions are defined as times when the economy is getting worse, but active fiscal policy is typically used both in the downswing and on the rebound. Henry Aaron mentioned what he saw as a more fundamental point. At least three of the recessions covered in the paper were caused by cutbacks in defense outlays. This reverses the causation altogether and undermines the relevance of the comparison between state and federal countercyclicality.

Wolfers also noted that when the federal government wants to respond to economic weakness, it can respond forcefully. Much of the time, however, the federal government does not respond at all, perhaps because of politics or gridlock. Aggregating across all states, then, the response of the states may be much more reliable than that of the federal government. Politics has not yet entered into the discussion, but it certainly plays a role.

Robert Hall pointed out that before the early 1960s it was illegal for state and local employees to unionize. Public sector unionization has become important only in recent decades, so that today a governor's job is to figure out how to make up the difference after powerful unions have taken one large share of the revenue needed to balance the budget, and stingy taxpayers have withheld another. In such an environment it is hard to see how a state could possibly act countercyclically. Following up on Parker's comment, Hall noted that another big change is the greater dependence of many states on a progressive income tax, which gathers

COMMENTS and DISCUSSION

abundant revenue in good times. He also agreed with Ball that focusing on recessions was not the right way of looking at the issue. The need for stimulus is after the end of a recession. A better analysis would be one that compared bad times with good times.

Gary Burtless argued that the discussion of countercyclical stimulus was incomplete without a consideration of the revenue side. As he understood it, the single biggest element of automatic countercyclical stimulus is the loss of income tax revenue from the corporate and personal income tax.

Burtless was also interested in the treatment of unemployment insurance and its allocation between state and federal responsibility. The UI program is essentially mandated by the federal government, but states set the benefit levels and the tax rates on employers to pay for the benefits. An unambiguously discretionary part of policy is the decision whether to provide extensions to UI during downturns. That is entirely a federal initiative, mandated and funded by the federal government, although the state governments write the checks. If such extensions are a large part of what the paper is counting as state stimulus spending, it may not be an accurate characterization.

Refet Gürkaynak was curious whether the difference that Hines observed between small and large states would be found among small and large member states of the European Union. The available history is not as long, but it would be informative to see whether the smaller European states have behaved differently from the larger ones during the last recession and its aftermath.

Donald Kohn noted that the depth of the recent recession and the length and severity of the output gap likely caused many states to run through their rainy-day funds, even if they had built them up as planned. He also wondered whether the dependence of most states on real estate taxes made a difference in this cycle. Because this recession started and was deepest in the real estate sector, the resulting steep loss in property taxes might have cut into state revenue deeper and more quickly than in other recessions. To the extent that states were constrained by a balanced budget, this would have forced them to cut back spending more aggressively than otherwise.

Robert Gordon observed that state and local real spending as a share of potential GDP dropped sharply between 1931 and 1933 and continued to drop throughout the 1930s. Roughly half of the federal stimulus in those years was thus offset by tightening at the state and local level, even before including the tax side. The nation's economic outlook was dismal in the second quarter of 1940, but then, in a little over a year, the total government share of spending doubled with the surge in wartime spending. In the recent period, the state and local share of potential GDP has drifted downward steadily since 2003, but the federal government has come nowhere close to offsetting this decline. In fact, it is hard to see any increase in federal government spending on goods and services through the second quarter of 2010. The spending has all been in transfer payments, and most of that in unemployment insurance.